OFFICE AT HOME

OFFICE
AT HOME

Robert Scott

Charles Scribner's Sons
New York

Copyright © 1985 Robert Scott Associates

Library of Congress Cataloging in Publication Data
Scott, Robert, 1918–
Office at home.

Bibliography: p.
Includes index.
1. Office practice.   2. Home-based business
I. Title.
HF5547.5.S38   1985   651.3   84–23605
ISBN 0–684–18212–2

This book published simultaneously in the
United States of America and in Canada—
Copyright under the Berne Convention.

1 3 5 7 9 11 13 15 17 19 V/C 20 18 16 14 12 10 8 6 4 2

Printed in the United States of America.

Contents

Acknowledgments

The information in this book has come from interviews, conversations, and correspondence with many persons in government, trade, and professional organizations and in private industry, as well as those with offices at home. All have been patient with my fumbling questions. To list everyone would be an impossible task, but I would especially like to single out the following persons for mention:

Dorothy J. Lander, library director of the Ossining Public Library, and the excellent reference staff of Marian Custons, Natalee Fogel, Joan Hraban, Jack Oxton, and Ruth Schwab; Helen Burnham, director of the Croton Free Library, and Nancy Rolnick, reference librarian; Charles and Diane Newman, of Books 'n Things, Briarcliff Manor, New York, and their knowledgeable staff, who kept up such a steady flow of source books and reference works as to cause my library shelves to sag.

Alexander Walsh, of West Windsor, Connecticut, gracious friend and dealer in American paintings, who supplied ideas on home-office operation, as well as paintings to brighten my walls; Robert Silkworth, for sharing his knowledge of office machines and office practice; Harry Mendez, for making the world of stationery and office supplies come alive; Peter Mills, for giving so freely of his knowledge of office design and decoration and working with me in making my home office what it is (a trucker delivering some office furniture here not long ago paid it a spontaneous compliment by exclaiming, "Why, this is the nicest home office I've ever been in"); George Treistman, who promised that I "wouldn't get hurt" in my home-office-equipment purchases, which assurance meant more than any manufacturer's warranty.

Detective Robert Scanlon, for information on security procedures; Harvey Seymour, of the Insurance Information Institute, as well as Russell Rogers and Marilyn Hauprich, for ensuring the completeness of the information on home-office insurance; Hermann Koelling, for help in understanding the intricacies of freight and shipping; Postmaster David Bolton and his accommodating crew, for making the mysteries of the postal service fathomable; Stuart O'Steen, for explaining the arcana of air express to me; Leonard Fristrom, for guidance on how to deal with banks and bankers.

Frank North, for advice on graphics and letterhead design; Dan Stovall, for help in sorting out typefaces; Robert Koumjian, for clarifying the terminology of printing; Angela Aiello, for painstakingly keyboarding the Sources and Resources section of this book; Lottie Nielsen, my former secretary, who long ago graciously put up with my experiments in office management and helped me to refine many of the procedures still used in my office at home.

Office-at-homers Isaac Asimov, Roger Caras, Denison Hatch, Harold Longman, John McCollister, Judith McQuown, Ray Ovington, and Mark Sosin for advice and comment. Special words of thanks are owed to Susanne Kirk, my editor at Charles Scribner's Sons, whose editorial judgment and wisdom run like a thread through this book.

To all who offered knowledge, anecdotal experiences, and suggestions: You helped to make the writing of this book such a pleasant challenge that I am sorry it is done. The book's merits owe much to you and to your generosity in giving of your time and information; whatever deficiencies it may have are of my own making.

Preface

~~~~~~

Intercity public transportation being non-existent, for ten years I commuted between my home and office by automobile—a distance of nearly fifty miles each way. To keep myself awake on that monotonous drive, I would occasionally work out arithmetic problems in my head.

One day I calculated that each year I was commuting by automobile over a distance equal to the circumference of the earth at the Equator; I was figuratively driving around the world each year in order to get to and from my office. A few additional mental calculations revealed that each year, in doing so, I was spending the equivalent of thirteen forty-hour work weeks mindlessly piloting an automobile back and forth over some of the most hazardous roads in the country.

From that moment on, the decision to change my work style became inevitable and only a matter of time. Traffic delays that had formerly been endurable became insufferable. The weather— ice and snow, rain, even the baking heat of summer—became my enemy. Finally, with more than a little trepidation, I decided to cut the hawser.

I now commute from my home to my office over the minuscule distance of ten feet, for I have an office at home. The hours I formerly spent in commuting are suddenly available for productive work. I am working longer and harder than ever on projects close to my heart, and I have never been happier. In fact, my problem has become one of forcing myself to spend less time in my office at home.

Setting up a home office was not easy. Library searches revealed the existence of dozens of books on how to incorporate or form a partnership and hundreds of titles on how to operate a small business. But no book existed on the very real problems that go along with setting up and equipping an office in one's home.

Office at Home is the result of hundreds of hours of research and frustrating trial-and-error experiments as part of a novel learning experience. It is dedicated to everyone who yearns to get off the treadmill, to escape from the demeaning routine of commuting, and to discover the special pleasures of an office at home. For you who have already taken the plunge, in addition to useful information, may it offer reinforcement of the wisdom of your decision. Winston Churchill knew whereof he spoke when he observed, "Those whose work and pleasures are one are fortune's favoured children."

Part One

IN THE BEGINNING

ONE

Get Off the Treadmill: Why Not Work at Home?

The president does it in the White House. Ann Landers and hundreds of other newspaper columnists do it in their homes. Tens of thousands of professionals—physicians, dentists, psychologists, lawyers, architects—also do it at home. And other hundreds of thousands of ordinary people are discovering the rewards of working at home and of having a home office.

Rising costs of commercial rentals, more generous tax advantages for home offices, and the introduction of sophisticated computer networks, telecommunications devices, and earth satellites have all contributed to the number, types, and locations of home-based workers. Even the rise in the number of babies being born each year, with a concomitant rise in the number of mothers, has increased the availability of those who can work at home and who find such work desirable.

Philip Fulton, chief of the commuting statistics program of the Census Bureau, estimates that about 2 million people, not including farmers, now work from their homes.

If you work at home now (or are planning to), it can only be for one of two reasons: because you choose to work at home or because, of necessity, you are forced by circumstances into doing so. You may be in the ranks of the unemployed and unable to find another job; you may be a parent with small children and unable to accept ordinary employment; you may be handicapped and even housebound.

According to Charles McClintock, an organizational behavior scientist at Cornell University, more than two-thirds of the home computers in America are today being used for work-related purposes. By 1990, he predicts more than 10 million American workers will be using computers and telecommunications devices at home to transfer information to the office.

McClintock believes this could result in a physical and psychological reversal of the Industrial Revolution, which took workers from their homes and put them into factories. Less office space will be required as more employees desert corporate headquarters to set up offices at home; additional handicapped persons and mothers with small children will enlarge the work force still more by working at home.

More than 1.6 million American mothers—one-fourth of the 6.5 million nonworking mothers with a child under five years old —would look for work if they could afford child care, a Census Bureau report reveals. An increase in homework opportunities would make this reservoir of skills immediately available.

In addition, those working at home will be required to become skilled specialists. In 1940, 50 percent of the American labor force was unskilled, as compared to 7 percent in 1980 and a projected 1 percent by the year 2000.

Many of today's large business enterprises started modestly as small operations at home. Perhaps the most dramatic example of the success of a home-based business can be found in Apple Computer, Inc., one of the leading manufacturers of personal computers. In 1977, it was a two-person venture in a garage. Seven years later, it ranked 299th on the Fortune 500 list and employed thousands of workers. In the history of American business, no other company has gone so far so fast.

A surprising number of profitable enterprises still operate from homes. As a base for business, the home offers many advantages: low overhead, tax savings, flexible hours, the ability to be with one's family, security, and convenience. In nice weather, many with offices at home can take their work outside. When asked to enumerate the disadvantages of working at home, home-based business owners were often at a loss to come up with valid disadvantages. The condition most frequently cited was the difficulty of keeping business and family matters separate. But even this problem can be overcome with a little effort on the part of all members of the household.

Not the least of the attractions of having a home office is the very considerable tax advantages that result from dedicating a portion of your home or apartment to office use. No one launches a home-based business to lose money, of course, but if your home office houses a business operating in the red, the losses may be deductible, if certain tests and conditions imposed by the IRS are met. Even if it is not used for your own home-based business—

whether sideline or full time—a home office in which you do work for your employer can still offer tax benefits.

In terms of commuting times and distances, nothing can beat a home office. A 1979 survey of heads of households showed the average distance traveled to work to be 11.1 miles and the time taken as 22.5 minutes. According to a Census Bureau survey of 96 million American workers sixteen years or older, the average commuter spent 21.7 minutes getting to work. New York workers spent 38.3 minutes, while those in San Diego spent only 18.5 minutes.

Assuming a daily round trip, a five-day week, ten holidays, and a two-week vacation each year, this meant that toilers in the Big Apple spent the equivalent of almost eight forty-hour work weeks of their own time in getting to and from work. Even those who work in San Diego, which bills itself as "America's Favorite City," spent the equivalent of almost four forty-hour work weeks in going back and forth.

Just imagine how much work could have been accomplished in that unproductive commuting time! If you spend your commuting time in an automobile—a not uncommon experience for many Americans—you cannot even read a book or a newspaper or do work of any kind, for you are occupied with driving.

With an office at home, not only will you be able to apply ordinarily wasted commuting time to productive work, but on any day you can decide whether you want to work full time or part time, literally setting your own hours for work and recreation. If you are a night person and work better in the quiet of the night and the small hours of the morning, you can opt to work during those hours, which will free you up for other activities during the day. (As many night workers know, significant savings on entertainment costs can be made by taking advantage of daytime prices; libraries, museums, and galleries are open; in fact, there are many other advantages of taking your recreation when others are working, not the least of which is the lack of crowds.)

With an office at home, you'll be freed of the requirement to follow a rigid or arbitrary dress code. One mistake you should not make, however, is to start the practice of going to your home office in pajamas or nightgown, bathrobe, and bedroom slippers. An occasional lapse is permissible, but experience has shown that you'll be more efficient and happier if you keep home and office as compartmentalized as possible. This is not to say that you should dress specifically for the home office as if it were outside your home. Nevertheless, there are demonstrable psychological advantages to be gained by treating the time in your home office as a separate and distinct work experience.

You can say good-bye to the hurried shower and the bolted breakfast, followed by a mad dash for train or bus or by a daily fight with traffic on the roads. There will be no more time clocks or sign-in sheets. You can forget Byzantine company politics and erstwhile friends who would stab you in the back to get ahead.

Another advantage of an office at home is that you won't have to face the shock of arriving at your office some morning to find it has been burglarized during the night or over the weekend. Security problems are reduced by the presence of your office in your home. That's a two-way street, of course; neither will you have to face the prospect of returning to a home that has been burglarized during your absence all day at a distant office.

Home offices can be made so pleasant and such enjoyable places in which to be that sometimes the home-based office worker's biggest problem is how to manage to spend *less* time in the attractive surroundings of an inviting office at home.

TWO

But Can You? Laws, Ordinances — and the Neighbors

Let's assume you have taken the plunge and have decided to create an honest-to-goodness office in your home or apartment. If you are an apartment dweller and if you have a lease, your first concern should be whether a home office is specifically prohibited by your landlord. Even if you had a lease at one time and now continue to remain in your apartment as a month-to-month tenant, the provisions of the now-expired lease may still apply.

For many years, loft dwellers in New York City occupied their commercially zoned spaces illegally and surreptitiously—until city fathers recognized they were actually pioneers in salvaging neighborhoods from urban blight. Recent changes in home-occupation regulations there allow loft residents to use a greater portion of their living space for work than is permitted in other places. The reasoning is—and it is well founded—that many loft dwellers are artists who genuinely need larger work spaces.

In many communities, a home occupation is characterized as a secondary, or accessory, use of a residential structure. Home-occupation regulations usually ban the sale of goods and the display of merchandise for two reasons: to minimize the commercial nature of the accessory use and to prevent aesthetic values of the neighborhood from being adversely affected. Most ordinances restrict the changes that can be made in the exterior appearance of residential structures.

Unless you are a professional—a doctor, dentist, or lawyer—you may not even be allowed to post a sign. And such signs are usually limited to a nonilluminated nameplate or professional sign with an area not exceeding two square feet.

"Accessory use" is usually interpreted as meaning that the occupation must be carried out in the owner's place of residence or in an accessory building (garage, studio, greenhouse). Generally speaking, the use of a house or apartment for a home-based business is limited to 25 or 30 percent of the space in the dwelling unit. The zoning ordinance of Denver, Colorado, for example, requires that a home occupation may not utilize "more than 20 percent of the gross floor area, but not to exceed 300 square feet in a single-unit dwelling."

It is no exaggeration to suggest, however, that many home businesses are carried on without the knowledge or notice of public officials. Your first task, therefore, should be to investigate the legality of a home office. For many communities, the regulation of home occupations is an unwelcome problem, largely because so many activities could be included. As a result of lack of funds and personnel and in the face of the sheer number of potential home occupations, many communities recognize the virtual impossibility of regulating every home occupation, and so they concentrate on the high-traffic and high-volume home occupations—those traditionally the most visible and the most likely to present problems. To put it another way, the authorities focus on those home occupations most likely to give rise to neighbors' complaints and so come to the attention of local planning or zoning agencies.

Examples of professionals who have usually been permitted to establish offices in residential structures include physicians, dentists, attorneys, music teachers, dancing teachers, and artists. Among those who have been prohibited from operating in residential structures are printers, real estate brokers (in California, Massachusetts, and Pennsylvania), and insurance agents—a Pennsylvania court ruled that licensing of an insurance broker by the state did not confer professional status.

Often, determination whether a proposed use may be conducted hinges on the nature and extent of the professional operation rather than on its exact classification. Pennsylvania courts ruled that a portion of a dwelling rented to five doctors, each practicing independently of the others, did not constitute a "medical center," a permitted use.

Courts disagree as to the exact meaning of "customary home occupations" in a residential area, and there's the rub. Some hold that the term refers to activities pursued at home on a family or personal basis, while others extend it to commercial activity or to the operation of a business.

A professional engineer, denied an office in his residence in Tulsa, Oklahoma, challenged in court the ruling that held that a professional engineer could establish an office in his residence as an accessory use and employ members of his household but could not practice his profession from it.

Courts in New York state sustained a finding by a zoning board that a karate school was not a home occupation but constituted a commercial enterprise.

A home nursery and baby-sitting service in Grand Prairie, Texas, was ruled a permitted use as a "customary home occupation" in an area zoned for single-family dwellings.

One method used by communities to bar certain uses in residential areas is to incorporate provisions limiting the kinds of equipment that may be used. Such ordinances usually prohibit the use of any mechanical or electrical equipment "not normally used for domestic purposes." A Wisconsin photographic studio was prohibited from operating in a residence for such reasons. Donnelson, Missouri; Davidson County, Tennessee; and Philadelphia, Pennsylvania, all banned beauty parlors in residences on similar grounds. But Louisiana courts held for a Baton Rouge beauty-parlor operator, noting that reclining chairs, tables, hair dryers, and other equipment were commonly found in many residences.

In the village in which I live, accessory use of a residence is limited to "customary home occupations," which are otherwise undefined and leave a great potential for conflicting interpretations. My village also makes provision for the use of a residence as a "professional office or studio of an architect, artist, dentist, engineer, lawyer, musician, teacher, physician, public accountant, chiropractor, city planner, insurance broker, real estate broker, or ladies' hairdresser, but not including veterinarians." A ladies' hairdresser seems strangely out of place among all of the professions listed, but this is the least of the faults with this zoning ordinance. Curiously, authors, of whom there are many in the village, are not specifically included.

The exclusion of veterinarians is not unusual—dogs do tend to bark. Of course, this does not preclude the occupation of commercial space by veterinarians. Psychologists constitute another group that is increasingly being excluded in many communities, although psychiatrists, as physicians, are usually permitted. Apparently, the rationale is that psychologists are more likely to engage in group therapy or group counseling sessions, while psychiatrists treat one patient at a time. Few zoning ordinances make provision for some of the newer marginal professionals, such as optometrists and physiotherapists.

Some zoning ordinances are narrowly restrictive, as Patrick and Leah O'Connor discovered in Chicago. The O'Connors perform word processing in their apartment. One day they were visited by a Chicago housing inspector, who told them, "We have received a complaint that you are violating the zoning laws by conducting a commercial enterprise in a residential area." After inspecting the premises, he left, but two days later the O'Connors' landlord received a formal complaint that the apartment was being used for an illegal enterprise and ordered her to appear at the office of the zoning administrator.

The O'Connors checked the wording of the ordinance and discovered that it reads:

> Home Occupations. A physician, dentist, lawyer, clergyman, or other professional person may use his residence for consultation, emergency treatment, or performance of religious rites, but not for the general practice of his profession and not for the installation or use of any mechanical or electrical equipment customarily incident to the practice of such profession.

Mike Royko, then a columnist for the *Sun-Times,* who became interested in the O'Connors' case, pointed out that if this ordinance were strictly enforced, even the use of an electric calculator would be illegal. Happily for the O'Connors, the matter has lain dormant, but there is no doubt that under the law the use of electric calculators and computers is illegal in a Chicago residence.

Dr. George Westmoreland, a psychologist in Maplewood, New Jersey, gained the right to practice from his home in 1981. He received a variance from the strict application of the local ordinance, but only after he had demonstrated that he treated children and adults for depression. The board of appeals considered this a needed community service that was not likely to generate excessive noise or traffic. Dr. James F. Gillespie, of Westport, Connecticut, was not so fortunate. Although his children are grown and his five-bedroom house is ideally suited to accommodate his professional office and give him relief from an $800 monthly rental for commercial office space, he cannot practice from his home.

Architects have been the targets of zoning restrictions in some communities. In 1982, the city of White Plains, New York, decided to tighten its home-occupation regulations, causing the Westchester County chapter of the American Institute of Architects to protest. A local architect, William A. Rose, arguing on behalf of the group, pointed out that more than half of its 130 members used their homes as their place of business. Architects were eventually included in the list of professionals allowed to operate from their homes, but in White Plains, as in many other communities, architects are still hampered by regulations permitting only one employee. An architect often needs two and even three assistants to do designing and drafting, particularly when several projects are being worked on at the same time. Anyone who has ever seen a busy doctor's waiting room would have to know that a physician, working alone under the definition of most ordinances, can generate much more traffic than an architect working with a small group of associates.

The nature of the workplace is changing so radically that the unrestricted *ability* to work at home could make a property more attractive to both the present owner and a potential buyer. In 1973, Leonard Weinberg, a White Plains architect, built a fifteen-by-twenty-foot addition to his home to serve as a home office. He now insists this office is so economical to operate and such a convenience he would never consider buying another house unless he could work at home. "With so many people working from home," Weinberg maintains, "it has to be an added attraction. Even if people don't want to use their homes as offices right away, at least they have that option."

According to Stuart W. Miller of the Research and Technical Services Department of the Chicago-based International Association of Assessing Officers, it is doubtful that a home office—even a custom-designed work space—would have a significant effect on a property's value, unless, of course, it would require major remodeling to turn the house back into a purely residential structure. "Any structural modification which makes the house less of a 'home,' might have an adverse effect on the property's value as a residence," Miller believes. "But any modification that increases square footage will probably have a positive effect (and, incidentally, will probably increase the assessed value)."

Not everyone is in agreement with the concept that working at home or a home-office capability necessarily makes a residential property more attractive. Albert Schatz, a realtor in Ossining, New York, and past president of the Westchester Board of Realtors, says, "A pleasant, quiet neighborhood is still what ultimately determines values. And allowing home-based businesses eventually downgrades an area."

Officials in Smithtown, a Long Island community in New York State, are drafting an ordinance to ban *all* home occupations. Frederick Meyer, Smithtown town planner, points out that about 10 percent of the 32,000 homes in the town are given over in part to home occupations, as compared with almost none ten years ago. "With all those extra people and cars coming and going all the time," he remarked, "you can change the character of town streets."

That many of today's zoning regulations are archaic needs little underscoring. In my village, a homeowner may employ four or even a dozen domestic servants without running afoul of the law; yet if a writer employs and brings into the home two typists to help in typing a book manuscript, this could be considered a violation of the zoning ordinance, which allows for only one nonresident assistant.

Nevertheless, provisions limiting employment in professional offices and home occupations have been upheld by the courts. A custom dressmaking business, operated as a home occupation in Millburn, New Jersey, was held in violation because the owner employed two nonresident workers. The ordinance requires that such business be carried on solely by residents of a residential structure.

One group concerned about the zoning implications of home-based occupations is the National Alliance of Home-Based Business Women. Headquartered in Norwood, New Jersey, the 1,400-member organization is led by Wendy Lazar, who has been working from her home for more than ten years. "Because of the increasing number of individuals, both men and women, working from their homes," she observed, "many neighbors and landlords are getting nervous. We find that businesses with a low profile do not create problems. But anything else, such as a dance studio, makes neighbors very uneasy."

Her organization has found that unions are becoming worried that taking work out of offices and factories, where terms and conditions may be regulated by contracts, could imperil wage scales and benefits. Some unions have even invoked zoning restrictions to halt work in homes.

A federal regulation dating from 1943 forbids work at home in certain traditional crafts: women's clothing (curiously, men's clothing can be made at home), embroidery, handkerchiefs, buttons and buckles, gloves and mittens, and jewelry. Also once prohibited, knitwear can now be made under certain conditions.

The restrictions were intended to keep domestic sweatshops run with cheap labor from undercutting established businesses—but American cheap at-home labor today can hardly compete with products manufactured in Haiti, Singapore, Hong Kong, Taiwan, and Korea. The Center on National Labor Policy, a North Springfield, Virginia, legal foundation (see page 281), is working to have this outdated legislation erased from the books.

Labor unions oppose attempts to lift the homework restrictions, claiming this will lead to new "sweatshops." But as Michael E. Avakian, senior attorney for the center, pointed out before a U.S. Senate labor subcommittee, "Sweatshops are nothing more than illegal *factories* where federal or state minimum wage, record keeping, health, and safety standards are violated. They do not exist in one's home; that is, workers do not live in a sweatshop."

Although the federal homework restrictions are limited to sewing and other craftwork, at least eighteen states and the District of Columbia have even more onerous prohibitions covering manufacturing and assembly work.

The AFL-CIO would like to see such restrictions extended to

include the most exciting area of new technology—the home computer—by promoting a federal ban on computer homework. Sol Chaikin, AFL-CIO vice-president and head of the powerful International Ladies Garment Workers Union, argues, "We cannot afford to wait for a new history of exploitation, wage and hour violations, child labor abuse, and loss of office and factory jobs to homework in that [the computer] field." With the decline of employment in male-dominated heavy industry, his concerns have a foundation in fact: today less than 10 percent of office workers and less than 15 percent of all female workers belong to unions.

Because the line between a hobby and a home occupation is such a fine one, many communities rely on the licensing of businesses in order to detect and to regulate home-based businesses. Therefore, your first step should be a discreet inquiry to the local planning board, zoning board, or licensing authority. You would be well advised to make your initial approach in the form of a personal visit or a telephone call rather than a letter and to couch your inquiry in the most general terms: "I'm thinking about setting up a home office, and I should like to obtain a copy of the zoning ordinance and other applicable regulations" is a good way to begin. If your home office would seem to be a violation, you should consult an attorney who specializes in real estate and zoning problems. Most communities have a zoning board of appeals set up specifically to grant variances and special permits in cases of hardship or other unusual circumstances.

Whether we like them or not, intelligently conceived and fairly applied zoning regulations can work to preserve the character of a neighborhood and even to protect from unfair competition those businesses located in districts zoned for commercial and office uses. The truth is that some home occupations, unregulated either by definition in a zoning ordinance or by a permit requirement, can indeed change the nature of a neighborhood. Unregulated home occupations lower the quality of residential life and tend to give a residential neighborhood commercial overtones, depressing real estate values for everyone.

It is impossible to predict what restrictions you'll find are on the books of your city, town, or village when you inquire about applicable local regulations. For example, although Glenview, Illinois, allows home occupations to be pursued, it specifically prohibits physicians, dentists, lawyers, and clergymen from practicing their professions in their residences.

San Rafael, California, permits various specific home occupations, but just as specifically prohibits others. In defining a home occupation, the San Rafael ordinance goes on to state, "Custom and tradition are intentionally excluded as criteria. In general, a home occupation is an accessory use so located and conducted that the average neighbor, under normal circumstances, would not be aware of its existence other than for a nameplate as permitted."

Fairfax County, Virginia, permits an occupation like cabinet making, often associated with noise-producing machinery, yet prohibits two of the quietest of all business endeavors: antique shops and funeral homes.

No matter whether your local ordinance operates by defining permitted and prohibited home occupations or makes provision for review and screening procedures and requires the issuance of a permit, you should be on the lookout for hidden pitfalls. An ordinance that limits employees to "members of the family residing on the premises" does not take into account whether the business is a partnership or that a physician's nurse is not usually a member of the family. Provisions calling for a restriction of the space utilized to 25 percent of the total area may not be practicable. A psychologist holding a group meeting at home may be forced to utilize more than 25 percent of the home for a brief period.

Ordinances prohibiting any change in the appearance of your home may operate to prevent you from adding a new room, a patio, or a porch. Prohibitions against the use of accessory buildings, such as detached garages and greenhouses, would have prevented many now-successful businesses from getting started. Restrictions on sales in connection with home occupations would prohibit many occupations the ordinance would otherwise permit: artists who sell their paintings from their homes and door-to-door salesmen who maintain offices at home are two examples.

Some communities regulate the parking of vehicles off or on local streets—the latter if the residence has no off-street parking facilities. Others, such as Redlands and Fremont, California, limit the use of, or parking of, trucks, vans, and other commercial vehicles that could serve to advertise the home occupation. If your home-based business is large enough to require even a small number of commercial vehicles, however, it has probably outgrown the home office.

Restrictions on the use of certain utilities may have some relevance (a beauty parlor could overburden community facilities by clogging residential sewer lines with hair), but such restrictions seem intrusive when extended to the use of utilities (telephone, electricity), which would receive increased revenues as a result of the operation of a home-based business.

Today the trend is toward putting less emphasis on defining acceptable and unacceptable home occupations in favor of clarifying the conditions under which a homeowner may operate a business or pursue a profession at home. Redlands, California, employs the permit process, with a clear-cut list of performance standards and a case-by-case evaluation of each application, giving the community complete control over home-based businesses.

This is a far cry from the time-honored precept enunciated by English jurist Sir Edward Coke in 1605 that "the house of every one is to him as his castle and fortress, as well for his defense against injury and violence as for his repose." Nevertheless, the permit process does have the significant advantage that many potential nuisance problems are uncovered and solved before the business can begin to operate. Complaints by neighbors usually do not arise.

If your community has detailed procedural steps leading to a permit, including a written application, filing fee, public hearings (with notices of your intentions mailed to neighbors), formal decisions, and elaborate appeals processes, plus provision for voiding permits once they have been granted and for renewal of permits at stated intervals, the best advice is to find a local attorney who understands the nuances of the permit ordinance and who, ideally, has had some success in preparing other applications and in obtaining positive action on them. The permit process can be costly and time consuming, especially for an applicant anxious to get started in business.

Gregory Longhini, senior research associate with the American Planning Association in Chicago, views the policy of allowing home occupations by special permit as preferable to letting people do whatever they want at home unless and until someone complains. He points out that many zoning regulations were written at a time when the majority of suburbanites were bringing up young children. "Today the mix of different individuals," he says, "suggests a different type of resident, who might be more willing to accept certain things that were discouraged for understandable reasons in the past."

Zoning ordinances occasionally prohibit "offensive" uses within a residential area or uses that place a burden on residents to their disadvantage. Such an ordinance, in Le Mars, Iowa, was held to be sufficiently specific to warrant the issuance of an injunction for abatement of use of a residence as a funeral home, since it did not deny the use of the building for residential purposes. Neighboring residents testified that the establishment was offensive to them, and the court pointed out that the ordinance did not have to spell out those things that were offensive.

Because most problems connected with home-based businesses and home offices arise as a result of the complaints of neighbors, the ideal home-based business would be one that is entirely self-contained, puts no strain on community services, and needs a minimum of external evidence of its existence. The more your home office or home-based business approaches this ideal, the greater will be its chances of getting started and operating without hindrance from the community.

Once you are past the hurdle of the local zoning laws and the applicable building codes of your community, you'll need to satisfy the registration requirements of your state and the federal government. You can get assistance in ascertaining what these are by visiting a local Small Business Administration office (see pages 282–86).

If you decide to incorporate, you'll have to apply to the appropriate department of the state in which you live or the state in which your corporation will be domiciled. This is usually the secretary of state (see pages 286–89). If you incorporate in a state in which you do not reside, you'll need a resident registered agent to represent your interests.

Licensed professionals (accountants, architects, dental hygienists, dentists, doctors, engineers, funeral directors, landscape architects, lawyers, life insurance agents, pharmacists, psychologists, shorthand reporters, social workers, surveyors, and veterinarians) may find that a professional corporation (P.C.) has advantages. But incorporating has disadvantages, too: more paper work, loss of management flexibility, lack of privacy, and an increased chance of state and federal tax audits.

In most states, if you are not operating as a corporation and your full name isn't contained in the name of the business, you'll have to register under the so-called fictitious name law by filing a fictitious-name statement with the county clerk of the county in which you will be doing business. You may also be required to publish the fictitious-name statement in a general-circulation newspaper. By so doing, you will be assured that no other business in the county will be able to use the name chosen. You may have to renew the registration of the fictitious name at specified intervals to keep protection in force. The fictitious-name statement will not be necessary if your own name is part of the name you have chosen.

Unless you live in Alaska, Delaware, Montana, New Hampshire, or Oregon, you'll also have to file for a state sales-tax and use-tax number, and you will be required to collect and remit taxes on any retail sales you make. Such a number is also needed to avoid paying retail sales taxes on any merchandise you buy for resale. In order to report your business income, especially if you expect to employ anyone, you should file Form SS-4, *Application for Employer's Identification Number,* with the Internal Revenue Service for an employer's identification number and ask the IRS for a "Going Into Business Tax Kit."

If you expect to engage in a mail-order business, certain specific legal requirements apply to businesses selling to customers by mail; you should write to the Federal Trade Commission (FTC) for its list of publications and order those that pertain to your business. If you will be selling food, you must write to the Food and Drug Administration (FDA) for information about regulations that apply to food-handling businesses.

THREE

Measure Twice, Cut Once: Planning the Home Office

Where you put your office in your home will probably be the least of your worries, unless you are moving into an unoccupied house or apartment and so have complete freedom of choice. A spare bedroom, now that the children have gone, a walk-in closet, a corner of the basement, or even the attic may represent the only possible sites. Today, with the wide availability of attractive modular units providing work surfaces and storage space, the only limits to the creation of a pleasant and efficient workplace will be your imagination and your budget.

One home-based business is housed in a magnificent nineteenth-century folding desk of burled walnut. When closed, this monstrous collectors' item, called a Wooten Patent Desk, resembles a cylinder-front desk with a cupboard base. Opened, it attests to the inventiveness of W. S. Wooten, of Indianapolis, Indiana, who was granted a patent in 1874.

Consisting of three units—the main desk and two hinged fronts about as thick as the doors on a bank vault—a Wooten desk puts modern counterparts to shame. Swing back the right-hand unit and it reveals forty filing compartments. Inside the left section is a letter box surrounded by pigeonholes and small shelves.

The main section is fitted with a drop-front writing flap concealing additional compartments and five shallow drawers. Wooten Patent Desks have sold for as much as $15,000 on the antiques market, and this could put a dent in anyone's home-office furniture budget.

There are several reasons for designating, designing, and decorating a specific work area within your home as your home office. Not only will it give a boost to your morale to have a well-designed and adequately equipped place to work, but your work efficiency will increase. There are other advantages, as well. The IRS won't recognize your kitchen as your home office if your kitchen table doubles as an occasional work space, but it will allow you to take credit for areas within your home that are furnished as an office and dedicated to the purpose of office work and records storage.

At-home offices can contribute to tax breaks only if the office is used exclusively as a "principal place of business." The exclusivity test usually requires that an entire room or rooms be devoted to business, but the office area can be part of a larger room if personal activities are excluded from the office portion. Many who work at home discover that home-office activities have a curious way of encroaching on the home, with correspondence waiting to be filed often being sorted in the dining room or unpaid bills being spread out on the kitchen table.

OFFICE LAYOUT

Two considerations are paramount in planning for a home office. The first, of course, is the nature of the business you will conduct in your home office. If your business is such that outsiders must come to your office to discuss or transact business with you, you'll have to make provision for receiving them and accommodating them. Remember that the best-laid plans go awry, and you may find yourself with the problem of two overlapping appointments. In such cases, a waiting area is a requisite. This does not have to be elaborately furnished, but it should provide seating space in a place where your conversations on the telephone or with an earlier caller or client cannot be overheard.

You should also provide some magazines (be sure they are current and have not become dog-eared) on appropriate subjects for browsing and page turning, not necessarily for lengthy reading. Ideal magazines for this purpose include *American Heritage, National Geographic, The New Yorker, Sports Illustrated, Time, Newsweek,* and *People.* These can be supplemented with regional magazines of local interest for your area. (The cost of such magazine subscriptions is chargeable as a business expense.) Don't display your professional or specialized trade magazines in the waiting area; they are for your use, not the entertainment of your clients.

Low-volume background music can be utilized in the waiting area to mask any business conversations that would otherwise be overheard. Your choice of music for this area should be innocuous. Rock, jazz, and country-western are out; you are more or less limited to the kind of music heard in the lobbies and elevators of office buildings, although you might get away with light classical music.

Home offices that need facilities for visits by the public may also require some alteration of the family living quarters or living arrangements. For example, you may have to close off a door within the living area if you are using a common entrance for both. A separate entrance for clients is ideal but not always feasible. For this reason, many home offices of professionals serve as temporary quarters until the practice gives evidence of being successful, at which time consideration is given to making structural changes in the house itself or an outside office is sought.

The home-office worker who deals with clients by mail or telephone is in an enviable position. The occasional caller can always be accommodated in the living area of the house or apartment. However, if your actual workplace is an area of your bedroom and is not set up to receive visitors, no one will fault you if you do not receive visitors there.

The other key consideration in home-office layout is contained in the phrase "work flow." Even in a small home office, this is important. Plan your home-office layout so that you expend a minimum of wasted motion and effort. A credenza or open shelves behind your desk on which to store work in progress is a good example. A file cabinet that you can reach merely by rolling backwards or sideways in your office chair is another. At the same time, if you are likely to be chairbound for long periods in your home office, a walk to the files might be a welcome relief and an opportunity to stretch your legs. The same would apply to a cabinet for the storage of stationery and office suppiles or a worktable with wrapping paper, mail scale, and postage meter or stamps.

Remember, too, that one objective of designing your home office is to create a pleasant working environment—after all, you may be spending half of your waking hours there every working day.

PREPARING AN OFFICE-LAYOUT PLAN

With the foregoing considerations in mind, it is now time for you to prepare a formal plan of your home office. This is especially important if you intend to have outside contractors do any remodeling. A plan can keep you from purchasing furniture and equipment that cannot be used because of lack of space. It can also keep you from endlessly rearranging the furniture and equipment you have bought. By "plan," I mean a drawing to scale and not merely a rough sketch. It's a good idea to take pains in making such a plan, for an error of a fraction of an inch on paper can throw you off by a foot or two in your home office.

A useful publication, *How to Read Architectural Drawings,* is obtainable at no charge from the United States Gypsum Company (see page 290). Although intended for those in the construction business, it will be useful to anyone who must deal with architects and contractors.

The first step in drawing a plan is to take measurements and to record them. Measure the distances from wall to wall and from baseboard to baseboard *at several places* in the room—the corners may not be right angles. A carpenters' or builders' flexible steel rule will be useful for this and better than the traditional six-foot folding rule. Measure all door openings (this information will be useful in determining whether furniture or equipment can pass through) and window openings. (Be sure to record the height of sills from the floor.) Measure the height of the room from floor to ceiling. If you can, ascertain the location of ceiling joists and the studs in the walls with a stud finder, sold by hardware stores. This knowledge will be important later if you are fastening heavy objects to walls or ceilings.

Note the location of all existing electrical fixtures and outlets. Ascertain which fuses or circuit breakers at the electrical service entrance control each individual outlet and fixture. To trace outlets to their fuses, plug in a vacuum cleaner, radio, or other appliance that can be heard when operating and turn it on. Then unscrew fuses or circuit breakers at the service entrance panel until you hear the appliance stop.

Repeat this at all other outlets and record the results. To identify the fuses on the lines serving light fixtures, you'll have to turn on each fixture individually and identify the specific fuse by a process of elimination. It's a good idea to record this information inside the cover of the fuse box for future use. Now calculate the total number of watts available to you in your projected home office by adding together the amperage shown on fuses or circuit breakers serving the home office and then multiplying this sum by the voltage of the house current.

For example, let's say you find that four 15-ampere fuses control the projected home-office area of your house and that the nominal voltage is 110 volts; $4 \times 15 \times 110 = 6,600$ watts—the total wattage available to you for air conditioners, office machines, lighting, and other uses. Do not plan on using every last watt; circuits operating at their maximum amperage often blow their fuses. Moreover, if you plan on using any equipment calling for a higher voltage (for example, heaters or heater/air conditioners operating at 208 or 230 volts), you'll need the services of an electrical contractor to run heavier electrical wiring to your home office and to install additional outlets. Higher-voltage equipment has special polarized line-cord plugs that will not fit standard duplex outlets.

Before drawing up your formal plan, buy a couple of architects' office-layout templates from a drafting-materials supplier. Available in scales of $\frac{1}{8}$ inch and $\frac{1}{4}$ inch to the foot, these will save a lot of time in laying out alternative plans, I prefer $\frac{1}{4}$ inch to the foot as a working scale. Not only does it yield a larger and more readable plan, but it is the scale with which architects, interior designers, and contractors work. This makes your plan instantly usable should you decide to engage an outside contractor to do any remodeling. You can choose from templates showing desks, chairs, tables, lamps, wastebaskets (both round and square), file cabinets (in banks or singly and showing the actual floor area occupied when drawers are opened), partitions, aisle widths, door-opening arcs, and miscellaneous furniture and equipment. Alternatively, you can buy self-adhesive outlines of office furniture and equipment for cutting out and affixing to your home-office plan.

Don't overlook the possibility of adapting commercial office panels and screens in your home-office design. Movable partitions may result in tax savings—they are considered office equipment for tax purposes rather than as a capital expenditure, so a larger deduction can be taken on their cost. Panels and partitions offer useful locations for shelves, desk tops, cabinets, and storage modules, which can be hung from them without taking up valuable floor space. Movable partitions interlock and may be attached to the floor for increased stability, although this tends to limit their mobility.

LIGHTING

Two major factors are involved in using light to provide efficient and comfortable seeing conditions: quantity of light and quality of light, including light color and diffusion to eliminate glare. Psychological effects, aesthetics, and economics will also play roles in decisions about lighting selection.

Lighting needs in the home office will differ from residential lighting requirements in several respects. Your eyes will be used at close range for critical visual tasks—reading such varied materials as typed letters, carbon copies, word processing screens, and books with texts ranging from large type to fine print. In addition, you may be preparing documents by hand or on machines under a variety of conditions. As a general rule, visual performance improves as the quantity (the level of illumination) increases.

Light Quantity

For purposes of interior design, the quantity of light (called "illuminance" by lighting engineers) is measured by special meters in footcandles, a unit equal to the amount of light produced on a surface one foot from a standard candle, a measurement usually taken thirty inches above the floor. (As a rule of thumb, one watt per square foot will provide fifteen footcandles. A 100-watt light bulb lighting an area ten feet by ten feet square would provide about fifteen footcandles of illumination.) Such meters are available, but a reasonable approximation of relative light values can be obtained with an ordinary photographic exposure meter. Ideal lighting for an office would be at the level of daylight, but this is virtually impossible to achieve with artificial illumination.

Before World War I, a light intensity of five footcandles was considered adequate in offices; between the First and Second World Wars, this was increased to fifteen footcandles; after the Second World War, some newly designed offices provided as much as thirty footcandles of illumination.

Today it is not unusual for offices in which exacting tasks are performed (a drafting room or art studio, for example) to provide 200 footcandles or more. Areas of less-exacting tasks may receive 150 footcandles, and even corridors and storage areas may get 20 footcandles, making them positively bright by Victorian office standards. Table 3.1 shows suggested quantities of illumination for efficient visual performance of selected office tasks.

Table 3.1. Suggested Illumination for Specific Tasks

Task	Foot candles
Bookkeeping, accounting	30–150
Filing	50–100
Drafting	100–200
Conference, waiting areas	20–50
VDT displays	5–10
Reading (at desk)	50–100

Light Quality

Providing for light in adequate quantity does not in itself guarantee comfortable vision or promote work efficiency. Light quantity is measurable, of course, but light quality and visual comfort are equally important, not determinable quantitatively, and much more difficult to achieve, especially where less than optimum conditions are present or difficult visual tasks must be performed.

The main consideration in achieving lighting of high quality is to keep brightness ratios low. This means that the brightness of the task and its surroundings should be of nearly the same degree, with no excessively high (or very low) brightness present. High brightness is often associated with glare, either direct or reflected.

Brightness Subjective brightness is the sensation produced by a source of light or by reflected light. When measured photometrically, it is called "luminance" and is a measure of the luminous intensity of a surface and depends on the amount of light that falls on it and on its reflecting characteristics. Everything visible has some luminance.

Brightness Ratio The degree of brightness is measured as a ratio between the luminances of two surfaces. For office work, the Illuminating Engineering Society suggests that the brightness ratios of certain areas should not exceed the values shown below. In fact, values *less* than these are desirable.

Table 3.2. Brightness Ratios

Objects	Maximum Brightness Ratio
Task and adjacent surfaces	1 to 1/3
Task and more remote darker surfaces	1 to 1/10
Task and more remote lighter surfaces	1 to 10

Table 3.2 underscores that what is to be avoided, therefore, in illuminating any task and work surface is a "spotlight" effect.

In order to reduce contrasts in brightness, the amount of light coming from fixtures can be reduced or increased, or their positions can be changed in the planning stage. Furniture, ceilings, walls, and floors can be utilized as secondary light sources by changing their surface-reflection qualities. Light colors have better reflective values than dark colors, and white has the highest, of course. Therefore, to reduce contrasts in brightness, use light-colored walls, floors, desk surfaces, and decorations. If your desk top or work surface is dark colored, a light-colored covering—a light-colored desk blotter or even a large scheduling calendar—can help to reduce brightness ratios between the task and work surface.

Glare For visual comfort, the sensation of glare must be eliminated from light, contrasts in brightness must be minimized, and the light must be diffused uniformly. Direct glare is intense light produced by a bright or insufficiently shielded light source within the visual field of the viewer. If the light is sunlight, it can be eliminated or reduced by the use of window curtains, drapes, blinds, or by means of sun-filtering screens applied directly to the window glass. Light fixtures should be shielded or of a type that gives off indirect light. Reflected (indirect) glare can be caused by highly polished furniture, glass desk tops, CRT (cathode ray tube) screens, mirrors, or pictures framed under glass. (A strategically placed mirror, however, can make a room appear larger or lighten a dark area if placed opposite a window or other source of light.)

Reflectance This is the amount of light reflected by an object or surface expressed as a percentage of the amount of light it receives. High-reflectance room surfaces and furnishings are desirable to achieve proper luminance ratios in the occupant's visual field. The reflectance of an object is important because it is the basis of seeing; it is affected by the surface finish and color of an object as well as the amount of light received by it.

Reflectances recommended for office use (in percentages) are: ceilings, 80–90; walls, 40–60; blinds, 40–60; desk and worktable tops, 25–45; and floors, 20–40. These are higher values than those usually encountered, but only because most offices are poorly lit in terms of reflectance values. High reflectances contribute much to pleasant visual surroundings.

Reflectance can be judged by visually comparing surfaces with color chips of known reflectance. One widely used system uses 100 color chips for convenient comparison with surface colors. Instruments called reflectometers also measure diffuse reflectance with a high degree of accuracy.

Lighting Systems and Fixtures "Direct," "semidirect," "general diffuse," "semiindirect," and "indirect" are the terms applied to lighting systems, based on the type of fixture employed. Illumination is usually the highest when direct and semidirect fixtures are used, but brightness ratios can range from ideal to excessive, depending on the fixtures installed. In contrast, indirect and semidirect lighting can result in low utilization of light but can give comfortable levels with little reflected glare.

You'll find that you have a wide choice in fixtures (called "luminaires") that will accept incandescent, fluorescent, and high-intensity discharge lamps. Luminous panels, coffers, courses, cornices, troffers, and downlights are examples of direct-lighting fixtures. Coves, wall urns, and units with opaque bottom reflectors are examples of indirect-lighting fixtures. In general, the more light you can arrange to have coming from the ceiling, the better will be your office illumination. Task illumination can be provided selectively by supplementary lighting, such as desk lamps.

Incandescent Bulbs

The filament of an incandescent lamp, heated to a high temperature by an electric current, gives off a steady light that accentuates reds and oranges and dulls blues. Incandescents are notoriously inefficient and emit much heat—only about 10 percent of their electrical energy is used to produce light. Generally speaking, incandescent fixtures and bulbs are less expensive than their fluorescent counterparts, but the bulbs have markedly short lives. A 60-watt bulb will last about a thousand hours, and a 100-watt bulb will last only about 750 hours. Long-life (rough-service) bulbs can be purchased; they are intended for use in areas in which lights burn continuously, as in a fire stairway, or in inaccessible locations, where frequent bulb changing is impractical.

Fluorescent Tubes

Fluorescent tubes in ceiling fixtures or desk lamps offer certain advantages: less heat, better diffusion of light because of their larger surface area, almost five times the light of incandescent bulbs of similar wattage, and a useful life twenty times as long. Fluorescent tubes cannot be operated directly from a power source but require a ballast, or current-limiting device. Oddly enough, the service life of fluorescents is extended by use. Fluorescents operating for twelve hours a day will last longer than those operated for less than three hours a day.

Standard cool-white fluorescent tubes are the most efficient in terms of light production, but they alter color values, tending to make blues and greens vivid and dulling reds. Fluorescents in the warm-white group blend more successfully with incandescent lighting.

Improved-color-rendition fluorescent tubes (also called "deluxe whites") are available in cool or warm styles. These add red to the spectrum to bring out a full range of object colors, but their light output is about one-third less than the standard types. If you are planning to use fluorescent fixtures and are concerned about the accurate color rendition of red objects, you should install warm-white or deluxe warm-white tubes.

Fluorescent light is produced by the action of ultraviolet waves on phosphors coating the inside of the tubes. As a result, they are momentarily "off," and some persons are acutely aware of and bothered by this stroboscopic effect, which is sometimes more noticeable as the tubes age or in single-tube fixtures. Because of their greater efficiency, however, fluorescents have one notable advantage over incandescents: at the planning stage and for a given equivalent wattage, a choice of fluorescents over incandescents makes it possible to increase the total amount of illumination without rewiring the electrical circuits in a room. The wattage of fluorescent tubes varies with their length; once fluorescent luminaires have been installed, wattage cannot be increased (or lowered), as it can with incandescent bulbs.

Fluorescents are not without other drawbacks. Although fluorescent ballasts have an average useful life of ten years, they will often buzz in operation or drip a gooey black liquid when they fail. In multiple fixtures operating on a single ballast, one tube cannot be removed without affecting the operation of the others.

Fluorescents are available in three types: trigger start, rapid start, and instant start, depending on the type of ballast employed. Rapid-start ballasts are always using electricity in small amounts to keep their cathodes warm.

It's just as easy to overilluminate a room as it is to underilluminate one, and overillumination can be costly in terms of electrical energy. Utilize daylight as a light source whenever possible; there's no better or cheaper source of illumination. Light colors on surfaces can increase the amount of light available from any source by up to thirty footcandles. Because incandescent lamps are only about a fifth as efficient as fluorescent lamps, the latter should be used whenever possible.

In planning the placement of fluorescent fixtures, it is preferable to align their long axes at right angles to the line of sight rather than parallel to it, especially in large rooms with many fixtures.

High-Intensity Discharge Lamps

A third type, high-intensity discharge lamps, is subdivided into mercury, metal-halide, and high-pressure sodium lamps, which emit light resulting from the passage of an electric arc through a tube under high pressure. High-intensity discharge lamps should not be screwed into ordinary household sockets; like fluorescents, they must have a ballast to control the voltage. Because of their high wattages and necessary start-up and cool-down periods, high-intensity discharge lamps are not suited for most home-office interior situations, although they have outdoor applications and find indoor uses in office-building lobbies and high-ceilinged industrial plants.

TEMPERATURE AND HUMIDITY CONTROL

Because your home office will be an integral part of your house or apartment, you'll probably have no way of independently controlling the heating and cooling. However, a newly created home office in a previously unoccupied area, such as an attic or basement, will give you an opportunity to make provision for separate heating or cooling. This can be accomplished by running additional ducts (for hot-air heating and central air conditioning), piping for hot-water heating, or wiring, if desired, for electrical baseboard heating. Don't overlook the tax advantages you can get for the energy-conservation devices and materials you add. These include insulation to reduce heat loss (or heat gain in summer) or heat loss from a water heater; storm or thermal outside windows or doors; caulking or weather stripping of outside doors and windows; clock thermostats or other automatic energy-saving setback thermostats; furnace replacement burners, ignition systems to replace gas pilot lights; flue-opening modifications; and meters to show the cost of energy use.

You should also investigate window-mounted room air conditioners that double as heaters. These year-around units feature built-in automatic timers, variable-speed fans, and night settings. Some are available as heat pumps (which reverse the normal air-conditioning cycle by exhausting cool air to the outside in winter) or with conventional heating elements. All are usually of high capacity and require 230-, 208-, or 230/208-volt circuitry.

Selection of an air conditioner of the correct capacity is dependent on the cooling load that will be placed on the unit. This involves such factors as geographical location, whether the unit is intended primarily for nighttime cooling, number of windows, exposure, wall insulation, and so on.

A simpler and less accurate method, the "square-foot method," is a quick and easy way to compute needed air-conditioner capacity. Forms for computing by either method are available from the Association of Home Appliance Manufacturers (AHAM; see page 290). You should also ask for a copy of their latest *Consumer Selection Guide for Room Air Conditioners.* (*Note:* this publication also covers heating units as well as cooling units and built-ins.)

A unit with too much cooling capacity will be inefficient and expensive to operate; a unit that's too small won't do a satisfactory job. There's also a relationship between cooling capacity and dehumidifying action. An oversized unit will cool the air without remaining in operation long enough to dehumidify it, and a cold, clammy feeling will result.

Because air conditioners are less efficient than heating furnaces, the potential for energy savings in summer is greater than in winter. By utilizing the thermostatic controls on your air conditioner, you can save 10–20 percent on energy costs. Ideally, you should keep the difference between inside and outside temperatures small. If it is ninety degrees outside and seventy degrees inside, every degree you raise the thermostat will cut your utility bill by 5 percent.

In the absence of an air conditioner, your options include turning off stove and furnace pilot lights and using vents and exhaust fans to draw heat and moisture from the work area.

Studies have shown that work efficiency is reduced when temperatures are too high or too low. A comfortable temperature range would be seventy to seventy-four degrees Fahrenheit in winter and seventy-four to seventy-eight degrees in summer. Comfort is additionally dependent on the relative humidity—the amount of water vapor in the air (expressed as a percentage of the maximum amount of moisture the air can hold at a given temperature). This should range between 40 and 55 percent. In many regions, humidity, especially in summer, can be excessive, reducing comfort levels, damaging furniture and equipment, and necessitating the use of dehumidifying appliances other than air conditioners, which must first reduce the humidity before cooling takes place.

Table 3.3 shows criteria to use in the selection of a dehumidifier, based on conditions without dehumidification. Values in this table indicate the dehumidification required in pints per twenty-four hours, based on the area of the space to be dehumidified and the conditions that would exist in that space when a dehumidifier is not in use during warm and humid outdoor conditions. Dehumidification variables also include such other factors as climate, laundry equipment, number of family members, number of doors and windows, and degree and intensity of area activity.

Table 3.3. Dehumidification Selection Guide
(Values in Pints Per Twenty-four Hours)*

Condition Without Dehumidification	Area in Square Feet				
	500	1,000	1,500	2,000	2,500
Moderately damp. Space feels damp and has a musty odor only in humid weather.	10	14	18	22	26
Very damp. Space always feels damp and has a musty odor. Damp spots show on walls and floor.	12	17	22	27	32
Wet; space feels and smells wet. Walls or floor sweat, or seepage is present.	14	20	26	32	38
Extremely wet; laundry drying, wet floor, high-load conditions.	16	23	30	37	44

* After AHAM.

Although relative humidity can drop to as low as 25 percent in winter without affecting comfort, sensitive electronic equipment may malfunction because of static buildup at low-humidity levels. Humidity can be measured by a simple instrument called a psychrometer, which consists of two thermometers, one of whose bulbs is kept moistened by a reservoir and simple wick.

Under conditions of low humidity, an appliance to increase relative humidity should be considered. This may be installed as part of the central heating/cooling system or may be freestanding and independent of it. But overhumidifying indoor air can be dangerous, especially in winter, causing structural damage and equipment failure because of condensation. Therefore, a humidifier should be controlled by an adjustable humidistat, which can be set at a level to prevent condensation on windows, sills, walls, and equipment. The humidistat should be reset whenever there has been a major change in outdoor temperature. Condensed moisture or frost on inside windows is a good sign that the controls are set too high.

You can place a freestanding humidifier almost anywhere in the house as long as the moist air can circulate freely through the house. When the humidifier begins to operate, it may run constantly for a day or so; this is because furniture, rugs, drapes, and other articles are absorbing moisture.

Table 3.4 shows the criteria to use in the selection of a humidifier, based on residence construction and size of the occupied area in square feet. Values shown are in gallons per twenty-four hours. An amount of approximately two gallons per twenty-four hours provided by sources of internal humidity (based on a family of four) has already been taken into account in calculating the values in table 3.4.

Energy Audits The principal enemy of efficient humidifier and heater/air conditioner operation is the exchange of inside and outside air that takes place through structural cracks and apertures and improperly sealed doors and windows. It will be to your advantage to apply caulking and weather stripping; if your local electric company offers an energy audit at no cost, arrange to have one made. Such energy audits can pinpoint areas of energy loss and suggest the best energy-conservation methods. In poorly constructed or older buildings, up to 30 percent of the heating, cooling, and humidifying (or dehumidifying) effect may be lost through leakage.

Energy Ratings Detailed data on model performances, configuration, electrical requirements, and other values can be found in publications of AHAM. When shopping for an appliance, look for the highest EER (energy efficiency ratio) on the label, which must be carried by all air conditioners, refrigerators, and similar appli-

Table 3.4. Humidification Requirements
(Values in Gallons per Twenty-four Hours)*

Construction	Area in Square Feet					
	500	**1,000**	**1,500**	**2,000**	**2,500**	**3,000**
Tight (well insulated; vapor barrier; tight storm doors and windows with weather stripping; dampered fireplace)	†	1.4	3.2	4.9	6.6	8.3
Average (insulated; vapor barrier; loose storm doors and windows; dampered fireplace)	0.5	3.0	5.5	8.0	10.5	13.0
Loose (little insulation; no storm doors or windows; no vapor barrier; undampered fireplace)	1.0	4.0	7.0	10.0	13.1	16.1

* After AHAM.
† Humidification unnecessary to maintain conditions of 70 degrees Fahrenheit (21.1 degrees Centigrade) and 30 percent relative humidity.

ances. This value is determined by the manufacturer under Department of Energy (DOE) test procedures and is reported to the FTC for labeling purposes. The EER, expressed in BTUs per watt-hour, can be calculated for any cooling appliance. It is the quotient of the cooling capacity of the unit in BTUs per hour divided by its electrical input in watts.

Another proportion—the ratio of sensible heat to total heat removal—is a useful performance characteristic in evaluating air conditioners for specific climatic conditions but is generally not provided by air-conditioner manufacturers. A unit with a low ratio will provide more dehumidification and would be more desirable on the Gulf Coast, while a unit with a higher ratio would be more appropriate in the dry climate of Arizona or New Mexico.

The latent heat removal of room air conditioners typically ranges from 25–35 percent of total capacity.

Do It by the Code Whatever plans for construction you make in connection with your home office, you should be prepared to follow the several safety codes and standards that apply to such work, including the National Electrical Code (sponsored by the National Fire Protection Association), Underwriters' Laboratories, Inc., and your own local building code. In Canada, the Canadian Standards Association is the national body that establishes standards for safety, fire protection, and shock hazards.

If your construction work and wiring are done by a professional contractor, all permits and inspections after completion by a building inspector should be arranged by the contractor. If you decide to do the work yourself, you'd be well advised to obtain the necessary permits and have your finished work inspected by the building inspector. In the event of a fire or other damage, failure to have done this won't result in refusal of your insurance company to pay your claim (they will cover you even for your own stupidity), but it could cause you to be regarded as an undesirable insurance risk in the future.

FOUR

To Your Own Taste: Decorating the Home Office

Despite the advances in office design that have taken place in recent years, many commercial offices are still drab places in which to work. But that doesn't mean your home office should duplicate such conditions. Your decorating plans can include the use of a number of decorating elements to produce a pleasant workplace: color, lighting, floor coverings, furniture, and the use of built-ins. Among the areas for special treatment are walls, ceilings, floors, and windows.

PAINT AND WALL COVERINGS

When it comes to covering your walls, nothing is better than paint. Not only is it something you can apply yourself, but paint gives you the widest latitude in colors, types, and finishes. If you ever tire of the appearance of a painted room, it can be done over quickly.

Old-fashioned oil-base paints have largely been replaced by alkyd interior paints because of the latter's better durability, appearance, and ease of application. (If you are applying alkyd paint over unpainted gypsum wallboard, use a latex primer—alkyd primers raise the fibers.)

Latex paints are still the most widely used because they go on quickly and easily, clean up with cold water, and are almost odorless. In addition, a second coat can be applied in a matter of hours. (But if you are applying latex paint to raw wood, use an alkyd primer.)

Special paint and paint finishes are available, such as cement paint, epoxy (waterproof) paint, texture paints, sand paints, and stippling paints. To reduce annoying reflections from painted surfaces, use flat or semigloss finishes rather than high-gloss finishes, even though the latter are easier to keep clean.

Flexible wall coverings are available in a variety of materials including wallpaper, grass cloth, burlap, felt, and other fabrics. Metal foil, cork tiles, and cork slabs are also available. Instead of traditional plaster or gypsum wallboard, you may elect to cover your walls with wood, plywood, or hardboard panels. Other coverings include glass and ceramic tile, brick, marble, and mirrors— none of these is very sound absorbent, and so they are not particularly desirable in an office environment.

COLOR

Psychologists have demonstrated a definite correlation between room colors and their effect on the moods of occupants. In one office, after the walls were painted blue, employees complained that they were cold, even though the temperature had been raised. Color can work both ways, of course. Another company heard fewer complaints about summer heat after it repainted its offices a light shade of blue. Employees in an office painted yellow and light green demanded a reduction in the amount of heat in winter.

If your home office gets little or no sunlight or has a northern or eastern exposure, warm colors—shades of beige, brown, tan, yellow, peach, or orange—should be considered. Rooms with a western or southern exposure can be painted in such cool colors as shades of blue or green. Color can also be used to change the apparent size and shape of rooms. Small rooms can be made to appear larger by painting the walls white or a single light color. If your home office is in one large room, consider using more than one color or shade of that color on the walls. Square rooms can be made to appear less square (and thus more interesting dimensionally) by using a lighter or darker color on one wall. (But do not use dark colors on a wall containing a window or windows.) Long, narrow rooms will seem wider if the end walls are painted in a dark color and the long walls in a lighter shade of the same color. High-ceilinged rooms can have their apparent height reduced by carrying the ceiling color down on to the upper parts of the walls. High ceilings also tend to appear lower when painted a darker color than the walls.

A simple color wheel or chromatic circle can be useful for selecting appropriate colors for a home office. The primary colors, of course, are red, yellow, and blue. Mixing two primary colors yields a secondary color. One of a pair of colors opposite the other member of the pair on the color wheel is referred to as a complementary color: green is the complement of red, orange of blue, and violet of yellow (Fig. 4.1).

Among color schemes that create pleasing effects without accompanying problems are:

One or Two Colors with Black, White, or Gray (It's virtually impossible to go wrong with this.) Remember, however, that professional decorators usually employ muted shades of colors and avoid the visually jarring effect of pure colors.

Complementary Colors Harmonious effects can be achieved by using complementary colors—two colors opposite one another on the color wheel (e.g., green with red).

Split Complements Takes the form of a Y on the color wheel, with two arms pointing to adjacent complementary colors and a primary color (e.g., blue green and yellow green with red).

Double-Split Complements Takes the form of an X on the color wheel. If two legs are selected indicating yellow orange and yellow green, the other legs will be red violet and blue violet.

Triads Employs three primary or three secondary colors equi-

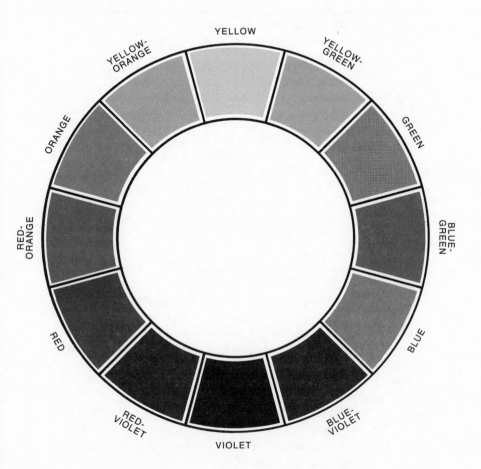

Fig. 4.1. Basic color wheel.

distant on the color wheel (red-yellow-blue or green-violet-orange).
*A Monochromatic Scheme Utilizing Several Shades of a Single
Color* (*Note*: this does not work for certain light colors that cannot achieve deep values for emphasis, such as yellow, orange, and
pale green.)
Analogous Colors Utilizes colors that adjoin each other on the
color wheel (but always in muted tones): yellow, yellow green,
and green; red, red orange, and orange.
Analogous Colors and an Accenting Complementary Color Usually, three analogous colors (e.g., yellow orange, orange, and yellow green) are set off with a complementary accent color, violet,
which grays and softens the three other colors.

Colors rise and fall in popularity in office decor. According to
the Color Marketing Group, a trend-setting organization, the "in"
colors are:
Grays The fastest-growing color group, grays are neutral yet
formal, suited to the latest postmodern interiors.
Blue An influence from the Orient, blues and turquoises are gain-
ing momentum. Navy and gray blue are also popular.
Green As an escape from the overuse of mauve—a color on its
way out—many shades of green are coming back in style. Blue
greens, yellow greens, gray greens, and aquas, as well as soft to
deep forest green.

Table 4.1 gives some *suggested* color schemes based on the color
of the office furniture selected. In choosing carpet colors, remember that a floor is a large area, and an entire floor covered with
carpet will intensify the color chosen, making it seem darker than
the sample swatch. Therefore, select a carpet color one shade
lighter than the target color.

*Table 4.1. Some Suggested Color Combinations
Based on Furniture Color*

Furniture	Carpet	Walls	Drapes	Accessories
Walnut	Green	Beige	Chartreuse	Red
Mahogany	Beige	Light blue	Dark blue	Dark yellow
Light oak	Light brown	Beige	Dark brown	Orange
Blond	Charcoal	Gray	Yellow	Coral
Mixed	Gray	White	Gray	Red

Color schemes and light sources are interdependent. The interior color scheme you choose should not be decided until consideration has been given to the kind of lighting that will be used. If part of the home office is illuminated by daylight, electric lighting should be chosen that blends well with daylight. This means you should choose sources that have a correlated color temperature above 4,000 Kelvins (the unit of color temperature; color-temperature values for a particular light source can be obtained from the manufacturer). The higher the color temperature, the cooler the light. Light sources should not be mixed without first establishing that their correlated color temperatures and their color-rendering properties match.

Because fluorescents have the widest range of effects on color rendition, table 4.2 should be used to select appropriate fluorescent lamp types.

DECORATING YOUR WALLS

What you put on your walls will tell visitors something about yourself and your taste in decoration. Of course, you may be required to display certain documents prominently in connection with your business: a license to practice or to conduct a business, a workers' compensation notice, insurance certificate, or authorization to collect sales taxes. These do not have to be displayed in your office but can be hung anywhere in the business portion of the premises. Unless you are a doctor, dentist, or lawyer, keep your diplomas and your other educational credentials to yourself. A political pollster might want to display photographs of himself shaking hands with former presidents or well-known political figures, as would politicians at any level. Still, if you display too many autographed photographs, your office risks looking like a barbershop in the theatrical district. Family photographs are also taboo. Works of art—especially paintings and prints—are all right if they are appropriate. But a reclining nude would be better hung behind the bar in a men's club or in one of those Victorian saloon-type steak houses that have sprung up everywhere.

Color-print enlargements from color-film negatives or slides are an often overlooked source of wall decoration. Perhaps you have a favorite shot of a landscape, a dramatic sunset, or a marine scene.

Table 4.2. *Color Effects of Fluorescent Lamps*

Fluorescent Lamp Types	Effect on Neutral Surfaces	Effect on "Atmosphere"	Colors Enhanced	Colors Dulled
Cool white[a]	White	Neutral to moderately cool	Orange, yellow, blue	Red
Deluxe cool white[b]	White	Neutral to moderately cool	All	None
Warm white[c]	Yellowish white	Warm	Orange, yellow	Red, green, blue
Deluxe warm white[d]	Yellowish white	Warm	Red, orange, yellow, green	Blue
Daylight[e]	Bluish white	Very cool	Green, blue	Red, orange
White[f]	Pale yellowish white	Moderately warm	Orange, yellow	Red, green, blue
Soft white— natural[g]	Pinkish white	Warm pinkish	Red, orange	Green, blue

[a] Blends with natural light.
[b] Best overall color rendition; simulates natural daylight.
[c] Blends with incandescent light.
[d] Excellent color rendition; simulates incandescent light.
[e] Usually replaceable with cool white.
[f] Usually replaceable with cool white or warm white.
[g] Usually replaceable with deluxe cool white or deluxe warm white.

A large color print suitable for framing can be made at comparatively low cost.

A few rules must be observed in displaying such prints: indirect illumination by incandescent lighting is best. Avoid direct sunlight and bright lights of any kind, especially fluorescent lighting. Excessive heat or humidity are also undesirable.

To mount color enlargements, use a photographic-mounting cement (Kodak Rapid Mounting Cement or Dry Mounting Tissue are both good). Do not use rubber cement or any mounting paste containing water or penetrating solvents. When color enlargements are mounted under glass, a slight separation should be maintained between the print surface and the glass. This makes a matted border desirable. Even when kept under optimum conditions, the dyes in color films and prints will undergo change.

FLOOR COVERINGS

You'll find a wide choice of materials, starting with linoleum or other sheet flooring materials and progressing through various kinds of resilient floor tiles to carpeting. Linoleum, widely used before the Second World War, has been largely superseded by floor tiles because of the ease of application of the latter.

But the old-fashioned monochromatic, unimaginatively designed roll linoleum (the name comes from the fact that it was made from linseed oil) has given way to very modern and pleasing decorative designs. If you are operating on a low budget, consider linoleum, by all means. Resilient tiles, offering almost the same degree of water impermeability and soil resistance as linoleum, is available in asphalt, cork, rubber, vinyl, and vinyl-asbestos in thicknesses of $\frac{1}{8}$, $\frac{3}{32}$, or $\frac{1}{16}$ inch, and sizes 9 by 9 or 12 by 12 inches.

If your floor is uneven, it is easier to conceal this fact with a thick carpet than with linoleum or resilient tiles. And not only is carpet more sound absorbent, with better insulating properties, but it will also help to prevent slips and to cushion falls.

CARPET CONSTRUCTION AND TEXTURES

Before 1950, virtually all carpet was woven. Today, 95 percent of carpet is made by a tufting process in which hundreds of tufts—pieces of yarn—are imbedded in a backing material. To lock the tufts into place, a latex coating is applied to the backing, and a secondary backing is then applied. These are the several tufting methods:

Level-Loop Pile The yarn on the face of the carpet forms a loop, with both ends anchored into the carpet back. The pile loops are of equal height and uncut, making a smooth and level surface with excellent wearing qualities. Soil tends to stay on the surface, making level-loop pile carpet easy to clean. Multilevel-loop pile carpets (called "sculptured" or "carved" because the different heights give a patterned effect) may have loops of two or three different heights and are not quite as wear resistant.

Cut Pile When the top of the carpet yarn loop is cut, two individual yarn tufts result; this is referred to as cut-pile carpet. Within this texture category are many of today's most popular types whose specific appearance is achieved by the amount of "twist" given to the yarn, its size and luster, and the type of heat-setting employed.

In heat-setting, after separate strands of yarn are twisted together to form a two-ply, three-ply, or four-ply yarn, the twist is set and made permanent in special machinery by means of heat or steam. Today most nylon and polyester cut-pile carpets are heat-set. The following are some of the types of cut-pile carpet:

Velvets or plushes are made from yarns with very little twist, giving a very level surface that creates a formal atmosphere.

Saxonies are yarns of two or more ply, twisted together and heat-set to lock the twist in the yarn, thus giving it stability and permanence. Because each tuft end is distinguishable in the surface, a distinctive look results; in the velvets, all tuft ends merge and blend together.

Velvets, plushes, and saxonies made with today's high-luster fibers have rich highlights and shadow effects. Footmarks are also more apparent in cut-pile carpets than in the other textures.

Friezé (pronounced "free-zay") carpets are made from tightly twisted heat-set yarns that create a dense, low-pile surface with a nubby effect. These are extremely rugged carpets suitable for heavy traffic areas.

Cut-and-loop pile uses a combination of cut and looped yarns to give a variety of surface textures and sculptured effects. They may be tip sheared, randomly sheared, or have a shag texture.

The backing and the pile of *woven carpeting* are interwoven simultaneously to lock both yarns together in a single fabric. Three styles of weaving are used: velvet, Wilton, and Axminster. Velvet is the simplest and is used mostly for solid colors. Wilton carpets are noted for their sharply delineated patterns and textures. Axminster weaving simulates the handwoven carpets of the Orient.

CARPET FIBERS

Carpet is available in nylon, olefin (polypropylene), polyester, acrylic, and wool. Approximately 97 percent of all carpet today is made from man-made fibers. As a fiber, wool is luxurious and expensive, but nylon is the strongest and longest wearing (and also the most subject to static electricity).

Because of its proven resistance to abrasion and staining and its ease of cleaning, nylon makes up about 80 percent of the pile fibers used in carpets today. So-called advanced-generation nylons feature built-in static control and yield even greater durability.

Olefin carpet yarns are strong, resist abrasion, soiling, and staining and are colorfast (because the color is built into the fiber). Also static-free and easily cleaned, olefin carpet is very resistant to moisture and mildew, making it useful in ground-level applications.

Polyester yarns are known for their luxurious, soft feel when used in thick, cut-pile textures. Readily cleaned, polyester yarns are resistant to water-soluble stains, but their use should be restricted to low-traffic areas.

Acrylic fibers give the appearance and feel of wool at lower cost. Acrylic carpets have a low static level and are moisture and mildew resistant, but only fair in soil and stain resistance.

Wool is the only nonsynthetic fiber still used in significant quantities to make carpets; its desirable qualities include luxurious appearance, high bulk, and wide color range. The wool used in carpets is a blend of fibers imported from many countries; domestic wool is too fine and too soft, making it better for clothing and blankets.

Carpet Quality

The best single clue to carpet quality is density—the thickness of the pile surface and the closeness of construction. A dense pile indicates long carpet life expectancy, but the pile should be resilient, not stiff. Bend back a piece of carpeting; the less backing you can see through the pile, the better the carpet. Pile weight, the weight of the pile yarn in one square yard of carpet, is useful in judging a carpet's anticipated performance but is less important than density.

Another test of density is to press down on the pile with one finger and note how much resistance you get to penetrating to the backing. Twist—the winding of the carpet yarn around itself—is another measure of quality. Compare the twist level of several cut-pile carpets by looking closely at the cut ends of the individual tufts. They should be even and well defined, not blossomed open.

Steer clear of carpet stores running perpetual sales; generally speaking, price is a good yardstick of value. So-called commercial grades may not offer any advantage for the home office. For an office environment, solid colors—free of patterns, designs, or texturing—are always in good taste. Widths of roll carpeting will range from fifty-four inches to twelve and fifteen feet and wider. ("Broadloom" means just that—the carpet was woven on a wide loom—and is not an indicator of quality.) Seams may be cemented or hand sewn. Be sure to inspect the carpet backing—synthetics have displaced cotton and jute, which tend to mildew in damp locations.

Good padding (called "carpet cushion" in the trade), either sponge rubber, foam rubber, urethane, or jute, is important. Carpet cushion does more than make carpeting feel better to walk on or extend its useful life. It also doubles a carpet's acoustical properties and improves its thermal-insulating qualities by a third. Carpeting laid over a separate cushion can also be more economical—less costly to install and replace—than that which is laid over glued-down cushions. Some roll carpeting already has a urethane-foam padding attached, making it ideal for installation by do-it-yourselfers.

For basement offices directly on a concrete slab, you may want to consider one of the indoor/outdoor grades of polypropylene carpet that are unaffected by moisture or dampness.

Avoid shag-type carpeting that will make your office look like a bedroom, especially if your office does double duty as a sleeping area. And don't overlook the decorating possibilities of area rugs, which can contribute to the ambience of a room and can also serve in high-traffic areas to preserve the carpet or the finish of the floor. A special "no slip" pad should be used under small area rugs over carpeting to prevent movement or rippling.

In terms of initial cost, among resilient floor materials vinyl is the most expensive to install, but is also the most durable and the easiest to maintain. Among carpets, wool is generally more expensive than synthetic fibers, and its luxurious appearance and good performance characteristics make it the fiber against which all others are inevitably compared, although it is exceeded in durability and resistance to wear by nylon and the other synthetics. Because advanced-generation nylon fibers cost more to produce, carpets made from them tend to be priced higher than equivalent regular nylon carpet.

In appearance, carpet looks better than resilient tile and sheet floorings. In terms of comfort and sound-absorbing properties, carpeting is preferable to floor tile and rolled linoleum. Because of some carpet's tendency to generate static electricity and damaging sparks, the floors of offices equipped with computers, electronic typewriters, and other business machines (whose circuit boards are expensive to service or replace) are being covered with resilient tiles and roll materials, which also tend to trap less dirt and are easier to keep clean.

SOUND CONTROL

Sounds may be airborne, structure transmitted, or both. Trucks passing by on the street are an obvious source of the noise that enters buildings through the windows, but many sounds of unknown origin can travel through pipes, ducts, or the structure itself.

In the home office, sound control usually means isolating the office from street noise and especially from the noise of the rest of the household. But it can also involve the elimination of noise generated within the home office itself in order to achieve a comfortable level of sound.

Medical research has shown that excessive noise dulls mental processes and can lead to fatigue. In actual tests, an insurance company discovered that efficiency increased 8 percent in work areas treated with sound-deadening materials. A communications company reduced message errors by 42 percent after machines were put in sound-reducing enclosures or in soundproof areas and other excessive noise was eliminated. Bare walls, hard floors, and nonabsorptive ceiling materials make for a "lively" office soundwise and can contribute to the propagation of unwanted noise.

The best way to prevent sound from moving through a building is in the initial construction or remodeling stages. If a room is to house noisy equipment, it is better to have two rows of studs in the walls between rooms so that the wallboard on one row is staggered and independent of that on the other. Additional Fiberglas insulation in the space between the two rows of studs will decrease resonance within the wall.

Sound-Absorbing Materials In these, you will be limited largely to acoustical ceiling tile, carpeting, and drapes. Suspended acoustical ceiling tile, $\frac{3}{4}$ inch thick, has a noise-reduction coefficient of .95; heavy drapes (eighteen ounces per square yard), pleated to half the overall area, have a noise-reduction coefficient of .60. Sound absorption is a reciprocal of sound reflection: materials that reflect sound well (concrete, marble, plaster, glass, and wood) all absorb sound poorly. In fact, a broad plaster or gypsum-board surface absorbs only 5 percent of the sound that strikes it, reflecting the rest. Consequently, it has a noise-reduction coefficient of .05. A cloth wall hanging or decorative rug hung on a wall can reduce wall-reflected noise.

Here are some specific potential sources of noise in the home office and the methods of combating them:

Street Noise Most outside sounds enter through windows and even through cracks in the window frames. Sound transmission through windows can be reduced by increasing the number of panes, as in double- or triple-paned thermal windows. Storm windows also improve outside sound control. "In general, methods that improve sound insulation also help save thermal energy," says Dr. Cyril Harris, professor of electrical engineering and architecture at New York's Columbia University.

Other sound-control methods include installing air conditioning so that windows may be kept closed and putting up heavy drapes to muffle street and traffic noises.

House Noise This often creates other problems. Instruct other members of the household to keep noise to a minimum, especially radios, TVs, and stereo equipment; restrict children's noisy games, particularly when visitors are present; have family members answer home telephones promptly; eliminate bare floors above the office area by installing deep-pile carpet and carpet cushion or even by adding rugs.

Office Equipment Wherever practicable, stopping sound at its source is preferable to trying to alter its pathways or absorbing it once it has started to travel. Install sound-deadening pads under all typewriters, computer printers, and other noise-producing equipment. Some automatic printers can be equipped with sound-reducing transparent plastic cover panels or can be placed within special acoustical enclosures. Service and lubricate all machines regularly for smooth and quiet operation.

Metal typewriter tables and printer stands are perhaps the worst offenders in generating office noise. Stands resting on uncarpeted floors should be equipped with rubber-tired casters or should have soft-plastic or rubber insulating cups placed under each leg or caster.

If machine noise persists, you should consider relocating the offending machines to an unused room nearby or to a closet in another part of the house, especially if they can be remotely operated. Separation from the office area will reduce the amount of perceived noise, but additional intervening soundproofing insulation may be needed. This is always more effective when installed on the walls and ceiling of the room where the noise has its source rather than on the other side.

Telephone Conversations If two or more persons must use telephones in your home office, you can purchase devices at stationers or telephone equipment stores that will reduce the noise level of conversations. One such device fits over the mouthpiece; intended to make telephone conversations inaudible to others, it also serves to reduce the level at which telephone conversations must be conducted. The other is a soft polyurethane cushion that fits over the earpiece and shuts out distracting room noises. However, these work best on conventional telephones; the newer electronic telephones often come in other-than-traditional shapes. Remember, too, that telephone bells or ringers can be adjusted to ring more quietly by changing the position of a switch in the base or handset. Some who want to work in their home offices undisturbed by noise or interruptions resort to earplugs. The telephone ringer is replaced by a flashing light, a device similar to that used by the hearing impaired and available in telephone stores.

MUSIC

Opinions differ on the subject of background music, but music can also be used discreetly to mask background noise. In addition, it has been demonstrated that music is an antidote to fatigue, particularly during the performance of monotonous and repetitive tasks.

If you choose to use music in your office work area, what you play is your own business, provided, of course, you have a way of silencing it when the telephone rings or a visitor calls on you. In my own home office, the radio is infrequently used; when it is used and because it is not within easy reach, a remotely controlled switch enables me to cut off the radio immediately. There's nothing more disconcerting to a telephone caller than to have to talk to someone while a loud radio plays in the background. Besides, inappropriate music can always make it appear that little real work is accomplished in your office. You probably won't be faulted on that score if it's classical music that can be heard in the background.

Also useful for masking noise are recordings, tapes, or sound boxes that produce so-called white or pink noise, with sounds resembling surf, rain, and falling water. White noise has more high-frequency sounds; pink noise, pitched lower, does not have the hiss of white noise and so has wider applications.

For some scriptwriters or copywriters for radio and TV, a radio or a television set is not a distraction but as necessary to their work as a typewriter. As such, these can be treated as business equipment for tax purposes. On the question of a radio or TV set as part of the furniture or equipment of your home office, you'll have to let the nature of work you do there, your conscience, and your work schedule or deadlines be your guides. In my own home office, use of the TV set is limited to occasional telecasts of special interest or in connection with a project on which I am working.

Part Two

~~~~~~

EQUIPMENT
FOR THE
HOME OFFICE

FIVE

On Paper: Stationery, Envelopes, and Business Cards

An old show-business adage advises, "When you're down to your last quarter, don't eat—get a shine." Inflation may have played hob with the purchasing power of the quarter, but in principle, that's still sound advice for anyone setting up a home-based business, particularly as it applies to the stationery and paper materials to be used.

Those who receive your correspondence, memoranda, reports, and other documents will form their first impressions of you and your business from these. You will communicate with many people —including clients and customers—only by means of the mails. This means that you'll want to create a serious image, especially in your initial dealings with potential clients, if only to overcome the stigma that sometimes is attached to an office at home.

You can achieve such an image if you stick with the old-fashioned tried and true standbys: white paper, white envelopes, white business cards. You may have started in business only last week, but the impression you want to achieve is one of solidity, even of permanence. Cheap paper, sleazy printing, lack of attention to details, and sloppy typing have doomed many home-based ventures before they had a chance to get started.

STATIONERY

Paper

Choose a bond paper of the best grade, even if your budget can't seem to stand it. In the long run, the difference in cost reduces to only a few thousandths of a cent a sheet, but the advantage gained will be incalculable. (Bond paper is so called because it was once used almost exclusively for the printing of bonds, where strength, durability, and permanence were requisites.) Bond paper is called "rag paper" if it contains cotton fibers made from new or reprocessed rags, but today's bond paper doesn't necessarily have to have a rag content. Until the end of the eighteenth century, practically all paper in Europe and America was handmade from cotton and linen rags, which accounts for the lasting and durable quality of so many early documents. Rag paper may range in cotton content from 100 percent to 25 percent.

Lower down on the scale of paper grades is paper made from wood chips cooked to a pulp under pressure in a solution of various chemicals. The use of wood pulp and the invention of continuous-sheet papermaking machinery satisfied the appetite of steam-driven mechanical printing presses and made possible the explosion of book printing that occurred during the nineteenth century; such paper is today the despair of archivists and librarians, confronted with books and documents that are literally disintegrating before their eyes.

If you hold a sheet of good-quality paper up to the light, you will probably see a design or words. That's the watermark, impressed on the paper by the raised pattern on the wire-mesh dandy roll, which gives texture effects during manufacture. The presence of a watermark is usually a hallmark of quality. (Large-volume buyers of paper can and do have their own watermarks impressed on their papers.) "Laid paper" contains fine parallel lines imposed during the papermaking process; "wove paper" exhibits a fine mesh pattern. Both are modern variants of hand-papermaking techniques.

Some high-grade papers are manufactured with a date code hidden in the watermark. From this, it is possible to establish the date of manufacture, making this a desirable paper for legal use in cases where the dating of a document might be questioned. As a consequence of the papermaking process, all paper has two "sides," and each side has individual characteristics. The side in contact with the woven-wire endless belt of the papermaking machine is called the "wire side," while the other side is the top, or "felt side."

The felt side usually has a closer formation, with less grain and better interweaving of the fibers, resulting in better-looking typed correspondence. (In contrast, the wire side is preferred by offset printers as a working surface because it deposits less loose paper dust and lint on the blanket cylinders of their presses.)

Always hold paper up to the light before typing a letter, and type on the side on which the watermark is readable. All water-marked paper is positioned the same way in a box or package, so you will only have to inspect the first few sheets in order to have your typing paper arranged correctly for the best appearance of your typed documents.

When you shop for paper, you'll hear the word "substance" used as a measure of weight. Substance (shortened to "sub" in some designations) is the weight in pounds of a ream (500 sheets) of standard size—seventeen by twenty-two inches. The higher the number, the denser the paper. Bond paper for letterheads is usually bought by the ream in sixteen-, twenty-, or twenty-four-pound weights. Because four reams of 8½-by-11-inch paper can be cut from a ream of 17-by-22-inch paper, these will weigh four, five, and six pounds, respectively. If the weight of the paper you are using isn't shown on the package, weigh a ream and multiply the weight by four to get the substance weight.

Avoid erasable papers, especially for letterheads, since these papers have little permanence. Erasable papers can often be recognized by their brand names, which emphasize this quality. Such papers are highly calendered (smoothed under pressure) to a hard finish, and some have special chemical coatings. Typed impressions lie lightly on the surface without penetrating into the paper, thus making the typing easy to remove by erasure. The use of erasable papers should be limited to rough drafts.

Try to avoid making erasures or other corrections on typed correspondence. If you must erase, however, you'll find that erasing can be done more easily on high-cotton-content bond papers. If you are a writer, you should know that most editors dread manuscripts submitted on erasable papers, because they tend to smear easily. (If you type your manuscript on erasable paper, submit a good photocopy and retain the original for later correction.) Moreover, such papers grow brittle with age. The same tendency to brittleness and poor erasing qualities characterizes nonbond papers.

Printed Letterheads and Envelopes

Unless you are in a creative side of the graphics arts, stick to standard sizes and to white as the color. Light shades of buff- and cream-colored papers and envelopes are increasing in popularity and acceptance, but remember that it is more difficult to make corrections on tinted papers and envelopes, especially if you use correction liquid. The chalk-type correction papers, intended to conceal typing errors on white paper, simply will not work on colored papers.

The standard size for business letterhead paper is 8½ by 11 inches, with the letter folded horizontally in thirds, and a no. 10 envelope (4⅛ by 9½ inches). Avoid the small no. 6¾ envelope (3⅝ by 6½ inches). Not only does a no. 10 envelope require less folding of the letter, but it also allows more and larger enclosures to be included. Another size, much used by federal agencies and the military, is slightly smaller, measuring 8 by 10½ inches, but still takes a no. 10 envelope. If you are terse in your letter writing, monarch-size letterhead paper (7¼ by 10½ inches) may be more desirable, with the letter folded horizontally in thirds, and a no. 7 (Monarch) envelope (3⅞ by 7½ inches).

Window envelopes are popular for several reasons: they save the time and trouble of typing the address twice and thus avoid the possibility of a transcription error in the address. But window envelopes are not without drawbacks. Unless the enclosed letter is folded properly and makes a snug fit, it may move within the envelope, thus obscuring the address. Some mailers staple through the envelope and contents after sealing the envelope and making sure the letter is positioned properly, but this detracts from the appearance and the personalized nature of the correspondence. Perhaps the strongest argument against the use of window envelopes is their widespread use for the mailing of bills, statements, and solicitations; letters in window envelopes risk not being opened and going straight into the wastebasket.

In the design of your letterhead and the choice of a typeface, you have several options. If your tastes are conventional, you'll probably be able to find a suitable typeface and point size from the selection of typefaces available at the print shop producing your letterhead paper and envelopes. Alternatively, you may want to have your letterhead designed by a professional designer, in which case you may have to locate a typesetting shop with a larger selection of typefaces. (The old-fashioned "hot metal" monotype and linotype typesetting machines have been superseded by computerized photographic typesetting techniques that reproduce or imitate most of the old standbys among typefaces and make available a host of new faces.) Once your designer-specified type has been set, you can take the job to a printer.

Make sure you select a typeface appropriate to your business. Thus, an uncluttered, modern, clean-looking sans serif typeface such as the now-overused Helvetica, News Gothic, or Optima would be quite appropriate for a consulting engineer or an aeronautical designer. Similarly, an antique dealer might prefer the period flavor of a typeface such as Caslon Antique. Traditional and more sedate faces include the old-style roman faces—Baskerville, Caslon, Century, and Garamond—or the modern roman faces—Bodoni, Bookman, Melior, Palatino, and Ventura. These are the so-called book faces and carry a feeling of solidity and conservatism. This book is set in Times Roman, a handsome face long favored for books. Some mixing of a roman face (your name on the top line) and sans serif faces (address lines) is permissible.

In choosing a typeface, be careful not to choose one that has become dated as a result of age or overuse in the past. Examples of faces that have seen better days are Franklin Gothic and Karnak (the latter in several look alikes—for example, Memphis and Stymie). Also to be avoided are the typefaces used for wedding invitations—Gothic faces more appropriate to a diploma and flowing imitation script. Avoid faces with a pronounced period flavor (Broadway, P. T. Barnum, Old Bowery, Jim Crow, Stencil) unless you have a sound reason to use them.

The type design you choose for your letterhead may also be usable as the return address for your envelopes. But a bold design that does not seem out of place at the top of a large sheet of paper can look awkward in the upper left-hand corner of an envelope. A design that's an appropriate size for your letterhead but too large for the envelope can be reduced photographically by the print shop.

When you select your letterhead paper, remember to have the printer supply additional paper of the same size, weight, and surface finish for letters that run to more than one page and for reports or memoranda. (The printer may refer to them as "second sheets," but they are more properly called "continuation sheets"; "second sheets" is a term usually applied to the thin papers used to make carbon copies.) In the beginning, you won't be able to estimate how many continuation sheets to order. Because you'll always have a need for plain bond paper, and paper is cheaper by the ream, you won't be overbuying if you order a ream or two. You should never use your letterhead paper for the second and subsequent pages of a letter.

If much of your correspondence will be sent overseas, you may

want to have airmail letterheads and envelopes printed to econ-
omize on postage. The substance of airmail papers is usually
between nine and eleven pounds; envelopes are of matching
weight, with red-and-blue borders and the printed word "AIRMAIL."
Because overseas airmail postage is calculated in half-ounce
increments, a considerable saving in postage charges can be made
if lightweight paper and envelopes are used.

One paper and envelope size you should avoid is called
"baronial." The paper measures a meager 5½ by 8½ inches;
envelopes are of a more formal appearance, with a deep, pointed
flap. Widely used for handwritten social correspondence, thank-
you notes, and announcements, there is simply not enough room
on such paper to type an adequate business letter.

Second Sheets

These are the sheets of thin paper used to make file copies of
letters and other documents. Such paper is often called onionskin
or manifold paper. The substance of these lightweight papers
varies from seven to thirteen pounds, and they are available in
smooth, glazed, and rippled, or cockle, finishes. (The latter finish is
produced by air-drying the paper after manufacture.)

Smooth-finish second sheets will take up slightly less room in
your files but tend to be harder to handle. They have the advantage
of being able to make more clear carbons than rippled-finish
papers. Manifold paper is glazed on one side for ease of filing and
dull on the other side so it won't slip in the typewriter.

Commercial stationers carry second sheets imprinted with the
word "COPY" in large open-block letters. If you type copies of
originals on plain bond paper or make copies on your copying
machine that cannot be distinguished readily from originals, self-
inking rubber stamps are available to identify such copies. Second
sheets are also available in colors to aid in sorting, filing, or rout-
ing carbons.

Timesaving carbon "sets" are available as individual sets or
multiple sets or pads containing one or more interleaved, snap-out,
one-time carbon sheets or "carbonless" paper and an equal number of second sheets. Carbonless papers avoid the smearing of
papers and smudging of hands that accompany copies made with
carbon paper.

If you use sets of either kind, be careful in handling and storing them before use. Because they can pick up any impression made on them, you should keep them off desk tops or worktables until they are to be used. In situations where confidentiality may be important, remember that onetime carbon papers discarded with your office trash could provide snoopers with a readable copy of what was written or typed.

With a home office, you'll be spared such traditional extras as interoffice letterheads and envelopes, memorandum paper, and other accoutrements of large corporations. A timesaving nicety is a supply of so-called speed letters, available in carbonless format or with interleaved carbon paper. Recipients merely write a reply on the original; their retained file copy contains both original message and response.

A supply of single sheets showing your name is also useful for short handwritten or typed notes. (A good size is 5½ by 8½ inches; the printer who prints your letterheads can print these up—the size is exactly half of a standard letter-size sheet.) But avoid such cute banalities as headings reading "FROM THE DESK OF . . ." lest you receive notes in response addressed to your desk.

Such abbreviated notes will be especially helpful for quick answers to letters not requiring a formal response. By using informal handwritten notes, you'll clear your desk more quickly. So that you'll always know what you said in your single-sheet notes, buy a box of pencil carbon paper, cut some of the carbon paper sheets in half, and make your own notepaper "sets."

Business Cards

If you look through any business cards you've accumulated from friends and business acquaintances, you'll notice that today's business cards tend to be less inhibited in design than letterheads, so you may want to be more creative in designing your business card.

The traditional card is usually "engraved" in a conservative typeface in black on thin white cardboard. This isn't the old-fashioned copper-plate engraving of the great masters but a more modern (and much less expensive) thermographic process that fuses the hot ink to the card and produces raised lettering. You won't be faulted, however, if you choose to have your business cards printed rather than engraved or if you select a deep blue ink or even choose two-color printing.

A typical business-card size is 2 inches deep by about 3½ inches long. Your name should be centered, and the card should carry the name and address of your business and its telephone number.

Your business card can play many roles. In addition to leaving it with receptionists and telephone operators on business visits, you'll find yourself including it with gifts, attaching it to items you mail (where it can almost serve in place of a handwritten note), and even sliding it under doors or leaving it in mailboxes as a token of your visit when the person called upon is out. Be sure to order enough business cards to take care of these situations.

Other Papers

Other specialized papers you should know about and may want to use include mimeograph paper, an opaque, relatively bulky, noncurling rough paper intended to absorb ink rapidly and to be printed on both sides without feathering or blurring. Mimeograph machines can duplicate on paper ranging from 9 to 117 pounds. Duplicator paper is designed to be used with spirit- or gelatin-type duplicating machines, with a smoother and slightly less absorbent surface than mimeograph papers and usually with less body. Xerographic papers are precisely cut to ensure trouble-free feeding and with a hard, smooth finish to reproduce well in copying machines. Copiers employing single-element toners must use special calendarized paper to obtain optimum image quality. The paper used on coated-paper copiers is treated to accept and develop direct images; it should not be used for any other purposes.

Other Envelope Styles

Other kinds of envelopes available include booklet envelopes, whose concealed seams make them ideal for direct-mail use because they can be imprinted front and back; bankers flap envelopes, made of brown kraft paper, a strong unbleached paper stock, sturdier than ordinary commercial white envelopes; clasp envelopes, with metal-clasp closures and gummed flaps to keep them sealed in the mails; large, open-end catalog envelopes of kraft paper with gummed self-sealing flaps, ideal for mailing magazines, catalogs, and bulky items. Avoid string-and-button envelopes, the kind used for interoffice mail in large corporations; these are not intended for mailing purposes, but are designed to withstand repeated opening and closing and to give easy access to the contents.

Whenever the protection of the contents is a prime consideration, use plastic envelopes. Made of tough, high-density polyethylene fibers bonded together under pressure, these have twice the strength of kraft-paper envelopes and half the weight. They are available in a variety of styles and sizes, all with pressure-sensitive seals.

Other specialized mailing materials include asphalt-laminated kraft envelopes cushioned with finely chopped paper or plastic air bubbles; Fiberglas-reinforced mailers; cloth mailing bags with drawstrings and sewn-in address labels, ideal for small items or samples; and mailing tubes.

You may be wondering why I have discussed your paper needs before describing such necessary items as typewriters and other office equipment. The answer is simple: quick-printing shops abound, but you should be looking for quality printing, which takes time.

Most reputable printers would rather not rush any printing job. A conscientious printer will show you "blue-line" proofs before a plate is made and the job is printed. Remember to examine proofs very carefully before giving your approval. Once you have initialed a proof and the job has been printed, any undetected errors that may have found their way into print are your responsibility.

You can make decisions about specialized furniture and equipment for your home office while your printing is being done—and it should be done carefully.

SIX

First Buy a Chair: Office Furniture

It may seem heretical, but your first major purchase should be a chair or chairs and not a desk. Choose your office chairs carefully —you'll probably be spending most of your working time sitting in one or another of them. The person who goes shopping for office chairs without doing some preliminary research will be confronted by what the French call *"un embarras de richesse."*

Do not let the wide choice dismay you; many office chairs or "posture chairs" that claim to have been ergonomically designed with the human body in mind have serious shortcomings, as you will discover when you apply the acid test and sit in them.

By way of preparation for this ordeal, I suggest that you read a few issues of trade magazines specializing in office furniture. Two good examples are *Interiors* and *Contract*, and both are read by commercial interior designers and architects. Only when you are familiar with office-furniture terminology and with what is currently being offered should you begin a shopping expedition.

Your first stop should be at a secondhand office-furniture store. With the increase in business failures and the realignment of American industry that has taken place, secondhand office-furniture warehouses are overflowing; it's genuinely a buyer's market. Next, visit the showrooms of dealers in brand-new office furniture. In that way, you'll be able to compare prices and values.

You'll find straight-backed visitors' chairs, chairs that swivel, tilt, and roll, upholstered or plain chairs in wood, plastic, and metal, and chairs with and without armrests.

Your desk chair needs only to be comfortable; it should swivel and should have casters so as to move easily. Unless you are a lawyer, it's a good idea to avoid one of those high-backed, uncomfortable leather monstrosities more appropriate to a black-robed Supreme Court justice.

Here are some things to look for in selecting a desk chair:

Seat Height When seated, your feet should be flat on the floor with thighs and lower legs making an angle just slightly larger than ninety degrees. A slight clearance should be evident at the front-seat edge under the legs. Given the wide variance in human body measurements, this calls for a chair of adjustable height. Take the time to adjust it properly. Some more expensive chairs are equipped with a gas-cylinder height adjuster, making the desired height easy to achieve. To adjust a gas-cylinder chair, raise the chair to maximum height and lift the seat-adjustment lever while applying gentle seating pressure on the seat. Releasing the lever when the desired height is reached locks the chair at that height.

Backrest This should provide support for the lumbar region of your back—the so-called small of the back—and is usually adjustable on posture chairs for height, attitude, and horizontal depth.

Tilt Tension This is usually adjusted to suit personal comfort and work demands. Tension should be sufficient to keep the chair from tilting backward when you are seated in an erect position.

Seat Depth The seat should be deep enough so that your body's weight on the seat is supported by the underside of the thigh muscles.

Cushions Look for chairs with rounded cushions. Avoid those with square cushions and an upholstered "bead" along the top front edge—a few hours on one of these and you'll think your hamstring tendons have been cut.

You'll need at least one chair for the occasional visitor, even if your home-office activities don't invite visits by outsiders. A simple straight-backed chair will do. If visits are frequent, keep this chair or chairs in front of your desk or table, facing you.

FURNITURE STYLES

Only a few years ago, office-furniture design was mired in the past. Desks, whether executive or secretarial, were of conventional design, materials, and finishes. With the introduction of the concept of "office landscaping," movable, freestanding panels and partitions, and the abandonment of the "bullpen" approach to clerical work, office furniture took on a whole new function and appearance.

The advent of the microcomputer into the world of business has meant that wooden furniture has come back into favor. The villain, of course, is static electricity, which can wreak havoc on computer circuit boards and disks.

In the furnishing of your home office, you will really be able to use your imagination and to express yourself. Whatever the style in which you choose to decorate your home office—antique, Parsons modern, or mixed—remember to strive for simplicity. Not only is a simply furnished office easier on your budget, but also it will prove to be actually more fun to work in and to operate. Even office cleaning and housekeeping chores will be a breeze. And a simply furnished office is always an affirmation of your good taste.

A good beginning rule for selecting furniture for your home office is this: if it's good enough for your home, it's good enough for your home office. Therefore, try to adapt some of your existing furnishings to your home-office design plan before buying any office furnishings. Unless you are a doctor, dentist, or architect, don't worry that callers at your home office will be expecting to see specialized furniture and equipment.

The desk you work at doesn't have to be a traditional office desk; it can be an elegant and graceful period table. If your desk is a table and lacks adequate drawer space, a credenza or other low storage cabinet or chest with doors or drawers can store needed papers and materials. Place it behind you for ease of access. In lieu of a credenza or chest, consider floor-to-ceiling shelves. These don't have to be built in; wall-mounted standards and shelf brackets with one-inch-thick painted or walnut-stained pine shelving or veneered composition shelf boards about eight or ten inches wide will serve nicely.

DESKS

We all have all seen photographs of captains of industry seated at desks totally devoid of a single scrap of paper; out of range of the camera is the small army of assistants needed by the same executives to achieve those paper-free desks. Because you may never be able to afford the luxury of clerical or secretarial assistance—certainly not at the outset—make sure your desk or worktable is large enough to accommodate your papers and equipment, and don't worry about appearances.

One frequently used desk substitute is a pair of two-drawer filing cabinets with a smooth door or thick plywood sheet laid across them. Hollow-core doors measuring twenty-four by eighty inches and sheets of plywood are available at lumberyards. A full sheet of plywood measures four by eight feet—this is too large for desk-top purposes, and you'll have to have it cut down. (Hollow-core doors cannot be cut down, so be sure to buy the exact size you need.) Ready-made desk-size tops in laminates, veneers, and solid butcher-block styles are available in home-furnishing specialty stores.

If you resort to any of these expedients, be sure to pay attention to the eventual height of the work surface that will result. In the past, tables and desks were made about thirty inches in height; typewriter stands, about twenty-six inches. Therefore, if your desk is to double as a work surface on which you will place a typewriter or computer keyboard, you should take this difference into account. (The average two-drawer file may be anywhere from twenty-seven to twenty-nine inches in height.) One way to adjust in part for differences in work-surface heights is with a chair of adjustable height.

When keyboards are placed so that elbows must be raised more than three inches, neck, shoulder, and upper-back muscles ache. The angle made by the wrist should be not greater than 10 degrees; the angle between the upper and lower arms should be between 80 and 120 degrees.

Traditional desks are available in a number of styles and grades. The standard metal desk usually has a composition wooden top measuring thirty by sixty inches, covered in laminated wood-grain plastic, with two pedestals containing drawers for small items and a larger file drawer or drawers for storing frequently used records. A wide, shallow center drawer is almost always provided. When space is at a premium, single-pedestal desks whose work surfaces measure thirty by forty-eight inches can be used.

The old-fashioned secretarial desk, with a foldaway or sliding typewriter shelf concealed by a large door when closed, has largely disappeared. Its place has been taken by a simple open desk with one pedestal or by a table, to which can be added a "return"—a work surface attached on either side at right angles. This puts the typewriter at convenient typing height and creates a versatile L-shaped desk.

"Conference desks" are conventional desks with a larger top, usually measuring thirty-six by seventy-two inches, arranged so as to give a six-inch-larger overhang on three sides. This allows associates or visitors to sit close to the desk and to share the work surface with the desk's occupant.

Office furniture comes in two grades—budget grade and general-office grade; price is usually the best indicator of grade. Budget-grade furniture may lack such features as central drawer locking (when the center drawer is locked, the side drawers also lock automatically) and full-suspension file drawers. The metal used in budget-grade furniture may be of slightly thinner gauge, and some construction features may be omitted.

Feel along the edges of desk tops and frames. Sharp or unfinished edges are a sign of cheap workmanship and should be avoided—the money you save on a cheap desk could easily be spent in reweaving ripped suits or dresses or in new hosiery over the years. You should also avoid desks whose tops or hardware are highly reflective, which could cause annoying highlights and glare.

RECEPTION-AREA FURNITURE

Commercial office furniture available for the seating of visitors tends to be unimaginative and limited to the following: two-person settees, three-person sofas, individual chairs, and occasional tables (corner tables or coffee tables—the latter for the display of magazines). You'll probably find a wider selection of more attractive furniture suitable for a reception area at dealers in home furnishings.

OTHER OFFICE FURNITURE

Among the other items of office furniture you may want to consider are bookcases (if you have a lot of books to shelve, built-ins are cheaper), coatracks, coat-trees, magazine racks, conference tables and chairs, and folding worktables and chairs. If you intend to have more than one person working in your home office, consider using an open-plan system, including movable, freestanding panels and panel-hung components, such as shelves, cabinets, work organizers, and sorters. Open systems provide better space utilization and greater flexibility; they keep costs down by requiring fewer structural and remodeling changes; energy benefits accrue from the increased efficiency of heating and air-conditioning systems and because fewer overhead light fixtures are needed.

When selecting furniture for your home office, don't overlook the possibilities of dual-use furniture: dining chairs you already own (or are contemplating buying) can double as visitors' chairs; an unused dining table can serve temporarily as a worktable or conference table in the home office. Built-ins, from wall cabinets and bookcases to carpet-covered storage banquettes around the perimeter of a room to increase seating space, represent practical ways of solving the furniture problem and also increasing the value of your home.

Use visual tricks, too, especially if available space is on the small side. For example, if you paint built-ins or cabinets along walls the same color as your walls, they will blend into the room and make it look larger. Half-height, one- or two-sided (back to back) modular wall units projecting into a room at right angles to a wall or used as an "island" can provide storage space and serve as a room divider. Half height is recommended to avoid the possibility of a unit tipping over. If anchored to a wall or to the floor, of course, such units can go all the way to the ceiling. If you are a renter, you should know that in theory your landlord can claim anything fastened to the floor or walls as having been made a permanent part of the house or apartment—and some landlords exercise this right when tenants announce their intention of moving.

SEVEN

Pa Bell's Wonderful Invention: The Telephone

On February 14, 1876, in one of those peculiar coincidences that haunt the history of science and invention, Scottish-born Alexander Graham Bell and American inventor Elisha Gray filed almost simultaneous patent applications covering devices for telephonic communication. It was to prove to be an invention with many fathers.

Prolonged litigation resulted during which the U.S. Patent Office was charged with corruption. In 1893, the Supreme Court finally ruled in favor of Bell. (Otherwise, we might today be referring to "Ma Gray.")

Paradoxically, despite their electronic tones and space-age shapes, many of today's telephones still work largely on principles that were known before the telephone was invented. Aside from replacement of the rotary dial with a push-button keypad, no changes have been made in most of the telephones in use in the United States and Canada since 1953, when the "500 set" was introduced. The standard push-button model has more than 120 separate parts in the push-button assembly alone. Most ringing continues to be done by means of a clapper and bells. The telephone is still essentially an electromagnetic instrument, although truly electronic telephones of surprising versatility are on the way.

Over the years, the telephone companies retained control of telephone equipment, including the instruments in subscribers' homes, so much of their capital was invested in equipment on lease. Because the telephone companies serviced this equipment, in theory, at least, at no charge to subscribers, there was every reason to build it to last. With virtually no competition to speak of, however, there was also little impetus to add innovations. It has been conservatively estimated that there are some 160 million standard telephones of various vintages in use in North America.

In 1969, the landmark Carterphone antitrust case, which was settled out of court, set the stage for the 1977 Federal Communications Commission (FCC) decision giving telephone subscribers the right to attach equipment of their own to the telephone network without installing a special protective device previously obtainable only from the phone company. This touched off a flood of telephone answering machines, followed by today's rush to subscriber-installed telephones.

Coincidentally, in 1969, Illinois Bell asked AT&T's Bell Laboratories to design a modification to wires and equipment so that company installers could plug connecting wires into telephones and wall outlets or junction boxes, thus keeping down installation costs.

At the same time, AT&T, the parent company, was creating the concept of company-owned stores where customers could choose the telephones the company would then install. With the development of the modular plug, however, a company decision to let customers install their own phones became inevitable.

Before long, other companies were manufacturing telephones and underselling the phone company's own stores. Delbert C. Staley, then chairman of AT&T's New York Telephone Company, who recalled the sequence of events for an interviewer, concluded, "We outsmarted ourselves." The rest, as the saying has it, is history.

In addition to having the legal right to buy equipment from vendors and connect it to the utility's lines, users are now able to obtain access to voice- or data-channels of a number of supplemental long-distance services. One benefit of the multiplication of equipment and companies is that it is finally possible for users to make cost-benefit analyses of the rates of competing suppliers.

TELEPHONE SERVICE

You'll probably want a telephone in your home office unless you are a writer who uses the office as a retreat in which to be undisturbed. The first decision you'll have to make is whether it should be an extension of your present home telephone or a separate line with its own number.

You'll also have to decide whether you want to lease or buy a telephone instrument from the phone company or to buy one from an outside source—a telephone store, department store, chain store, or mail-order catalog. The Consumer Affairs Department of New York State has estimated that if all New York telephone users decided to buy telephones instead of leasing them, the saving would amount to some $600 million.

The calculations involved in deciding to buy a telephone are simple. Call your phone-company business office and ascertain the monthly charge for the model of your choice (or the model you are leasing now). Determine the purchase price of a comparable model. Divide the monthly-use charge (including taxes) into the cost of purchasing the same telephone instrument (also including taxes), and you will have the payback period (in months). Now multiply the monthly rental charge by twelve to get the annual saving you will make by owning your own telephone—once the payback period has passed. One factor you won't be able to take into account is that leased telephones are serviced or replaced by the phone company at no charge to the subscriber. Offsetting this, perhaps, is the knowledge that standard tabletop telephones have had a service life of fifteen to twenty years and need repairs on the average of once every seven years.

According to a survey of communications executives conducted by the Chicago-based Arthur Andersen & Co., more than two-thirds of all business and residential customers will own their own phones by 1990. By then, we'll be buying 7 million phones a year for home use (a 233 percent increase over 1980) and 5 million business systems (a 150 percent increase).

The entire question of the rental of new equipment may become academic in the light of the divestiture agreement worked out between the phone companies and the federal government. Because of the economics of phone leasing, AT&T (which inherited the equipment of the former individual Bell telephone companies) could eventually decide to stop leasing telephones to subscribers altogether. Certain questions still remain to be resolved, however. For example, senior citizens, the handicapped, and the infirm may prefer the advantages of leased equipment simply because of the associated repair provisions.

The telephone of the future will have more mobility, do a host of different tasks, and be part of a complex, far-reaching information network. Some phone models now available give a hint of things to come, displaying the date and time or the number of the phone being called, timing calls, forwarding calls, storing and remembering numbers, and even restricting outgoing calls.

At one time, all telephone equipment was manufactured by AT&T's subsidiary, Western Electric, and built to very high standards. Consumers are discovering that "genuine Bell" is no longer as exclusive as legend has it; today's telephone company equipment may be manufactured by outside suppliers, but to no less exacting standards. The big difference is that the same telephone supplied to the phone company may also be marketed by the manufacturer under another name. A good example is the Electra Corporation of Cumberland, Indiana, which manufactures the phone company's Nomad 1000 model. Electra also sells the same telephone under its own label as the Freedom 4000.

Do not be confused by the multiplicity of telephones now being offered. Telephones are of two basic types: pulse and tone. Pulse phones include the old-fashioned rotary dial or push-button phones, as well as many newer electronic push-button phones). Despite the presence of a sophisticated keypad, such electronic phones are not designed to be usable on tone lines. (They employ semiconductor chips to do electronically what a standard push-button or dial phone does mechanically—that is, they send out electrical *pulses* rather than electronically generated *tones*.) These pulses have a standard rate of ten per second, which limits the speed of pulse dialing, so that even with push-button dialing, calls take just as long to be placed.

Tone phones, the second type, will also accept calls initiated on either rotary dial or push-button pulse phones, but not the other way around. Therefore, existing rotary or push-button pulse telephones will always be usable on tone lines, even if they are not able to take advantage of the speed of such lines in placing calls. All numbers take the same length of time to be generated on tone phones, so calls to numbers made up of low digits are placed no faster than calls to numbers made up of high digits, and there is no longer any advantage in dialing such low numbers.

Because their computers can only receive initiating signals from tone phones, you won't be able to use rotary or other pulse instruments for some time to come with alternative long-distance dialing services, such as MCI, Sprint, or Metrophone, although you can purchase a small, hand-held tone generator that will give you access to these services over pulse telephones. Moreover, the pulse telephones won't be usable for other computerized functions that are expected to be introduced, such as home banking and universal bill paying.

"All consumers can save money if they own their own phones," according to Samuel Simon, executive director of the Telecommunications Research and Action Center, a Washington-based nonprofit group. "But the savings from not paying a monthly rental fee," he cautions, "can turn into a loss with a single bad purchase."

Linda Rosenblum, director of the consumer services division of the New York State Public Service Commission, counsels potential buyers in workshops across the state to treat the purchase of a telephone as they would any other appliance.

In deciding whether to buy a telephone and where to buy it, because of the proliferation of cheap telephone instruments, an important consideration should be the nature of the warranty that accompanies the instrument you buy. The manufacturer's warranty may be good for anywhere from ninety days to one year, but does the store offer a warranty extending beyond this period? Does the store do its own repairs, or must you ship the instrument back to the manufacturer? Will the store supply you with a substitute telephone while yours is being repaired? How long will it take before you get the phone back? What will be the charge for repairs once the warranty period has expired? In deciding which telephone to buy, the warranty policy of the manufacturer and the store is almost as important as the purchase price.

Any phone you buy should carry a label showing the FCC registration number, the ringer equivalence number, and the date of manufacture. You are required to report the first two of these numbers to the phone company when you begin to use the phone. (This reporting requirement does not apply to phones directly purchased from the phone company.) Although all non-phone-company telephones must be registered by the manufacturer with the FCC to assure that they will not damage the telephone network or interfere with other calls, the presence of such a number does not signify FCC approval of a particular instrument.

If you elect to make your office phone an extension of your present home telephone service, you can have the phone company do the wiring, in which case you'll pay an additional monthly charge for the wires they place in your house or apartment for as long as you keep the extension. (The telephone company calls these "wire-investment charges" but does not so specify them in your bill; you can find out how much you pay each month for the use of the wiring already installed or to be installed in your home by calling your local telephone business office.) Alternatively, you can do the interior wiring yourself.

Some telephone companies are offering "wire insurance" covering repairs to inside wiring, although in apartments and some homes inside wiring may be measurable in inches. The average repair frequency for inside wiring, according to Pennsylvania Bell, is once every 13½ years. Not only are the chances slim that your inside wiring will ever need repairs, but most such repairs can be made by anyone familiar with basic do-it-yourself techniques.

In addition to removing equipment-rental charges from your monthly telephone bill by buying your own telephones, you can get out from under paying the monthly wire-investment charges on wires previously installed by asking the phone company to install a network interface at the point where the phone line enters your house. They will install such a device for a nominal charge—but they will also disable or remove all existing phone-company wires and jacks in the house.

You can calculate how long it will take you to recover your initial investment in wire, jacks, and other devices by totaling the cost of these when purchased from an outside source and dividing this figure by the monthly wire-investment charge you are now paying. The resulting number (it will probably be less than twenty-four) is the number of months that it will take you to break even. Before you decide to ask the phone company to remove their wires, it would be a good idea to trace the existing phone-company interior wiring. If it passes through some inaccessible areas of the house, you might have difficulty snaking new wires to replace those disabled or removed.

A SECOND NUMBER

Your choices as to who does the wiring are similar if you decide to have a second line installed for a home-office telephone. The phone company offers three options: (1) a phone completely installed and wired by them, with wire-investment charges and instrument-rental charges included in your monthly telephone bill; (2) the same arrangement as in (1), except that the telephone instrument or instruments will be supplied by you; or (3) a network interface installed at the point where the phone line enters the house, with interior wiring, jacks, and telephone instrument(s) supplied by you. Network interfaces are of two kinds; for a slight additional cost, the phone company will install one with the capability of testing the lines from the central office. In the event of trouble, this interface could pinpoint whether the fault was in your lines or theirs and save the cost of a service call.

A second telephone line will give you greater communications flexibility and avoid the possibility of the situation that every office-at-homer dreads: the important phone call answered and mishandled by a member of the family. If you elect to have a second number, you have no choice—you must have the line installed by the phone company, at least to the point where it enters your house or apartment.

If your business does not require you to advertise, consider the advantages of having the second line as an unlisted number. Ordinarily, the phone company adds an extra charge for an unlisted number, but this charge is waived when the second line is at the same address as the listed line. By giving the unlisted number only to clients, you'll know it's a business call you'll want to answer when the unlisted phone rings. Another method of avoiding payment of the special monthly charge for an unlisted phone is to list the telephone under a fictitious name; this can be tantamount to having an unlisted number.

EIGHT

Ma Bell's Offspring: Auxiliary Telephone Equipment and Services

No matter whether you have opted for an extension phone or a separate incoming line, there are a number of items of auxiliary equipment that can make the operation of a home office easier. Alphabetically arranged, here's a selection of those with applications to the home office:

Amplifiers Amplifiers may include headset amplifiers and adapters for hearing aids with a telephone pickup feature. Most frequently encountered will be two-way amplifiers that free up your hands. Some two-way amplifiers use the loudspeaker as both speaker and microphone; they cannot transmit and receive at the same time, as the transmission mode is controlled by a voice-activated switch. Both parties cannot talk at the same time as on a telephone.

Amplifiers provide an inexpensive way of allowing more than one person to take part in your side of the conversation. Perhaps the biggest complaint about amplifiers is their tendency to make voices sound as though they are coming from the bottom of a well.

Alternate Services Many alternate long-distance telephone services are available, but access charges, rates, discounts, and places served are so variable that it is impossible to say which service will be the best and cheapest for you. You'll have to make your own comparison of carriers, and your long-distance telephone bills for the past year are a good place to start. Compare the rates of several carriers for the kind of calls you made within the past twelve months. Don't neglect to take into account your need for ancillary services that some carriers may not offer, such as operator assistance or directory service.

Answering Machines See chapter 9.

Automatic Dialers Available as stand-alone items or as part of sophisticated electronic telephone instruments, automatic dialers allow you to dial frequently called numbers by pushing previously programmed and coded buttons. Button codes may be letter-number combinations or mnemonic codes ("MOM," "DAD," "COPS,"

"FIRE," etc.). The storage capacity of these small computers can go as high as 176 individual seven-digit numbers. You may find, however, that such capacity is more than you need or can fill with frequently called numbers. Also, if the number of code designations you create exceeds your ability to remember them, you'll still find yourself having to look up your own codes, even though you will be spared the task of dialing the numbers.

If you purchase an automatic dialer, make sure it matches your present phone service—models are available for pulse-dialing systems and for tone service, but tone-service dialers will not operate on pulse lines. Because many phone numbers are now accessed by dialing a prefix and pausing before entering the main number, any automatic dialer you consider should be able to observe the pauses in such sequences.

The stated capacity of automatic dialers can be deceptive. Thus, an automatic dialer that can hold 176 seven-digit numbers is only capable of accepting sixty-eight eleven-digit numbers and fifty-five twenty-three-digit numbers. (Low-cost long-distance dialing services can consume as many as twenty-six digits for each number dialed.)

Automatic Directories Battery-operated desk-top and portable directories are available that will hold several hundred names and telephone numbers, displaying them at the touch of a key.

Beeps, Chimes, and Lights Devices are available for attachment to your telephone that silence the loud bell and substitute electronically generated sounds or a light to signal an incoming call. In addition to two different sequences of beeps, Heathkit's "Pleasant Ringer" even plays tunes like Beethoven's "Für Elise" and Rubenstein's "Romance."

Call Forwarding Available in some areas from the phone company, this is a service that enables you to have calls made to your number automatically transferred and ring on another number. It is widely used by businesses with offices in several locations to consolidate night and weekend calls at one monitored number. If you use a pocket pager, calls can be diverted to your pager. Call-forwarding devices are also available for sale or rental from non-phone-company sources.

Call Screeners Occasions may arise in which it would be desirable for you to screen calls; devices are available that receive calls only from callers who know a preliminary coded sequence. Some harassed types—mostly delinquent bill payers—regularly utilize telephone answering machines as call screeners, allowing callers to identify themselves after hearing the "I'm not in" message and then interrupting the message-leaving caller to take the call.

Cordless Telephones These have been the Cinderellas of the telephone equipment marketplace, capturing the public's imagination. Since their introduction a few years ago, however, they have not been without problems. Sound quality has been a major complaint, along with interference from fluorescent lights, motors, and other electrical equipment. Cordless handsets actually broadcast to and receive their signals from the base station. The antenna for transmission and reception is either built into the handset or is a folding or telescoping rod attached to it; the latter can be awkward, although external antennas do increase the operating range.

Cordless telephones are coded to show the operating frequency; if you experience difficulty because neighbors with cordless phones are on the same frequency, return your phone as quickly as possible; a cordless telephone operating on one of the other frequencies may solve the problem. The FCC has increased the number of channels available, and manufacturers have introduced cordless models that enable the user to switch channels until a clear channel is found.

Another problem has been "dial-tone theft" by strangers with cordless phones who tour neighborhoods in automobiles looking for a random dial tone. (This can only be done with older cordless telephones.) If your cordless telephone has its keypad on the base set, dial-tone theft cannot take place, since the phone is "hung up" for all practical purposes when the handset has been returned to the base.

Once a dial tone is heard—yours—thieves can either eavesdrop on your conversations or make costly long-distance calls at your expense. You will not even be aware of such calls until you get your monthly phone bill or if you happen to pick up your telephone during their conversation. To combat this situation, manufacturers of cordless telephones now offer a new generation of instruments incorporating security codes.

An even more serious problem affects some cordless telephones. The ringer in most cordless telephones is in the earpiece; to answer the phone you must move a switch from "ring" to "talk." If you forget to do this and simply place the phone to your ear, "the next ring may blow your mind," according to Stan Morrow, project manager for the Consumer Product Safety Commission. The American Academy of Otolaryngology says it has received reports of about a dozen cases of permanent hearing loss from this cause.

Among the innovative features offered on cordless telephones are automatic last-number redialing, ten-number automatic dialing, clear-channel selector switch, built-in digital clock and call timer, dialed number display, mute button, automatic hang-up at the base station (if you forget to do so at the handset), and the ability to function as a two-way intercom.

Facsimile Transmission Facsimile transmitters enable the user to to send a copy of a document over phone lines from one location to another, provided the second location is also equipped with a compatible facsimile machine. Facsimile transmission is ideal for the transmission of photographs, illustrations, statistical material, or lengthy documents—in fact, any material that would take time to keyboard again.

Machines may be rented or bought. The quality of the transmitted image is determined by resolution, or the number of lines per inch. Early machines transmitted relatively coarse pictures, comparable in quality to screened newspaper halftones; machines available now are capable of higher quality.

If you do not have direct access to a machine, material can still be sent anywhere in the world. Western Union maintains Facsimile Service Bureaus in New York, San Francisco, Washington, Miami, and New Orleans. And if the intended recipient does not have access to a machine, Western Union will transmit the document to the nearest Western Union office overseas, which will deliver the facsimile by the fastest means.

The U.S. Postal Service offers an identical service called Intelpost. Anything that can be photocopied can be transmitted from designated U.S. post offices to selected foreign cities.

Headsets If your business requires that you spend a lot of time on the telephone, if you need both hands free while phoning, or if you are physically handicapped, a headset will enable you to have hands-free conversations.

Several models are available: a fully adjustable model allows positioning of the microphone and receiver; another model becomes a lightweight handset when the headband is removed; a third type weighs less than two ounces and requires no headband. Some headsets can be plugged directly into modular jacks.

Hold Module Added to single-line phones, this device enables you to put an incoming call on hold without losing it (while you look up something, consult with someone, or go to an extension phone to take the call). The chief advantage is that you no longer have to go back to the first phone to replace it on the hook or risk the possibility that the phone will be left off the hook, tying up the line.

Added to two incoming lines, a similar device enables you to carry both lines on one instrument; it holds either line while you talk to the other or puts two calls on stand-by.

If you are losing clients because your single line is often busy when they call, a phone-company service (called "call waiting") signals you that a second call is coming in over your line so you can put the call in progress on hold and answer it.

Intercoms You can save time, steps, and avoid distracting interruptions from other members of the household with an intercom system. Intercoms are of two basic designs: the less common wired systems and the more versatile "wireless" models. With a wired system, you'll have to string two-conductor bell wire between the stations; such installations are less flexible, and the locations of instruments are not easily changed. With the "wireless" models ("wireless" is a misnomer; the signals are actually transmitted over the house wiring), you merely plug them into any 110-volt outlet and turn them on. The utmost versatility can be achieved with three or more "wireless" instruments and two-channel operation. A lock-in transmit switch enables an intercom to function in a "baby-sitting" mode, transmitting all sounds from that location.

If your office is in a remote part of the house, an intercom setup can monitor the front door so that you never miss callers or deliveries. "Wireless" intercoms, which transmit via the home's 110-volt lines, give great flexibility, since they can be used anywhere in a house or apartment simply by being plugged into the nearest electrical outlet.

Jacks and Plugs In telephone parlance, a jack is a receptacle designed to receive a plug. (The terms "male" and "female" are frowned on in today's sexist-conscious world, but the analogy is appropriate.) You'll find four-prong plugs and jacks (now being phased out of use) and smaller modular plugs and jacks. In addition, you'll find a host of special plugs and jacks designed to enable you to adapt or mate existing lines and equipment to modular use, as well as to diversify their usefulness. Thus, once you have installed a modular jack, you can buy a duplex jack that will enable you to plug two modular plugs (from telephones, amplifier, or answering machine) into a single modular jack. Further expansion is possible with additional wires and jacks, making the possibilities almost unlimited.

Locks You may have occasion to want to prevent unauthorized use of your telephone. The easiest way to do this, of course, is simply to unplug the telephone instrument from the line and lock it away. Locks of various kinds are available, however, ranging from simple key-operated dial locks to sophisticated locks for tone phones.

Modems See chapter 14.

Multifunction Telephones Telephones incorporating clocks and clock radios; telephones featuring on-hook dialing, color-coded and illuminated single-button memory dialing of from two to sixty numbers, last-number redialing, and ringer silencers; telephones equipped with two-way speakers—these are the innovations available now, and more are on the way. Some instruments are versatile and can be switched either to pulse or tone dialing. In the future, telephones will incorporate computer-access capabilities, making the home or business telephone a veritable information center.

Outdoor Ringers If you like to work outside during good weather, a weatherproof outdoor ringer can be mounted outside your home. This is an electronic amplifier that converts the ringing voltage into a loud sound.

Pocket Tone Dialers Should you need tone dialing to access alternate long-distance services or computer services and you are at a pulse-dialing telephone, the answer is a battery-powered pocket tone dialer. Simply hold it against the transmitter of the telephone instrument and press the appropriate keys. Models are available with memory and thirty-two digit number capacity.

Remote Controllers You can control lights and appliances in your home from a distance with a remote-control system. This consists of a central control station that commands modules at lamps, switches, and appliances, plus a remote signaling unit that is used to transmit coded tone signals over telephone lines. With such a system, you can turn on lights, TV set, or radios to discourage burglars; you can start dinner in a microwave oven or turn on air conditioners or space heaters in advance of your return home.

Ringer Silencers There may be times when you will want to silence the bell or ringer on your telephone. Switches are available to enable you to do this: one mounts directly on the phone's base set, while the other is contained in a seven-foot cord that plugs into the phone's modular jack. With either in operation, the caller hears what appears to be a ringing tone, and you hear nothing. But if you forget to switch the silencer off, you could miss an important call.

Speakerphones (*see also Amplifiers*) These enable hands-free telephoning and are useful if you want more than one person at your end to take part in a phone conversation. Some speaker phones use infrared light and require no wiring between them and the telephone instrument. Separate speaker phones will eventually disappear as these devices become incorporated into multifunction telephone instruments.

Specialty Telephones The emperor of Japan owns a Mickey Mouse watch, so there's no reason why you shouldn't have a Mickey Mouse telephone in your office, if you want one. Decorator telephones are available that imitate ornate French phones, rural crank-type phones, or the candlestick telephones of the roaring twenties. Telephones are now concealed in boxes and have bases of wood, leather, cane, or onyx or even resemble a tiny rolltop desk. Others have giant-sized buttons and numerals or black-boards for scribbling messages. If you want to express your personality by means of your telephone, there's something for everybody.

Telex and TWX Telex (now called Telex I) and TWX (now called Telex II) are both owned by Western Union. Telex began in Germany in the 1930s and rapidly spread throughout Europe and the rest of the world. Today, it includes 84,000 subscribers in the United States, 90,000 in other parts of North America, and another 1,500,000 elsewhere in the world.

Internationally, Telex I messages are handled by IRCs (International Record Carriers), such as RCA Global Communications, ITT World Communications, Western Union International (which is not affiliated with the Western Union Telegraph Company), TRT Telecommunications, and FTC Communications. Recently, the FCC granted Western Union permission to offer international Telex I service; the IRCs were also granted permission to begin domestic services.

The initials "TWX" stood for "teletypewriter exchange." This service was owned by AT&T until the 1960s, when it was acquired by its competitor, Western Union. Telex and TWX were incompatible, but the new owners have connected all subscribers by means of devices that resolved code and transmission speed incompatibilities.

Western Union also offers a message service called Infomaster under which a message or messages (up to a limit of 450) can be sent.

Home-based businesses requiring a written record of all messages sent and received (Telex I and Telex II can transmit and accept messages without an operator being present) or businesses engaged in international trade should consider Telex. Experts expect computers to supplant these services, however, as computer terminals increase in number and wider use is made of telephone networks for data and message transmission.

Toll-Call Timers When you look at your first long-distance bill, your initial impulse may be to purchase a timer. One home office I have visited is equipped with a simple three-minute kitchen egg-timer hourglass. I have used a jogger's stopwatch on calls that are likely to run long. Another device makes an audible beep every three minutes, but this may be too infrequent for most marathon long-distance talkers. Some multifunction telephones and automatic dialers incorporate timers with digital displays of elapsed minutes and seconds.

Voice Mail Telecomputers offering computerized storage and delivery of a phone message to another person (especially the same message to a number of different recipients) and the recording of their responses are still too expensive for the average home office. In the future, this telephonic equivalent of the Mailgram could become a monster, inundating millions of telephone subscribers with unsolicited and unwanted "junk" phone calls.

"People are fascinated, even if they're not interested in the message," maintains Irv Kadet, vice-president of New York–based RIKA Electronics, one of about a dozen American manufacturers of the machines.

Not everyone who is called finds listening and talking to a machine attractive, however. "We had to devise a feature that disconnects the recording if the person doesn't answer two questions in succession," Kadet explained. "It's the ultimate insult—a computer hanging up on you."

In 1980, the FCC decided that nationwide controls on telecomputers would be unworkable, but more than a dozen states regulate them, and others are expected to follow suit. Most restrictions require a human to get permission before playing the taped message.

Voice Scramblers Many long-distance phone conversations travel via satellites or over microwave relay links and are subject to interception and eavesdropping by enterprising listeners, often with no more than a scanner able to tune across the operating frequency. It is not unlawful to listen to such conversations, although it is a violation of FCC regulations to impart to another the substance of such a conversation.

If your phone conversations are of a kind you would prefer to remain absolutely confidential, the answer could lie in a voice scrambler and descrambler, much like those made famous in wartime by President Roosevelt and Prime Minister Churchill and still used by intelligence agencies. These devices are expensive; you'll need one, and so will everyone else with whom you have a conversation on confidential or sensitive subjects, so equipment costs could be prohibitive.

NINE

I'm Not In Now:
Answering Machines,
Answering Services, and Pagers

Sales of answering machines are increasing by about 15 percent annually, with current sales volume at about a million units a year. Despite the average person's aversion to talking to a machine, answering machines do enable callers to leave a message that can be retrieved later. Occasionally, callers will fail to leave a message on a machine; when that happens, you can conclude that the call was unimportant or the caller needed an immediate answer.

Answering machines can serve as effective protective devices for persons with high-visibility careers, anyone who receives annoying phone calls, and women who live alone. The monitoring switch on many answering machines makes it possible for you to know who is calling and to decide whether you want to talk with the caller. Annoyance callers quickly lose interest in pestering a machine.

Basically, an answering machine is nothing more than a tape player/recorder triggered by incoming calls. Although answering machines are provided with a modular jack into which a phone can be plugged, both the telephone and the answering machine can operate independently. If quiet working conditions are necessary for you, you can unplug the phone and let the answering machine do the answering. By turning down the volume control, the answering machine can be silenced without interfering with its ability to answer.

Answering machines may be categorized by price into two main groups: inexpensive machines selling for under $150 and more expensive models costing over $150. The only significant differences between the groups is the number of conveniences offered. Here are the features you are likely to find and an estimate of their desirability:

Announce-Only Mode Useful, especially if you don't want to receive messages but do want callers to be given information, such as another number at which you can be reached. Inexpensive, nonrecording, announce-only machines are also available.

Automatic-Answer Switch Useful. Turns the machine to the answer mode automatically regardless of the mode it has been left in.

Battery Backup Desirable if your machine has a built-in calendar or clock display devices and the electric current in your area is erratic.

Call Screening Desirable and now almost standard. Allows you to listen to the caller's message and to decide whether you want to interrupt by answering the phone.

Cue Feature Allows the listener to locate specific messages for quick playback.

Dual-Message Tapes Some machines are equipped with two outgoing message tapes that allow the user to change messages.

Last-Message Alert Because answering machines return to the beginning of the message-taking tape when you have played back your messages, it is annoying not to be able to know where today's messages leave off and older messages resume. This feature is particularly useful if you do not erase old messages from your tape.

Manual Erase Useful, especially if your machine does not have a call counter or last-message alert.

Memo Mode Allows you to record notes to yourself, a feature of doubtful value.

Message-Received Indicator Necessary. Signals visually that one or more messages have been received and sometimes indicates the total number of new messages on the tape. Some sophisticated machines show the date and time each message was received.

Remote Access This hand-held tone-generating device is useful if you are away from your office and want to listen to the accumulated messages from another location. More expensive machines have triggering devices that are security coded to prevent others with similar devices from causing your machine to play back its messages for them. Newer machines dispense with beepers entirely and use tone phones for accessing machines.

Some machines offer a special ring delay for use with remote access devices. If your machine ordinarily answers on the third ring, it will not answer a remote-access call until the fifth ring, thus signaling to you that no new messages have been received and saving on toll-call costs.

Ring-Delay Adjustment Desirable. Allows you to adjust the machine to answer after a predetermined number of rings. A machine that cannot be adjusted for the number of rings before answering (some inexpensive machines answer too quickly—after the first or second ring) or one that is adjusted to answer too quickly puts callers at a disadvantage. What is worse, if left in the answer mode while you are at home, such a machine may answer calls before you get to the phone, causing delays and much fumbling with switches while callers wait.

Two-way Recording Useful. Allows your answering machine to double as a tape recorder during a conversation. This electronic note-taking feature is especially valuable if you must take down complicated information or if you want to interview someone on the telephone. (FCC rules require that a beep be inserted on the line every fifteen seconds to let the caller know that the conversation is being recorded; machines with a two-way recording feature do this.)

Is it illegal to record conversations made on your own telephone? Is this the same as wiretapping? In a 1947 tariff, the FCC required telephone companies to prohibit the recording of interstate or international telephone conversations without the knowledge of the other party unless all parties consent or a beep tone is sounded every fifteen seconds to make known the fact that a recording is being made.

Phone companies are required by the FCC to state this in their tariffs; the phone companies are also charged with the enforcement of this rule. The severest penalty for violation is termination of the telephone service of the person making the unauthorized recording.

Unfortunately, this is a regulation that is apparently honored more in the breach than in the observance. In the nation's capital, the beepless telephone recorder is reputed to be as omnipresent in some government offices as the carafe, water glasses, and serving tray on the credenza. Many high-level conversations are conducted with the expectation that they may be surreptitiously recorded or transcribed.

If you must record a conversation over your own phone for any reason and your answering machine makes no provision for this, small induction coils that attach to the handset by means of suction cups are available. More sophisticated devices connect directly to the modular jack on the telephone instrument and begin recording when the handset is lifted. Either type can be connected to an ordinary cassette tape recorder.

It is not a crime under federal law for one party to tape a telephone conversation without telling the other. It is a crime to do so under state laws in effect in California, Delaware, Florida, Georgia, Illinois, Massachusetts, Maryland, Michigan, Montana, New Hampshire, Pennsylvania, and Washington. Therefore, *where* the telephone call is being recorded makes a big difference. A person in Bethesda, Maryland, telephoning someone in the neighboring city of Washington commits a crime if the call is recorded in Maryland, but no crime is committed if the person in the District of Columbia records it.

VOX The abbreviation is borrowed from radio and stands for "voice-operated transmission," now altered to mean "voice-operated switch"—a most desirable feature. VOX models record messages for as long as the caller continues to talk and "hang up" only after the caller stops talking. Machines without this feature record for a prescribed time—usually thirty seconds. If your caller is a poor judge of time or feels hurried by your message that only thirty seconds are available, you may get a truncated or incomplete message, or the caller may be forced to call back one or more times to complete the message. Most VOX machines can also be set to record messages of fixed duration.

The VOX circuit in answering machines has a time-lag feature to allow for short pauses and does not disconnect instantaneously. One disadvantage to VOX is that the unit is sometimes fooled by spurious signals (line noise, cross talk, or a dial tone) and continues to record. Other drawbacks to VOX include long-winded callers who drone on and on and pranksters who will cause an entire tape to run out by placing the telephone handset near a radio.

Some answering machines offer "calling party control" (CPC) and only disconnect when the caller terminates the call by hanging up.

Recording an Outgoing Message

When recording a message for the outgoing cassette, practice what you will say before attempting to record it. A written "script" may assist you in timing it correctly. It's a good idea to keep your outgoing message short and to consume most or all of the tape time with your message. There's nothing more frustrating for a caller than to listen to your hasty message and "Now listen for the beep tone," only to be made to wait ten or fifteen seconds before being able to begin speaking. Outgoing message and announcement tapes are available in lengths of ten, fifteen, twenty, thirty, forty-five, and sixty seconds.

Your message should be appropriate to the nature of the business you are in. If a caller is expecting to reach a professional, he should not be greeted with a humorous tape. Unless you are Burt Bacharach, you should avoid musical backgrounds that sound as though you recorded your message in a piano bar. Similarly, celestial music would be inappropriate for an undertaker.

CAUTION: answering machines provide an easy way for thieves to scout for prospective victims from a distance without exposing themselves to observation by the police or alert neighbors. If you are away from home regularly for extended periods, your answering machine can be an invitation to breaking and entering. Your phone message should stress that you have left the house *briefly* and that you will return shortly—no matter how long you expect to be away. To foil burglars, some messages state that the machine is being used to screen calls, implying that someone is indeed at home. This may infuriate some callers, who then neither leave a message nor call back.

If you are going to be away on a long vacation trip, do not make the mistake of announcing this on your answering machine's outgoing message tape. The incoming message tape hasn't been made that can accept an unlimited number of messages; more importantly, you may find both your office and your home empty of furniture and valuables. And no answering machine.

ANSWERING SERVICES

There are two alternatives to an answering machine: to have none at all or to employ an answering service. Answering services offer certain advantages, for the caller is able to talk with a living person, albeit someone who sometimes seems to be singularly uninformed about your schedule, your whereabouts, or even your intention of calling the answering service. Nevertheless, speaking with a living person can be reassuring, especially in an emergency or crisis situation. Answering-service operators usually know more than they are willing to let on to callers and often will immediately communicate a message to the client if it seems important. Answering services are also much used by physicians and other professionals because they offer a way of screening calls without seeming to do so and of sorting out calls by their degree of importance before responding.

Answering services serve many clients, so waiting times before the phone is answered tend to be longer; operators are likely to be busier, often putting callers on hold while they answer another call. The person with a long or complicated message to leave will often fare better at the hands of an answering machine with the VOX feature.

Every client of an answering service has experienced situations involving lost or garbled messages and uncivil operators. One professional checks up on his answering service from time to time by having friends call with prearranged messages. Although many answering services, particularly in smaller communities, are mom-and-pop enterprises, at one time or another the same problems seem to afflict all answering services, large or small.

When should you employ an answering service? If your business is such that immediate action must be taken in response to a call—that is, if you are a physician, surgeon, or someone in an emergency service—my advice is to employ an answering service that can and will find you and pass messages to you. Otherwise, an answering machine is an economical and totally acceptable substitute.

PAGERS

At one time, the sound of a beeper going off in a crowded theater or restaurant meant only one thing: the person wearing it was a doctor who was being summoned to a nearby phone because of a life-threatening emergency, and audiences or diners gawked. With their proliferation, pagers have ceased to be a status symbol.

Today, the call could be for a plumber, computer repairman, or even a call girl.

The belt-attached, comparatively cumbersome pagers of the past have become compact and pocketable. Pagers are still only miniature FM receivers, but sophisticated models are on the way. Look for pagers that will display the caller's phone number or store the numbers of a series of callers and those that will give you stock-market quotations and the prices of commodities futures.

Anticipating a surge in demand, the FCC has already doubled the number of frequencies available. The technology to manufacture two-way pagers that can function as portable extensions of your own telephone is here, according to Randall Tobias, president of AT&T Consumer Products. The only element missing is the long-life battery needed to power them. Then the Dick Tracy wristwatch radio, first dreamed up by cartoonist Chester Gould in 1946, will have become a reality.

National paging anywhere in the country is the next step. Experts have predicted that as many as 18 million pagers may be abroad in the land by 1990. Pager prices, now high, inevitably will plummet, but access costs and service charges will rise. Nevertheless, for the office-at-homer with a small staff or no employees, a pager can mean that you will never be unreachable again.

TEN

The Impact of a Machine: Electric and Electronic Typewriters

The typewriter has a long history—longer than you may suspect. Several machines for imposing type on paper were proposed toward the end of the seventeenth century. In 1714, Henry Mill received British patent no. 395 for "an Artificial Machine or Method for the Impressing or Transcribing of Letters Singly or Progressively one after another, as in Writing, whereby all Writing whatever may be Engrossed in Paper or Parchment so Neat and Exact as not to be distinguished from Print." That's as good a definition of today's typewriting objectives as you'll find anywhere. Little is known of Mill's machine, but from its patent description it had to be crude and cumbersome.

Another attempt in the eighteenth century, in 1784, in France resulted in a machine for embossing characters for the blind, a forerunner of Braille machines. Interestingly, the history of invention is studded with devices designed to help the handicapped; Alexander Graham Bell's employment of visual aids to teach the articulation of sounds by deaf children led to the theory from which he derived the principles of telephony.

Genuine "firsts" among inventions are often difficult to identify, but the most famous of the early typewriter patents was that of Christopher Latham Sholes, Carlos Glidden, and Samuel W. Soule in 1868. It covered a machine with understroke type bars that registered an impression from beneath the platen, just as standard typewriters do.

The Sholes machine was more than just the first practical typewriter. It also gave birth to the phrase that everyone seems to use to test the speed of typewriters. According to Charles E. Weller, a court reporter and a friend of inventor Sholes, he was asked to try the prototype machine. A hotly contested political campaign was being waged in Milwaukee in the summer of 1867, and so Weller typed, "Now is the time for all good men to come to the aid of the party."

James Densmore, a financial backer of Sholes and his associates, later negotiated a contract with Philo Remington, of the Ilion, New York, arms company of the same name, and the office typewriter was born in 1874. It wasn't until the typewriter showed itself as able to produce letters faster than handwriting that it caught on. The Remington was the first machine to feature the modern standard arrangement ("QWERTY") of keyboard characters.

In 1933, IBM introduced the first practical electric typewriter, which slowly but surely displaced manual machines in business offices. The next milestone came in 1961, which saw the introduction of the first replaceable, interchangeable single-element typewriter. The honor of being the first electronic typewriter goes to the Qyx (now Exxon) Intelligent Typewriter, introduced in 1978, which stole a march on IBM. The Qyx machine offered text input into memory and an optional twenty-four-character LED (light-emitting diode) display.

ELECTRIC AND ELECTRONIC TYPEWRITERS

Nothing distinguishes business letters from personal communications more than the use of a typewriter or printer of some kind. Today the words "electric typewriter" and "electronic typewriter" are almost synonymous with business communications.

Just as your letterheads, envelopes, and business cards will be the means by which outsiders—for the most part, strangers—will learn of you and the services you offer, so, too, the look of your letters will tell them much about you. If meticulousness and accuracy are qualities of the service (free-lance proofreading, for example) you offer to clients, you'd be foolish to produce a carelessly typed letter. Your correspondence should display neat typing of the kind best produced by an electric or an electronic machine.

Does this mean you should trade in your mechanical machine for an electric or an electronic typewriter or even give it away? Not at all. The next time the power to your home office goes off during a storm or other emergency, you'll be glad you kept your mechanical clunker.

If you have an old-fashioned mechanical typewriter, dust it off and try it. If the keys work and are not misaligned, cleaning may work wonders. First, buy a new nylon ribbon of solid black color. Avoid two-color red-and-black ribbons; unless your machine is in perfect working order, such ribbons tend to mix the colors at the bottoms of lines.

Next, clean the type itself using a solvent-type liquid cleaner and an old toothbrush (but watch out for spattering). Other cleaning materials you can use include a plastic, putty-type, kneaded material or a specially treated fabric that picks dirt from the keys as you type on it (without the ribbon, of course). Hardened and encrusted dirt is more easily softened and removed with a liquid solvent.

If the type levers move sluggishly or stick in one position because of accumulated lubricant and eraser droppings, you should clean and lubricate the machine thoroughly. Accumulations of old lubricant can be removed from a machine in otherwise good condition by spraying the moving parts with TV tuner cleaner, obtainable in aerosol cans at radio and TV stores. This cleaner and degreaser not only loosens and removes caked oil and dirt but will lubricate the machine. Place the typewriter on an opened newspaper and spray it until the solvent drips down, carrying old oil and accumulated dirt with it. This treatment, the same used by typewriter repairmen, works wonders in restoring mechanical typewriters to operating condition.

If you are about to buy a typewriter—either new or used— you'll want to consider an electric or electronic model. All current electric and electronic machines have one feature in common: the carriage no longer moves; instead, the typing element (a metal ball or a metal or plastic wheel) travels back and forth. For those who are accustomed to moving the carriage by hand, this feature may be difficult to adjust to at first. The addition of correcting tapes that literally lift the typed characters off the page has meant that fewer eraser droppings are created to clog typewriter mechanisms. You'll find that simple electronic typewriters cost only a little more than good electric typewriters but offer many more features.

If electronic typewriters have begun to supplant electric machines because they now approach them in price, they can also be regarded as a sound investment because of the increased productivity they permit. Once you have tried an electronic typewriter, you may never be happy with anything less.

In addition to their wider range of functions, the electronic components of electronic typewriters offer greater reliability than the electromechanical parts of electric typewriters. Flexibility in the choice of ten-, twelve-, and fifteen-pitch typing, as well as proportional spacing, is another advantage. Instead of the levers or type elements of electrics, electronic typewriters employ daisy-wheel printing disks, which are less expensive and more durable. Again, because of the fewer moving parts in an electronic typewriter, service problems are less.

Industry studies have shown that an electronic typewriter can provide an increase in speed and a consequent increase in typing output from 20 to 50 percent. The tasks for which it is best suited include general correspondence and memos, statistical typing, and short documents and reports, especially if all or part of the information must be repeated.

According to estimates of industry research firms, the annual growth rate of electronic typewriters until 1986 will be around 28 percent. During the same period, the growth in personal computers and word processors is expected to be about 54 percent and 26 percent, respectively. Some manual machines may survive in special areas, such as unheated warehouses and truck terminals, where extreme operating conditions could be hard on electronic components.

Electronic typewriters are the offspring of the marriage in the late 1970s of the electric typewriter and the microprocessor. They may be classified as basic, intermediate, and advanced machines. Basic electronic typewriters will automate some tasks, such as margin setting, decimal tabbing, carriage return, centering, and underscoring. The correction buffer (where characters are stored in memory and subject to correction) on some low-level machines can go as high as 400 characters.

Intermediate machines offer all of the above features but add greater text-handling capabilities, such as default-format settings, stop codes for repetitive-letter printout, and columnar layout. Machines in this category tend to offer larger correction buffers and increased phrase-format storage.

Advanced electronic typewriters may offer internal storage capabilities that retain up to ten pages of text, in addition to more text manipulation features, such as text move/insertion/deletion, text assembling, search-and-replace functions, and the ability to paginate. CRT screens and cassette or disk storage are usually offered as options. At this stage, such electronic typewriters approach word processors in versatility.

Here are some features to consider when shopping for an electronic typewriter:

Automatic Carriage Return Performs a carriage return automatically when the last word able to fit on a line is typed.

Automatic Centering Centers individual lines between set margins. Desirable if you often type tables, charts, or material for display.

Automatic Error Correction Universally available. Deletes corrected errors from the machine's memory.

Automatic Line Spacing Can usually be set to space at 1–, 1½–, and 2–line intervals. Now universally available.

Automatic Relocate Desirable. After errors have been corrected, automatically returns to the original position before correction was initiated.

Automatic Underscoring Desirable, especially if copy contains material that must eventually be set in italics. (Underscoring is the way typesetters are instructed to set typed copy in italics.)

Automatic Word Wrap Desirable. Places a word on the next line automatically if it will not fit in the space remaining in the line being typed.

Boldface Makes letters heavier for emphasis.

Correction Buffer Its size determines how far you can backtrack in already typed text to enter a correction and still return to the point you left off (see also "Visual Display").

Decimal Tabulation Automatically aligns decimal points in columns of figures. Useful if you do much columnar typing of quantities involving decimals or figures expressed as dollars and cents.

Double Print Strikes each character twice. Useful for making multiple carbon copies.

Hyphenation Some electronic typewriters allow the user to break a word at the end of a line with a "soft" hyphen. If retyping puts this hyphenated word in the text away from the right margin, the hyphen will not appear.

Keyboard Just as an automobile buyer test drives a car before buying it, the serious typewriter buyer should test type any typewriter before making a purchase. The "feel," "click," and responsiveness of typewriters varies markedly. The keyboards of electronic typewriters are electronically operated rather than mechanically controlled, giving a faster and more efficient response time; as a consequence, most typists report an increase in typing speed.

Memory Desirable. If the memory feature is offered, it may be phrase-format memory or combined with text memory. Phrase-format memory gives the machine the ability to store often-used words, phrases, or even entire sentences in a special memory for call-up at any time. If text memory is present, bigger is better. The text memory of some expensive electronic typewriters can approach that of simple word processors.

Memory Protection Very desirable. Enables the electronic typewriter to preserve the material stored in its memory or memories during periods when the power is shut off or accidentally cut off.

Mode Refers to the method of impressing the type on paper: may be a typing element (a metal ball somewhat resembling a golf ball); it may be a print wheel called a "daisy wheel" of plastic or metal (so named because the characters are at the ends of thin "petals") or a "whisper disc" (a daisy wheel with preprogrammed impression control).

Pitch Refers to the number of characters per inch. The most common values are ten, twelve, and fifteen, although some machines also offer six pitch and proportional spacing. (The older terms "pica" and "elite" refer to ten and twelve pitch, respectively.)

Playback Speed The speed at which an electronic typewriter will automatically type the material stored in its text memory. Varies between twelve and twenty characters per second.

Price Generally speaking, price will reflect the number of features available on a particular machine. List prices for electronic typewriters range from $700 to $2,500, and discounts are widely available.

Ribbon May be nylon or other fabric, multistrike film, single strike for intense black impressions, and correctable film in a lift-off or cover-up formulas. May come in cartridge, cassette, or spool form.

Right-hand Margin Justification Increases the spacing between words to extend each line so as to align vertically at the preset right margin.

Search and Replace Desirable. Enables a user to search the memory for a particular word or misspelling and to replace it with another word, phrase, or sentence.

Type Comes in several versions: standard, in which letters and symbols correspond directly to the keys on the typewriter; bracket, including square brackets and a degree symbol in place of the numeral 1; degree, including degree and plus and minus symbols in place of fractions; and legal, including paragraph and section symbols in place of @ and ¢, plus the options of the above bracket version. "Dual" keyboards with provision for additional characters and symbols are now available on many machines.

Visual Display Some electronic typewriters have a time-lag feature that enables them to display characters as the keys are depressed but before they are impressed on the paper, allowing the typist to change or correct spellings before they reach the printed page. As an alternative to typing a document in its entirety and then correcting it before final printout, visual display is useful, but it can be a mixed blessing, since it actually slows down some typists.

ELEVEN

It All Adds Up: Printing Calculators

Conventional hand-held calculators in any one of a thousand manifestations are omnipresent in today's society. They have been slimmed down to visiting-card size; they come as part of checkbook covers; they have even been made small enough to fit in watchcases.

Nevertheless, such calculators have one major drawback in common. Because they do not preserve entries and only show totals, the user has no way of verifying whether the entries were keyed correctly.

Adding machines and printing calculators overcome that objection. Today, noisy adding machines—hand cranked or electric—are virtually obsolete. Their place has been taken by printing calculators, which have come down in price to a point where they are within the reach of every home office. Here are some features to consider in buying a printing calculator:

Display One of four kinds of displays is used in calculators: light-emitting diodes (LEDs), liquid-crystal display (LCDs), gas-discharge display (also called "plasma display"), and fluorescent display.

LEDs are semiconductors that emit excess energy as light instead of heat. LEDs offer three advantages: lower voltage requirements (six to ten volts), longer operating life, and ease of reading under ambient light conditions. LEDs form seven-segment line or dot-matrix characters when excited by an electric current. Colors available are red, yellow, and green.

LCDs are nonemissive and require external illumination to be read. The chief advantage of LCDs is their low power requirements, making them especially popular in hand-held units; they are less likely to be encountered in desk-top units operating on 110-volt current. To determine whether your calculator uses LCDs, take it into a darkened room and turn it on. If you cannot read its display, it employs LCDs. But LCDs are more visible in bright light or direct sunlight than any other display type.

Neon and other gases emit a glow when an electric charge is passed through them, and this characteristic is utilized in gas-discharge displays. These are also emissive and, because of their brightness and their size, offer excellent readability under any light conditions. Their power consumption is greater (upward of 150 volts) than other displays. Display colors are red, red orange, or amber.

Fluorescent readouts resemble gas-discharge types. Instead of causing gas above the anodes to glow, the fluorescents' anodes are coated with phosphors that glow. Many display colors are available, but green is most often encountered.

The number of digits displayed may vary from eight to as many as twenty; eight is more than adequate for most nonscientific purposes. Although the quality of the readout of a printing calculator is not necessarily a primary consideration, in choosing any calculator you should look for large numerals that are readable at normal office lighting levels. Avoid models with angled readouts that may reflect room lighting.

Keyboard Keyboards will be either an electromechanical (movable key) or a pressure-sensitive (membrane) type. The raised electromechanical keyboards are preferable for heavy use because they provide tactile and aural feedback upon entry of figures. The flat-membrane keyboards are made of layered sheets of polyester and do not return tactile signals to users. To overcome this objection, manufacturers have installed noise-feedback devices—small speakers that produce a tone or a click when a key is touched.

One advantage of the membrane type is that they are dustproof and moisture resistant, but a dust cover over an electromechanical keyboard can perform the same function when it is not in use. As for spills, coffee or soda and electronic instruments simply do not mix.

Therefore, you should prefer a machine with tactile keys that let you feel (and sometimes hear) a distinct click. Nontactile keys can more easily be keyed twice for the same entry. The keys should have some degree of resistance when they are pushed—keys that respond to a light touch can easily cause a double entry; too much key resistance could result in no entry being made at all.

Because keys can be positioned farther apart than on hand-held models, desk-top calculators are subject to fewer keying mistakes, such as hitting the wrong key or hitting two keys simultaneously, which can also result in no entry being made.

Power Most printing calculators will operate on 110-volt house current; these are preferable to battery-powered machines for office use. If you choose a battery model, use rechargeable nickel-cadmium or alkaline batteries. Over time, rechargeable batteries will prove to be less costly than alkaline or ordinary batteries. Nickel-cadmium batteries can be recharged upwards of five hundred times, and many calculators allow use during the recharge cycle.

Price List prices range from $35 to $400, and discounts are widely available. A good printing calculator, suitable for any home-office need, can be bought for well under $100.

Printing Printing calculators record calculations either on thermal paper or by means of a ribbon and roller, with impact printing on ordinary paper. Impact printing has been carried over from the former adding-machine technology. Thermal printing is a non-impact process in which figures are "burned" on treated silver paper; it does not yield figures as intensely dark as impact printing.

Among their advantages, thermal printers are virtually silent in operation; thermal printheads are less expensive to manufacture than impact printheads and take up less space, making them more desirable for hand-held printing calculators.

Thermal printers have one significant disadvantage that could affect your buying decision. In heavy use, the thermal printhead tends to need replacement more frequently; on the other hand, industry estimates give fifty years as the expected useful life of an impact printhead. Moreover, the calculations printed on thermal paper retain their readability for a comparatively short time—as little as a year, even if kept away from heat and light. This could be an important consideration if calculator tapes are a part of records intended to be preserved for long periods.

Programmability Like their hand-held counterparts, a small number of desk-top printing calculators are user programmable, making them the most sophisticated and powerful calculators available. Such machines perform all the basic functions and, in addition, offer the capability to be user programmed by keystroke or from previously programmed instructions in software packages. User-programmable calculators can often be linked to printers, video interfaces, and external storage devices. They find their most frequent applications in accounting, finance, and engineering.

Special Features If you perform many calculations involving sales taxes, choose a machine equipped with a decimal roundoff switch (sometimes called a "5/4 switch"). When this is set, the machine will increase the last decimal in an answer by one if the next number to the right is five or greater. Most machines apply an automatic constant to additions and subtractions, but you should select a machine than can apply an automatic constant to all functions.

If your calculations include many discounts, commissions, taxes, and other percentages, you should choose a machine equipped with a special percent function key to provide answers expressed as a percentage. Some machines have "markup/markdown" or "gross margin" keys, making them ideal for wholesalers and retailers.

The ability of a calculator to do repetitive calculations without the operator having to hit the equals key is called "chain calculation." You should examine the calculator's punctuation—the way the display and printout sequence of figures are made easier to read. On some calculators, groups of three digits are separated by a space; other calculators actually display and print a comma.

Ordinarily, a safeguard built into many calculators makes two keys hit simultaneously record or enter no numbers. One feature to look for, called "rollover indexing," prevents errors in keying. This allows the depression of a second key before the first key has been released, permitting faster entry of numbers. So long as the first key is depressed, the entry of other numbers is prevented, but the value of the second key will be entered as soon as the first key is released.

TWELVE

One More Time: Copying Machines

No area of office equipment has seen more spectacular growth than that of copying machines. So sudden and so great has been the explosion, we tend to forget that not many years ago the only truly reproductive copying technique available to business, large or small, was the now-outmoded photostat machine.

Today's office copying machine had its origins in the 1930s, when Chester F. Carlson patented a new technology based on what he called "electrophotography," in which an image was transferred to a sensitized plate electrostatically. The process was improved by the nonprofit Battelle Memorial Institute, of Columbus, Ohio; in 1948, through the joint efforts of the institute and a photographic supply company in Rochester, New York, the Haloid Company, the first copier embodying Carlson's principle became commercially feasible—a manually fed model.

Two years later, the company changed its name to the Xerox Corporation, and the process was named "xerography." The term came from two Greek words, *xeros* (dry) and *graphein* (writing). In 1960, Xerox introduced the first automatic copier, the Model 914.

Paralleling this, in 1955, the Radio Corporation of America's laboratories in Princeton, New Jersey, developed a coated-paper copier. Copies were produced on charge-sensitive paper rather than on Carlson's intermediary drum, giving stiff competition to plain-paper copiers. Eventually, the faster copying speed and higher copy quality of plain-paper copiers enabled them to capture a major share of the copier market.

Although copying machines are widely available in public libraries, post offices, banks, and copy centers, the time will come when you must consider the advantages of a copying machine, whether bought or leased, for your home office.

The quality of copies made on today's machines is infinitely better than those made on copiers costing two or three times as much five years ago. Does this mean that the technology is steadily improving and you should wait to add a copier to the complement of equipment in your home office? Not at all. The truth is that copier technology has now begun to level off and that most of the features added to machines in the near future will be refinements of existing technology.

The majority of copying machines available today are plain-paper copiers (referred to as PPCs). For many years, coated-paper copiers (CPCs), which utilized special papers and liquid toners, were the only copying machines a small business could afford.

Thanks to such technical developments as microprocessors to

control and monitor machine functions, automatic toner control to give more consistent reproductive quality, waste-toner recycling to increase toner yields, single-element toners that eliminate the need for separate developer, and cold-pressure fusing that does away with warm-up delays, copying machines are well worth considering as a tool of the home office.

As cost has dropped, so, too, have size and weight been shed. Solid-state electronics have eliminated many mechanical moving parts, and fiber optics are replacing lens/mirror systems, resulting in more compact designs.

The principal copying processes used in today's copiers are electrostatic, thermographic, and diazo systems.

Xerography is an electrostatic process that operates in the following fashion: (1) a drum or belt, coated with photoconductive selenium or zinc oxide, accepts a positive (+) charge as it rotates past a shielded corona wire or wires; (2) by means of fiber optics or a system of mirrors and lenses, the drum is exposed to the document to be copied, and light reflecting off the nonimage areas discharges the positive charge applied previously; (3) toner (a mixture of carbon and plastic particles), carrying a negative (−) charge, is cascaded over the surface of the drum or belt, adhering to the positively charged image and being repelled by the open negative areas; (4) a sheet of paper is positively charged and pressed against the drum or belt, pulling the toner onto the paper; (5) a high-temperature heater fuses the toner to the paper.

Direct-image electrofax processes work in largely the same way, with the exception that the transfer of the toner from drum to paper is eliminated. Instead, each sheet of paper has a special photosensitive coating of zinc oxide or a similar substance—thus, the reference to electrofax machines as coated-paper copiers.

Originally, this process employed liquid toner to develop the image and then a heat-drying system to evaporate the toner solvent. Today most CPCs use dry toner and cold-pressure fusing.

Thermographic copying takes advantage of a widely known physical fact: dark colors absorb more heat than white colors. Thermographic copiers use coated and translucent paper; the coating discolors to reproduce the image because it reacts to heat at a certain temperature.

The diazo process requires exposure by ultraviolet light through a translucent original. Light passes easily through the clear areas and decomposes a diazo compound in the copying paper, but the compound remains chemically active in those areas not reached by light. At this point, "dry" or "wet" development can take place. The sheet is either exposed to ammonia vapor or moistened with an alkaline solution to develop the latent image.

Whether your decision is to buy or lease a copying machine, you'll want to know something about the types of machines you should consider. Here are some features to investigate:

CPCs or PPCs You'll probably prefer a PPC for many reasons. You'll be able to make copies on any paper and even on your own letterhead. This feature makes it easy to send identical letters to many different recipients. Conversely, you'll be able to apply your own single-color letterhead to any letter paper after letters have been typed. PPCs will accept pencil, marker pens, or ball-point writing without skipping.

CPCs use special paper that costs more than plain paper; the coating is also easily marked and damaged by heavy metal objects. Moreover, a CPC cannot produce copies on both sides of the paper. In the past, copies made on CPCs have cost less than PPCs, but this advantage has been eroded by the increasing number of relatively inexpensive PPCs. Copies made on CPCs with liquid toner are generally suitable only for record copies and filing, at best. The introduction of dry toner into electrofax copiers has made them somewhat more desirable for all-around use.

Color Copying in color is achieved on some machines by means of interchangeables cartridges. Colors include black, brown, and blue.

Dry or Liquid Toner Dry toners are powdered inks used primarily in xerography. Liquid toners are suspensions of toner particles in a vehicle. These are applied to paper surfaces, where the toner particles are attracted to the positively charged image on the sheet. With liquid toner, the surface of the paper is wet only until the vehicle evaporates.

Maximum Size of Original The usual maximum size is 8½ by 14 inches, 10 by 14 inches, or 11 by 17 inches. The largest size encountered (one manufacturer only) was 14 x 17 inches.

Reduction (and Enlargement) This feature enables users to reduce large-sized originals to a smaller or uniform size, resulting in a saving in filing space and making it possible to include otherwise unwieldy sheets (such as computer printouts) in letter-size reports. Some copiers can also enlarge originals.

Speed (Copies Per Minute) Ranges from a low of 6 to as many as 283 in a double-sided format (the latter on a machine listing for

$64,000—hardly intended for the home office). The average number of copies per minute is about twelve.

Special Features If the following features are important to you, you should ascertain whether they are available on each copying machine under consideration: the ability to make multiple copies and the limit of such duplication (sometimes limited by the dial or readout); the ability to make offset masters; the ability to make transparencies; and the ability to copy bound-book pages. (Some copiers only accept single sheets.) Document feeders are available as standard or optional features. It would be an unusual home office that would need a sophisticated feeding device.

Two-sided copying Also called "automatic duplexing," this feature can save filing space, keep reports to a smaller number of sheets of paper, save on postage, and reduce copying-paper expenses and per-copy costs.

Copier Tips

If you buy or lease a copier, your first impulse will be to abandon the practice of making two carbons of outgoing correspondence in favor of photocopies made on your newly acquired machine. Soon after my copier arrived, I started this practice—to my sorrow. In my haste to get letters to the post office before it closed, on several occasions I mailed letters without having made photocopies. Now, even though I make photocopies of some outgoing correspondence, I always rely on two carbons as a backstop. This will avoid the embarrassment of writing to some recipients of your letters to ask them to send you a copy.

If you keep newspaper clippings in your files, you've already discovered how quickly newsprint turns brittle and disintegrates. If you copy clippings on a good grade of copy paper, however, their life will be extended immeasurably.

OTHER COPYING PROCESSES

When we think of copying processes, we inevitably think of today's copying machines that have revolutionized office practices. But processes for making copies of or from originals have been around for a long time. The older processes were largely duplicative; here are a few of them:

Carbon Paper

A staple office product for centuries, the first carbon paper was made by Ralph Wedgwood, who received British patent no. 2972 on his process in 1806. Wedgwood called his invention "duplicate paper," and made it by oiling ordinary paper and coating this with an ink made of carbon black or other coloring. Writing was done with fine-tipped points made of agate or other hard substance.

Carbon paper is still the most widely used duplicative process when the need is for no more than about a dozen readable copies. Today's carbon papers have overcome most of the objections to traditional carbon papers and are practically smudgeless; they are actually ultra-thin plastic sheets on which the medium has been deposited chemically, rather than mechanically. "Carbonless" paper (always in two parts) is chemically treated to show an image where an impression has been made. The contrast is usually not as good as in carbon-paper copies, but smudging of hands or paper is no longer a problem.

Hectograph

Employing a gelatin process, this "machine" was originated in Germany in 1880 by Alexander Shapiro. In its simplest form, it consists of a flat rectangular tray containing a gelatin compound. Special carbon paper or pencils in several colors (purple is the most common and seemingly characteristic color) apply the image to a master, which is then placed on the moist gelatin. Plain paper placed on the gelatin picks up the image. Usable for up to 100 copies.

Stencil

The first practical office duplicating machine was the mimeograph, built in the United States in 1887 by A. B. Dick. Stencils are usually typed, although a stylus can be used for lettering or signatures. The finished master is mounted face down on a fabric ink pad on the cylinder of the duplicator. Where the protective plastic surface has been cut to expose the fibrous tissue base, these openings allow ink to pass through so that mimeograph paper in contact with the stencil receives the image. Mimeograph paper has a bulky, comparatively rough surface that takes and holds ink without blurring. Stencils can also be produced in an electronic scanner or in a thermal copying machine. Usable for up to 5,000 copies; electronic stencils yield up to 10,000 copies.

Direct or Liquid (Spirit) Process

The image to be copied is transferred by means of stylus, pen or typewriter to a master sheet backed by carbon paper; this places the image in reverse on the back of the "master," which is mounted on the cylinder of the duplicating machine. As a sheet of paper moistened with spirit (methyl alcohol) passes through the machine, the spirit dissolves a small amount of aniline dye from the master and forms the image on the paper.

Spirit duplicators can copy on smooth, lint-free paper ranging from 16 to 90 pounds; the paper is treated with sizing compounds to limit its absorption of moisture and to strengthen the fibers which must be exposed to the alcohol solvent. Usable for up to 500 copies; purple dye yields the longest runs.

Offset Lithography

The original to be reproduced must be transferred to a thin aluminum plate photographically (or typed or copied by means of xerography on a paperlike master) and printed on a special offset press. The principle is an old one, having been used in stone lithography since its invention in 1798 by August Sennefelder of Austria. It makes use of the fact that oil and water do not mix.

The plate, or master, is mounted on the press cylinder and moistened with dampener rollers. Because moisture adheres to the non-image areas, these repel ink applied by inking rollers. The inked image on the plate is transferred, or "offset," to an intermediate roller (called the "blanket"), of rubber, which, in turn, prints on the paper. Because the plate or master does not come in direct contact with the paper, wear is kept to a minimum. Also called "photo-offset printing" and "planography." Masters can produce up to 10,000 copies each; aluminum plates can generate up to 50,000 copies each.

THIRTEEN

Now Hear This: Dictating and Recording Equipment

The first dictating machine, called the "Graphophone," was introduced to the business world in 1887. Developed by prolific inventor Alexander Graham Bell, his cousin Chester A. Bell, and Charles Sumner Tainter, it recorded sound by means of a spiral groove cut into the circumference of a hollow wax cylinder.

Variants of this machine were used until the Second World War and after. Among my duties on my first job as a messenger for the Chase National Bank during the Depression was the preparation of such cylinders for reuse. I operated a shaving machine that turned the cylinder on a mandrel while a cutting blade moved along the cylinder and removed a thin layer from the surface in an endless spiral. The shaved cylinders were then replaced in felt-lined cardboard containers and delivered to the bank's officers.

Modern dictating machines used the same essential principle of recording sound on a medium cut or scratched with a stylus. Plastic belts and disks replaced cylinders after World War II and then gave way to magnetic belts and disks. These were superseded by magnetic tape cassettes—the same cassettes used in home tape recorders and their miniaturized counterparts.

In the corporate world, the information to be transcribed or typed is usually delivered and picked up by messenger as rough drafts or dictation tapes. The ultimate in flexibility is achieved in arrangements where the transcriber has a dictating machine with a telephone-recording attachment. The dictator dials the transcriber's telephone extension and dictates letters, memos, reports, and other tasks over the telephone. The transcribed material is later delivered to the dictator's office, often on the same day.

Because an office at home is usually self-limiting in terms of the number of employees permitted or budgeted for, many home-office operators are turning to off-the-premises secretarial, stenographic, and typing services. Dictation is done in the home office and tapes are delivered to the transcriber. The only requirement is that the transcriber's equipment be compatible with the dictator's equipment. This does not necessarily mean that they both must be made by the same manufacturer. In fact, tapes made on business dictating equipment can usually be played on any tape recorder of the same type (i.e., standard cassettes on standard recorders, minicassettes on minirecorders, and microcassettes on microrecorders).

The selection of the machine on which the material will be dictated is usually made by you, perhaps after you have made arrangements with a transcriber to do your typing. With almost two dozen manufacturers and systems to choose from, what criteria should you apply? Here are some features to look for in a dictating machine:

Configuration Machines are classified as pocket, portable, or desk-top models. Because pocket machines are so easily kept at hand, many people use them as notebooks or idea jotters. One owner of a small business keeps one at his bedside table. Even in the small hours of the morning, it is ready to take down a whispered idea and to do it in the dark. In a pinch, with a telephone amplifier available, an operating pocket tape recorder can be pressed into service to record both sides of a phone conversation.

Correction Method The universal method of correction is voice-over automatic erasure in which subsequent recording obliterates what was previously recorded.

Indexing Method At best, methods to assist the dictator or transcriber in finding a particular place on a tape present problems for the user. No dictating machine has the capability of opening a "window" into the recorded tape (as do computers, word processors, and memory typewriters) and making provision for the insertion of new material by shifting previously recorded material. Therefore, the dictator must add corrections, changes, and emendations at the *end* of the material already recorded and indicate— by the use of an indexing device—where the change should be made or the correction should be inserted. It is important, of course, that the transcriber be made aware that a correction or change will be made at a particular point, the nature of which will be forthcoming later on. This avoids the typing and retyping of several preliminary drafts before the final version can be typed.

Various indexing methods are available: audible, visible, electronic, and automatic indexing—all designed to mark and to call the transcriber's attention to places where new copy starts or a change or correction must be made. Because most unhappiness with indexing systems arises with transcribers, you should seek the transcriber's opinion when selecting a machine and thus its indexing system.

Mode Does the machine serve as both recorder and transcriber, or are individual machines required to perform these functions? A dual-purpose machine will give greater flexibility, of course. In a pinch, any machine and tape can be handed to the transcriber. Not only do dual-purpose machines afford interchangeability, but a transcriber can literally send messages or queries back to the dictator on the recording medium.

Recording Medium Most frequently encountered will be capstan-drive standard cassettes, capstan-drive microcassettes, or rim-drive minicassettes, in that order. Endless-loop machines are not for home offices but are intended for central systems in large offices. Your dictating machine will only be recording sounds within the range of voice frequencies, so high fidelity is not a consideration, and the least expensive tape cassettes can be purchased.

Dictation machine manufacturers claim that cassettes intended to be used with dictation and playback machines should be designed to withstand the frequent starting and stopping they undergo. You may therefore prefer to use dictation tape cassettes that minimize tape slippage, stretching, or breaking. Leaders are strips of reinforced nonmagnetic plastic attached at each end of the tape and intended to prevent tape breakage. Care should be exercised when using tape with leaders that no dictation is lost and positioning indexes register correctly.

Standard cassettes come in 30-, 45-, 60-, and 90-minute versions; 120- and 180-minute standard cassettes are also offered but may present problems with tape breakage because thinner tape is employed.

The customary playing time of microcassettes is thirty minutes to a side, or a total of sixty minutes, although cassettes with total playing times of thirty minutes and ninety minutes are also available. Some microcassette machines offer a choice of two tape speeds. When operated at 1.2 centimeters per second (instead of the standard speed of 2.4 centimeters per second), cassette capacity is doubled. With a ninety-minute cassette operated at the slower speed, total recording time available could be up to three hours.

The usual limit for minicassettes is thirty minutes (fifteen minutes of recording on each side). One manufacturer, Stenocord, introduced a fifty-minute minicassette with twenty-five minutes per side, and sixty-minute versions (thirty minutes per side) are now available.

Recording Time Because of the wide variety of recording media available, total recording time is also variable, ranging from a low of 30 minutes to a high of 180 minutes. In general, recording time is a function of recording speed and the capacity of available tape cassettes.

Speaking Device What you talk into may be built into the unit (generally less desirable), a separate microphone, or a handset with controls mounted in the handle. A clip-on microphone is a convenience if you like to have your hands free while recording or if you dictate while driving your automobile.

Special Features Among the features you may want to look for are unlimited review of a tape (almost all machines now offer this), audible scanning (to find a particular word or phrase), and a telephone attachment for recording from a telephone handset.

Transcription Device What you listen to on playback may be a unit-mounted speaker, the microphone in the handset (functioning in reverse as a small speaker), or an earphone-headset combination. For the transcriber, a foot-activated switch or pedal is a must and allows the transcriber to keep both hands on the typewriter.

VOX Highly desirable. The recorder operates only when the dictator speaks and pauses when the speaker pauses, giving the user time for thought between dictated segments and obviating the need for manipulation of hand controls.

In the absence of a dictating machine, a portable tape recorder or even a hi-fi tape deck can be pressed into service (although recording on the latter would be like using an elephant gun to kill a flea). Portable tape recorders usually have built-in microphones of poor quality. None will have the ability of office dictating machines to "backtrack"—that is, to rewind the tape briefly so that the last few words or phrases will be repeated when resuming play.

Digital counters are useful in locating previously recorded material on the tape. Some tape recorders offer a cue/review feature to enable you to hear the sounds (speeded up and distorted) on a moving tape and to know where recording segments ended. Searching on a tape recorder equipped with the cue/review feature is much faster than using the fast-forward and rewind buttons. If your portable tape recorder is battery operated, it's desirable to have a meter or a light to indicate remaining battery strength. (Meters are more precise than lights.)

One thing is certain: no one—dictator or transcriber—is ever lukewarm on the subject of dictating machines. They either swear by them—or have sworn off them. Correctly used, dictating machines can save significant amounts of time.

One way to increase the usefulness of dictating machines and tape recorders as an adjunct to the home office is to hone your own dictating skills. Here are some tips:

Before You Start Dictating

Read the manufacturer's manual and familiarize yourself with the equipment you are using. Know the function of every button, switch, and control on your machine.

Have at hand all the dictation materials you will need: files, reports, memos, letters, but also a dictionary, thesaurus, ZIP code directory, and other reference works you may have to consult.

Organize the items in an order of descending priority; the transcriber should not be made to jump back and forth within a tape to locate the more important items that must be typed first.

Visualize the addressee of the communication you are dictating or the potential reader of the document. There should be a difference in how you address and what you say to an individual, a group, or a general audience. Establish in your own mind, also, the purpose, tone, and impact you want your communication to have (firm, apologetic, insistent) and make sure you are consistent.

Organize your thoughts before starting to dictate; if necessary, make brief written outlines of your letters. These will keep you from digressing, making your dictation well organized and smooth flowing.

When Dictating

Avoid making distracting sounds. Do not clear your throat into the microphone before starting to speak. Be careful not to strike the microphone or drop it. Keep the sound of radios and other noisemaking appliances out of the background of your tapes.

Speak clearly and slowly. Enunciate distinctly. Speak in a conversational tone at a steady pace. Avoid speech mannerisms, particularly the "holy tone" some dictators adopt when confronted with a microphone.

Don't use jargon or industry-specific terminology. You may be familiar with "stet" (let it stand), "ital" (italics), and "caps" (capital letters), but these may be unintelligible to the transcriber.

Emphasize words likely to be misunderstood: plurals and past tenses (sound the final *s* and *ed*) and any letters that could be confused (*b* for *p*, *d* for *t*, *f* for *s*, *m* for *n*).

If there is any likelihood that the transcriber will be in doubt about a word, spell it. But announce, "I spell," before you spell the word. To clarify and reinforce any individual letters that could be confused, use one of the easily recognized word lists, such as the International Telecommunications Union list, which is familiar because it is employed by the military and all airlines:

A—Alfa	N—November
B—Bravo	O—Oscar
C—Charlie	P—Papa
D—Delta	Q—Quebec
E—Echo	R—Romeo
F—Foxtrot	S—Sierra
G—Golf	T—Tango
H—Hotel	U—Uniform
I—India	V—Victor
J—Juliette	W—Whiskey
K—Kilo	X—X-ray
L—Lima	Y—Yankee
M—Mike	Z—Zulu

Also spell easily confused words (principle/principal; affect/effect; capital/capitol).

Number the items as you dictate and announce the number to the transcriber beforehand. This reference number does not have to appear on the typed copy, but it will make it easier for the transcriber to locate an item on the tape if a correction or change should be necessary.

Identify your instructions and keep them separate from the text of letters and documents. You can do this by changing the tone of your voice and by addressing the transcriber by name, which is attention getting, stating, "Edith, here are the instructions;" or, "Angela, this ends the instructions. The document starts here."

Identify the nature of the document to be prepared and the stationery to be used. Tell the transcriber whether it is a business letter to be put on letterhead paper, a personal letter with your home address shown, a report, or a memo. If you want a particular typing style used (block, semiblock, indented, hanging indented, or simplified style), now is the time to tell the transcriber. Indicate whether you want a finished copy or a double- or triple-spaced rough draft on plain paper for correction by you that will be returned to the transcriber for final typing.

Also indicate whether any copies are to be distributed and to whom. (Do this *before* dictating any letter, for it tells the transcriber how many carbons should be made.) If additional envelopes must be prepared, indicate this fact now.

Indicate any special qualities about individual letters. It is customary, for example, to type "VIA REGISTERED MAIL" and "RETURN RECEIPT REQUESTED" above the name of the addressee on letters sent by this means—for example, letters containing cash, valuable papers, or requiring such special protection to assure safe delivery.

Dictate the *specific* address (box number or street address) of the addressee, including the ZIP code. If you don't know the ZIP code, look it up before beginning to dictate.

Indicate the salutation desired (Dear Robbie, Dear Mr. Rhodes, Dear Sir).

Indicate paragraphs by saying "Paragraph" before each new paragraph is to begin.

Indicate punctuation (period, comma, semicolon, colon) and capitalization, especially if you are fussy about these and are unfamiliar with the grammatical skills of the transcriber. If you want a particular convention observed, specify it. For example, the usual way to form a dash in typing is by means of two hyphens joined to the words they link (and not a single hyphen with a space before and after).

Indicate whether numbers are to be spelled out or shown as numerals. Indicate, too, your preference in typing large numbers. (Should it be 1,560 or 1560?)

Indicate the closing you want (Very truly yours, Cordially, Sincerely). The formality or informality of the closing should match the tone of the salutation at the beginning of the letter.

Indicate whether enclosures will be included with the letter when it is mailed, what they will be (check, money order, application), and who will supply them.

Indicate that the document has ended. Also indicate when your last dictated item on a tape has been concluded.

When You Receive the Typed Letters or Documents

Proofread everything carefully before signing or initialing. If you detect an error, resist the temptation to slash an angry line through the letter with a scribbled request to do it over. (Anyway, the mistake may have been yours.) A typed document containing a minor error often can be salvaged; therefore, mark your correction *in the margin* in a soft (no. 2) lead pencil. The transcriber will be grateful to you.

Compare the envelope with the address in the letter. Sign the letter (or intital the document). If the job has been done satisfactorily, remember to thank the transcriber.

Review your dictation techniques from time to time. Occasionally ask the transcriber how you can improve your dictating skills to increase efficiency.

Pay the transcriber's invoices promptly.

FOURTEEN

Bytes Dog Man:
Computerizing the Home Office

At the end of the Second World War, the number of computers could be counted on the fingers of one hand. A decade later, there were 600. By 1966, they totaled 30,000, reaching 400,000 by 1976. Computers today number in the millions. It is estimated that in 1990 half of all American households will have a computer.

Completed in 1946 at the University of Pennsylvania, ENIAC, the first electronic computer, contained 18,000 vacuum tubes of sixteen different types, about 70,000 resistors, 10,000 capacitors, and 6,000 switches.

ENIAC was 100 feet long, 10 feet high, and 3 feet deep. In operation, it consumed 140 kilowatts of power. One observer reported that the gentle clicking of the thousands of relays and switches in such primitive computers "sounded like a roomful of ladies knitting."

Today, computers of tremendous power weigh in at less than ten pounds as portables and silently perform their prodigious calculations in milliseconds. If the aircraft industry had reduced cost, increased speed, and decreased energy consumption as the computer industry has in the past twenty-five years, a giant jet would cost $500 today and could circle the globe in twenty minutes on five gallons of fuel.

With personal computer sales in the millions annually and in the face of a drumbeat of insistent advertising claims, sooner or later you will want to explore the desirability of a computer for the home office. Although computers are capable of a wide variety of tasks, their usefulness in the home office will be limited by the nature and volume of the work performed. At the outset, you should distinguish between a computer's ability to process data and its capability to generate information.

The terms "data processing" and "information processing" are sometimes used interchangeably, but purists now prefer to restrict use of the first term to what was formerly described as record keeping, paper work, or clerical work. "Information" is coming to mean specific data that have been organized, processed, and converted to meet specific needs. It is in this ability to *convert* mere data to useful information that the computer excels and makes it invaluable to the person with little or no staff and a great need for information on which to base decisions.

The first question you must ask yourself is "Can I really profit from a computer?" Here are some possible home-office applications of microcomputers:

Word Processing Traditionally, typewriters have been the office machines of choice for letter writing and document preparation. Today, typewriters are being displaced by "dedicated" office-type word processors, by microcomputers capable of word processing, and by electronic typewriters that almost qualify as word processors.

Because word processing programs with merging features are usually integrable with mailing-list programs, users can now generate personalized letters in mass mailings. These are invaluable in the creation of new business and in selling by mail. Even the chore of mailing employment-application letters and résumés can be simplified by such programs.

As a program, word processing is not limited merely to the typing of letters or memos. It is now a part of the editing functions of many spreadsheets and integrated software packages.

Data Management Data management systems permit the manipulation, storage, and retrieval of lists, names, and files and facilitate the generation of information in various forms.

Spreadsheets Perhaps the most appropriate and widely used business application for the personal computer in the home office, such programs enable the user to create financial models, to ask "what if" questions of the computer, and to study the consequences of various business strategies under changing economic or financial conditions.

Graphics Graphics programs can translate financial data from electronic spreadsheets into line and bar graphs and pie charts (sometimes in color) to give a graphic picture of conditions.

Accounting Accounting programs are much used in business but also subject to the widest modification to meet individual needs. Programs offering traditional accounting-related functions (accounts receivable, payroll, accounts payable, general ledger, and invoicing) are available, as well as more specialized functions: inventory control, order/entry, and industry- or profession-oriented programs (i.e., to complete tax forms by accountants).

Accounting software for a small business must necessarily be different from that used by large corporations. For example, packaged programs that generate income statements reporting income as earnings per share are useless in small businesses, few of which are incorporated.

Integrated Software Until recently, one criticism of microcomputers was the separate and compartmentalized nature of available programs. This required the changing of disks in order to go from one program to another. Integrated software is now available that permits data to be exchanged between application environments such as word processing, data-base management, spreadsheets, and graphics.

Computer-Aided Design In these special graphics programs used by architects and engineers, the user is interactively coupled to a display screen with a graphic data base and analytical programs stored in the computer. An architect designing a building on the graphics display can have an instantaneous comparison of costs, and a civil engineer can do stress calculations while designing a bridge.

Data-Base Retrieval Systems Computerized information services open up a tremendous world of data previously inaccessible to the home office. Data-base retrieval systems are of three types: current information services offering news and stock information; vertical data bases, which concentrate on a single profession or area of interest, such as law, medicine, or census data; and data banks, which offer many data bases through a single organization.

The use of data-base retrieval systems requires that the user learn search techniques; since the user is billed for access time and rates are not cheap, learning how to use such systems can cost money as well as time. Often hobbyist oriented, computer bulletin boards offer an inexpensive way of exchanging ideas or of making personal contacts.

Electronic Mail Also known as E-Mail, electronic mail offers exciting possibilities for the home office equipped with a computer. With E-Mail, you can send messages computer to computer anywhere in the world, send messages to special printing and mailing centers near an intended recipient who does not have a computer, or send and receive messages via computer networks linked to 1.6 million Telex machines worldwide.

Competition is keen among the several companies offering E-Mail service. MCI Communications Corporation, GTE Corporation, and International Telephone & Telegraph all offer it. Western Union's EasyLink boasts some 10 million users.

You'll need an external modem (or a modem card installed in your computer) and communications software in order to initiate telecommunications with electronic mail services and data-base retrieval systems.

Determining Your Computer Requirements

Despite predictions of the inevitable spread of computers throughout the land, should every home office have one? Many valid reasons can be cited for *not buying* a computer for your home office. Let's examine some of them:

1. *Everyone you know owns a computer.* Unless you have explored your own need for a computer and thought about specific uses for it, lemminglike behavior is the world's worst

reason for buying a computer. If it is indeed true, however, that all your friends now own computers, this gives you a marvelous opportunity to try out several kinds of computers before making your own purchase.

2. *Computers are coming down in price.* Yes, they are, and they will continue to do so. If this is your feeling, you should wait, by all means. You won't be happy with your purchase as you watch prices drop in years to come.

3. *You only want something simple.* As with so many other things, you get what you pay for. A $500 computer with tape-cassette drive may be fine for arcade-type game playing, but it will not handle complicated programs—and you will have wasted your money.

4. *Your records are a mess.* If they are, it's probably for a number of reasons of your own making: your inefficiency, your neglect, your failure to plan intelligently, your failure to record necessary data, or your failure to identify objectives—in short, your own fault. If that's the case, no computer of any size or versatility will be able to solve such fundamental problems. Instead of cleaning up the mess with a computer, you'd only be digging yourself in deeper.

5. *You only want a computer to take care of your bookkeeping and accounting chores.* But so can a small-business bookkeeping service or a computer service bureau—and at much less cost. Just because you occasionally fly to another city, you wouldn't buy a small plane and take flying lessons, would you?

6. *Computer graphics will help you to solve business problems.* Nonsense. Visual data can provide few conclusions that the original numerical data could not provide. Line and bar graphs and pie charts have been around for many years, and a computer will add little except cost to such visual presentation.

7. *You've heard there's a lot of software out there now.* That's correct. And much of it may not be for you. Despite the proliferation of software, it's a mistake for you to think that off-the-shelf packaged software can do the same job as custom software tailored for your specific needs. Custom software and the services of an experienced software consultant aren't cheap.

8. *Okay, then you'll learn to do your own programming.* You

are foolish if you think that as the new owner of a computer you'll be able to achieve enough proficiency quickly to write your own programs. In the beginning, you'll be lucky if you can understand and tame your computer.

Some Aids to Decision Making

In making your decision as to whether your home office needs a computer, consider the following:

1. If you are thinking of buying an electric typewriter or an electronic typewriter, you should consider the advantages of the word processing capabilities of a computer. Electric typewriters, which have no memory capabilities, can be bought for as little as $400. Electronic machines, featuring small memories and automatic typing, cost about $700. For about twice this amount, you can equip your home office with a computer, monitor, and dot-matrix printer. If you own an electronic typewriter, you should inquire about its ability to be used as a printer in association with a computer; some electronic typewriters have "hot" keyboards, which preclude their receiving and printing computer information.

2. Can you identify the tasks that would benefit from the availability of a computer and the frequency with which you do them? How much typing do you do? How much data do you record? Could you use an electronic spreadsheet? How often do you write checks? How often do you send invoices? Statements? How frequently do you generate reports? How do you now record and update current-account information? Inventory? How do you handle credit information on clients?

3. Can you project the future growth of your home-office activities with and without a hypothetical computer? If your only use of a computer will be to replace a typewriter for occasional letter writing, you probably don't need one. Conversely, an author working at home whose only use for a computer could be as a word processor would be foolish not to have one, so superior is it to a typewriter for the generation and editing of large quantities of manuscript.

Generally speaking, a home office or small business can use a computer if it must store extensive data, if it keeps elaborate bookkeeping or other records, or if many letters, reports, or other documents are typed.

4. Acquisition of a computer for the home office may be further justified if its capabilities can be extended to home-management activities. These include home budgeting, tax planning, tax calculation and filing, kitchen recipe storage, investment analysis, home banking, and personal finance. The home-office computer can be used for computer-assisted instruction in typing, languages, mathematics, logic, programming, and even kindergarten subjects (learning the alphabet, numbers, or fractions). If there's a teacher in the family, the computer can be used for curriculum analysis, classroom scheduling, and homework-assignment scheduling.

5. Don't overlook a computer's game-playing capabilities, including arcade-type games; adventure, action, and puzzle games; and strategy games—poker or chess played with the computer as the opponent. Although this has to be a subsidiary reason for acquiring a computer, recreational use of a computer can offer a welcome respite from work-related activities.

Assuming that you have not ruled out a computer on the basis of the preceding informal survey, your next step will be to collect information about the kinds of programs and computers available, their capabilities, and their specifications.

Select Software First

1. Define and list your needs in order of their importance. Your needs will, of course, determine the features you should be looking for (i.e., mailing list, word processing, inventory management, accounts receivable). For each of the listed functions, you should know how many transactions or documents would be involved daily, weekly, and monthly. If one of your needs is for a program capable of sending personalized identical letters to a list of names, this rules out of consideration any word processing programs not capable of file merging.

2. You should obtain specifications and prices of currently available software for each home-office function you have identified. Software, of course, is the most critical link in the

computer chain, which is why I have placed it first. Regrettably, most buyers choose a computer on the basis of hardware and find themselves locked into the software available. The intelligent approach is to determine the applications software you will need and only to consider buying a computer that runs the programs you have selected.

This can be a tall order. For example, in the word processing area alone, there are more than a hundred programs of varying levels of versatility, priced at between a few dollars and several hundred. Therefore, you may want to narrow your search to the more popular programs.

3. Justify your purchase. An income-tax-preparation program would be a luxury if you only use it once a year, yet the same package would be a must for a tax-consultation service. If you have no employees, a software package with payroll and tax-withholding features would be useless and a waste of money.

4. List and investigate only those products whose specifications meet your needs. A program may have unique features, but these should be subordinated to your specific requirements.

5. Read documentation carefully. Manuals should include all operational aspects of the program, instructions on the use of the system's special features, and procedures for handling unusual or exceptional conditions (such as a power outage in the middle of the program).

6. Compare costs. You should not forget to include in your cost calculations the cost of converting existing files or records to computerized formats.

7. Anticipate growth. This may be difficult to do before you have had experience with your computer, but anticipation of future needs and expansion can affect your decision. For example, if you buy a particular word processing program, can you buy a spelling checker later (if one is not included in the package)?

Questions to Ask Before Deciding on Applications Software

1. Is it appropriate for the desired application? Buying powerful software with more features than you need or expect to need is a waste of money.

2. Is it simple to learn to operate, and is it user friendly? Some

programs are so complicated that it could take weeks for you
to learn their intricacies. User-friendly software anticipates
errors you might make and even gives you a chance to recover from an error without losing the data.

3. Is the documentation clear and understandable? Carelessness
   in writing a manual can signal carelessness in writing a program. Don't be misled by the elaborate presentation and slick
   binders of most manuals. It's the contents that count.

4. What kind of support does the manufacturer offer for the
   applications software? Is a "hot line" available for your questions in the event you get into trouble?

5. Which operating system does it operate under? All applications software is designed to run under other software (called
   an operating system) built into a computer. It is highly desirable that all of the applications software you select should
   run under a single operating system (even though some software is able to run under more than one operating system).

Among the operating systems you'll encounter frequently are
Digital Research's CP/M, most often found on eight-bit microcomputers; MS-DOS from Microsoft, widely used on sixteen-bit
machines (IBM's PC-DOS is a functionally equivalent system designed for the IBM Personal Computer; Heath-Zenith's Z-DOS, an
equivalent for their computers); UNIX, a powerful multiuser system from Bell Labs; and XENIX, Microsoft's adaptation of
UNIX. Some computer manufacturers—Commodore, Tandy, and
Apple, for example—use their own operating systems and thus
have set their own standards, in effect, through sheer numbers.

In your survey of microcomputers and their capabilities, you
should look for and prefer those with operating systems that are
widely used, since they will have the largest number of applications
software programs available.

Questions to Ask Before Deciding on Operating System Software

1. Can you choose your own operating system software, or are
   you locked into the computer maker's own operating system?

2. Will the operating system software (whether manufacturer-

specified or selected by you) operate the applications software you have selected? Many manufacturer-specified systems offer a limited range of applications software, thus narrowing your choices.

Now Investigate Hardware

Next, you should obtain specifications and prices of currently available hardware, its expansion capabilities, and its compatibility with other hardware and software. At a minimum, hardware will include a stand-alone computer or components—keyboard, computer, and monitor).

These are the aspects of hardware you should investigate:

Keyboards Keyboards are of two types: membrane and mechanical. Membrane keys are raised areas (sometimes called "bubbles") of a pressure-sensitive plastic membrane; mechanical keys resemble those on an electric or electronic typewriter.

There is no substitute for trying the keyboard of any machine you are considering. IBM, deviser of the widely used and near-standard Selectric keyboard, came up with a keyboard for the IBM PC that puts the shift and return keys in unusual locations and perplexes users. The original keyboard on the PC Jr. was regarded as virtually unusable by serious typists. Many keyboards provide an audible click or beep to indicate that a character has registered; this can be disconnected on some computers.

Among the exciting developments in keyboards is the availability of an alternative keyboard arrangement to replace the "standard" QWERTY keyboard (so called because of the sequence of the first six keys at the left of the second row of keys), which was originally designed to slow typists down. The first typewriters were clumsy machines whose crude keys tended to jam up if typists worked too fast. To offset this, inventor Christopher Sholes moved the most frequently used letters as far apart as possible.

In the early 1930s, August Dvorak, a University of Washington professor of education, whose special interest was time and motion studies, devised a keyboard with the most frequently used letters in the "home" row.

With Dvorak's keyboard, champion typist Barbara Blackburn,

of Salem, Oregon, has achieved 194 words a minute. After about forty hours of practice, a 40-words-per-minute typist can easily do 80–100 words per minute on a Dvorak keyboard. A beginner with no typing skills can get up to 40 words per minute in eighteen to twenty hours—one-tenth the usual training time. And, with the Dvorak key arrangement, thirty-two times as many words can be typed without moving the fingers from the "home" row. Thus, a typist's fingers will only travel one mile in eight hours as compared with sixteen miles during the same period typing on a traditional keyboard.

Many alternative keyboards have been proposed, but standing in the way have been the specifications of the American National Standards Institute, which was founded in 1918 and develops safety, engineering, and industrial standards. In 1982, the institute approved the Dvorak keyboard as an alternate standard; since then, some keyboard and computer manufacturers are offering keyboards in the Dvorak configuration.

Much has been written about the desirability of a separate keyboard, and some users are pictured using keyboards on their laps or in bed. Because of greater flexibility in placement, separate keyboards may offer the greatest advantage to handicapped users.

Of greater importance than keyboard placement, however, is the ability to adjust the placement of the screen (to avoid glare or annoying reflections). This would argue for a separate monitor as being more desirable. To increase a separate monitor's utility, you can place it on a lazy susan-type rotating and tilting stand.

Display Variously called a CRT (cathode ray tube), VDU (video display unit), or VDT (video display tube) and available in monochrome or color. Capacity is measured in number of "columns" (characters per line) and number of lines. Resolution, an important element, is governed by the number of pixels (a phonetic shortening of "picture elements"). Resolution is often overlooked as a factor in computer selection, but it is important; the greater the number of pixels, the sharper the resulting image.

Memory Measured in kilobytes. One kilobyte contains about 1,000 (actually 1,024) bytes. How much memory should you look for? The answer is, as much as you can find. Some personal computers are now offering up to 512 kilobytes of RAM (random access memory) in floppy disks and up to 25 megabytes in hard disks.

Storage Measured in kilobytes, storage can be by means of tape

*Fig. 14.1. Dvorak keyboard arrangement. Copyright © 1983
Dvorak International Federation.*

cassettes, floppy disks, or hard disks. Floppy disks, the most common, come in sizes of $3\frac{1}{2}$, $5\frac{1}{4}$, 8, and 14 inches. Most widely used in microcomputers are $5\frac{1}{4}$-inch disks.

Interfaces The places at which peripheral devices such as printers or external disk drives are attached to the computer, usually as I/O (input/output) ports on the back of the computer. I/O ports are of two standard types: the RS-232-C serial port and the IEEE-488 parallel port. A higher number of interfaces is more desirable.

Printer The device that produces permanent ("hard") copies of what is displayed on the screen. Printers are of several types: letter-quality printers, which print like a typewriter from a ball element or daisy wheel; dot-matrix printers, ink-jet printers, and thermal printers.

The first two types are impact printers in which a hammer strikes a metal or plastic type element, causing it to press against a fabric or film ribbon and to transfer its image to paper. Impact printers are simple but slow and noisy. Within the next several years, inexpensive printers that write by means of heat or beams of laser light are expected to supplant those that rely on hammering and work like typewriters.

Documentation As with software, hardware documentation is important. A survey of 6,000 owners of microcomputers found that one-third of them rated their computer's instruction manual as only fair or poor.

Terms You should obtain details of warranty terms and coverage periods, the availability of technical support and training, purchase cost (of the components separately and as a package—many vendors will give discounts on packages), and monthly or annual leasing charges, if lease terms are offered.

Compatibility Your decision to buy a computer should be independent of the *total* amount of software available for it, but this fact will color any choice you make. The lure of compatibility will inevitably be a strong component in any decision, and compatibility does not only mean compatibility with the IBM PC; several computers claim "Apple compatibility."

Compatibility can mean many things to many people—especially computer manufacturers. In some cases, "IBM compatible" means only that the competing computer uses an Intel 8088 chip, as does the IBM PC. No other computer can be identical with the IBM, since this would infringe on IBM's copyright protection. The obvious question to be asked about any computer is not "Is it compatible?" but a question that would be perfectly at home on the "Tonight Show," "How compatible is it?"

Computers have different degrees of compatibility. *Operationally compatible* computers can run off-the-shelf software designed for the IBM PC and may also use peripheral hardware designed for it (examples: Compaq, Panasonic Senior Partner, Heath/ Zenith 150 series, Columbia Data Products computers).

Functionally compatible computers are based on the IBM internal design but may have different keyboards and function keys, video screens, or other features. Software for the IBM PC can be run with modification or through the use of an accessory software package that allows the emulation of many IBM features (examples: Radio Shack 2000, Texas Instruments Professional Computer, Data General 10).

Data compatible equipment will run on the IBM operating system but can only exchange data with IBM machines. Ordinarily, software for the IBM will not work (example: Hewlett Packard 150).

If you are considering the purchase of a computer because it is represented to be IBM compatible, the way to find out is to try the prospective computer and programs designed for the PC. Two frequently used programs are Lotus 1-2-3 (which tests the compatible's disk controller) and Flight Simulator (which tests the compatible's internal architecture). Other good tests are PC-DOS 2.00 (which indicates if the ROM and DOS are implemented in a manner similar to the IBM PC) and Wordstar 3.30 (which determines if the compatible's video display is mapped to the same memory addresses as the IBM PC).

In general, those programs whose PC version use direct-screen access (those bypassing the ROM) will work. Others have sophisticated copy-protection devices encoded in them; one, PC Visi-Calc, cleverly deactivates any debugger that might be used to find the cause of the problem. However, programs are constantly being rewritten, and what runs today might not run tomorrow. By 1988, some experts predict three-quarters of all microcomputers in use will be IBM compatible to some degree. Nevertheless, if your needs are specific and the machine you are considering can run the desired programs, IBM compatibility assumes less importance. By the same token, if total IBM compatibility is critical to your needs, no computer is more compatible with the IBM PC than the IBM PC.

Questions to Ask Before Deciding on Hardware

1. How much money do you have in your budget? Microcomputers come in several price ranges. For under $500 you can buy a popular model of limited storage capacity, but these are not for a home office.

   The next group, costing to $2,500, includes some of the most popular microcomputers available with eight- and sixteen-bit microprocessors and true capabilities for the home office. Memory may range from 64 to 128 kilobytes, with expansion capability.

   Systems costing to $5,000 offer built-in hard-disk drives and storage capacities of ten megabytes or more—the equivalent of several dozen floppy disks. In addition to offering huge storage capacity, such systems dramatically decrease data retrieval and processing times.

2. Will you want to assemble components from several sources, or are you interested in a packaged system from one manufacturer?

3. What size (8-, 8/16-, 16-, or 32-bit) microprocessor are you looking for? If cost is a consideration, you may find that an 8-bit machine is adequate for your needs and much less expensive than newer 16-bit machines. But you should know that in addition to being slower running, most 8-bit microprocessors are limited to 64 kilobytes of memory.

4. Is portability an important feature? If you intend to take your computer with you on trips, you should only consider a portable.

5. How much memory (RAM) do you need? This may be difficult for you to determine at this point; generally speaking, more is better. Can the memory be upgraded in the future? Most manufacturers make provision for memory expansion by the later addition of circuit boards in internal slots.

6. Does the computer have one or two disk drives (or one disk drive and a permanently installed internal hard-disk drive)? Two drives increase system flexibility and make the transfer of information and disk copying easier.

7. If you are planning to expand your activities, will the computer accommodate this? For example, if your spouse or an associate were to join in your home-office venture, could you add another terminal to the computer you have under consideration?

8. Do you need a color monitor? If so, your computer will need color capability, which may entail the addition of a color video RAM chip at an extra charge.

9. What kind of printer do you need? If much of your hard copy must be of letter quality, you should only consider a letter-quality printer. Letter-quality printers are generally more expensive and slower than dot-matrix or thermographic printers, although the latter are adequate for preliminary drafts and work of less demanding quality.

10. Will you use the computer for accessing public data systems? If so, a modem and communications software can be added to most computers.

11. What kind of warranty covers your purchase, and for how long is the coverage? Can you purchase an extended warranty? A service contract?

Questions to Ask About the Vendor

1. Is the vendor a manufacturer or a retailer? If a retailer, is the vendor part of a franchised chain? Has the vendor been in business for a long time? The answer to these questions could have a bearing on the support and service you can expect to receive.
2. Does the vendor supply a complete line of hardware (computers, monitors, printers, modems)? Does the vendor supply software as well as hardware? One-stop shopping could be to your advantage, enabling you to negotiate the best prices and the most favorable terms for a package deal.
3. Does the vendor offer a *reasonable* amount of support and problem solving to buyers in the period immediately after purchase? Try calling the vendor with a question before you make your purchase and see how it is handled. Also, if the vendor's phone is always busy, imagine trying to get through when you have a problem.
4. Does the vendor have service facilities for routine maintenance and in the event of breakdown? On what basis (i.e., customer carry-in or a service call at your home) is service offered? How long will service take? What hourly rates are charged for labor? Are replacement parts marked up in price or charged at cost?

Where to Get Information

Finding reliable information about computer systems and their characteristics is not easy. Computer books are often brand oriented and so are not of much help. Few book publishers can keep up with the rapid changes in the computer field. Computer magazines present a different problem: hardware and software manufacturers are major advertisers in computer magazines, and so hard-hitting comparative product reviews are rare.

In the past, computer magazines have contributed to the confusion surrounding the availability of new models by publishing information supplied by manufacturers long before the machines were even in production.

Because computer stores are a comparatively new phenomenon, business know-how, merchandising techniques, the expertise of sales personnel, and even decorum can vary widely. Most computer dealers will let you "test drive" a computer—certainly one of the models on display. Try the software packages you are considering (software comes in sealed packages, but most dealers have open samples of the more popular packages on hand for customer testing), assess the keyboard, the display, the hardware and the software manuals, and then the performance of the program in a few routines.

In researching your computer decision, you should be on the lookout for manufacturer-applied buzzwords, such as "compatible" and "user friendly," both of which have been overused. Beware of slick packaging, whether in software or hardware. You'd be surprised at what the innards of most computers look like. Similarly, steer clear of sleek manuals full of bad grammar and typographical errors. One of the best data-base management programs I own (titled "Query!^{2}") costs $29.95 and comes in a simple package put together absolutely without frills. But it is a superb program nonetheless.

Among the best sources of information are users of the computers or software you are considering. Most computer manufacturers support and encourage user groups. You can find out from dealers or manufacturers when a nearby group will be meeting and attend. You'll find most users loud in their praise of the computers and programs they have chosen; a few will even point out defects and features that could be changed. Surprisingly, machines and programs are constantly being upgraded by hardware manufacturers and software packagers in response to user feedback.

AFTER YOUR PURCHASE

Computer Furniture

Once you have purchased your computer, you'll want to consider alternatives to a typing stand, a coffee table, or the dining-room table. Because of the length of time you will be spending with your computer and peripheral equipment, care in the selection of furniture is important. Incorrect height of keyboards and incorrect placement of monitors and screens have given rise to chronic eyestrain, fatigue, headaches, and pain in the neck, shoulder, back, arms, and legs.

Desks and tables Unfortunately, the so-called average person doesn't exist, although office-furniture manufacturers try to accommodate this mythical being. One thing is certain: the thirty-inch height of traditional office desks and worktables is too high for comfortable computer use. The obvious answer is to select furniture of adjustable height, if possible.

Some suggested ranges are:

> Table height: twenty-five to thirty inches
> Chair-seat height: fifteen to twenty inches
> Eye-to-screen distance: sixteen to thirty inches
> Eye vertical-rotation angle: thirty degrees maximum, with center of the screen twenty degrees below the horizontal

The most comfortable positions and the relationship between seat height, keyboard height, and monitor height will vary from individual to individual and are only determinable by trial and error. It has been shown that keyboards positioned so that elbows are raised more than three inches may cause neck, shoulder, and upper-back pain. The angle between wrist and keyboard should be no greater than 10 degrees, and the angle made by the upper and lower arms should be between 80 and 120 degrees. Forearms or wrists should be supported for greater efficiency and the reduction of fatigue.

In purchasing computer desks or tables, do not make the mistake of thinking you will no longer need room for traditional paperwork tasks; if anything, your paper handling may increase. Because some computer-generated documents are produced by continuous feed, your desk or worktable should be adequately deep. For this reason, L- and U-shaped "work stations" are becoming popular; in an L-shaped arrangement, the location of the keyboard (on the section at a right angle, called the "runoff" or "return") should be lower and to the right of the work surface for a right-handed person.

Chairs Look for castered posture chairs that offer chairback-attitude adjustment, seat-attitude adjustment, as well as seat-height adjustment; all adjustments should be able to be made without special tools. Adequate back support in the lumbar area is important. Your thighs should be parallel to the floor, and your feet should be flat on the floor when you are seated. Seat depth should be appropriate to thigh length but should be short enough so that contact with the back of the knee with the chair seat is avoided; pressure at this point can constrict blood vessels. The best way to test any chair is to sit in it for a while in the posture you expect to be using. Manufacturers now design chairs with five legs; these effectively keep a castered chair from tipping over.

Storage One of the biggest problems to overcome will be clutter around the computer. You'll need shelf space nearby to store manuals—in the beginning, you'll consult these frequently. For disks, I find I need three kinds of storage: active storage for disks in everyday use in an open plastic sorter that holds them upright with labels visible; intermediate storage for less frequently used disks in a lift-top plastic storage box; and inactive storage for master disks in a loose-leaf binder with pocketed vinyl pages.

Computer Lighting and Vision

Proper lighting of the computer work station is the most often overlooked aspect in the planning of an electronic home office. One consequence is lighting that by default is either too bright or too dim. Each condition can lead to problems. Poor lighting is unlikely to cause long-term damage to your eyes, but according to Alan Safir, chief of ophthalmology at the University of Connecticut School of Medicine, "The thing to be concerned about is comfort."

In the opinion of experts, three areas deserve attention: the reference material (manual or document being used), the keyboard, and the screen. Ideally, these should be at the same distance from your eyes to avoid having to change the focus when looking from one to another. Each time the eye's focus is changed, muscles inside the eye must work, and this can be a cause of eye fatigue.

Proper lighting utilizes a high level of concentrated lighting to illuminate the reference materials and the keyboard and a low level of illumination elsewhere. Reference material should be placed close to the VDT screen to avoid frequent movement of the eyes and head over a wide angle.

Lighting needs will vary with individuals, of course. In general, overall illumination for VDT operation should be between thirty and fifty footcandles—less than half the usual office lighting levels. VDT screen brightness should be three to four times the general room lighting level. Lower levels of room illumination can be achieved by using fewer or smaller-wattage incandescent bulbs. If fluorescent tubes are already installed, replacement of cool white tubes with deluxe cool white tubes will provide less light and more comfortable lighting.

Characters on the VDT screen should be at least ten times brighter than the screen background. Ambient room illumination should be three times brighter than the VDT screen background. VDT screens tend to attract dust and dirt, so they should be cleaned frequently, as recommended by the manufacturer. (Some have protective coatings.)

A major problem will be glare reflected from shiny surfaces, particularly the screen. You can minimize reflected glare on the screen's surface by spraying it with an antiglare spray and by positioning the screen so that windows and other sources of bright light are not behind you—but do not sit facing an unshaded window. Use drapes and shades or blinds to control and reduce outside light. If glare is caused by overhead lighting, a cardboard hood can be improvised to shield the screen.

Task lighting should be such that the light will not shine directly on the monitor. This calls for localized lighting, such as that provided by an adjustable lamp, mounted so that it can be angled and titled as needed. I use a Luxo Lamp Corporation Model Lil-E, which has a two-foot horizontal radius of adjustment and takes a 40-watt incandescent bulb. As an alternate to a base that takes up useful space, a mounting clamp attaches this lamp to the edge of the worktable.

Fluorescent lamps made specifically for work near a screen use a principle called asymmetric lighting, which directs light at an oblique angle rather than straight down. A compromise is the Luxo Combination Model, which combines a sixty-watt incandescent bulb with a twenty-two-watt circular fluorescent tube, simulating daylight; either or both light sources can be used.

In addition to task illumination, you should provide the area around the computer with a low level of illumination. One way to achieve this is with floor lamps (called "torchieres") that direct light upward toward the ceiling.

One often-overlooked solution to the problem of eyestrain caused by the VDT is the practice of taking rest breaks. Because VDT use generally requires intense concentration, the National Institute of Occupational Safety and Health (NIOSH) recommends a fifteen-minute alternate-task break after two hours of continuous VDT work for users under moderate workload (i.e., less than 60 percent of time spent in looking at screen). A fifteen-minute alternate-task break every hour is recommended for those under high visual demands, high work loads, or who handle repetitive work tasks.

I have found two methods useful in combating eyestrain and eye fatigue. These were originally recommended by W. H. Bates and described in Aldous Huxley's 1942 book *The Art of Seeing*. "Palming" involves closing the eyes and covering them with the cupped palms of the hands. This excludes light and bathes the eyes with blackness, causing passive relaxation. Do not press, rub, or massage the eyes.

Another useful Bates technique is to hang on a distant wall a large calendar or chart whose words, letters, or numerals are perfectly familiar. Incipient eyestrain and eye-muscle fatigue caused by focusing your eyes at the same close distance for long periods can be alleviated by focusing your eyes on the calendar or chart.

Wiring the Computerized Home Office

Computers do not consume a lot of electricity—in fact, their electrical requirements are surprisingly low. Nevertheless, wires tend to abound in the electronic office, which usually are of three kinds: wiring to supply electrical power to outlets in several locations in the room, wiring and modular jacks for the connection of telephone lines (important if you expect to add a modem), and wiring to link components of the computer system.

If you have not provided enough outlets to supply electrical power to potential computer and printer locations in your home office, flat wiring systems are available for installation under carpeting. Such systems include flat wire capable of carrying up to thirty amperes, insulating materials to make joints impervious to moisture, floor-mounted receptacles, and transition boxes to tap into existing outlets.

In some installations, the existing acoustical ceiling can be used to run wire to the computer location. Decorative "power poles" bring wiring from the ceiling to the work station.

Computer Protection

Today's computers are remarkably sturdy machines. The most vital and most sensitive part and the one weak link in the computer component chain is the floppy disk, or diskette, itself. Computers are sealed, and you'll have no reason to open yours. The floppy disk, however, is something that you will handle frequently.

Remove a floppy disk from its protective paper envelope and you'll find a flat, square object. This is not the disk but the vinyl jacket that protects the disk from dust. Inside the jacket is the disk itself—a round, flat doughnut made of mylar and coated with a thin layer of metallic oxide. At the upper right corner is the *write-protect notch* (if you seal this with a protective tab, nothing can be changed on the disk) and two small *alignment notches* at the bottom. The jacket has three holes: the large *spindle hole* at the center, a small round *index hole* to the right of the spindle hole, and a *read/write access window* near the bottom.

Here are some rules of diskette care:

Never touch the exposed magnetic surfaces with your fingers or a rough surface.

Don't spill liquids on a diskette.

Never leave diskettes in bright sunlight or near heat.

Never place a diskette on top of the computer or other peripheral hardware that might contain a magnetic field.

Avoid magnetic paper-clip dispensers that can magnetize paper clips. Never place paper clips on or near diskettes—nonmagnetic plastic paper clips are preferable.

Smoking at a computer can deposit a layer of dust particles on the surface of the diskette.

If your computer is not equipped with built-in electrical surge protection, consider adding power-line protection in the form of plug-in devices that protect against power surges, spikes, and line noise. More expensive devices are equipped with constant-voltage transformers to protect against brownouts and voltage sags. If your area is troubled by electrical blackouts, you'll need an uninterruptible power supply, which contains a battery to give voltage at a normal level for about twenty minutes—long enough for you to save keyboarded data and shut down the computer without loss of information.

Static electricity is a constant danger in dry climates or in the centrally heated air of winter. Antistatic sprays are available for spraying on rugs and carpeting; acrylic and polyester carpet fibers have good static resistance; special antistatic carpeting is available, with copper, aluminum, or stainless-steel wire woven into the rug fabric.

If you can, it's desirable to provide your computer with its own separate, "dedicated" power line. This guarantees that electric coffee makers, dryers, irons, or copying machines will not cause power surges or electrical "noise" that can affect some computers. Also, a dedicated line is less likely to be turned off accidentally.

Like any other electrical device, a computer is most likely to fail when it is being turned on. Therefore, it's better to leave your computer on all day, rather than to turn it on and off repeatedly. This is especially true if your computer has a hard-disk (Winchester) drive; these are very delicate and also take time to "spin up" to running speed when the system is turned on.

Most 5¼-inch disk drives turn themselves off when not in use, and most 8-inch disk drives do not. With 8-inch drives, you can open the door of the drive and withdraw the disk when not in use. This will reduce wear on the disk and has the added advantage that the drive will be "off line" in the event the system should "crash" for any reason. (Your 8-inch disk drives can be modified to turn themselves off when not in use.)

If you can, leave the monitor screen blank when your computer is running but not in use. This will reduce the possibility of "burning" an image into the phosphors of the VDT.

A Few Kind Words

The story is told of the traveling salesman who stopped overnight at a hotel in a small town in western Kansas. The weather was dreary, the hotel was noisy, and sleep had been impossible.

In the hotel dining room the next morning, he ordered breakfast. "I'll have orange juice, eggs, toast, and coffee," he told the waitress. Then he added brightly, "And a few kind words."

The waitress said nothing as she placed his breakfast before him. He looked up at her expectantly. "And the kind words?"

"I wouldn't eat them eggs" was her whispered reply.

Because of the nature of the software and hardware jungle—and it is a jungle—the reader may appreciate a few kind words at this point. This chapter embodies the thinking that went into my own decision to buy a computer and the choice I made. This book was keyboarded on a Heath/Zenith Z-100 low-profile computer, with 128 kilobytes of RAM and two 5¼-inch disk drives. The manuscript occupied nine disks, with chapters distributed more or less evenly throughout. The huge on-line storage capacities of hard-disk drives have distinct advantages, but I find the floppy disks adequate for my purposes. Revisions are easy to accomplish, and the risk of loss is minimized by the distribution of the manuscript over many disks. The computer has operated perfectly from the first day and has not sustained a minute of down time. The word processing program used was WordStar. More detailed and with many more commands than simpler and less expensive packages, this best-selling program is extremely versatile. In my opinion, it should be the program of choice for serious writers.

Should I Buy a Computer Now? If you have made up your mind to buy a computer and have selected one, by all means complete the purchase. Don't wait until a "better" system appears—there will always be better systems standing in the wings. You should accept the fact that any computer you buy will be obsolescing faster than any other electronic products or home appliances on the market today. Nevertheless, any machine you buy now on the basis that it meets your present and near-future anticipated needs should serve you well for many years to come. This is true for those who have made a recent computer purchase. It is more important that you join the computer revolution and take advantage of its benefits than that you wait for prices to come down.

Because one of the benefits you will derive from a computer will be savings of time and money as a result of increased efficiency and higher productivity, waiting a year or two to save a few dollars could actually cost you money. And the other benefits of immediate computer availability—more free time, self-tuition, household budgeting, and personal bookkeeping—are benefits on which no price tags can be placed.

So even if you have chosen an eight-bit machine that is not "compatible" but has the applications software you need and an operating system to handle it, be happy with it and think of the money you saved over newer sixteen-bit models. Today's newest computer will be tomorrow's discontinued model.

A good parallel can be found in the early days of the automobile. You who desert your manual or electric typewriters and the drudgery of paper shuffling are not unlike those who abandoned the horse and buggy for the horseless carriage at the turn of the century. You have made the big and important leap, and questions of eight bits, sixteen bits (thirty-two bits are now upon us), and compatibility are of relatively little consequence.

The comparison of today's computers with the early automobile industry is quite appropriate in another way. As were early automobiles, all computers are assembled by their manufacturers from components bought from outside suppliers. The several computers you are considering may have many parts—chips, disk drives, keyboards—in common. With the exception of the internal circuitry of the microprocessor chip, the case in which each computer is housed may be the only other major difference between one computer and another.

FIFTEEN

One Day at a Time: Bookkeeping Systems

It is no exaggeration to say that at the heart of every successful home office or small business is an efficient system of records, forms, and reports. Business records are of two kinds: those a business is required to keep and those it is desirable for it to keep. The line between them is not always clear.

Surprisingly, the Internal Revenue Service is not of much help here. It prescribes no specific accounting records, documents, or systems. However, the IRS does require that any business maintain permanent books of account that can be used to identify business receipts, expenses, and deductions. When transactions involving inventories and assets are used in determining income or when travel and entertainment deductions are taken, special supporting information must be supplied.

The failure of the IRS to be specific about the nature of the records you keep should not be taken as an invitation to neglect the keeping of records. The IRS can afford to be unspecific, for the burden of proof is on the taxpayer—in this case, you, the operator of a small business or an office at home.

The easiest way for a small business or an office at home to keep records is in twelve large manila envelopes, one for each month, which can be reused from year to year. This way of record keeping is also called "the shoe-box method," and a shoe box or shoe boxes can be used, but large envelopes are better. You can mark invoices "Paid" and show the date and check number; alternatively, staple returned checks to paid invoices, since the cash-disbursement record will show the dates of payment and invoice numbers. Your income tax return can be prepared directly from the papers accumulated in these envelopes. Despite its simplicity, however, this method cannot be recommended wholeheartedly for any but the most primitive of home offices. It is too easy to mislay or to lose valuable documents, which may be the only record of a transaction or evidence of payment.

Your income tax return can be prepared directly and more quickly without recourse to the original documents if you keep more traditional bookkeeping records. Such "books" will also make an IRS audit easier to defend against than a loose collection of accumulated receipts, canceled checks, and other papers, even though the system will require more attention on your part in its operation.

Ideally, the best time for planning any bookkeeping system for your home office or small business is the moment you decide to embark on the venture. Adequate records give an instant picture of the financial health of a business at a particular time. Undoubtedly, more small businesses have foundered because of unreliable information caused by incomplete or inexact records than have gone under because of lack of sufficient capital. Poor bookkeeping is the first sign of bad management. A good bookkeeping system should be simple to use, easy to understand, reliable, accurate, consistent, and should provide the information you will need to operate your business and to meet your tax obligations.

The first decision you'll have to make is whether your bookkeeping will be on a cash or an accrual basis. If most of your business is transacted in cash, you'll probably prefer to be on a cash basis. The cash method of bookkeeping is used by most individuals and many small businesses, especially service businesses with no inventories.

The determining factor in the decision to operate on an accrual basis usually depends on whether or not you extend credit to clients or customers. Accrual bookkeeping is defined as "a method of recording receipts and expenses, in which each item is booked as earned or incurred, without regard to when actual payments are received or made." Thus, sales on credit are immediately credited as sales and charged to accounts receivable. When payment is made, accounts receivable receives a self-canceling credit. Interest expense on a note payable is recognized at the end of each accounting period, based on the time elapsed, even though the interest may not be actually paid for several months. Depreciation is recorded as assets are used, even though the cash expenditure for the assets may have occurred several years before. The accrual basis is also desirable because expense items payable in the future, such as annual or semiannual interest, can be entered immediately. Accrual accounting is used by most large corporations.

Regardless of the basis you select for your accounting records, you should have a separate bank account from which to make payments for expenses and in which to deposit receipts. If you have formed a corporation, you'll need a corporate resolution to which must be affixed the corporate seal before you will be able to open an account.

SOLE PROPRIETORSHIPS

A sole proprietorship is the simplest form of business organization. The business has no existence apart from you, the owner. Its liabilities are your personal liabilities, and your proprietary interest will end if you die. You risk all your assets, whether used in the business or personally owned.

When you figure your taxable income for the year, you must report the profit or loss on Schedule C (Form 1040) and add any profit or subtract any loss as a result of your sole proprietorship.

Each asset in your sole proprietorship is treated separately for tax purposes rather than as part of one overall ownership interest. For example, a sole proprietor selling a business as a going concern must figure gain or loss separately on each asset.

These are the minimal records you should keep if you are operating as a sole proprietorship:

1. A record of sales made or work performed.
2. A record of cash receipts listing cash sales and money received from outstanding accounts receivable. (If your business uses a cash register, items 1 and 2 may be combined in a single sales and cash receipts journal.) Enter each item to show date, name of payer, invoice number, and amount. Receipts should be deposited immediately in the exact amount received. (Do not pay small expenses from receipts, but use a petty cash fund.) By making deposits in the same amount received, you will be able to reconcile the cash receipts journal with your business bank account statement and checkbook each month.

   In everyday usage, "income" is used to describe any inflow or receipt of money without a reduction for associated expenses; in accounting, the meaning is more restrictive and covers the excess of revenues over all related expenses for a given period.

   Revenue that is not true revenue—for example, advertising allowances—should be separated from receipts that must be reported as "gross receipts or gross sales." Similarly, sales or other taxes you collect for remittance to state or local authorities are not business income and should be kept separate.
3. A record of payments. Make all disbursements by check (but do not merge your business and personal funds). Enter in your business checkbook the date, name of payee, check number, amount of each check, and the reason for the payment. Bank service charges (from the statement) should be entered in the same way that checks are entered, but without a check number. Use the petty-cash fund for the payment of small items. Columns can be provided in the disbursements journal for recurring types of expense items to show the distribution of expenses: postage, stationery, freight, utilities such as electricity and gas (if these are separately billed to your office; if not, these expenses can be apportioned from your household expenses, based on the percentage of the space in your home used as a home office), telephone, and miscellanous charges.
4. A petty-cash fund and record. Many small expenses will not be covered by invoices and can be paid in cash. First buy

a petty-cash box and a supply of petty-cash disbursement
slips. Next draw a check on your business bank account for
an appropriate amount—say, $100 in bills of various denomi-
nations—and put the money in the petty-cash box.

As payments are made for postage, freight, bus, and taxi
fares and other small disbursements, a petty cash slip should
be completed and deposited in the box in place of the cash
removed. At all times, the cash remaining in the petty-cash
box plus the total amount disbursed should equal the amount
of the petty-cash fund.

When the petty-cash fund is nearly exhausted, write another check to cover the amount expended. If you are re-
plenishing the petty-cash fund too often, you should increase
the amount you are carrying in petty cash.

PARTNERSHIPS AND CORPORATIONS

If your business is set up as a partnership or corporation, your
record keeping must anticipate situations that do not occur in a
sole proprietorship. If the business is a partnership, it is not a
taxable entity as a corporation is, but it must file an information
return on Form 1065 (Schedule K-1) indicating the income (or
loss) assignable to each partner. The partners then include their
share of the partnership income on their individual income tax
returns. A corporation's records must show the fees paid to its
directors, the salaries paid to its officers, and the dividends paid to
stockholders. As an officer of the corporation, if you are the owner-
manager, it's your responsibility to file an income tax return for
the company (Form 1120). In addition, you'll have to file a personal return on the salary and dividends you have paid yourself
from the corporation (or to include it on your income tax return if
you have income from other sources) and to remit partial tax
payments to the IRS if you do not withhold income tax from this
salary.

Record-Keeping Systems

Formalized bookkeeping and accounting systems are available
to help you manage the finances of your home office or small
business and to uncover hidden sources of profit or loss by analyz-

ing receipts and expenses. These take several forms; many consist of separate printed and ruled pages for journals, trial balances, ledgers, receipts, expenses, payroll records, and summaries—all in a convenient, loose-leaf binder. One widely used system available from many office stationers is manufactured by the Dome Publishing Company, Inc., of Warwick, Rhode Island. For my own home-office bookkeeping, I like the well-planned and comprehensive Data-Rite System, manufactured by Data Management, Inc., of Farmington, Connecticut. For many home offices and smaller businesses, Data Management's concise Alpha System is ideal.

OTHER RECORDS

To supplement the four basic records, you'll also want to keep: *An Equipment List* For many reasons, it's a good idea to keep individual lists of assets that have a useful life of a year or longer —furniture and fixtures, office machines, buildings, tools, and automotive equipment. Show the date the item was purchased, the vendor, a brief identifying description of the item, the check number by which it was paid, and the amount paid. If necessary, break down your lists into categories such as automotive equipment, furniture, fixtures, and office machines. Such lists provide the basis for calculating depreciation and to provide supporting data for fixed-asset accounts.

On your books, a charge to expenses should be made at the end of your fiscal year to cover depreciation of fixed assets (other than land). Corresponding credits are made to accumulated depreciation. Fixed assets are items normally in use for a year or more and which are held for use in the business and not for purposes of sale. They are valued at cost and reported at cost, less any amounts recognizable as depreciation.

You will probably want to use "straight-line depreciation" based on the expected life of the item. A building may have an expected life of eighteen years; the depreciation of the prorated cost of that part of your home used for your office is chargeable as a business expense. To calculate this, determine the square footage of the space devoted to your home office or business as compared with the total square footage of the house. Thus, if your home contains 3,500 square feet of usable space (you must include attic and basement areas in this) and your home office or business occupied 700 square feet of this, for eighteen years you would be entitled to deduct 20 percent of 5.55 percent of the total cost of the house (not to mention a proportional amount of other expenses). Alternatively, you can calculate the percentage on the basis of the number of rooms used for office purposes.

Here are some expected lives of depreciable items:

3 years: automobiles, light-duty trucks, and certain special manufacturing tools are depreciated at 33.33 percent a year.

5 years: most items of equipment, including office furniture and fixtures, are depreciated at 20 percent a year.

10 years: manufactured homes, including mobile homes, may be depreciated at 10 percent a year.

18 years: includes all real property, such as structures and buildings (other than any designated at ten-year property). Real property should be depreciated at 5.55 percent a year.

These recovery periods are considerably reduced from the depreciation periods previously accepted by the IRS and tend to speed up the write-off of these items.

A Record of Business Insurance Your home office or business may have certain kinds of insurance coverage. If so, list each policy, showing the nature and amount of the coverage, name of insurance carrier, name of broker or agent, expiration date, and annual premium.

Financial Statements If you have more than a very small business, you'll need an outside accountant to prepare these. The most important financial statements—the balance sheet and the profit and loss statement (also called an "income statement")—are prepared from the above-described basic records. The balance sheet is a picture of the business at a given moment (usually at the end of the fiscal year). It lists assets, liabilities, and capital (also called the "owner's equity"). The profit and loss statement presents an analysis of what happened over a selected period of time. In essence, it shows the amount of income received, from which expenses and taxes are subtracted, the balance being profit (or loss).

A General Journal and Ledger An easy way to consolidate useful records is in the form of a journal or book of original entry that records every business transaction chronologically as a debit or a credit. In effect, it is the financial diary of your business.

The information for each journal entry can be derived from original sources or from the basic records described earlier. In some small businesses, copies of such transaction records are incorporated into the journal, each record standing as an entry.

A general ledger should also be kept and posted with the dollar amounts of transactions and balances of separately captioned accounts, such as assets, liabilities, capital, receipts (or sales), and expenses. Posting permits the accumulation of all dollar activity relating to a particular account and provides a running summary of such activity for comparison with budget projections. Here's a sample classification of some typical ledger-account categories, called a "chart of accounts": (Each account is assigned a number and is given a separate page in the general ledger. New numbers can be added as needed.)

ASSETS

100—cash in banks
101—petty cash fund
102—accounts receivable
103—inventory
104—material and supplies
107—prepaid expenses
108—deposits
120—land
121—buildings
122—accumulated depreciation—buildings (credit)
123—tools and equipment
124—accumulated depreciation—tools and equipment (credit)
125—automotive equipment
126—accumulated depreciation—automotive equipment (credit)
127—furniture and fixtures
128—accumulated depreciation—furniture and fixtures (credit)
130—organization expenses (to be amortized)

LIABILITIES

200—accounts payable
201—notes payable
205—sales taxes payable

206—FICA taxes payable
207—federal withholding taxes
208—state withholding taxes
209—federal unemployment (FUTA) taxes
210—state unemployment taxes
211—other deductions (health insurance, pension, savings plans, etc.)
220—long-term debt—mortgages payable
221—long-term debt—bank loan
225—miscellaneous accruals

CAPITAL ACCOUNTS

300—capital stock
301—preferred capital stock } for corporations

or

300—proprietorship account
301—proprietor's withdrawals } for proprietorships

SALES (REVENUE) ACCOUNTS (CREDITS)

400—retail sales
401—wholesale sales
402—income from services
405—miscellaneous income

EXPENSES (DEBITS)

500—salaries and wages
501—contract labor (independent contractors)
502—payroll taxes
503—utilities (electricity, gas, water)
504—telephone
505—rent
506—office supplies
507—postage
508—maintenance expense
509—insurance
510—interest
511—depreciation
512—travel expense
513—entertainment
514—advertising

515—dues and contributions
520—miscellaneous expenses

You should avoid the use of too many subdivisions of accounts for expenses. But revenue sources should be separated into enough finite categories so that you get a clear picture of your sources of gross income. All small and unrelated expense items should be lumped under miscellaneous expenses.

Once a system of record keeping has been set up, the thorniest question sometimes becomes "Who will keep the books?" In a one-person organization, the answer is simple: you will keep the books. Part-time bookkeepers and accountants are available who will perform this service for a fee. You should weigh the cost of such services against your net income, remembering that professional advice often can increase your profitability and more than offset its cost.

RECORDS RETENTION

How long should you retain records? There is no firm answer to this question. Generally speaking, you should keep records for as long as their contents may become pertinent in any inquiry by the IRS into your home office or business. Under ordinary circumstances, the statute of limitations expires for such records three years after your return was due to be filed.

Again speaking generally, the IRS cannot bring assessment or collection proceedings for a given taxable year after three years have elapsed from the due date of the return or the date it was filed, whichever is later. The time period is six years in cases where the taxpayer has omitted more than 25 percent of gross income and is unlimited in the case of fraud.

The three-year period should be regarded not as a limit but as a minimum. Many records should be kept for a longer period. Among the records considered to be permanent are cash books, depreciation schedules, the general ledger, journals, financial statements, and audit reports. Records that should be retained for six to seven years include accounts payable and receivable, canceled checks, inventory schedules, payroll records, sales vouchers, and invoice details.

Records of income taxes withheld from employees wages, social security (FICA), and federal unemployment (FUTA) taxes should be kept for four years. Records of state and local income tax withheld and state unemployment insurance taxes should also be kept for four years.

You should always retain copies of your income tax returns. It is sometimes possible to use carry-back claims or to file an amended return, but only if you have your returns from previous years.

SIXTEEN

Gone but Not Forgotten: Filing and Storage

If you have not resorted to the use of two freestanding file cabinets to create a desk, an important purchase will be a file cabinet or cabinets for the files you will create.

File cabinets have come a long way from the old-fashioned and cumbersome golden-oak pull-drawer monstrosities of grandma's day. Paradoxically, these behemoths are today widely sought by collectors and are even being reproduced by office-furniture manufacturers. Not only were they built like battleships, but their drawers were commodious.

An important point to remember is that filing encompasses the storage of, but also the quick and efficient retrieval of, many types of information, not only correspondence and documents.

Here are the types of filing equipment you may want to consider for the home office:

Pull-Drawer File Cabinets These range from small one- and two-drawer card files for desk tops or tabletops to two- to six-drawer letter-size and legal-size cabinets. Wide, multidrawer flat-plan files are much used by architects and engineers.

A side-by-side series of two-drawer file cabinets makes a work surface at approximately desk height, and a similar series of three-drawer file cabinets makes a work surface of counter height. The usual placement of a two-drawer cabinet is alongside a desk and within reach of the desk's occupant.

Details of construction will vary from manufacturer to manufacturer, but, in general, most quality pull-drawer file cabinets feature a ball-bearing-equipped progressive sidearm suspension that allows the drawer to roll smoothly and to open and close easily. For certain filing applications, hanging folders offer greater ease of file location and nonslumping folders. Note, however, that suspended folders will double your work, for labels must be made for both the file folders and the suspended folders, which always remain in the files. Because the hanging folders always remain in the drawer, any empty hanging folders offer clues to the identification of file folders that have been removed and must be replaced.

Lateral Files Imagine a pull-drawer file with drawers or doors that open on the long side and you have a lateral file. Advocates of this type claim that it offers the advantage of faster handling and retrieval of stored materials, plus a saving in utilized floor area—their depth is about 60 percent of a conventional vertical file. Because the drawers open to the side, lateral files are especially useful in areas in which access is limited—along the side of a narrow room, in a long closet or corridor, or as work-space dividers or even as walls in open-office arrangements.

An open drawer in a lateral file cabinet extends at most sixteen inches, as compared to the twenty-six-inch extension of a typical vertical file. Some models feature shelf doors that lift and slide into the cabinet, allowing the drawer to roll out for full access.

Lateral files are available in shelf types, with open drawer sides into which folders are slid and removed from the side; the open doors (hinged at the bottom) serve as work surfaces when open. Lateral suspension files of extremely simple construction are also available. In these, folders with labels along the front edge are suspended by hooks from a pair of metal rods. Another lateral file, a variation of the simpler work sorter, consists of boxes hung at a slight angle (to make file tabs more visible).

Tub files are based on hanging file folders suspended from the top rails of a rolling stand, offering the added advantage of mobility. In terms of the unit's filing capacity, tub files are comparatively expensive. Because they can be moved easily from place to place, many users find the higher cost is justified. The notes and data that went into this book were assembled in two tub files containing legal-size hanging folders.

Other storage files include reciprocating files, movable files (motorized on tracks), and wheellike rotary files, which give several workers access to them at the same time. All can accommodate more records than your home office is ever likely to handle.

Card Files Available for various card sizes, including 3 by 5 inches, 4 by 6 inches, 5 by 8 inches, tab/mag card (7½ by 3¼ inches), microfiche (4 by 6 inches), and ledger or inventory cards in various sizes (6 by 4 inches and 8 by 8 inches are popular sizes).

Visible Files If your business requires access to at-a-glance visible information, you may want to investigate visible files, available in horizontal and vertical types. In these, cards are mounted in pockets in trays that slide out horizontally for posting or are mounted vertically for easy access. Visible files are ideal for posting information quickly and for presenting updated information requiring close follow-up, such as inventory records. Such files, however, have largely been superseded by computerized record keeping. Where posting and updating are not necessary, microfiche readers are frequently used.

As you create materials for filing, you will discover that correspondence, documents, and other information fall into two types: active and inactive, with the progression usually from the former to the latter. The average home office, therefore, will need only a small amount of active storage space; in some cases, this can be accommodated in a single two-drawer file cabinet. One cabinet you should consider investing in is a two-drawer insulated file cabinet: a legal-size cabinet, the bottom drawer of which is letter size and insulated for protection from fire. Insulated file cabinets will withstand an exterior temperature of 1,700 degrees for a minimum of one hour; their interiors will maintain a temperature not exceeding 350 degrees and keep the contents in good condition.

If you buy an insulated file cabinet, look for the Underwriters Laboratories label reading "Insulated Filing Device, Class 350—1 hour." This was formerly called "Class D." If your office is on the ground floor or in a fireproof environment, this will be adequate. The next-higher classification, "Fire-Resistant Safe, Class 350—1 hour" (formerly "Class C") gives the same protection but also includes a thirty-foot drop test (equivalent to the safe or cabinet dropping three stories).

For inactive storage, it makes little sense to spend money on filing cabinets that will seldom be used. Commercial stationers offer a wide variety of fiberboard storage files, also known as "transfer files." These range in styles from all-fiberboard files for shelf storage to stackable steel-framed and steel-fronted drawers and sleeves. Some feature coated surfaces on drawers and sleeves for easy opening and closing. Through the use of steel bases and connectors, a reasonable approximation of a bank of steel filing cabinets can be achieved inexpensively. Fiberboard storage boxes with lift-off lids are even lower in cost.

Filing Materials

Despite technological advances in many areas of filing and records retention, the old-fashioned file folder has not really been improved upon.

Thickness Like all card stock, file-folder thickness is measured in points; one point is equal to $\frac{1}{100}$th of an inch (0.01). Typical file folder weights are pressboard (25 points), tag stock (18 points), heavy weight (11 points), and medium weight ($9\frac{1}{2}$ points).

Stock Recognizable by its characteristic light tan color, manila is the most frequently used folder stock. It takes its name from the fact that formerly it was made from Manila hemp; it is now made from wood pulp and other fibers. The usual weights are $9\frac{1}{2}$ and 11 points. Kraft is brown in color and made from unbleached wood pulp; its usual weight is 11 points. Pressboard is a strong, thick pasteboard that can withstand frequent handling. Its weight is 25 points, and the usual colors are blue and gray.

Size Folders may be letter size or legal size. "Body size" refers to the top-to-bottom dimension exclusive of the tab; "overall size" includes the tab. Letter-size folders are $11\frac{3}{4}$ inches in width, with 9-inch body height and $9\frac{1}{2}$-inch overall height. Legal-size folders have similar body height and overall height but are $14\frac{3}{4}$ inches in width.

Tabbing The tab is that part of the folder that projects above the folder body. It may run the full width of the top of the folder (called straight or full cut) or be expressed as a fraction. For example, one-third cut folders have a tab one-third the width of the folder body. When placed in files, it is customary to stagger folders so that several tabs can be seen and read at the same time.

Table 16.1 shows the approximate number of typing characters that can be typed on labels for each size tab.

Table 16.1. Number of Character Spaces Available
on Tabbed Folders

	Full Cut	1/2	1/3	1/5
Letter-Size Folders				
Elite	135	68	43	26
Pica	113	57	36	22
Legal-Size Folders				
Elite	159	85	56	33
Pica	133	71	47	28

Hanging Folders Sometimes called "suspension folders," these have two flat metal inserts along the top of the folders; hooks enable them to hang from parallel metal frames. Plastic tabs set at an angle of forty-five degrees for better readability can be inserted in any one of eleven positions in legal-size folders and in any one of nine positions in letter-size folders. If file drawers are not equipped with rods to accommodate suspension folders, self-standing frames in letter size or legal size can be purchased and installed in drawers. Large-capacity hanging folders are also available.

Folders for Special Purposes File jackets are file folders whose sides are joined; they may be flat or with expansion gussets that allow expansion of up to $3\frac{1}{2}$ inches. The back of the file jacket is usually about a half inch higher for labeling. File pockets are file folders whose sides are joined at the lower half, making it easy to open the top of the folder and to have access to the contents. File wallets are gusseted and have elastic continuous loops or tie strings to secure the top flap. Expansion capability of file wallets is $3\frac{1}{2}$ inches.

For doctors and dentists, special file jackets are available to hold medical and dental records or large X-ray negatives. Filing envelopes for attorneys' documents are of legal size in heavy stock, with space on the front for recording data about court orders, court papers, and other pertinent information.

SEVENTEEN

It's the Little Things that Count: Office Supplies

Not long after you set up your home office, you may find yourself becoming an office-supplies junkie. Just as the first-time home-owner often haunts hardware stores in search of new gadgets, you will begin to frequent stationers and office-supply stores looking for timesaving aids to more efficient operation. You may be surprised to discover that office supplies comprise more than paper and envelopes. Here are some items to consider in outfitting your home office:

TAPE

Modern office tapes are a far cry from the transparent tape of the past that became brittle and turned yellow with age. The usual tape lengths are 1,296-inch (108-foot) rolls to fit 1-inch core dispensers and 2,592-inch (216-foot) lengths to fit 3-inch core dispensers.

Cellophane Tapes

Clear transparent tape is now nonyellowing and should be used where other physical changes because of aging are not a factor. It is useful in packaging and in general mending and holding.

Frosty tape becomes almost totally clear when applied to most surfaces and offers other advantages in permanent paper mending. It resists moisture, cracking, and yellowing. Unlike clear tape, frosty tape accepts writing done with an ordinary pen or pencil.

Double-coated tape comes in clear or white and has adhesive on both sides. It is useful for fastening two sheets of paper together or for mounting pictures in albums or frames.

Filament tape is superstrong tape for packaging. Made of polyester, it is reinforced with glass threads running through it longitudinally.

Book tape is a transparent tape made specifically for repairing, reinforcing, protecting, and covering edges and surfaces of books, magazines, pamphlets, and albums.

Paper Tapes

Masking tape has a wrinkled (crepe) surface; it peels off surfaces easily, making it useful for masking or covering areas that should not be painted or airbrushed. Masking tape is not desirable for packaging because it is less strong and less adhesive than tapes made specifically for packaging purposes. Not only doesn't it hold well, but because it can be easily removed, it makes the contents of packages on which it has been used subject to pilferage.

Drafting tape is similar to masking tape except that the adhesive is even less tacky. It is widely used by artists and in drafting rooms —hence, the name.

Paper package-sealing tapes, plain or reinforced by filaments, are available with traditional gummed backings and find their greatest use in preparing packages for shipment. Gummed tapes can be ordered with gummed side in or gummed side out, depending on how the sealing machine feeds.

Moisteners are still a feature of warehouses and mail rooms and are available in lever-action dispense-and-cut models with water bottles feeding water reservoirs, as well as simpler pull-and-tear models with refillable water reservoirs. All use a replaceable brush as the moistener.

Package-sealing tapes of plastic are self-adhesive and made of tough, thin, waterproof vinyl. They are gradually supplanting gummed paper tapes in package shipping and have the added advantage of stretching to conform to edges and corners.

Tape Dispensers and Moisteners

Dispensers for pressure-sensitive tape are available in two basic sizes: 3-inch core for 2,592-inch-long single rolls up to 2 inches in width or two 2,592-inch-long rolls 1 inch in width, and 1-inch core for 1,296-inch-long rolls ½ and ¾ inches in width.

DESK STAPLERS

The stapler has become a fixture in most offices. Staples overcome a major disadvantage of paper clips—the tendency for sheets of paper to slide under paper clips and to become part of a group of papers already clipped.

Today's desk stapler is a rather sophisticated instrument of many uses. Here are some points to look for in buying one: all desk staplers are able to make a permanent stitch in which the two legs of the staple are bent toward one another behind the last sheet of paper or material to be joined. (The horizontal part of the staple joining the two legs is called "the crown.") Many people are unaware that most staplers can make two kinds of stitches: the permanent stitch just described and another "pin stitch" for temporary stapling. By rotating the anvil (the flat metal plate on the stapler), you can create a stitch in which both legs of the staple are turned outward. In effect, the staple becomes a straight pin, and removal is facilitated without the need for a staple remover.

Most desk staplers can also be used as tackers. Merely swing the stapler head away from the base; you may have to release a catch underneath the base, and in some cases the head can be removed completely. Using your stapler as a tacker, staples can be inserted into cork boards, bulletin boards, or soft wood. Because the staples are not clinched, their holding power is small, and they can be easily removed.

Desk staplers usually load staples in strips of 105 or 210 staples, depending on the depth of the stapler's throat. The loading method may be rear loading, in which the spring-operated mechanism is removed from the back of the stapler and a staple strip is inserted, after which the follower compresses the spring.

Alternatively, loading may be by the open-channel method, in which the channel holding the staples is exposed by opening the body of the stapler and inserting a strip of staples. When this is closed again, a spring forces the staples forward. Some desk staplers feature a reloading signal, usually a window near the front of the stapler that shows how many staples remain.

Electric Staplers When the volume of stapling to be done is large, you should consider buying an electric stapler. Some are activated by insertion and contact with the sheets to be joined; others are operated by push-button manual switches or by foot pedals for volume production. One model makes its own staples—the equivalent of forty-eight strips of staples—from a single roll of wire stock.

STAPLERS FOR SPECIAL USES

Heavy-Duty Staplers In warehouses and shipping rooms, there is always a need for tough staplers employing heavier staples. For office use, heavy-duty staplers are available that can fasten as much as a half inch of paper. Many of these are power assisted.

Long-Reach Staplers With a throat longer than the four-inch reach of the standard desk stapler, long-reach staplers can accommodate wider materials or can staple at a greater distance from the fore edge of the paper being joined. These are used primarily for binding booklets and pamphlets and for mounting materials on larger display sheets.

One variation of the long-reach stapler is the *saddle stapler*, whose V-shaped anvil is specifically designed for fastening booklets and pamphlets in the center fold. Widely used in print shops, this process is called "saddle stitching."

Plier Staplers Operated by squeezing them like pliers, these staplers are familiar from their use at the checkout counters of discount department stores and supermarkets to seal purchases in bags. Plier staplers are also widely used by dry cleaners and florists.

"Stapleless" Staplers These "weld" up to six sheets of paper together by notching them—in effect making a staple from the paper itself. The sheets are not as obviously stapled, nor is the joint as permanent as one made with a metal staple.

Staple Guns These powerfully built tools are usually associated with the home craftsman or the building trades and are generally not employed for fastening paper to paper but to staple into wood, soft metal, gypsum board, and other construction materials. Staples for such staple guns are available in lengths from $\frac{1}{4}$ to $\frac{9}{16}$ inch. Among the business uses of staple guns are upholstering, carpet laying, display-window trimming, display mounting, and price tagging.

Staple removers usually operate in one of two ways: some squeeze claws together in order to open staples and remove them. Others, described as "beer-can-opener types," are thin, angled blades that can be pushed under the staple's crown. Some removers of the latter type are attached to the staplers themselves.

PENCILS

The prosaic pencil is still the workhorse of the world of business, but no longer is it merely a simple cylinder of graphite enclosed in a shaped piece of cedar.

Pencils are available in round or hexagonal shapes. (The hexagonal beveling is intended to keep pencils from rolling off sloping surfaces.) In choosing a general writing pencil, four qualities—all governed by the core material—should be considered: hardness, smoothness of writing, strength of lead, and durability.

The hardness of pencils is defined by numbers indicating increasing degrees of hardness, ranging from no. 1 (soft) to no. 4 (hard). Soft pencils (nos. 1 and $1\frac{1}{2}$) make a heavy black mark and are useful for marking, note taking, and editing. Although the lead tends to smear, the points won't gouge thin or hard papers, as will harder leads. Medium pencils (nos. 2 and $2\frac{1}{2}$ or F) are the most popular for office, school, and home use. Firm pencils (no. 3) take a strong, sharp point and are best suited for fine lines or for writing figures, as in accounting and bookkeeping. Hard pencils (no. 4) are preferred for drafting and for making multiple carbon copies.

Drawing Pencils Drawing pencils and leads (for use in mechanical drawing pencils) come in seventeen degrees of hardness, as follows:

Soft: 6B, 5B, 4B, 3B, 2B, B
Medium: HB, F, H, 2H, 3H, 4H
Hard: 5H, 6H, 7H, 8H, 9H

Unlike general writing pencils, drawing pencils are traditionally marked on most or all of their sides because users are likely to have an assortment of hardnesses and the pencils resemble one another.

Here are some uses for drawing pencils of specific hardness:

6B–3B: used by editors for proofreading and marking copy and by artists for quick sketches. Useful wherever a heavy black mark is needed.
3B–B: used by stenographers for shorthand notes and for all who like the feel of a medium-soft lead.
HB–H: the most popular hardness for general writing pur-

poses. Approximates the no. 2 general writing pencil in
hardness and intensity.

2H–4H: used by accountants, bookkeepers, engineers, and
draftsmen.

4H–6H: for mechanical drafting and for making large numbers of carbons.

7H–9H: used by draftsmen, engravers, stonecutters, and pattern makers for marking on glass tracing cloth, marble,
and stone.

Colored Pencils Available in thick or thin leads and as fast colors
or as colors dissolved by water. Also available as paper-wrapped
grease pencils for marking on china, porcelain, glass, plastic, or
highly polished metal surfaces.

Mechanical Pencils For many years, the development of thin-
leaded mechanical pencils was hindered by the annoying tendency
of leads to break under writing pressure. Leads come in two thicknesses: standard, .9 millimeters (.035 inch) and thin, .7 millimeter
(.028 inch). The introduction of new plastic leads of greater
strength has enabled manufacturers to produce even thinner leads
—as thin as .5 millimeters (.020 inch) and .3 millimeters (.012
inch). Mechanical pencils for such leads require a protective sleeve
over the lead—either fixed or retractable—to prevent breakage of
the lead under the pressure of writing. Available sleeve lengths are
5 millimeters (.020 inch), 4 millimeters (.016 inch), or 2 millimeters (.008 inch). If your work requires the use of a thin-lead
mechanical pencil with straightedges, templates, or other drafting
instruments, you should make sure that the mechanical pencil you
select has a sleeve long enough to clear the edges of these.

MISCELLANEOUS OFFICE SUPPLIES

Paper Clips The lowly paper clip comes in a surprising number of
materials, sizes, and finishes. In its traditional shape, the jumbo
size measures two inches in length with wire gauge of .050. The
no. 1 size comes in two grades: premium, with wire of .041 gauge,
and standard, with wire of .036 gauge. Both measure 1⅜ inch in
length. All are also available in a "nonskid" corrugated finish. The
no. 3 size, which measures only ¹⁵⁄₁₆ inch long, has the lightest-
gauge wire, .032, and is only available in the bright finish. Still

other clips are available in oval instead of round wire; this puts more clip surface in contact with the paper being held.

Medium-size and large-size wire clamps come in lengths of $1\frac{1}{2}$ and $2\frac{5}{8}$ inches, in .0615 and .072 wire gauges, respectively. So-called regal clips, of rectangular shape, come in lengths of $\frac{5}{8}$, $\frac{3}{4}$, and 1 inch; their double prongs grip paper firmly and lie flat.

For really demanding holding tasks, spring clips are available in a variety of sizes and equipped with permanent magnets for mounting on a steel surface. Black binder clips have nickel handles that fold flat against a surface (or can be removed entirely). Tempered stainless-steel spring clamps in lengths of $3\frac{1}{4}$ and $5\frac{3}{4}$ inches have no sharp points or edges; their upturned edge keeps fingernails from breaking when they are removed.

Plastic clips, because they cannot carry magnetic charges as metal paper clips do, are finding favor in areas where computers are used. Their flat surfaces makes them more desirable for use on photographs, film, and artwork; their colors (red, white, blue, green, orange, and yellow) make them ideally suited for color coding. A giant version of these plastic clips is perforated to allow suspension from a nail or thumbtack.

Rubber Bands Don't overlook these old standbys when you buy supplies for your home office. Rubber bands come in a range of sizes, from no. 8, measuring $\frac{7}{8}$ inch in length and $\frac{1}{16}$ inch in width, to no. 107, which is 7 inches long and $\frac{5}{8}$ inch in width. No. 33 is a widely used size. Rubber bands are sold by the pound or fraction of a pound.

Carbon Paper Old-fashioned carbon paper of carbon-impregnated wax on a paper backing is still available in typewriter and pencil-carbon versions. More modern carbons are now made by a solvent process on mylar or paper backings and are also available in typewriter or pencil-carbon types; because the ink actually impregnates the copy paper (instead of lying on the surface), copies made with solvent carbon paper tend to smudge less than standard carbon copies.

Pencil Sharpener If you do a lot of writing with old-fashioned lead pencils, a pencil sharpener—even an electric sharpener—will seem more like a necessity than a luxury. Some electric sharpeners now stop automatically when a pencil has been sharpened or signal that fact by means of an indicator light.

Postage Scale An inexpensive but reasonably accurate postage scale can pay for itself many times over. Because first-class post-

age rates are lower after the first ounce, if you do not have a
postage meter, you can save money by having a supply of postage
stamps in appropriate denominations. Direct-reading scales are
available that show not only the weight but the necessary postage
for various classes of mail. Replacement scale faces are available
at a nominal cost when postage rates change.

Scissors Even here you will be presented with a bewildering array
of styles. Banker's shears are extra long, presumably for clipping
bonds. Editor's shears are also long but with finer blades, making
them popular with paste-up artists and with editors for more accurate cutting between lines of type in galleys; so-called dress-
maker's (bent) shears are useful for clipping newspapers because
they hug the table or desk.

Adhesives Glues now come in bottles, in stick form, in plastic
tubes with sponge applicators, and as spray adhesives in aerosol
cans. Rubber cement, that old standby of the artist's studio, is
still widely used because any excess can be rubbed off surfaces
quickly and cleanly.

EIGHTEEN

Take Care:
Safety and Security

It goes almost without saying that your home office will only be as
safe and as secure as your home is. If conditions in your home
do not comply with sound construction practices or safety rules
and so constitute a hazard, your home office is also at risk.

SAFETY

Electrical If you have any reason to suspect that the electrical
wiring in your home does not conform to the National Electrical
Code, you can always ask the local building inspector or an elec-
trician to inspect the premises.

But there are many precautions you can take yourself. If fuses blow frequently, it's a sign the circuits are overloaded. The answer is not to increase the size of fuses but to survey the number of appliances on that circuit. When several heavy-duty appliances are being operated at the same time on the same circuit, it's a good idea to "feel" the plugs, outlets, and outlet cover plates. If any of these is warm to the touch, it's a sign that the equipment is overloading the lines or that the wiring is not heavy enough.

It's a bad practice to use two-prong lightweight extension cords to connect heavy-duty equipment to outlets; instead, you should purchase three-prong, heavy-duty extension cords specifically made for such purposes. An inexpensive three-prong circuit tester should be plugged into each outlet to determine whether it has been wired correctly. Such testers reveal whether the "hot," grounded, or neutral sides of a line are open or whether the hot and grounded sides of a line may have been reversed. This is important because many pieces of equipment with metal cabinets have polarized plugs that ground the cabinet to the presumed grounded side of the line. A circuit in which these have been reversed could very well mean that the metal cabinet is electrically "hot" and constitutes a severe shock hazard.

Telephones The telephone company advises against using a telephone during an electrical storm in the immediate area, and calls—only those of an urgent nature—should be kept brief. Although devices are installed on phone lines to keep abnormal electrical surges from entering a building, absolute protection is impossible, and so there is always the remote risk of an electrical shock during a nearby electrical storm. Telephones should never be used in situations where the instrument or the user might be immersed in water.

Housekeeping

Fires often start in wastebaskets and spread from there. Plastic wastebaskets may even contribute to a fire. Special fire-retardant wastebaskets made of Cycolac do not fuel fires, and their walls actually collapse under heat to smother the fire.

Regardless of their construction, it's a good idea to get in the habit of emptying waste receptacles regularly. Certain oily materials—furniture-polishing rags are a frequent offender—have been known to combust spontaneously in closed containers in the absence of air.

Most houses and apartments tend to accumulate quantities of combustible and flammable materials. You should survey your home, particularly closets, the basement, and attic and remove these potentially dangerous materials before a fire starts. Look for old newspapers, cardboard cartons, holiday wreaths stored for use next year, old rags, and similar items. Among flammable and combustible liquids, look for gasoline, benzine, paint thinners, mineral spirits, turpentine, cans of oil-based paint and stains— opened or unopened (such cans may explode when subjected to the heat of a fire), aerosol cans of lacquer and enamel for spray painting, charcoal starter, and white gasoline. Flammable and combustible liquids should only be stored in approved safety cans, never in glass containers. Read the labels on innocuous products, furniture polish and adhesives, for example—they may contain combustible substances. You'll probably shudder when you see the number of dangerous substances you have collected.

Office-Materials Storage Artists' materials—rubber cement, rubber-cement thinners, wax for adhesive-wax applicators, and inflammable liquids—should be kept in metal cabinets.

Fire Extinguishers

Because different extinguishing agents must be used on different kinds of fires, the National Fire Protection Association classifies fires into the following four types:

Class A Fires in ordinary combustible materials (such as wood, cloth, paper, rubber, and many plastics) that require the heat-absorbing effects of water or water solutions, the coating effects of certain dry chemicals that retard combustion, or the interruption of the combustion chain reaction by halogenated agents.

Class B Fires in flammable or combustible liquids (gasoline, oils, paint solvents, cooking fats and oils), flammable gases, greases, and similar materials, which must be put out by excluding air or interrupting the combustion chain reaction.

Class C Fires in live electrical wiring and equipment; the safety of the user requires the use of electrically nonconductive extinguishing agents. (When electrical equipment is not carrying electricity, extinguishers for Class A or B fires may be used.)

Class D A fourth class of fire involves fires in certain combustible metals (such as magnesium, titanium, zirconium, sodium, potassium) and requires a heat-absorbing extinguishing agent that does not react with the burning metals. You are not likely to encounter such a fire around your home, although the increasing use of magnesium and aluminum in automobile engines may increase the likelihood of this class of fire in vehicles.

The size of the fire an extinguisher can handle is shown by the number that precedes the Underwriters' Laboratories class rating, shown as a letter or letters. Thus, an extinguisher rated 1A must be able to put out a test fire of fifty pieces of two-by-twos, twenty inches long. If rated 2A, it must be able to extinguish a fire twice as large. A 1B model can extinguish $3\frac{1}{4}$ gallons of naphtha burning in a $2\frac{1}{2}$-square-foot pan. C-rated extinguishers carry no numerical prefix; the rating signifies that the extinguishing agent does not conduct electricity, and so is safe for use on electrical fires.

Halon 1211, a DuPont product, is a gas used as the fire suppressant on the Space Shuttle and on aircraft engines. Halon-filled extinguishers are excellent for fighting fires in delicate electrical equipment and computers because they leave no contaminating residue of powder or liquid.

Extinguishers utilizing gas under pressure to propel the extinguishing agent should be equipped with dials showing the internal pressure. Units that have been fully or even partially discharged must be recharged by a fire-extinguisher dealer.

Your home or apartment should have several extinguishers, distributed in kitchen, living area, sleeping area, home office, and if appropriate, in basement and garage. Statistics show that most dwelling fires start in the living room or kitchen, so at least one extinguisher should be located where it can be reached from either room. It is best to locate extinguishers near exits so that if the fire cannot be controlled, a quick escape can be made. Extinguishers should be easily accessible and hung on brackets rather than hidden in closets or other places difficult to reach.

The manufacture of all inverting-type extinguishers, including the soda-acid type, was discontinued in 1969. Many had failed in use; in the event of blockage, the possibility of explosion was great; they could not be turned off once they were actuated; the stream of water was a good conductor of electricity and more corrosive than plain water, making them potentially dangerous to the user. Millions of such inverting extinguishers are still in use; if you are relying on any for protection, they should be replaced.

Similarly, vaporizing liquid extinguishers employing carbon tetrachloride and chlorobromomethane have become obsolete. The toxic properties of their fire-fighting agents exposed users to health hazards.

It isn't enough to distribute fire extinguishers around your house or apartment—you should also understand how to use them and what to do in case of fire. Most household fire extinguishers have a discharge time of eight to twelve seconds in actual use. Therefore, you cannot wait until a fire occurs to learn what to do.

Before using any extinguisher, you must release a safety device that prevents the unit from discharging prematurely. Once the safety has been released, most extinguishers are activated either by squeezing two handles together or by depressing the upper handle with the thumb. A discharge of about two seconds' duration from a medium-size extinguisher will blanket a large fire localized within a room. Extinguishers should be fired in short bursts, and every extinguisher should be recharged and tested after any use, no matter how brief.

To fight fires involving grease and flammable liquids, you should stand well back—about ten feet from the flames. The pressure from an extinguisher discharged at close range may actually spread the burning material. With all other fires, get as close as you can without endangering yourself. Aim the nozzle at the base of the flames and sweep it back and forth. You should always keep your back to an exit to the outside and never let a fire get between you and the exit.

If you are alone when you discover a fire, it's best to phone the fire department before doing anything else. If someone is with you, they can summon help while you fight the fire. Too often people attempt to put out the fire, neglecting to call the fire department until the fire has become too big to fight. Better that the firemen arrive and discover that you had mastered the fire *after* calling them than that they never arrive at all.

Smoke Detectors These home fire-alarm devices the size of ceiling light fixtures provide timely warnings that can save lives. Two types of smoke detectors are available: ionization and photo-electric.

Ionization smoke detectors use a minute amount of radioactive material to ionize the air in the sensing chamber, rendering it conductive and permitting a flow of current between two electrodes. When smoke particles enter the ionization chamber, they decrease the flow of current, eventually triggering the alarm.

Photoelectric smoke detectors direct a light beam into a chamber containing a light-sensitive photoelectric cell placed so that the beam of light does not fall on it. The cell detects the light only when smoke enters the chamber and causes the beam to scatter, triggering an alarm.

Smoke detectors may be battery powered or operate from the house current. Although battery-powered models require replacement of the battery at regular intervals (about once a year), they give wider choice in placement because they do not have to be close to an electrical outlet and will continue to operate in the event of a power interruption.

Ionization smoke detectors are quicker to detect fast-burning fires such as burning paper or flammable liquids. Photoelectric smoke detectors afford the best protection against the fire most likely to occur in the home and the most frequent cause of fire deaths—the slow, smoldering fire caused by a cigarette dropped in bedding or upholstered furniture. Ionization models, on the other hand, are likely to give a quicker warning of fast-flaming fires fueled by flammable or easily combustible materials.

When installing smoke detectors, place them on or near ceiling areas where smoke is likely to rise—for example, at the top of a stairway. Most fatalities from fire occur at night, so be sure to place a smoke detector *outside* the room in which you sleep. If your home has several levels or if separate areas are closed off by doors, place a smoke detector on each level or in each area. And remember to test smoke detectors regularly—all smoke detectors have built-in test buttons.

HOME-OFFICE SECURITY

Entire books have been written on the problems of home security, which are growing at an astronomical rate. Consider some of the staggering statistics: Every nine seconds someone's home is burglarized. Every four seconds a crime against property—larceny or theft—is committed. Every seven minutes a woman is raped—and 36 percent of rapes take place in the victim's home. Every twenty-five minutes someone is murdered. Nearly one home in three is a target of some kind of violent crime or theft.

Solve the problem of the security of your home and you will

automatically solve the problem of the security of your home office. Three basic elements comprise successful home-office security: concealment, deterrence, and awareness. Your first step should be to look carefully at your home and home office through the eyes of a burglar. Criminals will be doing just that.

Concealment

If banks, protected by some of the most sophisticated security devices ever invented, are unable to keep thieves from breaking in, what chance do householders and apartment dwellers with home offices have? Even without the banks' alarms and vaults surrounded by concrete and steel, you can still improve the chances that your home office will be able to resist a burglary.

Banks are frequent targets because, as Willie Sutton explained, "that's where the money is"—and thieves know it. As do many businesses, thieves operate with an eye to the cost/benefit ratios of their actions. They are more likely, therefore, to burglarize a location where the potential rewards are known to be great. You may have accumulated a lot of the world's goods, but it's to your advantage to be modest in proclaiming that fact.

Concealment is the security component easiest to achieve, yet is the most often ignored aspect of good security practice. It can be summed up in the expression "What *they* don't know can't hurt *you*." Your objective should be to conceal your life-style, your personal property, your habits, and your movements from prying eyes.

With this in mind, you should keep delivery people at the front door and out of the house, where they can observe your furnishings and life-style. All windows of your home at ground level into which anyone can look should be equipped with shades, blinds, or curtains, and it's a good idea to get in the habit of keeping these drawn. Callers who cannot peer into your house cannot tell whether you are at home (and not answering the door) or out.

In little-used areas, such as basements and garages, you can apply old-fashioned water-removable whitewash to the windows. This will allow light to penetrate but keeps outsiders from seeing what you have inside. Adhesive-backed pressure-sensitive vinyl film is available that will give windows the appearance of frosted glass. You are inviting trouble if outsiders can see valuables at any time from the outside—oil paintings or antiques, for example.

Because most burglaries are committed on premises when the occupants are away, you should take great pains to ensure that no one can conclude from external evidence that the premises are unoccupied. Therefore, you should get in the habit of always closing the garage door and locking it. A radio-controlled garage door opener (and closer) is desirable for two reasons: not only does the hand-held transmitter enable you to close the garage door from anywhere within range without getting out of your automobile, but it increases security, for a mechanically closed door is also a locked door.

A locked garage will also mean that thieves will not have access to your tools and ladders with which to gain entry to your home. Daring thieves, passing themselves off as roofers or house painters, have been known to travel in a ladder-equipped van or truck. For this reason, windows on upper floors should always be kept locked when you are not at home.

An unlocked attached garage makes your home especially vulnerable. Thieves have been known to drive a car into such an unlocked garage; after closing the garage door behind them, they have been able to gain entry to the house through the usually minimally locked door connecting house to garage or by literally smashing through the gypsum board wall between house and garage. After ransacking the house of valuables, they drive off with a carload of loot. Not infrequently, they will lock the garage door after the crime to further confuse the victims and the police.

Keep your name off your home, lawn signs, and mailbox. Thieves have been known to read such names on houses that appear to be unoccupied and to call the house from a nearby phone booth. By allowing your phone to ring and returning to the house, they can verify that the phone is not being answered and that no one is indeed at home. You should turn down the volume of the ringer on your telephones so that outsiders cannot hear an unanswered phone.

A better idea is to take your phone off the hook whenever you leave the house for short periods. Alternatively, you can dial your own exchange and number or dial any exchange in your area and the number 9970; you'll hear a busy signal in the receiver. Leave the phone off the hook until you return. It's far better that your friends think you are a chatterbox on the telephone than that thieves be able to verify your absence.

If you have an answering machine and can do without messages while you are away from home, it's a good idea to disconnect it and leave the phone off the hook. If you must leave it operating while you are gone, your outgoing message should say that you are only temporarily unavailable. Despite the not uncommon practice of using an answering machine to screen telephone callers, thieves regard an answering machine as a good sign that you are probably away from the premises.

Thieves have a well-developed information-gathering network. If you are planning to be away from home for an extended period, avoid innocent references to your upcoming trip in gasoline stations, in checkout lines at local supermarkets, or the lobby of the post office. This also applies to announcements in the social columns of the local newspaper about your impending trip to attend a wedding, graduation, or funeral.

If you plan to be away from home for more than a day, DO NOT draw the blinds in every window, giving your house a closed look and thereby practically announcing to outsiders that you are not home. In fact, DO NOT change your living habits in any way. DO NOT notify the post office to hold mail or ask the newspaper circulation department to cancel the delivery of your newspaper. Instead, ask a responsible neighbor to collect them each day. DO NOT advise the electric company or the lawn-maintenance company that you will be away. DO NOT leave notes on your front door or in your mailbox for deliverymen. These only advertise to the world that you are away.

Some careful householders even provide neighbors with garbage bags and arrange to have token trash put out in front of their houses for them on garbage-collection days. If you plan to be away during the winter, have your sidewalk shoveled and your driveway plowed. In summer, have the grass cut. Place any valuables you have in the house—jewelry, cash, credit cards, and unused checks—in your safe deposit box. Why unused checks? Burglars often remove two or three checks from the back of a householder's checkbook during the course of a burglary; the victim does not immediately detect the loss until the next month's bank statement arrives, revealing that the account has been cleaned out.

Whether you should tell your local police department that you will be away is a moot point. This is not to suggest that your police department may harbor dishonest members. Some police departments post notices about "dark houses" (police parlance for an unoccupied house) in a conspicuous place so that officers on each shift will be informed about houses that should receive special attention. Some departments make it a practice to radio a suggestion to a patrol car to check your premises because the desk sergeant knows you are away. The easy availability of scanners and knowledge of police codes used in messages enables thieves to eavesdrop on such police radio transmissions. In principle, the fewer people who know the house is unoccupied, the better.

Once thieves have reason to believe that a house may be unoccupied, it is very easy for them to pay close attention to it and to verify that no one is home. Most thieves have highly developed powers of observation, as well as intimate knowledge of the external evidences of home occupancy. During the summer, all your prearranged signs of occupancy can go for nought if a burglar notices that air conditioners are not operating on hot days or nights. If you use timing devices, they should be set up to cause air conditioners as well as lamps in various portions of the house to go on and off at *appropriate* times. This calls for lights in the kitchen and living area in the evening, lights in the bedroom areas in the late evening, and perhaps a light in the bathroom during the small hours of the morning. Timers are available that enable random programming of on-off times; these will assist in defeating any attempt by thieves to detect the pattern of the timers by observation of the house.

Similarly, radios strategically placed within hearing distance of front or back doors can be connected to timers that go on and off at intervals.

If you are away from the house for an extended period and there has been a lengthy interruption of electrical service because of a storm or other reason, timers may have to be reset. Outside lights should be operated by photoelectric devices rather than by timers, for outside lights burning during daylight hours would be a telltale sign of an unoccupied house.

One family with a dog has an ingenious arrangement. Because the dog is taken to a boarding kennel when the family is away, a tape recorder has been set up to play a tape of the dog barking whenever the doorbell is rung. The tape is an endless loop and resets itself after each playing. Noise is a burglar's enemy. Most thieves agree that a yapping dog that runs under the bed and barks incessantly constitutes a bigger threat to the successful accomplishment of a burglary than does a fierce guard dog.

By the way, if you own a computer, don't advertise this fact with an automobile bumper sticker reading, "I love my computer." As computers become more popular, they will join stereos, TVs, VCRs, and other portable electronic items as the targets of thieves.

Deterrence

Because time is also a burglar's enemy, it's a good idea to slow down and discourage would-be intruders by making your home (and thus your home office) seemingly impregnable, thereby encouraging them to seek easier pickings elsewhere.

The three greatest aids to the deterrence of burglary are (1) the strength of materials at the thieves' place of entry, (2) adequate locks, and (3) an alarm system. Attention to all these categories will deter even the most determined of thieves.

Burglary is an unlawful entry to commit a felony or theft, and no force need be used to gain entrance. Paradoxically, 42 percent of all household burglaries occur without forced entry; in the face of such monumental carelessness, it is no wonder that almost 80 percent of burglaries go unsolved. The first rule is to keep doors and windows locked at all times. And do not leave keys in obvious locations, such as under the door mat or over the lintel. If you must stash a key for emergency use, place an unmarked extra key in a small glass jar, tape it shut, and bury it in a location in the garden known only to you and your family.

Contrary to conventional wisdom, most unlawful entries into homes occur through doors rather than through windows or other openings. One reason for this statistic is that a stranger standing at the door to a house or even entering through it may not arouse suspicion, but a stranger at or near a window is certain to attract attention, and a stranger observed in the act of entering a house through a window will need an explanation for the police who may be summoned by an alert neighbor.

Here are some tips on particular areas of houses and apartments that deserve your attention.

Doors

Check the doorframe for sturdiness. Reinforce or replace weak, spongy doorframes. Burglars have been known to use a small hydraulic jack and some lengths of two-by-fours placed between the frame uprights to spring the doorframe enough to bypass the latch.

If your outside doors are of hollow-core construction or have thin wooden panels, replace them with solid-core or panel doors of 1¾-inch thickness with a minimum panel thickness of ¾ inch. Hollow steel doors and Kalamine doors (solid core wood doors with steel sheets laminated to both sides) are even better.

A key-in-the-knob lock is next to useless for keeping thieves out. A pair of vise-grip pliers or a pipe wrench is usually the only tool needed to twist the knob off and gain access to the lock mechanism.

If the outside doors are equipped with key-in-the-knob locks, use them only for latching purposes when you are home, but add a sturdy deadbolt lock with pick-resistant cylinder and guard plate. (A deadbolt is a lock bolt that is not beveled, has no automatic spring action, and is operated by turning a key or a thumb turn.) The hardened bolt should have a throw of at least one inch—long enough to prevent it from being pried out of the strike or frame. Always lock the deadbolt whenever you leave the house.

A new type of door lock is useful in high-security areas. It employs a push-button or dial-type mechanism that opens on the entry of the correct combination of three or more digits. Because there are no keys, nothing can be lost or duplicated, and the lock is impossible to pick. The combination can be changed in a matter of seconds should unauthorized persons learn the entry code.

An ingenious thief could possibly detect wear patterns on buttons that are regularly used, thus reducing the number of potential combinations of digits needed to be tried randomly. Manufacturers therefore suggest that combinations be changed regularly to equalize the wear on button surfaces.

Make sure the hinge pins on outside doors are *inside* the house. (If the doors open inward, the hinge pins will always be on the inside.) Pins on the outside in so-called loose-pin hinges can often be removed by inserting a knife or screwdriver blade underneath the pins and tapping upward, making entry by thieves a simple matter. For added security, you should replace loose-pin hinges with non-removable-pin hinges or add screw-in jimmy pins in the doorframe that extend into matching holes in the door itself. You can also substitute such pins for one screw in each hinge; special hinges with such pins already installed are available at hardware stores.

You can reinforce the lock area of solid doors by drilling a series of deep horizontal holes into the doors above and below the locks. Using epoxy glue, cement steel rods in the holes and cut them off flush with the door edge. This will make it impossible for anyone to bypass your locks by chopping or drilling around them.

Keep the clearance between doorframes and doors to a minimum, defeating any attempt to insert pry bars or hacksaw blades in the space. If a lock with a deadbolt having a one-inch throw is installed in a door separated from the jamb by an opening of a half inch, the effective length of this bolt has been reduced to a half inch.

Protect protruding cylinders of rim locks and deadbolt locks with steel guard plates bolted through the door or with a rotating cylinder guard.

Vertical-bolt rim locks, which are mounted on the surface of the door rather than being mortised into it, make excellent secondary locks. The complete interlocking of the bolts and the strike make such locks high resistant to forcible entry.

Avoid large mortise locks in thin wooden doors. So much wood must be removed to install these that doors are weakened and can easily be kicked in.

Although they may seem unsightly, auxiliary bolts, such as sliding surface bolts mounted at the top and bottom of a door or lever extension bolts for double doors, can make doors more secure. They can only be activated from the inside—a disadvantage.

Use a bar lock on seldom-used doors or doors remote from observation by neighbors. One type places a two-by-four across an inward-opening door and is virtually burglarproof.

Sliding-glass doors are extremely vulnerable to prying and jimmying, not to mention glass cutting. Locks for such doors are available, but you should look for those that can be keyed to existing locks and that have stainless-steel deadbolts. Bar locks can be installed in the track of a sliding door, making it virtually impossible to open the door from the outside.

Door Braces Additional protection for doors you do not intend to enter from the outside can be provided by door braces, also called "buttress locks." In these, a steel rod is fitted with a yoke-like device at one end; this fits into a metal-reinforced slot immediately under the doorknob. The other end fits into a similar slot set in the floor. For carpeted floors, a buttress lock with a rubber tip is available.

Windows

Thumb-set crescent rotating window locks—whether keyed or unkeyed—and held in place on double-hung wooden windows by short wood screws are virtually useless for keeping thieves out. The reason is that the short screws cannot resist the force of a pry bar. A good technique for reinforcing such windows is to drill a small hole through the inner and outer sash and to insert a $2\frac{1}{2}$-inch-long carriage bolt in the hole, which should be angled slightly downward toward the outside to keep the carriage bolt from being worked out.

Large, nonopening windows provide good security if glazed with laminated vandal-resistant glass (wired glass is unsightly and should only be used in commercial or industrial settings). Small-paned windows with sturdy mullions are even more secure than large-paned windows, because entry is impossible even if the panes are broken.

Louvered (jalousie) windows allow for the regulation of air circulation but also offer the least security. Add decorative grilles or grates inside louvered windows for better protection.

Casement windows should never be allowed to remain partially open when you are not at home; they can easily be forced open completely. Removing the crank handle will afford a measure of extra protection for little-used casement windows.

Even though a snug-fitting stick or cutoff broom handle will keep them from being opened in the usual manner, sliding windows—like sliding doors—can be lifted out of their tracks, making them very vulnerable. One expedient is to place partially driven screws into the overhead track so that the windows will slide past them, yet protruding enough to prevent the windows from being lifted out. Thus protected, sliding windows can also be held together with a metal pin, top and bottom.

One technique used by burglars is to press a sheet of wet newspaper against a pane of glass and to push it in—the newspaper keeps the pieces from tinkling when they fall. Strips of drafting tape have been employed for the same purpose. Who would dream that someone carrying a newspaper or a roll of tape could be carrying burglar's tools?

Burglar-resistant glass will resist shattering when struck with a sledgehammer, baseball bat, or other heavy instrument. The highest resistance is to be found in vinyl-bonded laminated glass $\frac{1}{2}$ inch in thickness or more and in sheets of acrylic plastic (with the trade names Plexiglas or Lexan). These are not inexpensive and can be penetrated with a drill, saw, or blowtorch. The installation of burglar-resistant glass, however, may reduce your burglary-insurance premiums.

Metal casement windows, unlike wooden windows, have panes that are installed from the outside. Burglars can easily remove the putty or glazing compound holding a pane of glass in a casement window and reach in and unlock the window. For this reason, casement window locks should be key lockable.

The best locks for double-hung windows utilize a steel bolt that fits into a steel strike. On casement windows, replace existing handle latches with key-locked handles. When ordering keyed window locks of any kind, be sure to specify that they are to be keyed alike, thus reducing the number of keys you'll have to carry and making it easier to locate keys and to open locks in the event of fire.

Sliding metal-gate window guards are unsightly, but for houses in high-crime areas and urban apartments they afford maximum protection against forcible entry.

Unlikely Entrance Points

Pay special attention to the security of skylights, basement windows, windows opening on fire escapes, vents, and transoms. Do not take comfort in the small size of an opening or a window. Many burglaries are committed by young people whose small stature makes it possible to enter through small openings denied to an adult.

Alarms

Alarm systems are of three basic types:

1. Local alarms that only sound an alarm—a siren or bell—in or around the premises. You'll have to hope that an alert neighbor will telephone the police when it sounds; because burglars won't know whether this alarm is part of a more elaborate system, they'll usually disappear as soon as it goes off.

2. Alarms that sound an alarm at a console in the local police station.
3. Central-station alarms that sound an alarm at the central station of an alarm company.

The average home handyman can install the first kind of system easily, but this is the least effective type of alarm. The bell box should be mounted high on the house or be unreachable from the outside. Some thieves have been known to defeat an outside alarm bell by filling the bellbox with aerosol foam-type shaving cream, thus muting the bell. Such alarm systems are not advisable in remote areas. Systems nos. 2 and 3 must be installed and maintained by a professional alarm company. Most companies offer the option of purchase or lease.

My own home and home office are protected by a three-way system offering fire, smoke, and intrusion detectors connected to a central station. Although our village has a console in the police station monitored by the police, my reasons for opting for a central system may be of interest. I had decided to explore the possibility of an alarm system on a day that happened to be Good Friday. The offices of the company that maintains the console in the police station and has the exclusive right to make connections to it were closed when I called.

Because burglars observe no regular working hours, I decided I needed a service that worked around the clock. As a consequence, I called the offices of a national alarm service in a nearby city whose telephone lines are monitored twenty-four hours a day and which also serves local banks and a watch factory.

Is a central station system better? Many police departments have come to regret their acceptance of the role of control-panel monitors, because it commands the time and attention of desk sergeants. In addition, so many false alarms have been received by police that many communities now have imposed stiff charges for false alarms that tie up vehicles and personnel.

My alarm system allows me to cancel immediately any false alarms by telephoning the central station and identifying myself by my code number. Since the central-station employees are essentially my employees and are looking out for my best interests, they are glad to have false alarms intercepted before they can reach my local police department. Moreover, police personnel are often occupied with other duties and are neither qualified nor paid to determine whether a particular alarm is the result of trouble with the system or a genuine break-in.

Alarms can be wired to protect the doors and windows of your premises (perimeter defense), using magnetic switches and sound detection to detect break-ins, or interior spaces, using pressure pads under carpets and ultrasonic or infrared devices. (Pets cannot roam freely when interior areas are protected in this manner.)

No matter which alarm system you select, attention should be paid to the possibility that thieves may defeat the system. Consequently, buried telephone wires are more desirable than overhead wires. Fail-safe devices are available to signal to the central office if the line has been cut or if protection has otherwise been interrupted. The most sophisticated alarm systems are now computerized and monitor the status of lines to all premises on the system at frequent intervals.

It has been said that the biggest deterrents to burglary are the stickers on windows and doors announcing that the premises are protected by an alarm system. Experts are divided on the subject of stickers versus "secret" alarms. Because your objective should be to deter a thief—not to capture one—it is my feeling that you should display alarm system stickers if your premises are indeed protected by a system. In a neighborhood in which some homes are obviously protected and others apparently not protected, the smart burglar will bypass an alarm-protected house and work on an unprotected dwelling. This may not seem like good neighborliness, but it is certainly enlightened self-interest on your part.

One word of caution: avoid those phony stickers of nonexistent alarm companies. Most thieves can tell valid stickers from false stickers. A phony sticker may be the opposite of a deterrent—an open invitation to the knowledgeable thief.

Safes and Fire-Resistant Containers

Given enough time, a safecracker can get into any safe. In other words, the burglarproof safe does not exist—only safes with varying degrees of burglar resistance. Safes are rated by Underwriters' Laboratories.

A safe visible anywhere in the house tells a burglar that valuables are probably inside, so it is not a good idea to advertise a safe's presence. A safe that can be concealed in a wall behind a painting or one imbedded in concrete in a cellar floor with a throw rug over it is more likely to escape notice.

Weight alone is no guarantee that a safe can't be stolen. Most safes for home offices can be carried off by burglars and worked on at their leisure. Safes weighing as much a ton have been removed by enterprising burglars. If you have a safe, no matter how much it weighs, it should be bolted to the building structure.

Instead of a cumbersome safe, you'd be wise to invest in one of the fire-resistant filing cabinets described in chapter 16, which are designed to prevent loss from a more likely hazard—fire. Fire-resistant files ingeniously protect their contents with water, or rather with steam; their thick walls are filled with an insulating material that releases steam when heated to high temperatures.

Birth certificates, discharge papers, marriage certificates, stocks, bonds, and other negotiable instruments or irreplaceable papers should not be kept in a fire-resistant file cabinet at home or even in a home safe. Instead, these should be placed in a safe-deposit box.

Awareness

Not all hazards to the home office pertain to disasters that occur while you are away from home. In today's violent world, the individual alone in a remote location is easy prey for violent criminals and crazies. Fortunately, there are a number of devices and procedures to increase your awareness of the presence of strangers on your property or near your premises.

Exterior Lighting Very desirable. Light is perhaps the number-one crime deterrent. First, check out the street lighting in your neighborhood. In suburban areas, tree growth sometimes obscures the lights; if so, ask the local public works department to trim the trees. Next, inspect your home's exterior lighting. All doors should be provided with outside lights to make it possible for you to identify any nighttime visitors.

Eliminate all dark areas immediately adjacent to the house. Side yards and backyards should be illuminated to make it impossible for burglars to take advantage of trees and shrubbery to shield them from view.

Optical Viewers Highly desirable for *any* solid door, not only the front door, and available in wide-angle models.

Mirrors Strategically placed convex mirrors can be mounted out-side of windows to give you a view of whoever is at your door.

Door Chains Useful, but only if you discard the screws furnished and substitute long, heavier-duty screws. Protected in this way, a chained door offers reasonable protection against the push-in type robbery becoming more prevalent today. You should know, too, that a chained door is not a substitute for a deadlocked door if you are away from the house. Using such simple and unobvious burglary "tools" as a thumbtack or a piece of adhesive tape and a rubber band, a clever thief can easily open a chain in a few seconds.

Infrared Beam Devices These consist of a light source and photo-electric cell relay in one unit, with a mirror placed at a distance to reflect the beam back to the device. When mounted across a drive-way, walkway, or at a doorway, interruption of the beam causes a light, bell, or other warning device to be activated. It can also be used to actuate intrusion alarms, signal the entrance of customers into a room, or to count objects passing a point.

Annunciators Some homeowners have installed annunciators at their doors. These are two-station intercoms, with one microphone/speaker mounted in the doorframe near the doorbell. When the bell is rung, the caller can be asked for identification before the door is opened.

Window-Mounted Air Conditioners Most people are surprised to discover that air conditioners in accessible windows are an easy means of unlawful entry to a house or apartment—and some find this out the hard way. The burglar merely pushes the air condi-tioner into the room, leaving the outer shell still anchored to the window frame. The appliance falls to the floor (or onto the piece of furniture under the window) with a tremendous crash, of course. After waiting to see whether the loud noise has caused anyone to investigate it, an agile thief now has a means of easy ingress. To forestall this, use heavy wire or small L-shaped angle irons to se-cure the air conditioner so that it cannot be pushed in.

Have a Disaster Plan

You should have a disaster plan formulated well in advance. Disaster can strike from many quarters: burglary, fire, flood, even accidental destruction of records. Here are some elements of a good disaster plan:

1. Copies of all valuable and irreplaceable documents should be placed in a fire-resistant safe or cabinet. These can include birth certificates, marriage certificates, contracts, patents, incorporation certificates, books of account, etc.
2. Originals of these documents should be placed in a secure location accessible to you, such as a safe-deposit box.
3. Lists should be kept of model numbers and serial numbers of all appliances and office equipment, names of manufacturers, their addresses, and telephone numbers; also, names of all banks with whom you have accounts, together with account numbers. Credit cards issued to you should also be listed, with addresses and telephone numbers of issuers for notification in the event cards are lost. (This information accompanies credit cards when they are mailed to you.)

Epitomizing the advice of this chapter, an old Turkish proverb reminds us, "Fortune favors the well prepared."

NINETEEN

How to Find Out: Research Facilities for the Home Office

"You could look it up." The immortal words of Casey Stengel should be the motto of the home-based business in need of information. Casey used the phrase in his explanation of how the New York Yankees could win 103 games in 1954 without winning the pennant. "We had a splendid season," he was fond of saying, "but 'the señor' (Al Lopez, manager of the Cleveland Indians, winners of 111 games that same season) beat us—and you could look it up."

Large corporations do just that, investing millions in corporate libraries, not only because such expenses represent tax write-offs. Big business needs information about industry developments in order to remain competitive, to gain knowledge of the activities of competitors, and for trend spotting to forestall technological surprises. Corporate libraries are the usual repositories of sources of such information. Small businesses have a need for information sources, too—often more so than big business—simply by reason of being smaller, less likely to be diversified, and thus more vulnerable to the unforeseen.

A HOME-OFFICE LIBRARY

You probably won't ever be able to afford more than a modest collection of reference books, magazines, and newspapers, but this chapter can assist you in assembling the nucleus of a basic home-office reference library. And don't overlook the information facilities available in your community. Knowing where to find information in public sources when you need it can be more useful than attempting to accumulate a large library of seldom-used books.

BOOKS

One book you should buy is *Reference Books: A Brief Guide,* 8th ed., by Marion V. Bell and Eleanor A. Swidan (Baltimore, Md.: The Enoch Pratt Free Library, 1978). This inexpensive paperback is the reference librarian's Bible—and will be yours, as well.

Almanacs

The cornerstone of any working collection of reference books is a good almanac. The *World Almanac and Book of Facts* (New York: Newspaper Enterprise Association, annual) has been published continuously since 1868. Other almanacs along similar lines include the *Information Please Almanac* (New York: A & W Publishers, annual), the *Reader's Digest Almanac* (Pleasantville, NY: Reader's Digest Association, annual), and the *Hammond Almanac,* a successor to the *New York Times Encyclopedic Almanac* (Maplewood, N.J.: C. S. Hammond, annual). Because almanacs are revised and updated each year, unless you give an almanac hard usage, the paperback edition should last until the new edition appears.

Dictionaries and Thesauruses

Next, a good dictionary is indispensable. *Webster's New Collegiate Dictionary,* 9th ed. (Springfield, Mass.: G. & C. Merriam, 1983), *Webster's New World Dictionary of the American Language* (New York: Simon & Schuster, 1981), and the *American Heritage Dictionary of the English Language* (Boston: Houghton Mifflin, 1981) are all reasonably priced desk dictionaries and adequate for most needs. The *Random House Dictionary of the English Language* (New York: Random House, 1983) is somewhat larger than a desk dictionary and more expensive; it received a boost in prestige when it was selected as the basis for several computerized word-processing programs for the quick verification of the spelling of words.

First introduced in 1961, *Webster's Third New International Dictionary, Unabridged* (Springfield, Mass.: G. & C. Merriam, 1976) is truly a behemoth among dictionaries, with 100,000 new entries (but with the total number of entries reduced to 460,000 from the 600,000 of the previous edition by dropping obsolete and rare words), some 200,000 usage examples, and about a thousand synonym explanations. It is also the most controversial reference book of recent times and has been both attacked and defended for its departures from previous practice. Paradoxically, despite the absence of definitions of more recent words and usages, some diehards cling tenaciously to their well-worn copies of the second edition, maintaining that its level of scholarship is higher.

A thesaurus can be useful for letter writing and report preparation. As with a dictionary, you'll consult it often for the exact word you need, so invest in a hard-cover edition rather than a paperback. Two good thesauruses are *Roget's International Thesaurus,* 4th ed. (New York: Thomas Y. Crowell, 1977) and *Roget's Thesaurus of English Words and Phrases* (New York: St. Martin's Press, 1965).

A pair of synonym books I have found helpful are *The Word Finder,* compiled and edited by J. I. Rodale (Emmaus, Penn.: Rodale Books, 1947) and *The Synonym Finder,* edited by J. I. Rodale and others (Emmaus, Penn.: Rodale Books, 1961). These overcome most of the limitations of traditional thesauruses by expanding the number of synonyms for key words and by including many "near synonyms" close to the meaning of the subject word.

Directories

If you do business with government departments and need help in finding your way through the Washington maze, the *Congressional Directory* (Washington, D.C.: Government Printing Office, annual) is a must. In addition to information on the makeup of Congress and congressional committees, it lists federal courts and judges, plus agencies and officers of the executive branch. Another volume with detailed information on each agency is the *United States Government Manual* (Washington, D.C.: Government Printing Office, annual). A one-volume adjunct to these is *The Washington Information Directory* (Washington, D.C.: Congressional Quarterly, Inc., annual).

One reference book I find extremely useful is *The National Directory of Addresses and Telephone Numbers* (New York: Concord Reference Books, annual), which lists addresses and telephone numbers (including toll-free 800 numbers) by category for businesses of every description and government agencies. Separate categories list accounting firms, advertising agencies, associations and organizations, banks, brokerage and investment firms, county, state, and federal government agencies, hospitals, law firms, media and information sources, messenger, courier, and express delivery companies, and office-equipment manufacturers. For travelers on business or for pleasure, its lists of airlines, car-rental agencies, railroad and bus stations, hotels and motels (including resorts) are indispensable. More than 60 percent of this handy volume is devoted to lists of corporations, arranged alphabetically and classified by type of business activity. Much used in my home office, it is the closest thing to a national telephone and address book.

Each year thousands of foundation grants go unclaimed because no one applies for them. Small businesses could be the recipients of some of these grants, especially if the business is engaged in research. Foundations and grants are described in *The Foundation Directory* (New York: Columbia University Press, biennial, in odd years) and the *Foundation Grants Index* (New York: Columbia University Press, irregular).

Biographical Sources

For biographical information on the president, governors, senators, and representatives, their voting records, and the boundaries and voting patterns of congressional districts, *The Almanac of American Politics,* by Michael Barone and Grant Ujifusa (Washington, D.C.: Barone and Company, biennial) is indispensable.

Who's Who in America (Chicago: Marquis Who's Who, biennial, in even years) gives detailed biographical information on prominent living Americans; it is supplemented with *Who Was Who in America,* cumulated at intervals of about five years.

Written in engaging style, *Everybody's Business: An Almanac,* edited by Milton Moskowitz, Michael Katz, and Robert Levering (New York: Harper & Row, 1980), contains unusual "biographies" of businesses and describes itself as an "irreverent guide to corporate America."

Sources of Demographic Information

Businesses interested in demographics for marketing campaigns, economics, finance, business, or sociological studies will find the *Statistical Abstract of the United States* (Washington, D.C.: Government Printing Office, annual) a useful source of quantitative information.

A more ambitious presentation of the 1980 census is to be found in *1980 Census: Population and Housing Characteristics,* edited by Thomas R. Gay and James D. Shaffer (San Diego: National Decision Systems, 1983). The Census Bureau is now selling computer tapes of census data at less than cost to private publishers for processing and publication. This 1,611-page, five-volume set costs a whopping $395 but may be worth every penny to a business that needs this information and cannot wait until it is compiled and released by the Census Bureau.

Business Books

The association of a home office with business activities is inevitable. Therefore, no matter how small a home office library may

be, it should have a few basic business books. Bibliographies make
an excellent nucleus for any collection; a good starting place is
Business Information Sources, by Lorna M. Daniells (Berkeley,
Calif.: University of California Press, 1976). A later variant by
the same author, entitled *Business Reference Sources,* published in
1979, is essentially an index to the Baker Library of the Graduate
School of Business Administration of Harvard University. Unfortunately, the annotations in both books are often too brief to be
genuinely useful.

A Business Information Guidebook, by Oscar Figueroa and
Charles Winkler (New York: AMACOM, 1980), lists sources of
business information, including reference books, government publications, and periodicals. More broad based is *The Guide to Small
Business Resources,* by David E. Gumpert and Jeffrey A. Tim-
mons (Garden City, N.Y.: Doubleday, 1982), which includes
sources of federal, state, and local aid, financial assistance, and
venture capital, among other topics. *The Small Business Index,*
edited by Wayne D. Kryszak (Metuchen, N.J.: Scarecrow Press,
1978), is a subject-oriented list of books, pamphlets, directories,
and periodicals containing information of specific interest to the
small-business owner but is beginning to be dated.

One bibliography that can lead business owners to sources of
information on specific subjects is *The Encyclopedia of Business
Information Sources,* edited by Paul Wasserman (Detroit: Gale
Research, biennial). This information-packed volume contains
more than 20,000 entries arranged under 1,200 subject headings,
classified by business activity or topic. It lists dictionaries, indexes,
statistical publications, and handbooks, plus names and addresses
of trade associations and professional societies. Another useful
business bibliography is *Where to Find Business Information,* by
David M. Brownstone and Gorton Carruth (New York: Wiley,
1979).

An excellent source of leads to small-business information is
Small Business Sourcebook (Detroit, Mich.: Gale Research Company, 1983). The first part contains information on a hundred
small businesses, with the accent on small retail ventures but including businesses that could be home based, including advertising
services, mail-order businesses, translation and editorial services,
and word processing services. The second part is a comprehensive
listing of federal, state, and local government agencies, educational
institutions, venture capital firms, and published sources of small-
business information.

Specialized dictionaries are always useful in a home-office library. Among such dictionaries are *A Dictionary for Accountants,* 5th ed., by Erich L. Kohler (Englewood Cliffs, N.J.: Prentice-Hall, 1975); *Dictionary of Advertising Terms,* edited by Laurence Urdang (Chicago: Crain Books, 1979); *Dictionary of Banking and Finance,* by Jerry M. Rosenberg (New York: Wiley, 1982); *Dictionary of Business and Management,* also by Jerry Rosenberg (New York: Wiley, 1978); *Economics Dictionary,* by Donald W. Moffat (New York: Elsevier, 1976); *Dictionary of Business and Economics,* by Christine Ammer and Dean S. Ammer (New York: Free Press, 1977); *McGraw-Hill Dictionary of Modern Economics,* 3rd ed., by Douglas Greenwald and Associates (New York: McGraw-Hill, 1983); *The VNR Investor's Dictionary,* (New York: Van Nostrand Reinhold, 1981); and *Black's Law Dictionary,* 5th ed., edited by James R. Nolan and Michael J. Connolly (St. Paul, Minn.: West Publishing Company, 1979).

MAGAZINES

There is no lack of information about business available from magazines, particularly news and ideas on effective management and small business. To keep abreast of the world of business and to improve your own operating skills, you may want to read one of the so-called Big Four magazines: *Business Week, Forbes, Fortune,* and *Nation's Business.*

Black Enterprise describes itself as a "survival manual for black business people trying to make it in the free market" and provides how-to articles for investors and entrepreneurs. With a circulation of a quarter of a million, it controls 5 percent of the business magazine market.

Canada's wide-ranging weekly, *Financial Post,* closer to a newspaper than a magazine, reports on more than just the Canadian business scene and has much to interest the casual reader.

As the operator of a home office or the owner of a home-based business, among the specialized magazines you may want to consider are *In Business,* a bimonthly designed to help small business owners manage their enterprises more effectively; *Inc.,* targeted at small business managers and investors; and *Venture,* specifically geared to entrepreneurs, featuring articles on start-ups, buy-outs, franchising, and venture capital.

Although primarily a semiweekly tabloid-sized magazine about advertising and marketing, *Advertising Age* can be read profitably by anyone in any business, if only for its wealth of statistical data.

NEWSLETTERS

Under the federal government's Fair Labor Standards Act, at-home workers making certain kinds of products are in violation of the law. These restrictions originated in the 1940s to keep domestic sweatshops run with cheap labor from undercutting established businesses—but American cheap at-home labor today can hardly compete with products manufactured in Haiti, Singapore, Taiwan, and Korea. Erasing this outdated legislation from the books is one of the objectives of the National Association for the Cottage Industry, a Chicago-based organization that publishes a quarterly newsletter, *Mind Your Own Business at Home,* well worth its subscription price for anyone with a home office or home-based business.

Buyerism, a monthly newsletter "protecting the interests of the small business owner," analyzes business trends and pinpoints areas of opportunities. Originally published to give readers advice on the purchasing of franchises, it now includes much useful information on nonfranchised small-business opportunities and business equipment.

Sideline Business, from the publishers of the magazine *In Business,* is a chatty monthly newsletter combining practical advice with accounts of the experiences of small-business owners and cottage-industry operators.

For a listing of newsletters and their addresses, consult the *Newsletter Yearbook Directory* (Coral Springs, Fla.: B. Klein Publications, 1979).

OTHER SOURCES OF BUSINESS INFORMATION

Soundview Executive Book Summaries provide executives and the operators of businesses with monthly digests of important new books on business-related topics, incorporating innovative ideas, management methods, and business-development techniques. The detailed and professionally written summaries condense a book's major ideas and include tables, charts, and other illustrative material. In addition to the summaries mailed to subscribers each month, briefer reviews call attention to other new business books.

Boardroom Reports, a biweekly newsletter, contains digests of news and articles culled from a wide range of business and technical publications. It also offers advice for business owners and executives.

NEWSPAPERS

Of course, you'll want to read your local newspaper regularly, especially if it is the "newspaper of record" for your village, town, or city. Careful perusal is important if you must keep abreast of notices about changes in local ordinances affecting your business or your home office, invitations to bid on contracts, or even about business bankruptcies that could include some of your clients who owe you money.

Among "national" daily newspapers to consider are *The New York Times, Washington Post, Wall Street Journal,* and *Christian Science Monitor.* A relative newcomer on the national scene, *USA Today,* offers abbreviated national coverage and features, including many off-trail statistics in chart form or as graphics.

The tabloid-sized newspaper, *Barron's: The National Business and Financial Weekly,* ranks behind the *Wall Street Journal* as the newspaper most widely read by the financial and business communities.

LIBRARIES AND HOW TO USE THEM

Your nearby library represents a valuable resource, but most small business operators do not realize how useful a library can be. It may be a library in the public library system (village, town, county, or state), a nearby college or university library, or a specialized library operated by a corporation, foundation, or research institution.

The first step in locating a library is to consult the *American Library Directory* (New York: R. R. Bowker, annual). Libraries are listed there geographically, making it easy to find those that are nearby. Specialized collections and special libraries are listed in the

Directory of Special Libraries and Information Centers (Detroit Mich.: Gale Research Company, biennial). Among its business-related indexes are subject headings for libraries specializing in business and business administration, business history, international business, business research, business statistics, management, and commerce and trade.

See also the Sources and Resources section at the back of this book. It contains a list of libraries specializing in books and magazines on business-oriented subjects, including university, college, corporate, and public libraries with extensive collections of business books and periodicals.

You should make an appointment to meet the library director or librarian in charge of the library you plan to use regularly to supplement your own modest reference collection. Introduce yourself and explain your needs. In making a request for specific assistance, it's a good idea to proceed from the general to the specific. Remember, too, that reference librarians know their collections and can find a fact or a statistic for you quicker than you can by browsing.

Most librarians are eager to improve their collections so as to meet the needs of library users. Suggestions about titles that could be added are always welcome. Some libraries even have printed forms for recording information about a suggested title. If you expect to be a frequent user of a particular book not owned by a library, don't hesitate to ask the librarian to buy it or to borrow a copy from another library through the interlibrary loan facilities.

WHERE TO BEGIN A SEARCH

The most logical place to start a generalized search for information is in *The New York Times Index* (1851 to present) or the *Reader's Guide to Periodical Literature* (1900 to present). Before using the latter publication, check the listing of magazines indexed in it; many specialized periodicals, including business publications, are not indexed.

Another good starting place for a narrower information search are the many specialized indexes that are issued monthly and in quarterly and annual cumulations. These include:

Applied Science and Technology Index (1958 to present) Successor in part to the *Industrial Arts Index* (1913–57). Covers about 225 American and British periodicals in the fields of aeronautics, automation, chemistry, construction, electricity and electrical communication, engineering, geology and metallurgy, industrial and mechanical arts, machinery, physics, transportation, and related subjects.

Art Index (1913 to present) Covers about 190 American and foreign fine-arts periodicals.

Biological and Agricultural Index (1964 to present) Successor to the *Agricultural Index* (1916–63). A detailed index to about two hundred periodicals in the biological and agricultural sciences.

Business Periodicals Index (1958 to present) Continues in part the *Industrial Arts Index* (1913–57). Subject index to about 170 periodicals in the fields of accounting, advertising, banking and finance, general business, insurance, labor and management, marketing and purchasing, public administration, and specific businesses, industries, and trades.

Education Index (1929 to present) Indexes about 240 periodicals covering all phases of education.

Humanities Index (1974 to present) Continues in part the *Social Sciences and Humanities Index* (1907–74). Indexes periodicals in the fields of archaeology and classical studies, geographical area studies, folklore, history, language and literature, literary and political criticism, performing arts, philosophy, religion, theology, and related subjects.

Index to Legal Periodicals (1908 to present) An index to more than 380 legal periodicals; earlier volumes also indexed bar-association and judicial-council reports.

Social Sciences Index (1974 to present) Continues in part the *Social Sciences and Humanities Index* (1907–74). Index to periodicals in the fields of anthropology, area studies, economics, environmental science, geography, law and criminology, medical sciences, political science, psychology, public administration, sociology, and related subjects.

The *F & S Index, United States* indexes reports, newspapers, trade journals, business magazines, and government publications containing business information. A similar volume, the *F & S Index, International*, does the same for world-wide business data.

Only larger libraries will have these specialized indexes. If you also use general periodical indexes, you will find some overlap in coverage, but not enough to be annoying.

To ascertain the titles of the books on a particular subject owned by the library you are using, consult its card catalog or microfiche subject catalog. You should also consult the subject guide volumes of *Books in Print* (New York: R. R. Bowker, annual). This massive set is in three parts and catalogs every book in print by author, title, and subject. Supplements are issued at intervals to update its ten volumes; a separate *Paperbound Books in Print* and supplements are also published. For information on books scheduled to be published, consult *Forthcoming Books*, all published by R. R. Bowker.

GOVERNMENT INFORMATION SOURCES

One of the most often overlooked sources of information is the office of your congressman or senator, who maintain staffs for the purpose of liaison with constituents. (Because of their smaller constituencies, congressional staffs may give faster service than senatorial staffs.) Members of Congress also have access to the highly efficient Congressional Reference Service of the Library of Congress.

If you are not sure of the federal agency to which to direct an inquiry, a good starting place is one of the thirty-seven federal information centers located in major cities. These will supply information about government agencies and programs and will assist with any question about the federal government or its activities. (See Sources and Resources Section for a list of federal information centers and their addresses.)

If the information you seek falls within the scope of an agency of the executive branch of the federal government, you should address the Public Information Office of that agency at the address shown in the previously cited *United States Government Manual*. Many states also maintain commerce departments for the specific purpose of encouraging business and industry.

Some public libraries are designated as depository libraries and maintain full or partial collections of government documents. The reference librarian at your local library can tell you which libraries in your area are designated as depositories.

The Government Printing Office (GPO) is one of the largest publishers of printed materials anywhere in the world, yet its publications are largely unknown to the public. To facilitate the distribution of GPO publications, six sales centers are maintained in

Washington, D.C., and twenty others have been set up in various parts of the country. (See Sources and Resources Section for a list of cities in which the GPO maintains bookstores and their addresses.) Such outlets carry the best-selling GPO publications plus a selection of those of regional interest. Each GPO bookstore maintains an updated microfiche file listing all GPO publications. Any in-print publication may be obtained by mail from the Superintendent of Documents, Government Printing Office, Washington, D.C. 20402. Titles of available GPO publications may be found in the monthly GPO catalog or the biweekly *Selected List of U.S. Government Publications.*

THE TRADE PRESS

Specialized trade magazines and directories are an important source of business information. You can search out names, addresses, circulations, advertising rates, and information about magazines and newspapers published in the United States and Canada in the *Ayer Directory of Publications* (Philadelphia: N. W. Ayer & Son, annual) and U.S., Canadian, and foreign magazines in *Ulrich's International Periodicals Directory* (New York: R. R. Bowker, annual); *The Standard Periodical Directory* (New York: Oxbridge Communications, Inc., annual) is an alternate source of magazine information. Trade directories are listed in the *Guide to American Directories,* edited by B. Klein (Coral Springs, Fla: B. Klein Publications, irregular), which includes about 5,500 educational, philanthropic, and similar activities, as well as business and professional directories. Another source of information about trade directories is *Directory of Directories: An Annotated Guide to Business and Industrial Directories, Professional and Scientific Rosters, and Other Lists and Guides of All Kinds*, edited by James M. Ethridge (Detroit: Gale Research, irregular).

TECHNIQUES
FOR THE
HOME OFFICE

Part Three

TECHNIQUES FOR THE HOME OFFICE

TWENTY

The Bottom Line: Budgeting to Get There

Budgets are the road maps by which businesses plan their moves into the future. They have been called the tools for turning expectations into reality. Properly performed, budgeting requires careful consideration of basic objectives, policies, plans, and resources. Budgeting, in short, forces you to think about where you are going and to establish proper control and evaluation procedures. It is the opposite of the "cookie jar" method used by many householders to control home expenses.

Regardless of whether your home office is part of a profit-making enterprise or not, you'll need two basic budgets: the budget under which you set up your home office and furnish it and another under which you will operate it.

For a start-up budget, if remodeling is involved, you should include such fixed costs as materials (wallboard, lumber, wiring) and contractors services or decorating costs (paint, wallpaper, carpeting, fixtures). These will represent more or less permanent changes or additions to your home. The money you spend for things that become a permanent part of your home (for example, a safe embedded in the concrete floor of your basement) are capital expenses and not subject to state sales taxes.

Other costs you should budget for will cover furnishings (desks, tables, chairs, curtains, blinds, shades, wall decorations), equipment (typewriter, computer, printer, copier, recording equipment, telephone answering machine), and miscellaneous costs (office supplies, letterhead paper, printed envelopes). Many of these can serve to reduce your tax obligation, either as assets to be depreciated or as operating expenses. Among the other expenses you should not overlook in your start-up and operating budgets are utilities (electricity, gas, telephone), fuel oil, supplies, legal and professional fees, and insurance (fire, theft, flood, public liability). You will be paying for many of these already as part of your household expenses, and a portion can be allocated to the expense of operating a home office, further reducing your income tax (see chapter 25).

In a sense, the size of your start-up budget will be governed not so much by your plans for the design and furnishing of your home office as it will be by the amount of start-up money available. If money is tight, you may have to do the decorating and

		JAN	FEB	MAR	APR	MAY	JUN
Auto	(B)	150.00	150.00	150.00	150.00	150.00	150.00
	(A)	279.96	159.15	179.32	41.86	63.20	200.00
Electric	(B)	100.00	100.00	100.00	100.00	100.00	100.00
	(A)	109.68	107.48	110.86	104.20	100.94	103.41
Ent'n't	(B)	100.00	100.00	100.00	100.00	100.00	100.00
	(A)		194.74	189.87		275.87	204.42
Fuel Oil	(B)		200.00		200.00		
	(A)	84.88	245.12		122.96		
Gas	(B)	50.00	50.00	50.00	50.00	50.00	50.00
	(A)	62.01	50.49	60.73	58.33	59.58	35.71
Insur.	(B)						800.00
	(A)						917.00
Equipm't	(B)						500.00
	(A)						
Supplies	(B)	30.00	30.00	30.00	30.00	30.00	30.00
	(A)				97.56		
Labor	(B)	50.00	50.00	50.00	50.00	50.00	50.00
	(A)						321.00
Postage	(B)	60.00	60.00	60.00	60.00	60.00	60.00
	(A)	74.37	41.60	77.30	37.05	21.19	83.27
Services	(B)	50.00	50.00	50.00	50.00	50.00	50.00
	(A)	50.00	50.00	50.00	50.00	50.00	50.00
Phone	(B)	150.00	150.00	150.00	150.00	150.00	150.00
	(A)	156.44	247.06	145.10	59.40	220.16	164.39
Tolls	(B)	5.00	5.00	5.00	5.00	5.00	5.00
	(A)	6.25	7.00	7.00	4.70	3.75	4.00
Travel	(B)	100.00	100.00	100.00	100.00	100.00	100.00
	(A)				318.00		

furnishing of your home office in stages. Your operating budget is another thing, since it may depend on future receipts generated by your home office, if any.

One method I use in budgeting is a fourteen-column chart. The first column shows the categories of expenses, broken down into fixed and variable expenses. The next twelve columns show the

JUL	AUG	SEP	OCT	NOV	DEC	TOTAL
150.00	150.00	150.00	150.00	150.00	150.00	1800.00
130.44	108.50	115.15	117.35	150.00	200.00	1744.93
100.00	100.00	100.00	100.00	100.00	100.00	1200.00
150.29	138.39	173.68	211.54	111.27	107.98	1527.72
100.00	100.00	100.00	100.00	100.00	100.00	1200.00
153.98	133.35	33.90	199.65	199.76		1585.54
					200.00	600.00
				49.70	63.33	565.93
50.00	50.00	50.00		50.00	50.00	600.00
31.27	29.88	32.29	16.85	44.28	54.53	535.95
						800.00
						917.00
					500.00	1000.00
	816.35					816.35
30.00	30.00	30.00	30.00	30.00	30.00	360.00
	144.50				110.00	352.06
50.00	50.00	50.00	50.00	50.00	50.00	600.00
280.00						580.00
60.00	60.00	60.00	60.00	60.00	60.00	720.00
44.20	147.38	122.20	91.06	6.47	20.90	766.99
50.00	50.00	50.00	50.00	50.00	50.00	600.00
50.00	50.00	50.00	50.00	50.00	50.00	600.00
150.00	150.00	150.00	150.00	150.00	150.00	1800.00
134.37	153.08	150.00	102.09	129.52	145.88	1807.47
5.00	5.00	5.00	5.00	5.00	5.00	60.00
3.00	4.50	1.50	2.00	3.75	4.00	51.45
100.00	100.00	100.00	100.00	100.00	100.00	1200.00
463.00			366.00			1147.00

Total-Budget 12,540.00
Total-*Actual* 12,983.40

months of the year, and the last column is reserved for totals, horizontally and vertically. Each horizontal category, whether fixed or variable, is made up of two lines, budgeted and actual. The reason for this is that even anticipated "fixed" expenses (e.g., taxes and utility costs) are subject to fluctuations, invariably upward.

The trick in budget control is to establish categories small enough to be kept under observation but large enough so that the budget does not need the services of a part time accountant or bookkeeper to keep abreast of it. The preceding table shows a hypothetical budget for a typical home office.

Even if your home office generates no income, you should keep track of expenses with a monthly budget so that you will know exactly what it is costing you to operate a home office (and its contribution to reducing your taxes, if you use it as a business expense).

Here are some tips to help you in budgeting for and operating your home office:

1. Understand your goals and formulate a spending plan for the things you are going to buy. Next, put this plan down on paper in the form of a budget and stick to it.

2. Comparison shop. Compare specifications in catalogs. Read labels. Obtain information from industry and consumer organizations. Ask questions. Find out the names of others locally who may have bought the same equipment. Has the item met their expectations? Have service calls been frequent? Has service been satisfactory? Has the warranty period been sufficiently long?

3. Ascertain from the vendor the protection you have under warranties and service contracts. What are the vendor's responsibilities? The manufacturer's? Is the warranty limited or unlimited?

4. Know when to buy. Seasonality often has a great effect on price. Knowledge of an impending model change (which is frequently only cosmetic) can sometimes be a good reason for waiting; a discontinued model at a reduced price can be a wise purchase.

5. Familiarize yourself with industry merchandising practices. If the item you buy turns out to be defective, will you be in a better bargaining position if you charge it on your credit card or buy it on credit terms? Can you negotiate a discount by paying for the item in cash?

TWENTY-ONE

In a Family Way: Separating Home and Office

The most successful home offices have invariably been those in which there is separation between home and office activities. This is not so much to ensure that home activities do not interfere with office activities as it is to afford a place to which the home-office worker can retreat when the day's work is over.

For some, however, a home office can put a strain on family relationships. Those who work at home soon discover that proximity brings closer contact with the spouse and with family members. Frequent traffic within the home near or through the home office invariably gives rise to incidents. At the same time, your isolation in a home office can bring on the resentment of other family members who may feel that their time with you has been curtailed or even totally robbed.

For couples, particularly those whose relationship is under stress for other reasons, a home office can lead to disaster. The often-quoted remark "I married you for better or worse but not for lunch" echoes the spouse's frustration with a mate who is always around and under foot.

A home office can be such an inviting place to spend one's time that you may soon discover that your problem is tearing yourself away from your home office in order to find relaxation.

One solution to this problem is to go to lunch as often as your budget will permit and so long as your beltline can stand it. On the plus side, you can use the lunch hour to combat the problem of visitors who telephone and ask to drop in. Instead, arrange to meet clients and callers at a restaurant near your home.

Proximity of one's home office to one's home presents what is perhaps the greatest danger: that of becoming a home-office workaholic. Coined by Dr. Wayne E. Oates, professor of psychiatry and behavioral sciences at the University of Louisville School of Medicine, the terms "workaholic" and "workaholism" were first used in his 1971 book *Confessions of a Workaholic*.

Oddly, the danger may be more to the members of your family than to yourself. Marilyn Machlowitz, who studied a hundred workaholics of both sexes, concluded that they are a remarkably healthy group. "Workaholics typically love what they do, and research shows that work satisfaction is linked to good health and longevity."

In her opinion, it's not workaholics who suffer; it's the people around them. When workaholics have satisfactory marriages or relationships, it's usually because their partners have adapted to the workaholic's work habits, schedule, and life-style.

"There is a difference between being a hard worker and a workaholic," Dr. Machlowitz insists. "Hard workers can slow down when the pressure is off or a goal is met. Workaholics persist in their toil in response to some inner need."

One of the major reasons for avoiding workaholism is that many workaholics share the traits and profiles of Type A personalities. Type A behavior patterns have been linked to heart disease in studies by two San Francisco cardiologists, Meyer Friedman and Ray H. Rosenman, who defined Type A behavior as "a complex of personality traits, including excessive competitive drive, aggressiveness, impatience, and a harrying sense of time urgency."

Type A personalities in the world of business are ambitious, hard driving, and highly competitive. Their intense drive forces them to get things done at all costs, and they habitually pit themselves against the clock.

By contrast, Type B personalities often work just as hard but are more easygoing, with an ability to balance work with leisure activities and with no feeling of racing against time. One result is that Type B personalities are often more efficient than Type As.

Although most of us are mixtures of the two, one or the other type is usually dominant. Paradoxically, Type A personalities often have no knowledge that the nearly constant pressures they operate under may come from within themselves and are self-imposed rather than caused by external circumstances.

David C. Glass, professor of psychology at the City University of New York, has concluded:

> The Type A person works hard and fast to succeed and in striving toward his goals, he suppresses feelings such as fatigue that might interfere with his performance. Type A gets angry if someone or something gets in the way of their suc-

cess. I submit that all of these traits suggest a person who rises to master challenges out of need to control his world.

Lawrence Susser, formerly a pediatrician, now practicing psychiatry in Nantucket, Massachusetts, says it's a myth that the workaholic is efficient. It takes workaholics twelve hours to do what others can do in only eight, he claims; workaholics refuse to accept that what they took twelve hours to do could have been done in eight.

In his practice, Susser treats compulsive workaholics with what he describes as "play therapy," which starts with a six- to eight-hour hike and includes a two-hour lunch. He also suggests using such measures as reading something not related to your work and showing appreciation to your family. He maintains that workaholics are committing slow suicide by refusing to allow the child inside them to come out to play.

"I don't want to make it sound simple," Dr. Susser says, "but look at it this way: workaholism is one addiction that can be literally fun to give up."

TWENTY-TWO

Sharing the Risk: Insurance for the Home Office

No one knows when insurance originated. Thousands of years ago, groups of Chinese merchants devised an ingenious way of protecting themselves against the hazards of river rapids and pirates by dividing their cargoes among several boats. This was not insurance as we know it, but it was remarkably similar in principle to modern insurance.

In the great fire that raged through London in 1666, some 14,000 buildings were destroyed and 200,000 persons were left homeless. One lasting effect of the conflagration was the founding of the first fire insurance company within a year.

Insurance got off to a shaky start in the New World; the first fire insurance company was formed in 1735 but lasted only five years.

In 1752, Benjamin Franklin, who seemed to have his hand in everything in those days, helped to form the Philadelphia Contributorship for the Insurance of Homes from Loss by Fire. Also known as "the Hand in Hand," this company is still in existence.

By their very nature and location, offices at home present special insurance problems. For most home offices, the protections afforded by a homeowner's or renter's insurance policy will afford all the coverage needed. However, there are several kinds of homeowner's and renter's packages, and it will be useful to review them here:

Homeowner's Policies HO–1, HO–2, and HO–5

As Table 22.1 shows, the basic homeowner's policy (HO-1) provides coverage against eleven specified perils on a "named peril" basis. This form is infrequently used because it provides only minimum coverage.

The broad form, HO-2, covers you against the same eleven perils plus seven more—all the perils shown in Table 22.1. This form is more popular.

The comprehensive form, HO-5, covers all perils except for a few that are specifically excluded. This is the Cadillac of homeowners policies and priced accordingly.

Special or All-Risk Policy (HO–3)

A special policy (HO-3) offers the same broad "all-risk" coverage on your dwelling and other associated structures as the comprehensive form, HO-5, but less extensive coverage on personal property.

Renter's Policy (HO–4)

This tenant's policy, or contents broad form (HO-4), is designed for renters of houses or apartments or owners of cooperative apartments. It insures the household contents and personal belongings against all perils included in the broad form (HO-2). Insurance on the building, of course, is the responsibility of the

Table 22.1

PERILS AGAINST WHICH PROPERTIES ARE INSURED UNDER THE VARIOUS HOMEOWNERS POLICIES

Basic HO-1	Broad HO-2	Special HO-3	Renter's HO-4	Compre-hensive HO-5	Condo-minium HO-6	Older Home HO-8	PERILS
■	■	■	■	■	■	■	1. Fire or lightning
■	■	■	■	■	■	■	2. Loss of property removed from premises endangered by fire or other perils*
■	■	■	■	■	■	■	3. Windstorm or hail
■	■	■	■	■	■	■	4. Explosion
■	■	■	■	■	■	■	5. Riot or civil commotion
■	■	■	■	■	■	■	6. Aircraft
■	■	■	■	■	■	■	7. Vehicles
■	■	■	■	■	■	■	8. Smoke
■	■	■	■	■	■	■	9. Vandalism and malicious mischief
■	■	■	■	■	■	■	10. Theft
■	■	■	■	■	■	■	11. Breakage of glass constituting a part of the building
	■	■	■	■	■		12. Falling objects
	■	■	■	■	■		13. Weight of ice, snow, sleet
	■	■	■	■	■		14. Collapse of building(s) or any part thereof
	■	■	■	■	■		15. Sudden and accidental tearing asunder, cracking, burning, or bulging of a steam or hot water heating system or of appliances for heating water
	■	■	■	■	■		16. Accidental discharge, leakage or overflow of water or steam from within a plumbing, heating or air-conditioning system or domestic appliance
	■	■	■	■	■		17. Freezing of plumbing, heating and air-conditioning systems and domestic appliances
	■	■	■	■	■		18. Sudden and accidental injury from artificially generated currents to electrical appliances, devices, fixtures and wiring (TV and radio tubes not included)
		■		■			All perils except flood, earthquake, war, nuclear accident and others specified in your policy. Check your policy for a complete listing of perils excluded.

■ Dwelling and Personal Property   ■ Personal Property only
■ Dwelling only

* Included as a peril in traditional forms of the homeowners policy; as an additional coverage in the simplified (HO-76) policies.

landlord or the cooperative association. The renter's policy does provide coverage for additional living expenses.

Condominium-Unit Owner's Policy (HO-6)

A condominium association usually buys insurance to cover the condominium buildings and liability. However, a special condominium-unit owner's policy (HO-6) is available for unit owners who wish to insure their personal property or to cover changes and alterations they have made that are not covered by the association's policy. The coverages are basically the same as those provided by the renter's policy (HO-4).

Older Home Insurance (HO–8)

Most homeowners policies provide for damage to the building to be paid for on the basis of replacement costs without deduction for depreciation if the policyholder carries insurance for at least 80 percent of the replacement costs.

Older homes, however, are usually so constructed as to make it economically unfeasible to duplicate them following a loss. For example, ornate woodwork, leaded glass windows, and carved plaster ceilings might be too expensive to replace (if the artisans could be found to do the work).

The HO-8 policy is designed so that owners of older homes can carry lower limits of insurance—such as the market value of the home—rather than the 80 percent of replacement cost used with newer homes. The idea is to return the dwelling to serviceable condition but not necessarily through the use of materials of the same kind or quality as in the original.

This policy insures the property against the same perils as the basic form (HO-1) but restricts coverage of losses by theft to a maximum of a thousand dollars.

Mobile-Home Owner's Policy

A special policy is available for those who own and occupy a mobile home that is at least ten feet wide by forty feet long. The mobile-home policy provides basically the same coverages as the homeowner's broad-form policy (HO-2). Because of the difference in construction and the greater susceptibility of mobile homes to wind damage, premiums for mobile-home policies are much higher than for those on a conventional house.

Simplified Homeowner's Policies (HO-76)

In 1976 the insurance industry introduced a series of simplified and abbreviated versions of policies HO–1 through HO–6, referred to as the HO–76 program. Revisions to the longer policies included some minor changes in the coverages, largely to take into account today's inflated values. Such changes have not altered rating or price structures, however. Thus coverage of trees, shrubs, plants, or lawns is increased from $250 to $500 in HO–76 policies, and credit card, forgery, and counterfeit-money coverage of $500 —offered as an option in the traditional policies—is automatically included.

Additional Coverages

When a house is destroyed by fire or other cause, certain expenses are incurred that go beyond the repair of the house itself. Six of the "after-the-fact" expenses are added to homeowners' policies:

1. Debris removal. The insurance company will pay reasonable expenses for carting the damaged property away.
2. Reasonable repairs. When temporary repairs are necessary to protect property from further damage (for example patching a leaking roof resulting from a fire), the insurance company will pay for this additional expense.
3. The insurance company will pay for certain insured perils (but not windstorms) for loss of any tree, shrub, or plant (or an overall maximum of 5 percent of the limit of insurance on the dwelling). Lawns are also covered.
4. In areas in which the fire department levies a service charge for fire department services, the insurance company will pay up to $250.

5. When property is rescued from a dwelling, this coverage protects it for up to thirty days against direct loss from any cause.

6. The insurance company will reimburse you up to $500 should you lose your credit cards and others charge purchases to your accounts. This same limit applies to check forgery or a loss resulting from the acceptance in good faith of counterfeit money. This coverage also applies to renter's, condominium, and mobile-home policies.

Personal-Articles Coverage

If you have certain property in your home that may be more valuable than the limits set under the personal-property coverage of a homeowner's or tenant's policy, you should purchase a personal-articles "floater" as separate coverage or as an endorsement to your homeowner's policy. The term "floater" derives from the fact that the coverage is in force no matter where the property is located at the time of the loss—it "floats" with the property.

Flood and Earthquake Insurance

Homeowners policies do not cover damage resulting from floods or earthquake (although a flooded basement caused by a broken water pipe is covered). If you live in flood-prone or seismically active areas, you may want to consider such coverages, subject to deductibles, against these perils.

Flood insurance is offered by the Federal Insurance Administration. Because flood insurance is marketable only to people who live in areas likely to be flooded, it is uneconomical for private insurers to offer such coverage. To qualify for flood coverage, the property must be located in a community that has agreed to put into effect land-use control measures to reduce losses from future flooding.

Earthquakes strike most frequently on the Pacific Coast, so it is not surprising that half of all earthquake policies are written in California. Many other states are vulnerable to earthquakes, however, and earthquake insurance is available through private insurers. Earthquake insurance is usually written as an addition to fire insurance, a homeowner's policy, or other property insurance.

Safe Deposit Insurance

Banks and your homeowner's policy provide only limited coverage of items kept in safe deposit boxes, so you may want to get a separate safe deposit insurance policy to supplement this protection. Such policies usually provide all-risk coverage for securities and burglary and robbery coverage for other valuables. But be sure to keep a list of the contents of your safe deposit box and keep it up to date.

Computer Insurance

Any computer used in the home for household or hobbyist uses is, by definition, a home computer. Generally, such computers are covered under your homeowner's policy, although computers are not specifically mentioned in such policies. Theoretically, a computer in the home is no different from any other household appliance or property that might be stolen or damaged. Some policies will pay for the loss on the basis of depreciated value; others call for replacement of the appliance with like merchandise.

Even with coverage under a homeowner's policy, you may want to obtain the additional protection afforded by a floater policy. Some insurance companies are issuing special computer floaters, although the standard floater form is adequate. To offset the cost of the additional premium, you can always reduce your personal-property coverage under your homeowner's policy by an equivalent amount.

Protection for software is quite another matter. In the event of a loss of diskettes—even those containing valuable data—your reimbursement will only be for the value of a blank diskette.

Business Insurance

If your home office is used for professional purposes (which brings visitors and callers to your home) or if you operate a small business from your home, your homeowner's policy will no longer cover you. For insurance purposes, it's a whole new ballgame, and you should investigate the kinds of insurance available.

There are several ways of looking at business insurance. The soundest and most practical from the viewpoint of someone with a

professional or commercial office at home is to analyze potential
areas of loss. Loss can occur in four major areas:

1. *Property loss*, resulting from physical damage, loss of the use
   of the property, or criminal activity. Physical damage can be
   caused by fire, windstorm, or vandalism—but these hazards
   may already be covered by your homeowner's or apartment
   dweller's policy.
2. *Liability loss*, as a result of bodily injury or property damage
   suffered by another. Again, your homeowner's or apartment-
   dweller's policy may cover this.
3. *Key-person loss*. If your home office is part of a business you
   operate, you should perhaps consider insurance to cover the
   loss of your services as a key person. A key person may be
   an owner with special talents, but it can also be an employee
   with special talents whose presence is necessary to assure the
   survival of the enterprise. A sole proprietor, partner, or major
   stockholder of a closely held corporation may be a key person, because death or disability for an extended period could
   impose serious financial hardship.
4. *Business-interruption losses* may occur as a result of fire or
   other disaster, but they can also be caused when an important
   supplier or customer suffers a loss or interruption of business.

Once you have analyzed your risk exposure, you can start by
practicing *risk avoidance*. If flooding is a not infrequent event in
your area, you'd be wise not to set up your home office in your
basement and fill it with expensive electronic equipment. Next, you
should decide which of the several risks you cannot avoid you will
cover yourself—this is referred to as being "self-insured"—and
which you wish to share with an insurance company.

Generally speaking, you'll need four kinds of insurance: fire,
liability, automobile, and workers' compensation (the latter only if
you employ someone). Among the other kinds of insurance you
may want to consider are business-interruption insurance, crime
insurance, glass insurance, rent insurance, employee-benefit coverage, group life insurance, group health insurance, disability in-
surance, and key-person insurance.

Here are some things you should know:

Fire Insurance

You can add coverage against additional perils—windstorm, hail, smoke damage, explosion, vandalism, and malicious mischief —to existing fire insurance coverage at a small additional cost. If you think you need such comprehensive coverage and have no fire insurance now, investigate a broad all-risk contract rather than individual policies.

Your insurance company has the choice of indemnifying you in one of three ways in the event of loss: it may pay you the cash value of the property at the time of the loss, or it may repair or replace the property with other items of like kind and quality.

You can insure the property of others. For example, editors reading manuscripts can obtain a valuable-papers policy to cover them while in their possession or in transit.

Even though you may have several overlapping insurance policies on the same property, you'll only be able to collect on the amount of the actual loss. Each of the insurers will pay a proportional share.

You may have a standard fire insurance policy now, but you'll need a special policy to cover the loss by fire of books of account, bills, currency, deeds, notes, evidence of debt, and securities.

Read the fine print: misrepresenting to or concealing from an insurer any material fact or circumstance pertaining to an insurance policy or the interest of the insured may cause the policy to be voided. If by any of your actions you increase the risk of fire, your coverage may be suspended for losses not originating from the increased risk.

Because you must furnish to your insurance company within sixty days (unless an extension is granted) a complete inventory of the destroyed, damaged, and undamaged property showing quantities, costs, actual cash values, and amount of losses claimed, it will be to your advantage to have such an inventory before a fire occurs. Of course, a copy should be stored in a safe place away from the premises.

If you and your insurance company disagree on the amount of loss, the dispute may be referred to special appraisers as described in your policy.

You may cancel your policy at any time without notice and obtain a refund of a portion of the premium you have paid. But the insurance company—on five days' written notice—may also cancel your policy and refund the unused portion of the premium.

Fire-insurance policies are designed to cover disaster situations. If you accept a coinsurance clause in your policy, your premiums will be substantially reduced. Such a clause states that you must carry insurance of a specified percentage of the total value of the insured property (usually 80 or 90 percent). If you carry less than this, you cannot collect the full amount of your loss, however small.

If your loss has been caused by the negligence of another, your insurer has the right to sue this negligent third party (or the third party's insurer) for the amount you have recovered. This is called subrogation. Insurers will waive this right at your request.

Liability Insurance

Liability limits of a million dollars are no longer considered large in the light of recent jury awards.

Most liability policies require that you notify the insurer immediately of any incident occurring on your property that might result in a future claim.

You can now get protection against personal injuries (libel or slander) as well as for bodily injuries—but only if specifically written in the policy and covered.

Even though a false or fraudulent liability suit has been brought against you, your insurer will also pay court costs, legal fees, and interest judgments over and above the judgments themselves.

You can be held liable for the acts of others under contracts you have signed with them. Such liability can be covered by insurance.

Automobile Insurance

Consider raising the amount of your deductible under your automobile policy. Doing so will reduce the size of your premiums.

Coverage of medical payments (including your own) arising from automobile accidents are paid without regard for the question of negligence.

Most states now require you to have liability insurance or to be prepared to provide other proof of financial responsibility (such as a surety bond) in the event of an accident.

You can purchase uninsured-motorist protection to cover any injuries to you caused by someone who has no insurance.

If the car or truck of an employee or subcontractor becomes involved in an accident, you can be held legally liable even though you do not own the vehicle.

Personal property left in an automobile (and not attached to it) is not covered under your automobile policy.

Workers' Compensation Insurance

Federal law (and some state laws, as well as common law) requires that an employer provide employees with a safe place to work, hire competent fellow employees, provide safe tools and equipment, and warn employees of an existing danger. An employer who fails to do these things is liable for damage suits brought by an employee and risks a fine and prosecution.

In most states, you are required to have workers' compensation insurance. Rates vary on the basis of the degree of safety of the workplace and the hazardous nature of the occupation. Not every employee is covered by workers' compensation laws, which vary from state to state.

Employers can save money on workers' compensation insurance by properly classifying employees and by keeping accident frequencies low. State law (not federal law) determines the size and kind of benefits payable under compensation claims.

Crime Insurance

Burglary insurance excludes property such as books of account, manuscripts, and other valuable papers in your possession. In addition to cash, burglary insurance can be written to cover inventoried merchandise or property damaged in the course of a burglary.

Coverage is in force under burglar insurance policies only if there are *visible* marks of forced entry into the premises.

Robbery and burglary are two different crimes. Robbery insurance will protect from loss of property, money, and securities by force, trickery, or threat of violence on or off your premises.

You should investigate a small-business comprehensive crime

policy. In addition to protection from burglary and robbery, it covers other types of loss by theft, destruction, and "mysterious disappearance" of money and securities, including thefts by any of your employees.

If your home office is located in what is considered a high-crime area and you have been refused burglary and robbery insurance or cannot obtain it without paying exorbitant rates, investigate the availability of getting help through the Federal Crime Insurance Program, instituted in 1971. (Twenty-seven states, the District of Columbia, Puerto Rico, and the Virgin Islands participate in the program, but one state—New York—accounts for 60 percent of the policies written and 70 percent of the dollar amount of the insurance in force.)

Key-Person Insurance

Proceeds of a key-person policy are not subject to taxation as income, nor are premiums a deductible business expense.

You can borrow against the cash value of key-person insurance.

TWENTY-THREE

Money Matters: Money and Banking

Money may be the root of all evil, but in one form or another, it is the indisputable lifeblood of everyday life, including that of your home, home office, or small business. Sooner or later, you will have to face the problem of money and deal with the usual repositories of money—banks—and you should know something about them.

If you want to start off on the right foot, your first move should be to open a checking account. It doesn't matter that you already have a checking account. Open another—a completely separate account into which you will deposit any income generated by the work you do in your home office and from which you can pay any expenses in connection with its operation. By not blending home-office income and expenses with your personal account, you'll make bookkeeping and the preparation of income tax returns much easier.

Most people choose a bank for the same reasons they shop at a particular store: force of habit or simple convenience. These are the worst reasons for using a bank. Now that banking deregulation has introduced competition into the banking scene, it will be to your advantage to shop around. Generally speaking, bank size and customer service do not go hand in hand. If you are looking for personal attention, you'll probably find it at a smaller bank at which you can establish a personal relationship.

What to Look for in a Bank

Don't be seduced by unimportant statistics, for example, the large number of branches in a bank's system. Chances are you'll be doing most of your banking at only one branch. If you have several banks from which to choose, ascertain the following:

Are the lines long at peak times at the bank of your choice? If you're thinking about banking with a bank in an industrial area or a downtown business district, for example, you can probably forget about transacting any business on Fridays at noon.

How large must the minimum opening deposit be? What is the waiting period before funds are available if you deposit cash? A check on a local bank for more than a hundred dollars? A check in the same amount from a bank in a neighboring state? Or a check in the same amount from a bank several thousand miles away?

Will the bank cash third-party checks? What is the fee for a deposited check that bounces? What is the stop-payment fee? Does the bank accept direct deposits?

On the basis of this information, you may be able to eliminate one or more banks. Now proceed to another round of questions:

Does the bank offer special (economy) checking accounts? What minimum balance is required to be kept in each type of account? Is it a minimum average balance (this is better for you) or a minimum dollar balance? What is the monthly service charge on an ordinary checking account? For a special account? What is the fee on each check written or deposit transaction? For a NOW (negotiated order of withdrawal) interest-bearing checking account? For a money-market checking account? (Also sometimes called a super-NOW account.) For a money-market savings account?

The answers to these questions will probably surprise you. You may find that some accounts, for example, super-NOW accounts, are unattractive because of the high minimum balance and service charges.

If you think you will be needing money at odd hours at locations away from your home, you may want to consider how many ATMs (automated teller machines) are in your prospective bank's system. Another consideration could be the bank's plans for hooking into banking networks in other areas—this could be important if you travel a lot.

If you decide on a bank because of its network of ATMs, be sure to visit the ones you are likely to be using, especially in urban areas. They may be in a separate building with a locked door, in the bank's vestibule, or out in the street. Assault and robbery of customers at ATMs has become an increasing problem, especially in cities, and security considerations should be paramount.

Be sure to inquire about each bank's special services for customers. Does the bank offer free checking? (Many banks offer this to senior citizens, students, and other eligible groups.) Does the bank offer coverage of overdrafts? This will allow you to occasionally write a check when the balance in your account cannot cover it. There's a charge, of course, but it avoids the embarrassment of a bounced check (for which there will be a charge).

My bank calls this "convenience credit," the Chase Bank describes it as "overdraft checking," and the Bank of California knows it as a "money check." Other special services may include free investment advice and free estate-planning services.

The lending policy of a bank is also worth investigating before you decide where to bank. Inquire what the bank's rates are for unsecured loans to preferred customers and nonpreferred customers. "Preferred customers" are those who maintain checking and savings accounts with the bank. The interest rate for them can be as much as $2\frac{1}{2}$ percent lower than for ordinary customers.

Definitions of a "nonpreferred customer" may vary from bank to bank. It can mean that the applicant for a loan has no account with the bank, or it may be used to describe someone with an account who has not yet achieved preferred status.

Understandably, bankers don't like to lend money to "walk-ins"

—people they don't know—so an unsecured personal loan is something you won't be able to get until you have established a relationship with the bank you select. Even so, ask about current loan interest rates at several banks; a bank whose interest rates are lower than others is likely to have lower rates in the future.

Once you have decided on the bank at which your new account will be opened, work at cultivating a relationship. If it is a small bank or a branch in a large system, invite the manager to lunch and discuss your plans for the future. Remember to keep the luncheon conversation relaxed. Above all, don't spend the entire lunch hour reciting a litany of your problems with your present bank. Bankers call customers who move from bank to bank "bouncers," and they usually have the same complaints wherever they bank. By keeping the luncheon conversation informal, if problems arise later, you'll discover that bank managers have wide discretionary powers and that your problems will be a lot easier to smooth out. So be sure to make a friend of the manager *before* you need help.

Don't repeat the mistake people frequently make in dealing with banks: if you want to transact any business with your banker in person, be sure to telephone ahead for an appointment. Bankers like to be treated like the professionals they are.

Make an initial deposit in as large an amount as you can afford —preferably larger than the minimum balance below which you must pay for service. You'll receive an account number and a supply of temporary checks to tide you over until your checkbook has been printed with whatever name you have chosen. If you are operating your home office or home-based business as a sole proprietorship, you should distinguish the account title from any other personal accounts you may have. For example, someone establishing a literary agency might include the words "Royalty Account" in the account designation to distinguish such an account.

If you are operating with one or more other persons as a partnership, the bank will ask to see the partnership certificate, as well as evidence that the business has been registered with the county clerk. If you are operating as a corporation, the bank will require a corporate resolution (on a form you can obtain from the bank); this form will have to be signed by an officer of the corporation, and you will have to make an impression of the corporate seal on it.

Making a Deposit

A deposit slip must be used when you want to add more money to your account. The deposit slips you receive as part of your checkbook are preprinted with your account number (but deposit slips you get at bank tables are not so preprinted).

Here are some rules for depositing checks:

Identify each check separately on the deposit slip by listing the ABA transit number (the fractional number in the upper right-hand corner of the check) and the amount of each check.

Endorse all checks for deposit with "For Deposit Only" (a rubber stamp can be used for this purpose), *followed* by your signature and your bank account number—never the other way around.

To receive cash back from a check deposit, enter the full amount of the check deposited. Then write "less cash" on the lower part of the deposit slip and subtract the "less cash" amount from the check total to get the net amount of your deposit.

Always get a receipt for your deposits and be sure to record them in your checkbook register immediately.

To avoid errors and subsequent disputes, never deposit cash in one of those "speedy deposit boxes" that most banks provide for depositors in a hurry.

Safeguarding Your Checking Account

Always reconcile your bank statement as soon as possible. Inspect all canceled checks to make sure no amounts have been raised or signatures forged. You should ascertain from your bank the time limit they will honor in accepting notification of errors. If you detect an error or find evidence of fraud or larceny, notify the bank manager immediately.

Keep your blank checks in a safe place and treat them as you would cash. If any of your checks are lost or stolen, notify the bank and the police immediately. Destroy any blank checks that will not be used and those from an account that has been closed.

When newly printed checks are received, inspect them to verify that your account number is correct. Make certain that all check numbers are included.

Protect your canceled checks. Never discard them intact or in a way that they could fall into the hands of others.

Notify your bank immediately if your address changes. Also notify the bank if your regular monthly statement has not been received as usual or if newly printed checks are late in arriving.

Don't hesitate to stop payment on checks that are old or appear to be lost. (You can stop payment by a simple phone call, but you must confirm this in writing if you want the stop-payment order to remain in effect for more than two weeks.)

Notify your bank if you subsequently recover a check against which a stop-payment order was placed by you.

Don't cross out or change the written part of any check. If you make an error in writing a check, write "canceled" across the face of the check and file it in numerical order with your canceled checks.

Accepting the Checks of Others

Never endorse a check that shows signs of having been altered. Your endorsement means that you have accepted the check and will be responsible for it to anyone who holds it after you.

Never accept a check written in pencil.

Verify that the check is dated fully with month, day, and year. Check amounts should be written in numbers and in words.

Do not accept an undated check.

Do not accept a check that is more than one month old unless you can verify its status with the bank on which it was drawn.

Be especially careful of checks drawn on out-of-town banks. Demand identification from the person presenting any check unless they are known to you.

When accepting cash or checks, never allow yourself to be hurried or to become distracted.

Cash checks or deposit them as soon as possible. In most states, checks are acceptable for deposit for at least thirty days from the date of the check if it was made out to you and at least seven days if it was endorsed to you.

If a Check Bounces

A check may bounce for one of three reasons: it was forged; the bank on which it was drawn has no account in that name or the account has been closed; or an account exists, but insufficient funds remain in the account.

If someone has passed a forged check, you must first notify the local police. This puts your complaint on the record—an important step for insurance purposes; the police may also know if this was part of a series of such incidents in the area (known in police parlance as "paperhanging"). You should also notify the U.S. Secret Service, an arm of the Treasury Department, if the forged check was a government check.

A check stamped "No Account" is also probably evidence of fraud; you should first telephone the bank on which it was drawn and ascertain background information, then attempt to collect from the check passer or report the matter to the local police.

Checks stamped "Insufficient Funds" should be redeposited immediately; a telephone call to the check passer may get you a plausible explanation.

Reconciling Your Bank Statement

Once a month you will receive a statement of your account with the bank. You should balance your checkbook as soon as you receive this statement. The back of the bank statement contains a reconcilement form with instructions on how to bring your checkbook and statement up-to-date.

Verify the amounts of the canceled checks in the statement by comparing them with the amounts you had written in the checkbook register. Also compare the deposit amounts.

Make sure you have not transposed any figures in recording amounts in the checkbook register. Add the integers horizontally in the adjusted checkbook total (checks returned plus checks outstanding and recent deposits) and in the adjusted statement total. If they yield the same number (example: $1,357 = 1 + 3 + 5 + 7 = 16$; $1,375 = 1 + 3 + 7 + 5 = 16$), you have probably transposed digits in recording them in the checkbook register. This is an accountant's trick; another is to subtract the smaller balance from the larger and to divide the result by 9. If the quotient is a whole number, the chances are digits have been transposed.

Double-check your arithmetic. If the difference between the adjusted statement balance and the adjusted checkbook balance is a whole number, such as $1, $10, or $100, it usually indicates an error was made in adding or subtracting. First verify the addition and subtraction in your checkbook register. If the error is not found there, recheck your calculations on the reconcilement form.

If you still haven't found the error, search for a missing item. Examine the statement and your checkbook register to see whether an item for the amount of the discrepancy has been skipped. Look back in the checkbook register for any "old" checks that may still be outstanding. Double-check for unanticipated bank charges. Perhaps you received a supply of new checks for which you were charged but the charge does not appear.

Double-check the bank's arithmetic—machines do make mistakes. Using an adding machine or a printing calculator, total the amounts of all checks shown. Total all deposits. Add the deposits to the opening balance. Subtract the total of checks included with the statement.

If you still cannot locate the error, visit the bank and ask for assistance.

TWENTY-FOUR

Make Your Own Rules: Office Procedures

To operate efficiently, every office, no matter how small, must have a set of procedures for handling details and paper work in a consistent manner, and your home office should be no exception. You won't need a formalized procedures manual—at least not in the beginning—but if your operations should grow and you must use temporary help or have employees, such a formalized manual would not be a bad idea. You can always show any temporary worker appropriate portions of *Office at Home* in lieu of such a manual.

In most offices, the work load will consist of routine, carry-forward tasks combined with the work necessitated by the day's incoming correspondence. You can increase the time available for the top-priority tasks resulting from the incoming correspondence by getting access to your mail early. Most home offices are located in exclusively residential neighborhoods, and usual carrier delivery may bring mail to you too late in the day for it to be answered that same day.

Investigate the availability of a lockbox in your local post office. My small-town post office affords access to the lobby lockboxes every weekday from 6:30 A.M. until 6:00 P.M. and from 6:30 A.M. until 3:00 P.M. on Saturdays. Carrier delivery to my home is in the late afternoon. Because I like to respond to letters quickly, I have a lobby box.

Incoming Correspondence

Handling incoming correspondence will be easy if you use these few simple procedures: first, date-stamp all incoming mail. There are several reasons for doing this. For one, if the letter is something that cannot be answered immediately, your date stamp will tell you how long you have been holding it for a response.

The date placed on the letter by the letter writer is often not a good clue to when you received it. Many correspondents date and type letters but hold them for several days before mailing them. The letter itself may have been delayed in its passage through the mail system. Sometimes correspondents fail to date their letters. In the latter event, in addition to date-stamping the date of receipt, you should transfer the postmark date to the letter itself and refer to "your undated letter, postmarked May 20," especially if it relates to matters in which dating is important (for example, legal notices, contracts, deadlines, delivery dates, order dates, etc.).

Not surprisingly, in most home offices, paper work probably will be the biggest hurdle to be gotten over each day. Regardless of how complicated some may try to make the handling of paper in the home office, there are only so many things you can do with each piece of paper that crosses your desk. You can scan it quickly or read it carefully and (a) throw it away; (b) act on it immediately by responding to it with a letter, a memo, or a note; (c) put it aside for future action; or (d) file it.

Accordingly, you'll need three empty file folders, which you can label "For Immediate Action," "For Future Action," and "For Filing." For ease of identification, these can be of different colors. The incoming mail you receive can be sorted into these categories, plus a fourth—items that can be discarded immediately, with or without reading. For the latter purpose, you'll only need a commodious wastepaper basket.

Items for immediate action can include those requiring a response or your attention during that workday. Your objective should be to have this folder empty or nearly so at the end of the day. Future-action items will be those that have been assigned a lower order of importance and on which action can be deferred. The folder of items to be filed should be emptied at regular intervals, as distasteful as that task may be.

According to some management experts, from two-thirds to three-quarters of the paper filed in business offices could have and should have been thrown out. If you use your wastebasket more often than your file cabinet, you'll be doing yourself a big favor. The chances are slim that you'll ever miss what you didn't file.

Follow-up

The best reason for keeping a piece of paper is because you know you will need it again. The best device for making a piece of paper surface at a designated future date is one of those thirty-one-compartment accordion folders (called "sorters" and sold in stationery stores).

Merely insert the piece of paper or letter behind the numbered divider marking the date it will be wanted again—but be sure to empty the appropriate compartment each working day, as well as those for Saturday's and Sunday's dates on Monday if you do not work on the weekend. Your "tickler file" is not only for papers and letters requiring action. You can insert short notes to yourself at appropriate future dates. To make doubly certain you do not miss an important date, mark it on your desk calendar as well.

Outgoing Correspondence

Your first step in handling outgoing correspondence should be to ascertain at what time the mails close at the local post office or what time the last pickup is made each day from the collection box near your home. You can then make sure that urgent and top-priority letters are deposited there in time to get into the postal distribution system. It's also a good idea to find out from your postmaster where the mail goes after it leaves your local post office. Some larger post offices are distribution centers and operate around the clock. A short drive to such a distribution center might speed important letters to their destinations, especially those that missed the last mail truck from your own post office.

Correspondence and Document Styling

Your home office may be in your attic or basement, but there's no reason why the correspondence and other material you generate should proclaim this to the world. The written or typewritten output of your home office should look professional and reflect a consistent style in organization and presentation. Even though more than one person is doing your typing, this should not be apparent to recipients other than by means of the identifying initials your typists append to their work.

Your correspondence may take one of the following styles, depending upon your personal preferences:

Fully Blocked Style In this style, all lines of the letter are flush with the left-hand margin.

Blocked Style To overcome objections to the imbalance of the fully blocked style, the block style, which is the most frequently used style in business letters today, moves the date, the close, and the signature to the right.

Semiblocked Style Indents the first line of each new paragraph.

Official Style Places the writer's name and address after the close and the signature, giving a more formal yet personal touch to business correspondence.

Indented Style Increasingly indents the lines of the inside address; little used today.

Simplified Style This is a variation of the fully blocked style and omits the salutation and complimentary close; a subject line (often typed in uppercase letters) is substituted for the salutation.

Filing

There is no aspect of the operation of an office at home that is more distasteful than filing—or more necessary. Entire volumes have been written on the subject of filing and records management.

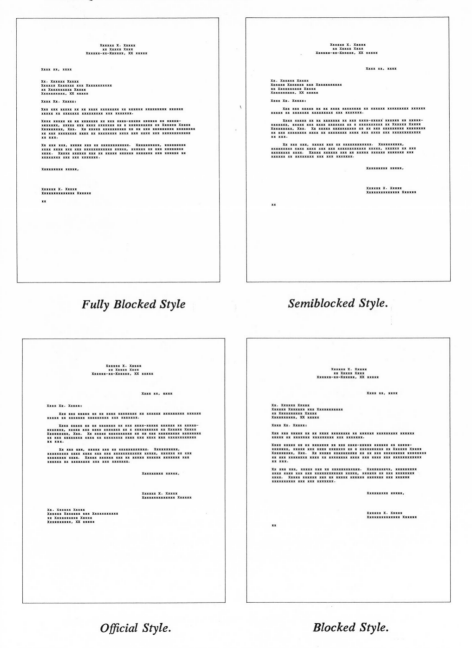

Fully Blocked Style   *Semiblocked Style.*

Official Style.   *Blocked Style.*

Fig. 24.1. Four letter formats.

Elaborate studies have been made of large business operations, with the result that some large corporations were able to throw out millions of pieces of seldom-consulted paper.

It should be obvious that the problem of filing will be quite simple for the office that eventually discards everything and considerably more complicated for the office that foolishly attempts to keep nearly everything. In the latter case, the major problems will be the physical labor involved in keeping the sheer mass of material that pours in. Headaches are also in store for the office that files some items and discards others indiscriminately. If you follow careless filing practices from the beginning without becoming familiar with your office's real needs for documents received or created by you, you'll waste a lot of time searching for something you may not have saved.

It will therefore be to your advantage to discard material by categories. A home-office mail-order book business should keep every publisher's catalog that arrives in the mail, no matter how small or obscure the publisher. Tax consultants, on the other hand, would be wise to discard most publishers' catalogs, perhaps keeping only catalogs from publishers specializing in accounting and finance books and the publications catalog of the national accounting membership organization to which they belong.

To complicate the problem of filing, certain records or documents pertaining to the operation of your office are required to be kept by law. (See chapter 15 for information on records retention requirements.)

Your Filing System

For the fledgling home office, it is best to begin the filing system by learning to be ruthless. Some items must be saved in the files (e.g., copies of your work and correspondence). Other things must be saved for future action, after which they can be jettisoned—for example, a printed notice from a client showing a new address or telephone number; you would discard the notice (after noting the new information in your address book or telephone-number file). Many things can be discarded immediately and won't be missed—this should be done at the time of mail opening. If jettisoning so much paper scares you, I suggest that you do what I do: save all home-office trash for one week in a large plastic bag; if you haven't discovered you discarded something by mistake in that time, you're probably safe in disposing of the bag and its contents.

The simplest home-office filing system will have two main parts:

1. A chronological file containing one copy of everything (letters, memos, reports, etc.) your home office generates. The importance of such a file cannot be overstressed. If your business bills clients at the end of each project, for example, such a file will be invaluable in backstopping whatever billing method you are using. The thickness of any month's chronological file will also give you some idea of the amount of activity your home office has had. A slim folder at the end of any month may galvanize you into increased effort the next month.

   It is important that the chronological file be regarded as sacrosanct and untouchable—copies of correspondence should not be removed from the chronological file under any circumstances. Another use of the chronological file will be to enable you to reconstruct the background of a letter or even to find a file or a name quickly. You may remember that you wrote a letter on a date close to Labor Day, although you cannot remember the name of the person to whom you wrote it. Your chronological file will enable you to locate it quickly and lead you to its other location in your files.

2. Start your filing system with twenty-seven alphabetical file folders labeled "A—Miscellaneous, B—Miscellaneous, C—Miscellaneous, etc." (The fourteenth folder, after "M—Miscellaneous," is for "Mc—Miscellaneous.") These folders will get your filing system started. As the volume of filed material increases, these folders can be emptied of their contents (but kept for filing material not warranting the making of separate folders). You can then add:

   Alphabetical company/individual files, supplemented by subject files when the volume warrants. It's usually a good idea to file by the name of the organization (company, firm name, agency name, etc.) rather than by the name of an individual within that organization as long as the file folders do not become unwieldy. Files captioned by organization name have the added advantage that they keep related correspondence together despite changes within the organization.

Of course, if the volume of material in any file requires it, there's nothing wrong with having entire files devoted to communications to and from individuals within an organization. (Index such folders on the tab by the name of the organization first and then by the name of the individual. They should be placed immediately behind the organization's main folder.)

When you make exceptions to your filing rules, you'll have to make sure that future correspondence is not filed in the wrong place in the files. When looking for something from Richard Roe of the Arista Company in your files, you should always start with the most general file folder and work toward the specific ("A—Miscellaneous"); next, look for a folder indexed "Arista Company," then for one behind it labeled "Arista Company—Roe, Richard."

Here are a few simple rules for indexing and filing that may help you to keep out of trouble:

1. Alphanumerical files should be in alphabetical order. Remember that anything misfiled or out of correct order is lost for all practical purposes.
2. File letters used as words before words. Thus, the file for the television station whose call letters are WPIX would be filed before any word beginning with a "W."
3. Put the last name of individuals first.
4. Consider prefixes as part of a name. (These include d', D', Da, de, De, Del, Des, Di, Du, Fitz, La, Le, M', Mac, Mc, O', Van de, Van der, Von der, and all variants of these. Exception: St. is alphabetized as if spelled Saint.)
5. Consider the hyphenated part of a name as attached to the first part.
6. Consider any abbreviated name as if written in full (county for Cty.; Jonathan for Jno., etc.).
7. Consider numbers as if written out in words.
8. File by organization name as written (thus, Bank of America, not America, Bank of; Charles of the Ritz, not Ritz, Charles of the).
9. File federal agencies under U.S. and the name of the department and exactly as written. (Thus, U.S. Department of the Interior, not Interior Department.)
10. File state and local government agencies similarly.
11. Ignore titles before a name (Dr., Capt., etc.). However, such

a title may be part of a corporate name, for example, Mr. Speedy Cleaners, Inc., in which case it should not be ignored.

12. Ignore articles, conjunctions, and prepositions (a, an, and, for, in, of, or the). An exception would be prepositions that are distinctive parts of a corporate name: After-Six Fashions.

13. Ignore the apostrophe in a possessive or contraction.

Subject Files

Subject files may be needed in your alphabetical filing system to bring together documents that do not pertain to an individual or an organization. Let's say you are a writer and are gathering information on the subject of the fluoridation of drinking water by communities. You engage in correspondence with a number of individuals and groups; you have also gathered some newspaper clippings and pamphlets. To scatter throughout your files this assorted material together with copies of your outgoing correspondence and the replies thereto would defeat your purpose.

Similarly, a subject file can bring together documents that would otherwise be filed in many places. For example, if you have been engaged to test products from a number of different paint manufacturers, it would make more sense to file everything pertaining to this project under a heading like "Paint-Testing Project" rather than have it distributed throughout the files under the names of the individual manufacturers.

Other basic filing systems of use in specialized offices are geographical systems and numerical systems. Some businesses, for example, real estate firms, concentrate their activities in specific geographical areas. Others are organized by regions or sales territories. Such businesses would find it advantageous to organize their basic filing systems geographically.

Generally speaking, in a numerical system, the file captions are numbers that have been assigned to names and subjects. If your business organizes its activities around particular legal cases, contracts, or unit operations that continue over long periods of time, a numerical filing system might offer advantages.

Numerical filing systems have an advantage when files are voluminous or material is scattered in files of related cases, as in a law office, for numerical systems lend themselves to the cross-indexing of documents filed in separate files or locations. Numerical filing systems offer advantages in certain businesses: Examples include businesses that file by voucher number, claim number, policy number, or order number.

In large corporations using numerical systems, file-department employees achieve familiarity with the system and eventually learn to identify specific numbers. In your home office, however, you are the one who will be doing the filing; if you institute a numerical filing system, you'll probably have to refer to an alphabetical card index file to find the number assigned to the name or subject you are seeking. With the exception of the applications to specific businesses described above, numerical filing systems offer few advantages for the home office.

Tips for Improving Mail Delivery and Reducing
Postage Costs, Envelopes, and Labels

For addresses, the postal service recommends the use of single-spaced uppercase letters and no punctuation in a flush-left block format.

Because the postal service now uses optical character recognition (OCR) devices to sort mail and these are programmed to scan a specific area on envelopes, be sure your typed address is within the area that will be scanned.

If you show the street address and P.O. box number on separate lines, remember that delivery will be made to the address or box on the next to last line.

The last line of the address should include only the city, state (use the approved two-letter state or provincial codes), and ZIP code designation. Do not show the ZIP code on a separate line.

Avoid any impediments to legibility and ease of sorting and handling. These include envelopes cluttered with advertising that make it difficult to perceive the address, dark-colored envelopes or labels, and peculiar, hard-to-decipher typefaces.

Chain-feed envelopes when typing. Before removing a typed envelope from the typewriter, insert a blank envelope behind the roller. The second will feed as the first is rolled out.

Speeding Delivery

ZIP code all mail. All mail is now sorted by ZIP code. (Pieces without ZIP codes tend to be delayed in a system geared to ZIP code sorting.) Purchase a ZIP code directory from your local post office, the Superintendent of Documents, Government Printing Office, Washington, DC 20402 or one of the twenty-six GPO bookstores or agencies at various locations throughout the United States.

Mailers to Canada requiring postal code information for Canadian addresses should write to: Mail Collection and Delivery Branch, Postal Coding Division, Canada Post, Ottawa, Ontario, Canada K1A 0B1.

If possible, presort mail before depositing it in the post office or collection box and avoid preliminary handling.

Your postmaster will be glad to tell you when mails close at the post office in advance of the departure of trucks to the distribution centers where sorting takes place. It's a good idea not to wait until the end of the day to mail your letters. If you deposit mail in a neighborhood collection box, make sure you know the current pickup schedule.

Rent a lockbox or post office box (which can also serve as your office address). In most post offices, mail is usually available in lobby boxes earlier than that delivered by carrier. Mail received in the afternoon at the post office that would not be delivered to your home on the following day is usually placed in lobby boxes immediately.

Use overnight package services, Express Mail, and Mailgrams to expedite delivery of urgent material or important messages.

If you regularly receive a large volume of mail or if you need a lockbox for a special reason (for example, the receipt of large amounts of cash and checks through the mails) and no lockboxes are immediately available, you should investigate "caller service." For an annual fee, the post office will assign a box number to you. Your mail can then be received by you at a lobby window or at the loading dock, but this service is considerably more expensive than box rent.

Invest in a set of rubber stamps: FIRST-CLASS MAIL, AIR MAIL, SPECIAL DELIVERY, SPECIAL HANDLING, DO NOT FOLD OR BEND, FRAGILE, etc.

Reducing Postal Expenses

If your letters, memos, and reports tend to be bulky, consider typing them on both sides of the paper. If overseas air mail constitutes much of your outgoing correspondence, buy lighter-weight paper and envelopes.

Weigh all mail; guessing weights can waste money and risks the return of letters or delay and the consequent loss of the goodwill of the addressee. A good postal scale can save its cost in less than a year.

Ask your postmaster for up-to-date rate charts for the classes of mail you use regularly.

Avoid sending stamped self-addressed envelopes when you must elicit a reply. Instead, use business reply envelopes or postcards and pay postage only on those returned to you (see page 257).

When special-delivery letters and packages reach the mail rooms of many large companies, they are handled routinely with the regular mail. Save money by using special handling for rush packages and Mailgrams for urgent messages.

TWENTY-FIVE

Capital Punishment: Taxes

In his *History of the Devil,* Daniel Defoe remarked on the certainty of death and taxes, and subsequent writers, including Ben Franklin, have underscored this observation. Many home offices that serve only as workplaces and not as business places or adjuncts to other business offices have no profit-making potential and thus offer no tax advantages.

If profit is your motive or you use your home office in connection with a business, however small in size it may be, your home office can offer significant tax advantages. Your "home" to the IRS may be a house, apartment, condominium, mobile home, boat, or similar property. For tax purposes, it also includes other structures on your property, such as a detached garage, studio building, barn, or greenhouse.

The IRS applies three use tests to any business use of the home: the space must be for exclusive use, for regular use, and be the principal place of business. If your home is used as *the principal place of business* for a trade or business operated by you or as *a place where you meet and deal with customers* in your business or if you use a separate structure that is not attached to your house or residence, you may deduct expenses for that part of your home used for business. If you work for someone else and you use a portion of your home as a home office to do work as an extension of the work you do in your employer's business, that use must be for *the convenience of your employer* and not merely because it is appropriate and helpful in your job that you take work home.

Exclusive-Use Test You must use a specific part of your home *only* for the purpose of your trade or business. For example, a den or recreation room cannot double as your office or place of business. For this reason, you will be wise to furnish the space allocated to business use with appropriate furniture and equipment.

The IRS is fairly strict in applying the exclusive-use test; this rules out any rooms or areas with mixed uses. If you prepare tax returns for clients or write a business newsletter in a spare bedroom of your home, that does not automatically constitute a business use, and you may not include it in the calculation of the area devoted to business use or deduct expenses on the basis of such inclusion.

If you use part of your home as a day-care center for children, handicapped persons, or the elderly, special rules apply, and you should consult IRS Publication 587, *Business Use of Your Home*.

The expenses paid to maintain your home may be directly related, indirectly related, or unrelated to its use in your business, and it will be up to you to allocate them properly when preparing your income tax return.

Direct Expenses These include alterations or repairs (including painting, papering, or plastering) to rooms used exclusively for business.

Indirect Expenses Examples of indirect expenses are real-estate taxes, mortgage interest, casualty losses, rent paid by you to the owner of a rented house or the landlord of an apartment house, utilities and services, including electricity, gas, and fuel oil, insurance, repairs, and depreciation. Depreciation should be allocated and shown on Form 4562. For a complete discussion of depreciation and instructions for use of Form 4562, consult IRS Publication 534, *Depreciation*. The personal portion of real-estate taxes and mortgage interest are deductible on Schedule A of your Form 1040.

Nondeductible Expenses Do not deduct any expenses that benefit that portion of your home *not used* for business purposes. These include repairs to nonbusiness parts of the house, landscaping, and lawn care (but you can deduct a portion of the cost of painting the outside of the house or of installing a new roof).

Regular-Use Test You must use that part of your home given over to business use on a continuing basis—not incidentally or occasionally.

Principal-Place-of-Business Test In order to determine that your home is your principal place of business for one of the trades or businesses that you may engage in, you should consider the following factors: the total time you spend regularly doing work there; the comparative degree of your business activity there; and the relative amount of income you receive from doing business at home.

Under an amendment to the law, "principal place of business" has been defined to mean that you can have a principal place of business for each separate trade or business in which you are engaged. If the regular- and exclusive-use tests are met, you can deduct the expenses attributable to using your residence as the principal place of business for one or more such businesses.

Many of your activities may have profit as a motive, but a profit-seeking activity that is not a trade or a business does not automatically qualify for deductions. Thus, if you set aside a portion of your home to read financial and business periodicals in order to manage your portfolio or to clip bond coupons, you will not be allowed to deduct any portion of your expenses.

Even if you incorporate and manage your portfolio as a corporation, the IRS may not allow it, for they may deem it a personal holding company if more than 60 percent of the corporation's income is derived from investments or personal services.

Deductions of expenses are allowed on the basis of the proportion of the area of your home used for business purposes as compared to the total area of your home. If the total square footage is 1,320 square feet (you should include kitchen, bathrooms, and hallways) and 507 square feet of this is devoted to business use, you would be entitled to deduct 38.4 percent of each applicable expense. In calculating areas used for business, you can include storage space in which records or inventory for sale at wholesale or retail are stored. Even though your basement is used for other purposes, that portion given over to the storage of records or inventory is considered to be devoted to a business use.

Alternatively, if your house or apartment has rooms of approximately the same size, these can be used as the basis of the calculation. If your house or apartment has six rooms and one is used as a home office exclusively for business purposes, you can consider that 16.7 percent is given over to business. You may also deduct the expenses for a separate structure near your home. An example of this would be the barn used by an antique dealer for the storage of items for sale or the greenhouse used by a florist to grow flowers in connection with a home-based floral business.

The IRS requires that the total deduction you make for business use of your home cannot exceed the gross income you receive from the business use of your home. In order to calculate this, first total the business portion of your real-estate taxes, mortgage interest, and casualty losses. If this is more than your gross income resulting from business use of your home, you cannot deduct any other expenses as a result of the business use of your home.

If your other expenses for business use of your home are more than your gross income from such use (after subtracting the business portion of your deductions for real-estate taxes, mortgage interest, and casualty losses), the order in which you may deduct other expenses is operating expenses and depreciation and the part of any limitation on your casualty-loss deduction that is due to a casualty loss on business property.

To demonstrate how this operates, consider the following example:

John Doe, a direct-mail copywriter, uses 20 percent of his home regularly and exclusively for business purposes. His home expenses for the year are:

Depreciation $ 200

Direct Expenses
   Painting business portion of home   200

Indirect Expenses

	Total	20%	
Real-estate taxes	3,000	600	
Mortgage interest	2,000	400	
Business portion of tax and interest			1,000

Other Indirect (Operating) Expenses

Electricity and gas	1,200	240
Fuel oil	800	160
Insurance	1,000	200
Outside painting	1,200	240
Roof repairs	600	120

Business portion of other indirect expenses	960
Total expenses for business use of the home	2,360
Less taxes and interest	1,000
Total expenses for business use of home *(other than taxes and interest)*	$1,360

If Mr. Doe's gross income from the business operated from his home is $25,000, he can deduct all of the $1,360 of expenses for business use of his home plus the $1,000 deduction for taxes and interest. If Mr. Doe's gross income from the business in his home is only $2,000, he can only deduct $1,000 of his $1,360 of expenses after deducting taxes and interest.

Mr. Doe cannot incur a loss as a result of the business use of his home. He must also deduct his operating expenses before he can deduct any depreciation. In the case where he has a gross income of only $2,000, he cannot deduct any depreciation and only $1,000 of his operating expenses.

TWENTY-SIX

It's About Time: Managing Your Days

No area of business literature contains more titles than that pertaining to time management. I should know; at one time or another, I've bought most of them and tried to operate by their rules.

In my experience, the major problem of most time-management books is their attempts to be too specific. By trying to solve every possible work-style problem, they usually solve none satisfactorily. My advice is to tailor your own home office time-management program to fit your personality, life-style, work habits, and goals. What follows are suggestions for a system that has worked for me in my own home office and for others who have used it.

What Is Your Time Worth?

One of the greatest aids to efficient time management is to create a set of reference values in your own mind by calculating exactly what your time is worth in dollars and cents. People who charge by the hour—psychiatrists, electricians, plumbers—are keenly aware of what their time is worth, and you should be, too.

Remember that any income goals you set are *gross* income goals, from which as much as 30–40 percent may be eaten up by your overhead, depending on the nature of your activities and the size of your expenses.

Let's say your eventual goal is to gross $50,000 a year from the work you do in your home office. You plan to work an eight-hour day, a five-day week, and you plan on taking a modest two-week vacation each year. On that basis, here's what your time is worth:

Per day: $200
Per hour: $25
Per minute: $0.42

These units can be put in more graphic terms of various non-productive daily activities: if you chat on the telephone for 144 seconds beyond the time it has taken you to accomplish the purpose of the call, that idle chatter has cost you the equivalent of one dollar in income. Five minutes dawdling over an extra cup of coffee each morning costs you $2.10, making it rather expensive coffee. If you spend twelve minutes in scanning the morning paper before getting started in your home office, you cost yourself $5.04. A fifteen-minute chat in the lobby of the post office, and you have lost $6.30.

If your income sights are set lower or higher, the dollar value of your time will change accordingly. Should your goal be to gross $25,000 a year, for example, divide the above amounts in half.

Nevertheless, unless you are working only for the fun of it, every second, minute, and hour that you waste represents a loss of potential income to you. But even with $25,000 a year as your gross-income target, those fifteen minutes gossiping in the post-office lobby still could cost you more than $3.00.

Working Time

You must set regular hours for working in your home office—and you must adhere to them. If you only work when the spirit moves you, you'll probably find a thousand reasons to put off getting started.

It's a good idea to keep track of your hours on a permanent record, such as a small desk calendar, whose pages turn over and are not meant to be torn out. Not only will it reveal how close you have been coming to your preset starting and stopping times, but if you bill clients on the basis of time expended, this record of time devoted to work will be an important document in preparing and supporting your invoice. By reviewing the pages of your desk calendar after a project has been completed, you will also be able to hone your time-estimating skills.

Be a Clock Watcher

There are 28,800 seconds in an eight-hour day, 144,000 in a forty-hour week, and 7,200,000 in a year of fifty working weeks. Since astronomers have calculated there are exactly 31,558,149 seconds in a year, your projected working time constitutes only 22.8 percent of the entire time available. This means that you have more than three-quarters of the rest of the available time to devote to other activities—eating, sleeping, recreation, TV watching, and the like. This generous portion of time available for other activities should make it easy for you to separate productive work time from nonproductive other time.

To make yourself conscious of the swift passage of your valuable work time, buy a clock for your home office, display it prominently, and consult it frequently as you work. For one thing, you will become a better judge of the time needed for the segments of tasks and will increase your ability to estimate more closely the time you will need in the future for similar tasks. In the beginning, if you are like most people, you will tend to underestimate the time needed to accomplish various jobs. A clock can be a potent weapon in the war against your most insidious enemy—procrastination.

Because you'll probably be working alone, without a secretary, a clock with an alarm feature will be especially useful. If you prefer a large clock on the wall and visible from across the room, battery-operated clocks with sweep-second hands or illuminated digital clocks are reasonably priced.

Organize Your Desk or Work Surface

In most offices, whether at home or in the biggest of big businesses, desk tops and desks are a veritable chamber of horrors, equipped with devices that have changed little since the days when office workers wore green eyeshades and sleeve garters. Traditional and infrequently used desk accessories only contribute to the clutter that characterizes the average desk. Your first move should be to attack this tyrannizing mess.

Photographs in standing frames should be hung on walls; keepsakes, souvenirs, and mementos (of doubtful usefulness in an office, anyway) should be displayed on shelves, if you insist on showing them. Even paperweights (relics of the days when ceiling fans were used for cooling and caused papers to scatter) can be retired altogether.

Pen and pencil clutter can be overcome with a few Dundee marmalade jars. (I use 600-milliliter glass laboratory beakers for this purpose.) The rule to apply to each object is the rule of use: if you do not use it at least once in the course of an average day's activities, relegate it to a less important location. Such infrequently used objects can include a tape dispenser, stapler, containers for paper clips and rubber bands, and any battery-powered calculator small enough to be put in a drawer.

At all costs, avoid those elaborate clerical desk-top organizing systems. Not only do they take up valuable space and are dust collectors, but their small trays and compartments invite filling, and so they become catchalls for useless small objects. If your desk or worktable is equipped with drawers, stationery holders, drawer dividers, and drawer trays can bring order to their contents.

One of the things you can remove from your desk is the elaborate card file most people use to record telephone numbers and addresses. Instead, use a small loose-leaf notebook with twenty-seven alphabetical tabbed separators. I like a six-by-nine-inch size that can be put in a briefcase or suitcase and taken on business trips.

Record all frequently used telephone numbers (and addresses) in approximate alphabetical order, leaving appropriate space between for insertion of new information. I write names and numbers on right-hand pages and reserve the empty left-hand pages for the spillover of additional entries. Unless you have the circle of friends of former Postmaster General Jim Farley (who had a prodigious memory and needed no address book or telephone-number directory), this notebook should be adequate.

Finding a number only requires the time it takes to find the appropriate page and to narrow your search to a portion of it. When a page begins to become too crowded, you can redo it or expand it at your convenience. In my experience, certain pages will require redoing because of frequent handling or overcrowding on the order of once every couple of years. This poses no problem, because you'll welcome the opportunity to weed out names not frequently consulted.

If you are in the process of furnishing your home office, a visit to a commercial stationer will open up a whole new world of efficient desk devices. A lamp or copyholder that clamps on the edge of your desk or worktable is more efficient and preferable to one that stands on it and takes up valuable space.

Don't overlook the possibilities of the many high-tech devices intended for the kitchen and elsewhere in the home. Plastic-coated wire baskets are available for under-shelf suspension or pegboard mounting and will increase the usable storage area as well as your efficiency.

Analyze Your Work Habits

Dieters are frequently advised to keep a diary of the time spent in eating and the quantities consumed—and the results are always surprising. Since you probably come to your home office with many bad work habits, keep a diary of your time expenditures over the first few days. Only in this way will you discover just how much time you actually spend in such nonproductive tasks as going to the post office, reading newspapers, taking a coffee break, or chatting on the telephone. Only with the knowledge about the way you apportion your time between productive and nonproductive activities can you begin to manage your time better.

Procrastination

At income tax time, the vice of procrastination becomes so rampant in the land that 3 million of us postpone preparing our income tax returns until after the April 15 deadline despite the penalties. Such dilatory behavior can be expensive. But procrastination in the home office is even more costly and can mean the difference between success and failure.

Let me first say a few words on behalf of procrastination: there are occasions when procrastination, intelligently used, can produce favorable results. Problems will inevitably arise about which you will not have enough information; it makes sense to wait for the needed information to be supplied. And some problems do diminish in size and even solve themselves and go away through inattention, but these are the exception. An acceptable form of procrastination that makes good sense is not to make a phone call or write a letter when you are angry. Problems arise and multiply, however, for those of us who make procrastination a way of life.

Current psychological research disputes the myth that procrastinators are lazy. "Scratch a procrastinator," says Dr. Lenora M. Yuen, a California psychologist and coauthor with Dr. Jane B. Burka of a recent book on procrastination, "and you'll find a workaholic."

Aside from a natural and understandable desire to defer unpleasant tasks, procrastination may stem from several causes: many who procrastinate have set high goals for themselves and fear failure and negative evaluation by society. Consequently, tackling any task becomes virtually impossible.

A Washington, D.C., psychotherapist, Dr. John C. Harris, believes that procrastination can sometimes stem from a desire to retaliate or from resistance to the authority and control of others. "You don't feel free to express your anger directly, but you show it by getting things done late," he suggests.

Some procrastinators find reasons to fear success and to court failure; for others, finishing a job just under a deadline is a way of skating close to the edge of the thin ice of disaster that provides adrenalin-boosting excitement.

Procrastination seems to be more prevalent when intellectual tasks are involved—tasks that will allow the person's work to be publicly evaluated and perhaps found wanting. This is so common among authors that it has come to be known as "writer's block," a staple subject for articles in writers' magazines describing the elaborate techniques used by famous authors to overcome it.

Oddly enough, procrastinators are not consistent. Some may be punctual in keeping appointments but delay in meeting deadlines. One characteristic common to all procrastinators, however, is a blind sense of invincibility and a willingness to delude themselves into thinking that the task being avoided will somehow get done despite the erosion of the time available in which to complete it.

If procrastination is one of your problems, try the following techniques:

1. Don't avoid the more difficult tasks or assign lower priorities to them. Always tackle all jobs in order of *importance*, not ease. If you only do the easy jobs, the genuinely important tasks may never get done at all. Humorist Bob Benchley once described this characteristic of procrastinators: "Anyone can do any amount of work, provided it isn't the work he is *supposed* to be doing."

2. Reduce your perfectionism. Every job doesn't have to be done perfectly—but it does have to be done.

3. Understand the consequences of procrastination. These may range from costly monetary penalties and fines to loss of future work from the same source. Internally, you may experience feelings of inadequacy, guilt, panic, and stress.

4. Think small. Divide the job into small increments and focus on them individually; the entire task will not seem so intimidating. Consultant Alan Lakein has dubbed this technique for punching holes in large jobs "the Swiss cheese method," and it works. Major wars are won by successes in a series of small campaigns and battles.

5. Set realistic subgoals and achievable deadlines for yourself. Avoid vagueness in identifying goals and deadlines; make them concrete and tangible.

6. If you work alone and report to no one but yourself, it sometimes helps to involve others (for example, members of your

family) by letting them know about project deadlines and asking them to check up on your performance.

7. Get started early. Don't wait until you *feel* like starting, but dig right in. Don't have another cup of coffee; forget the morning newspaper; put off tying up the tomato plants until the evening hours.

8. Be flexible as you go along. If you discover that your plan of attack has hit a snag or isn't working, don't give up. Modify your plan.

9. Expect interruptions, but try to avoid them. If they occur, remember every interruption will be potentially another excuse for not resuming the task.

10. Procrastinators tend to feel they really haven't accomplished anything until the entire job is done. Give yourself small rewards for meeting subgoals and big rewards for meeting major goals and deadlines. For example, reward yourself with a coffee break, but only after completing a targeted portion of an assigned task. Withhold rewards and penalize yourself for missing deadlines.

11. Avoid the "New Year's resolution syndrome"—the making of promises to yourself that you know you have no intention of keeping. This inevitably leads to the making of promises to others that you also know you have no intention of keeping.

12. Procrastinators often have low self-esteem. Avoid feelings of guilt; learn to feel good about yourself. Convince yourself you are more competent and better organized than you give yourself credit for being.

13. Learn to estimate the time it will take to complete tasks. People tend to underestimate the time needed for distasteful tasks, thus increasing the tendency to procrastinate.

14. Remember that the tendency to procrastinate can be reversed. Procrastination is a learned bad habit, and overcoming it involves learning a new habit while you are unlearning the old.

Planning Your Day

The unit of time you must concentrate on is the individual workday. The first thing you *must not* buy (and you can discard yours if you have one already) is one of those fancy leather-bound loose-leaf appointment books. Such books are fine for professionals—doctors, dentists, lawyers, interviewers—who must schedule and see a veritable parade of people each day. But in your home office *you* can be in intelligent control of your time, and a detailed plan of how you will spend each day is unnecessary.

The chief advantage of a home office, in fact, is the very flexibility that it makes possible in each day's schedule. Why throw this flexibility away and lock yourself into a rigorous and unyielding system?

For years I used just such an elaborate appointment and time-planning book, which sat impressively on my desk. It included facing pages for each working day and showed scheduled appointments (by quarter-hour increments), space for recording the tasks to be done that day, space for notes and memos to myself, and a page for the tasks accomplished (in six-minute increments). Eventually, I realized that I was becoming a slave to this ritualized form of record keeping. More often than not, I never consulted the book afterward for the information I had so dutifully recorded about what was to be done or what had been accomplished. Like the Watergate tapes, however, a detailed record would have been invaluable for reconstructing my days had I wanted to write my memoirs.

This is not to say you should not plan each day. By all means, have a plan, but keep it simple. Graphics designers have long referred to the admonishment to simplification in design as the KISS principle, a term now preempted by computer programmers. It stands for "Keep it simple, stupid."

You'll need two ordinary clipboards and two lined yellow pads, although you can get away with one clipboard and two yellow pads. Preferably on the night before the next working day, you should put on the top sheet of the first pad the words "To Do" and the next day's date. Then list in any order all the tasks you know of that should be done the next day. Once you have recorded the next day's tasks, categorize them in terms of importance by using the letters A, B, and C, with sequential numbering to indicate relative importance within each category and your estimate of the approximate time each should need. You can flag important target times or completion points; in this way, you'll know a particular task should be done by 11:15 A.M. or that another should begin by 2:30 in the afternoon in order to have the results in the afternoon's last mail.

The reason for making your list the night before is that it's best not to have anything impede your momentum in tackling the first important task the following day. In addition, a list prepared the night before gives you the opportunity to go over some of the tasks in your own mind during quiet moments in the evening and to make a battle plan for attacking them.

In outlining tasks, the trick is to avoid making your task breakdown and time schedule too finite. Management consultant Peter Drucker counsels the scheduling of time in large chunks rather than making an intricate, minute-by-minute plan of your activities during the day.

As an afterword, I should point out that according to Dr. Tom Ferguson, editor of the magazine *Medical Self-Care*, compulsive list making is regarded by experts as one of the signs of a workaholic. The operative word here is "compulsive," and you should not allow the daily list you make to become anything more than a planning tool.

When assigning priorities, you may discover the truth of what has come to be called "the Pareto principle." Vilfredo Pareto, a nineteenth-century Italian sociologist and economist, studied the distribution of wealth and economic power and discovered that most of it was in the hands of a few, while the vast majority were powerless and existed in poverty.

In his book *Managing for Results*, Peter Drucker suggested that many management problems follow this pattern. "In the marketplace, a handful of products in the line produce the bulk of sales volume; a few salesmen out of the total roster produce two-thirds of all new business." The ratio was quantified as "the 80/20 rule" by Alan Lakein: "80 percent of sales come from 20 percent of customers; 80 percent of file usage is in 20 percent of files; 80 percent of sick leave is taken by 20 percent of employees, etc."

By assigning priorities to tasks on the basis of genuine importance to you and your objectives and not because of some sense of hypothetical "urgency," you won't get trapped in the 80 percent of low-value activities and can concentrate on the vital 20 percent.

The second yellow pad is intended to record *future* projects as they arise in the course of each day's work. If their number is small, future tasks can be entered in no particular order as long as the starting date, due date, and time estimate are shown. Of course, if future projects become so numerous as to require that they be arranged in date order, merely make separate pages in your "future" pad for each date for an appropriate time period into the future.

As a backstop to your "future" pad and to your tickler file, a small desk calendar or wall-type month-at-a-glance "work-organizer" calendar is recommended. This will be useful as the place for jotting reminders to yourself about future appointments, important documents or dates, and similar memory-jogging information.

Preparing for Tomorrow

At the end of each working day, cross off all tasks you have accomplished. Those you have not done should be transferred to the following day's "To Do" page and assigned priorities along with the other tasks you have accumulated for the next day on the "future" pad.

Carrying forward too many planned but unstarted or unfinished tasks from one day to the next (and especially if any are high-priority tasks) is a signal that you are either biting off more than you can chew each day or you are using your time inefficiently, and you should resume the keeping of a time diary again for a couple of days.

Increase Your Time-Use Efficiency

Here are some suggestions for increasing your time-use efficiency:

Telephone calls Have you ever received a phone call just as you were rushing to catch a train or a plane or to keep an important appointment? You had almost no time for anything but the essentials; you were pressed, yet you were not rude.

Phone calls are usually a three-part sandwich: the opening, the message, and the closing. Not surprisingly, the message portion is usually succinct and to the point; it is in the opening and the closing that many of us tend to lose track of time. You should, therefore, set the tone of the call by avoiding an opening that invites too much exchange of personal information. Keep the message brief and to the point by knowing the exact information you want to impart or to receive.

You should also learn how to end a conversation. No one has devised a better way of doing this than by merely saying, "Good-bye," at an appropriate point to the person on the other end of the line. "Thanks a lot" and "Let's talk again" are courteous but definite ways to convey that you are at the end of the conversation without offending the other person.

Although there is no hard-and-fast rule about who should take the initiative in ending a call, if you placed the call, in principle you are responsible for ending it. After all, unless you are returning another's call, you should know when you have obtained whatever information you called about. "Thanks for the information" is a polite but firm way of indicating to the other person that you are about to terminate a conversation you initiated.

If you are the recipient of a call, assist the caller in terminating it by means of some easily perceived closing phrases or sentences: "I think that's what you wanted to know." If you can't supply the information needed by the caller, "I'll get back to you" is reassuring. But if you say this, mean it, and make it a point to get back to the caller.

In a pinch, no matter who called whom, and especially when a caller still hasn't perceived your not-so-subtle signals about the approaching end of a conversation, there's nothing wrong with saying, "Thanks and good-bye," and waiting for the other person's response.

If people at the other end of your telephone conversations are saying, "Let me go," "I've got to get back to work," "I've got to go now," or similar sentiments, chances are you have fallen into the habit of talking too long. Try making and taking telephone calls as though you had to catch a train as soon as you hang up, and you'll probably find the conversations are much shorter—and more welcome. Moreover, your phone bills will be smaller.

Another solution to the lengthy-phone-call problem is a small pocket countdown timer that can be set to a specific number of minutes and seconds and started when your phone rings. These beep audibly when the elapsed time is up; countdown timers are especially useful if you want to limit the length of expensive long-distance calls.

Insulating yourself from interruptions If incoming phone calls are keeping you from important tasks, consider adding a ringer silencer to your telephone, as described in chapter 8, or using your answering machine to intercept calls, as described in chapter 9.

If callers phone frequently, you can let them know you prefer to receive your calls at designated times—for example, between 11:00 A.M. and noon and between three and four in the afternoon.

One of the greatest aids to avoiding interruptions is to learn to say "no." Peter Drucker responds to much of his mail with an all-purpose printed reply card that reads:

MR. PETER F. DRUCKER
GREATLY APPRECIATES YOUR KIND INTEREST, BUT IS UNABLE TO: CONTRIBUTE ARTICLES OR FORE-WORDS; COMMENT ON MANUSCRIPTS OR BOOKS; TAKE PART IN PANELS AND SYMPOSIA; JOIN COM-MITTEES OR BOARDS OF ANY KIND; ANSWER QUES-TIONNAIRES; GIVE INTERVIEWS; AND APPEAR ON RADIO OR TELEVISION.

Learning to say no takes time; it sometimes means hurting the feelings of others, and it may even involve not doing things you like to do, because you should also be able to say no to yourself.

Visitors Interruptions by unannounced visitors are somewhat more difficult to handle. You can, of course, refuse to answer a knock at the door or the ringing of your doorbell. If this is your decision, it helps to have a viewing system (a one-way through-the-door optical viewer or a convex mirror mounted outside the house giving a view of the front door) to enable you to screen callers—you wouldn't want to turn away a registered letter or an important air-express package.

If failing to answer the ring or knock of an unwanted visitor offends your sense of good manners, you can salve your conscience by remembering that an unannounced business visit is itself an example of bad manners. As with telephone calls, you may find it desirable to limit the hours to a fixed period during which visitors may call.

If you must receive unexpected visitors and if the geography of your office permits, always see them in your reception area or in a room other than your office. Once you invite a visitor into your office, you limit your ability to control the situation and to ter-minate the visit gracefully.

When all else fails, you can always make a flat statement to the unannounced arrival at the start: "I can give you exactly ten minutes." A countdown timer or pocket alarm watch will be useful for signaling that the visitor's allotted time has expired.

As with telephone conversations, you can control the tone of the visit (and to some extent its length) by avoiding excessive curiosity about the visitor's family, health, recent vacation, and similar visit-prolonging subjects.

Knowing how to terminate a visit gracefully is also useful. This can range from maintaining silence and pointedly not responding to the visitor's remarks to a direct statement, such as, "Thanks for calling on me." That failing, you can stand abruptly and extend your hand—an unmistakable signal to the visitor that it's time to depart.

The telephone that rings while you have a visitor in your office presents a special problem. The best course is to take the call and to tell the caller immediately, "I'm in a meeting. I'll call you back." Do not ask the caller to call *you* back in ten minutes; this may make an important visitor feel that a time limit has been placed on the duration of the visit. Anyway, under the rules of business etiquette, by taking the call, you have accepted the responsibility for placing a call in return.

It is rude and usually awkward to try to hold a conversation about an important matter while a visitor is in your office. If you absolutely must take the call, however, courtesy dictates that you take it at another extension, if possible.

A Novel Way to Make More Time: Sleep Less

Sleep researchers have discovered that the traditional eight hours of sleep is not an inherited trait of the human species. Despite these findings, respected medical organizations run advertisements and distribute literature advising everyone "to get seven or eight hours of sleep every day."

As a result, it's not surprising that most of us are convinced that we need that much sleep for health and well-being, while one-third of the population who get less (or more) sleep than this "standard" believe they have cause to worry.

Many of history's leaders have been short sleepers: Frederick the Great, the Duke of Wellington, and Napoleon. Among contemporary political leaders, Harry Truman, Lyndon Johnson, and John F. Kennedy were all short sleepers.

Virgil, Horace, Darwin, Spencer, and George Bernard Shaw all

got along on little sleep, but perhaps the best-known figure was
Thomas A. Edison, who averaged between four and five hours of
sleep every night.

Among contemporary personalities, TV announcer Ed Mc-
Mahon gets only four or five hours of sleep a night. Actress Cloris
Leachman, comedians David Brenner and Jackie Gleason, drama
critic Clive Barnes, and writers Brendan Gill and George Plimpton
all need little sleep. So does prolific writer Isaac Asimov, who
explains that he accomplishes so much because he sleeps for only
five or six hours a night. "I hate sleep," Asimov says. "It wastes
time."

Michael DeBakey, the heart surgeon, and Alton Ochsner,
founder of the respected New Orleans clinic that bears his name,
are short sleepers. Shipping tycoon Aristotle Onassis and insurance
millionaire John D. MacArthur both believed their habit of sleeping only a few hours a night contributed to their success.

Experiments in cutting back on sleep have demonstrated that
sleeping can be curtailed with no ill effects and with eventual
adaptation to the reduced sleep period. According to Dr. Abra-
ham Weinberg, cofounder of New York's Sleep and Somatic Therapy Center, those who want to have an extra hour or two each day
for more living can do so without risk of damage through simple
behavior modification.

Consider these statistics: the eight-hour sleeper who sleeps two
hours less each night achieves the equivalent of 730.5 extra hours,
or 40.58 extra 18-hour days of living each year. If you began the
practice of sleeping for only six hours each night at the age of
twenty, you would have achieved 36,525 extra hours, or 2,029.2
extra eighteen-hour days of being alive and aware by the age of
seventy. You would have had the equivalent of 5.55 extra years of
being awake, of being capable of producing income for yourself, or
of simply enjoying the wonders of the world around you.

Reduce those six hours of sleep to only four hours of sleep each
night (and the evidence is the human body can be trained to get
along on four hours of rest) in the fifty years between twenty and
seventy and you would achieve the equivalent of 73.05 "extra"
twenty-hour days of living each year. If you started the practice of
sleeping four hours a night at the age of twenty, you would have
achieved 3,652.5 "extra" twenty-hour days of being awake and
aware by the time you reached seventy. You would have had the
equivalent of ten more years of being "alive." If this gained time

was treated as working time (i.e., fifty weeks of forty hours each per year), you would have added the astonishing equivalent of more than thirty-six additional working years! Wake up, sleepy head. Your first billion dollars awaits you.

TWENTY-SEVEN

Uncle Sam, Partner: Using the Mails Effectively

The U.S. Postal Service is today the world's largest communications system, with 600,000 employees and 32,000 post offices, branches, and stations. Because many users do not take the time to familiarize themselves with the services offered by this newly vitalized system, customer complaints are not uncommon but often are not justified. The postal customer who makes a point of understanding how the system works and discovering the things it can do will profit handsomely.

The U.S. Postal Service was created by the Postal Reorganization Act, which set up a quasi-independent government-owned corporation within the executive branch to replace the former Post Office Department, and was signed into law on August 12, 1970.

As a concomitant to the Postal Reorganization Act, mechanization and updating of distribution facilities were instituted. Perhaps because of increased competition from private package-delivery services, the volume of packages handled by the postal service has decreased, as has the total number of pieces of mail handled.

The first step in understanding and using the facilities of the postal service intelligently is to make the acquaintance of your postmaster. In former times, the postmaster's job was often a political sinecure, and the postmaster was a political hack or crony. This is no longer the case. You'll find that today's postmaster is often a savvy business manager interested in increasing the performance and the revenues of his post office.

Your postmaster has literature available explaining some of the special services now offered by the postal service, including consultation with mailers on their problems. Most users are not aware, for example, that they can obtain supplies such as trays, labels, and even rubber bands without charge from the postal service. Trayed mail bypasses separate handlings within the post office; when volume is large, it is even possible to arrange for free pickup of bulk mail by a post-office vehicle.

The postal service classifies mail into the following categories: express mail, first class, second class, controlled-circulation publications, third class, fourth class, priority mail, official and free mail, mail for the blind, and mixed classes.

Express Mail

In 1972, the postal service announced a group of specialized postal services oriented to business use. A high-speed delivery network was created to link more than fifty major cities in the United States and also cities in England. After a slow start, express mail has mushroomed in the last several years into an important part of the services offered to the business community.

Four levels of service are offered:

Next-Day Service Available in more than 1,200 cities. Get your package or letter to a post office by a designated acceptance time (it is posted in the lobby) and your articles will be available for pickup at the destination post office by 10:00 A.M. of the following day or (for a somewhat higher charge) will be delivered to the addressee by 3:00 P.M. the following day. If by the promised time delivery has not been made or if the package is not available for pickup, full refund of postage paid will be made upon application by the sender.

Shipments are insured against loss, damage, or rifling at no additional charge. Merchandise is insured at no charge for up to $500, except for negotiable items, currency, or bullion, in which cases indemnity is limited to $15.

Same-Day Airport Facility to Airport Facility Service Available between designated airport mail facilities in fifty-eight major cities on a next-available-flight basis. If your shipment is not available for pickup at the destination airport by the time promised, full refund of postage paid will be made.

Custom-Designed Service Available throughout the United States on a twenty-four hour basis, 365 days a year. This service is offered between any combination of airport facilities, post offices, and the customer's premises, based on a prior agreement between the postal service and the customer. The postal service guarantees that mail in this service will be delivered or available for pickup within twenty-four hours, or full refund will be made.

International Service Available to twenty-one countries under an arrangement comparable to custom-designed service and to seventeen countries as international on-demand service, which does not require prior agreement.

First-Class Mail

First-class matter includes letters or other handwritten or typewritten matter (including carbons and photocopies of letters), postcards, sealed greeting cards, business reply mail, and anything in written form in part (such as invoices and checks). First-class mail can also be included with other classes of mail by the sender, in which case it travels at the slower rate even though, as is required, first-class postage has been paid on the material enclosed. First-class mail is sealed against postal inspection of its contents.

The telephone company and other utilities send their monthly bills in large-volume mailings of presorted first-class letters at preferential rates. An annual presort first-class mailing fee must be paid.

Of course, anything may be sent as first-class mail at the sender's option, although you should weigh the trade-offs (speed of delivery against cost) before electing to use first-class mail for larger packages and parcels.

Any first-class mail that must travel a long distance is automatically sent by air. (For all practical purposes, the old classification of domestic air mail no longer exists.) The postal service has established service standards for each individual post office. Your postmaster can tell you which mail destinations receive overnight service from your post office and which receive second-day and third-day service. In theory, no location in the United States is more than three days away from any other location in terms of first-class mail delivery.

Certain-size standards—minimum and maximum—have been set for first-class mail. A piece of first-class mail weighing one ounce or less is nonstandard if it is larger than $6\frac{1}{8}$ inches in height, $11\frac{1}{2}$ inches in length, and $\frac{1}{4}$ inch in thickness.

A surcharge is assessed on each piece of mail that exceeds any of these standards, in addition to the applicable postage and fees. This is an important consideration if you are designing envelopes for your business or for a client.

Pieces of mail that are ¼ inch or less in thickness are unmailable unless they are rectangular in shape, at least 3½ inches high, at least 5 inches long, and at least .007 inch thick (about the thickness of a postcard). Exceptions to the minimum-size rule are hotel and motel keys (often carried away by guests and returned through the mails) and identification devices. Mail not meeting these standards will be returned to the sender.

TIP: if you send large-size envelopes of gray or brown kraft paper usually associated with other categories of mail, it's a good idea to stamp them FIRST-CLASS MAIL front and back to call attention to that fact. Better still, buy large white envelopes preprinted with green diamond borders for first-class mail. These are instantly recognizable by postal sorters as first-class mail.

Priority Mail

All first-class mail weighing more than twelve ounces is classified as priority mail. Unlike first-class mail, charges are based on weight and distance to be traveled. Your post office can furnish you with a priority-mail-zone chart for your area. Priority mail receives overnight service to designated cities and second-day service nationwide.

Maximum permissible weight of priority mail is seventy pounds. Size is limited to 108 inches in combined length and girth (the distance around the parcel at its thickest part). A parcel weighing less than fifteen pounds and measuring over 84 inches but not exceeding 100 inches in length and girth combined is charged at a rate equal to that for a fifteen-pound parcel. Priority mail stickers are available at post offices.

Second-Class Mail

This category includes printed newspapers and magazines that travel at special rates. However, to obtain such rates, it is necessary for the publisher to file forms and to pay a fee for the privilege of "entering" such mail as second-class matter and mailing it in bulk. When such publications are mailed singly by the publisher, they are charged at a higher single-piece rate. Recipients may forward complete copies of second-class publications at the second-class nonsubscriber transient rate or at the fourth-class rate, whichever is lower.

Controlled-Circulation Publications

Magazine-type publications of twenty-four pages or more circulated largely without a subscription fee are classified as controlled-circulation publications and are charged a special rate.

Third-Class Mail

Third-class mail (sometimes called "advertising mail") is mail weighing up to one pound that cannot be classified as first- or second-class mail. If over one pound, such mail must go at priority or fourth-class rates.

To be mailable at third-class rates, such mail must be clearly marked THIRD CLASS or BULK RATE—the latter only if a bulk-rate permit has been obtained—and this notation must be shown on the front of the envelope. Often it is included as part of the permit indicia, or meter stamp, sometimes abbreviated BLK RT, especially by large-volume mailers conscious of the public's aversion to what has come to be unfairly called "junk mail." (The postal service prefers to refer to this as "bulk business mail.")

One of the commonly held beliefs of the public is that this kind of mail clogs the postal system, making it difficult for more important mail to pass through. As your postmaster will tell you, this is a myth. Presorted mail from large-volume mailers actually requires less handling than do individual letters. Consequently, it generates profitable revenues for the postal service that reduce the need for federal subsidies—profits that can be applied to other classes of mail. It's the carelessly addressed, indecipherable or illegible pieces of mail without ZIP codes that take time and trouble to sort and handle.

Third-class mail includes merchandise such as seeds, cuttings, bulbs, roots, scions, and plants; by far the largest volume of third-

class mail is in the form of printed matter—subscription-solicita-
tion letters, newsletters, catalogs, advertising circulars, and bro-
chures.

Not-for-profit mailers (including political committees) may
qualify for mailing at special bulk-mailing rates, with three levels
of presorting and charges. These include presorting by carrier
route, five-digit ZIP code, and all others. "ZIP coding" refers to
the Zoning Improvement Plan instituted by the postal service in
1963, which gave a five-digit number to each post office. It has
been supplemented by a voluntary ZIP plus four-digit code that
took effect in 1983. Postage must be paid and applied by meter
stamp, permit imprint, or precanceled stamps. (The latter are
preferred by some large-volume mailers because they make the
mailing piece look less like bulk mail.)

Fourth-Class Mail

You know this by the more familiar designation of "parcel
post." It includes all mailable matter not in first, second, or third
class or priority mail weighing more than a pound. Fourth-class
rates are governed by weight and the distance the piece must
travel. Domestically, the United States is divided into eight zones.
(This division of the country into postal zones is one reason early
mail-order catalog houses had their beginnings in the centrally
located Midwest.)

Limits are set for both weight and size of fourth-class packages,
which can be as heavy as seventy pounds and can measure 108
inches in combined length and girth. Your post office can furnish
you with a chart showing the zone structure from your post office.

A special fourth-class rate exists for books of twenty-four pages
or more, at least twenty-two of which are printed and consist
wholly of reading matter. What makes this special mailing rate so
attractive is that zone rates do not apply. Similar special treatment
is given to book manuscripts, reels of positive film 16 millimeter
or narrower, printed music in sheet or bound form, printed objective test materials, sound recordings, educational reference charts,
and medical information for doctors, hospitals, medical schools,
and medical students. A special rate also exists for books lent or
exchanged between schools, colleges, universities, public libraries,
museums, herbaria, and not-for-profit religious, educational, sci-

entific, philanthropic, agricultural, labor, veterans, or fraternal organizations.

Such packages must be marked SPECIAL FOURTH-CLASS RATE—BOOKS, SPECIAL FOURTH-CLASS RATE—MANUSCRIPT, or LIBRARY RATE.

Mixed Classes

It is sometimes desirable to send two pieces of mail of different classes together as a single mailing. A good example of this would be a parcel containing a defective item returned to the manufacturer with a letter of explanation. The package would take fourth-class postage, but minimum first-class postage should be applied to the package, which should also be marked FIRST-CLASS LETTER ENCLOSED.

Alternatively, a first-class letter may be put in an envelope bearing first-class postage and affixed to the outside of the package. Such an envelope should be clearly marked LETTER ENCLOSED so that the recipient will not mistake the envelope for a mailing label. Invoices or sales slips may be included in or on fourth-class mail. (These are often placed in a window envelope attached to the outside of the package.)

In principle, all mail, with the exception of first-class mail, is liable to inspection. The mailing of a sealed package at fourth-class rates implies that the sender consents to inspection of the contents. (This inspection is not intended to be a moral judgment of the contents of the parcel but a verification that the parcel indeed qualifies for mailing at that rate.) Because of this implied consent, the old printed notation MAY BE OPENED FOR POSTAL INSPECTION is no longer necessary. However, unless a package is sent as first-class mail and conspicuously marked FIRST-CLASS MAIL, it risks being treated as parcel post and subject to inspection.

Foreign Mail

Surface mail and airmail services are available to foreign countries. *Note*: First-class postage rates to Canada and Mexico are the same as rates within the United States. Airmail postage to other foreign countries is charged at half-ounce increments rather than in one-ounce steps.

Special services, such as registry (maximum foreign indemnity, $25.20 to Canada, the maximum indemnity is $200), return receipt, and special delivery are available. Special-delivery mail to foreign destinations must show in red near the name of the country of destination the word EXPRES or bear an EXPRES label obtainable from the post office. "EXPRES" is an internationally recognized designation for special-delivery mail.

Parcels for overseas destinations are handled as parcel post or air parcel post. Rates, weight, and size limitations and other rules vary from country to country. (International COD service is not available.)

Small sealed parcels, called "letter packages," can be sent at letter rates if marked LETTER. A customs declaration form, obtainable at the post office, must be attached to each letter or parcel containing merchandise and must describe the contents.

Special air letters, or aerogrammes, are available at post offices. These are lightweight prestamped single sheets that can be folded to form their own envelope (much like early letters in the eighteenth century, when postal systems had their beginnings).

Forwarding of Mail

If you change your address, the post office will forward your mail for the following periods:

First-class mail: eighteen months at no charge.

Second-class mail: ninety days locally at no charge; if a move is nonlocal, mail will be forwarded for ninety days, but only if the customer pays the postage and a written guarantee to that effect is on file at the forwarding post office.

Third-class mail: one year if endorsed "Forwarding and Return Postage Guaranteed." Otherwise, such mail is disposed of as waste or sent to the dead-letter or dead-parcel office.

Fourth-class mail: one year, with postage collected from the addressee.

Express mail: one year.

SPECIAL SERVICES

Not only does the postal service accept and transport various classes of mail, it also offers a variety of special services, all at extra cost.

Registered Mail

Registering a letter or a parcel guarantees the security of valuables and gives the sender the option of purchasing insurance up to a stated level. (You'll have to declare the full value of the contents, whether or not postal insurance is purchased.) Exceptions would include a situation in which the mailer has outside insurance for valuations above $1,000 or if the contents are declared to have no commercial value (in which case the minimum registry fee will be charged). For valuations in excess of $25,000 (the limit of postal insurance), special outside insurance can be obtained for the specific mailing during transit. Only mail prepaid at first-class rates may be registered (but you may register COD parcels).

To be acceptable for registration, each piece of mail must be tightly sealed on all edges with mucilage or glue and must show the complete address of both the sender and intended recipient. Because the sending and receiving post offices stamp their postmarks on the flaps or seals of a piece of registered mail, plastic tape should not be used for sealing registered mail. Use plain paper or cloth tape that will absorb a postmark impression and will adhere in such a manner as to destroy the envelope or wrapper if it is removed.

Registered mail, because it is under complete postal service accountability and control en route to its destination, offers one feature other kinds of mail do not offer. Once it has been dispatched, the sender can direct that a piece of registered mail be sent to a new address if, for example, it was discovered that the intended recipient had moved to another address.

Registered mail offers several other features. The sender, of course, receives a receipt showing that the mailing has been accepted for transmittal and delivery. It is sometimes desirable for the sender to have proof of delivery. In such cases, for an additional fee, the carrier will obtain an additional signed receipt (called a "return receipt") for any piece of registered mail. A receipt can be requested after mailing, but the charge for it is doubled.

For an additional fee, the sender may designate that delivery of a piece of registered mail be restricted to the addressee only. Registered mail may be forwarded to another address (if known to the postal service) with the address of ultimate delivery recorded on the return receipt, which comes back to the sender. Such special services may be useful in tracing creditors who have moved and left no address.

Certified Mail

In some cases, the sender only needs a record of delivery of a letter without the special protection that registered mail offers. Certified mail may be the answer. Certified mail costs less and is ideal for mail that has no intrinsic value (for example, a notification letter to your landlord, an invoice or statement, or a nonnegotiable bond). Certified mail carries no insurance, but it can give the sender a receipt for a letter. Delivery is made individually by the carrier; for an additional fee, a signature will be obtained on a return receipt that comes back to the sender. Because the recipient cannot deny having received a certified letter and because it carries with it a certain sense of importance and urgency, certified mail is a widely employed and useful tool for the collection of overdue bills.

Insured Mail

Any piece of third- or fourth-class mail or first-class or priority mail containing third- or fourth-class matter (provided it bears the endorsement CONTAINS THIRD-CLASS or FOURTH-CLASS MATTER) may be insured for up to $400. Reimbursement will be made for any insured mail that has been lost, rifled, or damaged in transit. Receipts are given, and the sender may request restricted delivery.

COD Service

Merchandise for which you have not been paid may be sent COD (the letters stand for "collect on delivery"), but the shipment must be in response to a genuine order or agreement made by the mailer with the addressee. Postage on the shipment and the COD fees must be prepaid by the sender at the time of mailing (although these may be included in the amount to be collected from the addressee). The addressee also pays for the merchandise plus the money order fee for transmitting the money collected to the sender. The maximum amount collectible on any shipment is $400.

Certificates of Mailing

It is not generally known, but for a nominal fee a sender may obtain proof of mailing of any kind of mail at a post office. This is given on a postal form completed by the mailer and presented at the time of mailing. When can such a certificate be useful? If you are under no obligation to pay the extra charges necessary to insure an item of value only to the recipient, this is a low-cost way of having proof of mailing. For example, it would be an inexpensive method of documenting that one's tax return had indeed been mailed to the IRS or state tax department on time.

OTHER SPECIAL SERVICES

Special Delivery

This service offers the fastest means of handling mail and can be used with all classes of mail. Such mail must be marked SPECIAL DELIVERY above the address. Unfortunately, this service has become less attractive because costs have gone up and delivery frequency has been reduced. Delivery to the addressee is still immediate and by messenger from the post office of final destination during the prescribed hours.

Use of special delivery conveys to the recipient that you consider this letter important and you have taken pains to see that it is received as quickly as possible. Special delivery can ensure delivery on Saturday or even Sundays or holidays at larger post offices (your postmaster will be able to tell you this) when regular carrier service to the destination address is less frequent or nonexistent. Special-delivery service is available to all addresses served by city carriers and to addresses within a one-mile radius of other delivery post offices.

It's a waste of money to send special-delivery mail to post-office-box addresses (unless you know that the box holder has left a standing order with the local post office for the delivery of special-delivery mail to home or office) or to APO (Army Post Office) or FPO (Fleet Post Office) addresses. Do not use special delivery to a business office if it will arrive on a weekend when the office is closed. Also, some large companies treat special-delivery mail as ordinary mail after it reaches their mail room and deliver it to the addressee routinely with ordinary mail.

Special Handling

This service is available only for third- and fourth-class mail at a cost much less than that of special delivery. In principle, such parcels are treated as first-class mail to the office of final destination, after which they will be delivered by the next regularly scheduled carrier or on the next package-truck trip. Such parcels must be marked SPECIAL HANDLING, and the fee must be paid at the time of mailing. Special handling is especially useful in the shipment of highly perishable items, such as plants, baby chicks or other poultry, and packaged bees, all of which require special care.

It's a waste of money to specify and pay for special delivery and special handling at the same time. All special-delivery mail is treated as first-class mail.

Return Receipts

A return receipt is proof of delivery of an item. Return receipts are available for mail insured for more than $20, certified, registered, COD, and domestic express mail shipments. It shows the article's postal service number, the signature of the person who signed for it, and the date of delivery. For an additional fee (in case the item must be forwarded), you can obtain a receipt showing the exact address of delivery.

Restricted Delivery

For an additional fee, you may also request that delivery of a specific item be made to the addressee only or to an individual authorized to receive the mail of the addressee (for example, an attorney). Exceptions are express mail and mail addressed to employees of the federal, state, or local governments.

Recall of Mail

You wrote a letter in the heat of anger, and you've since had time to reflect on the lack of wisdom of your act. Or you wrote a strong letter of complaint, and you have since discovered that you had the facts wrong. Relax—all is not lost. Mail deposited in a collection box or a post office may be recalled on proper identification of the sender. But you must agree to pay all expenses of the recall, including the cost of any necessary telegrams or long-distance phone calls and the cost of return postage for returning the letter to you. You'll find your postmaster knowledgeable as well as sympathetic about this—it happens frequently.

Delivery of Mail to a Designated Agent

Celebrities find it useful to have their mail delivered to an agent. Even if you do not receive fan mail, you may want to avail yourself of this service. But you must notify the post office in writing so they will have the agent's name on file. To revoke this, you'll have to write still another letter.

OTHER SERVICES

Business Reply Mail

For volume mailers, the old-fashioned stamped, self-addressed envelope is a thing of the past. Mailers who want to encourage response by paying the postage now use business reply mail, which is returned from any U.S. post office to the address shown on the preprinted envelope or card. The advantage is that the mailer only pays for those replies received. For the privilege of using business reply mail, an annual fee is charged; in addition, postage must be paid at the regular first-class rate plus a business reply charge (based on size) for each piece received.

Mailgram Service

Mailgram is an electronic communications service offered by Western Union and the U.S. Postal Service. Mailgrams are telegramlike messages transmitted over Western Union's communications network to printing devices located in about 150 larger post offices. The printed Mailgrams are then placed in distinctive window envelopes and delivered by regular mail carrier on the next business day anywhere in the United States.

Mailgrams can be sent from Telex terminals by means of a direct computer connection with Western Union, from computer magnetic tape, or by telephone. For the latter purpose, Western Union provides a toll-free telephone number. Charges for this service will appear on the next month's telephone bill or may be charged against one of the standard credit cards.

A business reply Mailgram is now available for those who want their Mailgrams to encourage a response from recipients. In addition to the Mailgram, they contain a built-in response device using a business reply envelope.

Stamps, Envelopes, and Postcards

Postage stamps in various denominations are available in sheet, coil, or bound-booklet form. (Unused stamps are exchangeable if received in a damaged state when purchased, but unused loose stamps or adhesive stamps fixed to unmailed matter are not exchangeable or refundable.)

Precanceled stamps and precanceled stamped envelopes are available to be used by special-permit holders (but only at the post office where they were purchased). The use of precanceled postage reduces the time and cost of mail handling and expedites delivery.

Stamped standard and window envelopes in two sizes (no. 6¾ and no. 10) and denominations (first class and precanceled) are available. For a nominal charge, the sender's name and address can be imprinted on orders for quantities of 500 or more. Up to two lines of advertising and a telephone number may also be included with the return address.

Postal cards are available in single or double (reply) format. To facilitate imprinting by customers, postcards are available in uncut sheets of forty.

Misaddressed, spoiled, or unserviceable, uncanceled stamped envelopes may be exchanged at face value for other stamps, stamped envelopes, or postal cards.

Mailing Materials

The U.S. Postal Service offers for sale three sizes of cushioned mailing bags and mailing boxes, called "post boxes." Bag sizes are small (6 by 9 inches), medium (10½ by 15 inches), and large (14 by 19 inches). Box sizes are small (8 by 8 by 8 inches), medium (6 by 12 by 18 inches), and large (10 by 12 by 18 inches).

Money Orders

Domestic money orders may be purchased at any post office, branch, station, and from rural carriers in the United States and its possessions (except for certain offices in Alaska). The maximum amount for any money order purchased is limited to $500. There is no limitation on the number of money orders that can be purchased at any one time.

The postal service will replace without charge a lost money order, provided it was completed by the purchaser, a mutilated money order, a money order voided by too many endorsements, or a spoiled or incorrectly prepared money order.

For a small fee, it is possible to obtain a photocopy of a paid money order within two years of its cashing.

International money orders may be purchased at most larger post offices but may only be sent to countries having an exchange agreement with the United States. With the exception of Great Britain and Norway, the maximum amount for an international money order is $500.

POSTAGE METERS

Introduced in 1920, the postage meter quickly caught on and has been a hallmark of business bigness ever since. Aside from the prestige value of a metered-mail postmark, a postage meter can be a useful adjunct to a home office for other reasons.

First, a postage meter eliminates the need for keeping postage stamps in assorted denominations on hand, with the possibility that they will be lost, stolen, or never used. (A stolen postage meter can easily be traced, because each imprints its identifying serial number as part of the postmark.)

A postage meter provides automatic accounting of postage expenses and quicker movement through the postal system. Because metered mail is already dated and canceled, it is processed faster; it does not require facing (arranging letters with addresses and stamps all facing the same way) and cancellation. With a postage meter, you can also add advertising slogans to outgoing mail as part of the process of applying postage.

The U.S. Postal Service has licensed only four firms to lease postage meters to mailers in the United States: Pitney Bowes, Friden Alcatel, Postalia, and IMS/Hasler. Rental rates may be as low as ten dollars monthly if paid annually in advance.

To ascertain what a postage meter will cost in terms of rental cost per letter or parcel mailed, divide the monthly rental charge by the average number of letters and parcels mailed.

Postage metering equipment consists of two parts: the meter, which stores and prints postage (either directly or on adhesive tapes) and records the amounts used and the balance remaining, and the mailing machine, which moistens, seals, and stacks the envelopes. Mailing machines offer such other features as sealing without applying postage, check signing (by means of a printing plate), and item counting (useful in volume mailings).

A home office can operate nicely with the postage meter alone; the mailing-machine base can be added later if mail volume warrants. Postage meters are only leased; mailing machines may be leased or bought.

Postage meters are available with hand cranks or automatic feed. A small, hand-held Postalia model, KF 1501, is operated by running the meter across the package or letter to be mailed, printing the postage directly on it—a useful feature when mailing stacked cartons in a warehouse.

The capacity of postage meters can vary from $100 to $10,000 and even $100,000, depending on size. When postage runs low on your postage meter, it will be reset by your local post office on prepayment of an additional amount of postage. Trips to the post office are unnecessary with some newer meters. By maintaining a postage-meter balance at a trustee bank, you can recharge such meters by means of a simple phone call on a tone phone to a data center for resetting authorization.

TWENTY-EIGHT

I Need It Tomorrow: Using Freight and Package Services

Anyone watching TV commercials could hardly be blamed for thinking that half of the country's population must be sending packages and letters to the other half by overnight delivery services. How else to explain the phenomenal growth of air express?

Not many years ago, the overnight air-express industry did not exist. To move a shipment by air, you called one of the two major air-freight forwarders, Emery or Airborne, which would pick up the package at your door and turn it over to an airline. The shipment was then flown to an airport near the destination, and the forwarders would deliver it to the consignee.

Thanks to an abundance of night flights, delivery schedules were excellent. Because the industry was closely regulated, air-freight forwarders were not allowed to own large aircraft, and the airlines were not permitted to truck freight very far from the airport.

In 1973, Frederick W. Smith founded Federal Express as the first true air-express company. Smith got around the regulation that kept forwarders and airlines separate by flying small corporate-sized jets. Another innovative idea was the company's centrally located sorting center, or "hub," at Memphis, Tennessee, where small packages from all over the country were brought by company jets, sorted, reloaded on the same planes, and delivered to their destinations the next day by company trucks.

Federal Express's first-night package total was only eighteen shipments. For the first two years, it was touch-and-go; with losses of $27 million, the company came within a hair's breadth of folding. Today Federal Express is a highly successful operation, with revenues of more than a billion dollars. Three factors made the difference: the oil crisis put a crimp in the number of night flights flown by passenger airlines; REA Express went bankrupt in 1975, taking with it its marginal air-express business; and manufacturers' shipping patterns changed, moving toward smaller, higher-value shipments (such as computer components) that required rapid and reliable distribution.

It was evident to Emery and Airborne that growth in traditional heavy air-freight traffic was slow, such traffic was painfully susceptible to fluctuations in the economy, and cutbacks in the number of passenger flights at night made it impossible for them to match Federal's delivery times. When the industry began to be deregulated in 1977, Airborne and Emery bought their own fleets of planes and became aggressive competitors of Federal Express.

All overnight air-express services operate on the same "hub" principle introduced by Federal Express. To keep costly and time-consuming errors to a minimum, elaborate verification and quality-control procedures are employed—sometimes a destination is verified by four separate sorters. Airborne Express, headquartered in Seattle and with its hub at a company-owned airport in Wilmington, Ohio, allows workers two errors before dismissing them. Understandably, mistakes are few.

Emery Air Freight, still the world's largest freight forwarder, also has its hub in Ohio at Dayton. The Buckeye State's appeal is explained by the statistic that two-thirds of the population of the United States lives within 600 miles of the state.

Other hubs are Indianapolis (Purolator Courier), Cincinnati and Salt Lake City (DHL Worldwide Courier Express, the largest carrier internationally of courier-escorted packages), and Louisville (United Parcel Service).

The acknowledged behemoth of the overnight-delivery industry, Federal Express, claims a 45 percent share of a market expected to grow at a rate of 20 percent for the next five years. But Purolator Courier actually moves more packages, and United Parcel Service has the largest fleet of vehicles, although not all are used in the overnight air service. In terms of package volume, Airborne is today the fastest-growing air-express company in the world.

Limits on the allowable weights of overnight shipments have increased steadily; they are now at 200 pounds for one carrier

(Airborne). Before shipping anything, check with the intended carrier to verify that your shipment does not exceed the carrier's weight and size limitations.

In 1984, Federal Express introduced ZapMail to transmit facsimiles of documents to selected destinations, with delivery within two hours of an initiating call for a pickup and delivery within one hour if the material is dropped off at a Federal Express receiving station. Experts believe that this service will capture no more than 15 percent of the overnight market.

Bigger is not necessarily better in this hyperactive industry. Some carriers offer quantity discounts for volume shippers. If you will be making shipments regularly, investigate and compare carriers before designating one. If you have two packages going to the same destination, send them by different carriers and ask the recipients when they arrived.

Once you have decided on a specific carrier, monitor its service from time to time by spot-checking with recipients to ascertain that deliveries were made on time. If you receive many incoming packages at your expense, suggest to shippers that they use the carrier you designate.

If you send several shipments to the same address, consolidate them. One big wire-strapped bundle of packages will cost less than several small packages sent individually.

Some carriers supply airwaybills with your name imprinted as the shipper—ask your air-express company for such time-saving preprinted forms.

Read and compare air-express service guides carefully, particularly the fine print. For example, if a shipment cannot be delivered, some carriers notify shippers by mail and make no effort to ascertain a forwarding address. By the time you find out about the nondelivery, any advantages of overnight delivery will have been lost. Other carriers assume no liability for delayed shipments.

Don't send air-express letters and packages to post-office-box or RFD addresses. And don't use air express if you don't need it. When it doesn't "absolutely, positively have to be there overnight," use a less expensive method of shipping. Nor is there much point in flying a package from your office to a hub somewhere in the Middle West if its eventual destination is only one street away from you.

As convenient as overnight letter and package services are, they may not represent the least expensive ways of getting something from one place to another when transit time is not a factor. Many air-express companies offer slightly slower service by air at lower rates. Federal Express calls this service "standard air" and UPS calls it "second-day air service." Businesses lose millions of dollars annually because of a lack of package-shipping know-how.

Here is a comparison of the other choices available:

Surface Services

1. *Parcel Post*

    Service: post office to door.

    Weight limit: seventy pounds.

    Size limit: 108 inches in combined length and girth.

    Insurance: may be insured to a maximum of $400 for a fee. Unless the item is insured, shipment cannot be traced for proof of delivery.

    Remarks: inexpensive, especially for items such as books and records traveling long distances at unzoned rates. Customer must bring shipment to post office.

2. *United Parcel Service*

    Service: door to door.

    Weight limit: seventy pounds.

    Size limit: 108 inches in combined length and girth.

    Insurance: to $100 at no charge if requested at time of shipment. All shipments can be traced.

    Remarks: comparatively inexpensive; all charges based on weight and distance. Next-day pickup available. May be cheaper than parcel post at some weights to certain zones; compare rate charts carefully.

3. *Intercity and Interstate Bus Lines*

    Service: bus station to bus station.

    Weight limit: varies with bus company (Greyhound: 100 pounds; Trailways: 150 pounds).

    Size limit: 141 inches in combined length and girth. Largest dimension: Greyhound: 60 inches; Trailways: 74 inches.

    Insurance: available; packages can be traced.

    Remarks: inexpensive.

4. *Amtrak Package Express*

    Service: railroad station to railroad station.

Weight limit: seventy-five pounds.

Size limit: 108 inches in combined length and girth.

Insurance: available.

Remarks: inexpensive; infrequently used.

5. *Motor Freight*

Service: door to door.

Weight limit: none, but governed by motor-truck capability.

Size limit: none, but governed by motor-truck capability.

Insurance: available.

Remarks: ideal for shipments over 100 pounds.

Air Services

1. *Priority Mail*

Service: post office to addressee.

Weight limit: seventy pounds.

Size limit: 108 inches in combined length and girth.

Insurance: available to $400; may also be registered.

Remarks: replaces the mail service formerly called "air parcel post."

2. *Express Mail*

Service: post office to addressee.

post office to post office.

airport mail facility to airport mail facility.

Weight limit: seventy pounds.

Size limit: 108 inches in combined length and girth.

Insurance: available up to $500 at no extra charge; to $50,000 for business records.

Remarks: zoned rates apply: post office to addressee packages are charged at a single rate up to two pounds.

3. *Airline Small Package*

Service: airport baggage counter to airport baggage counter.

Weight limit: seventy pounds.

Size limit: ninety inches in combined length and girth.

Insurance: available.

Remarks: must be at airport baggage counter thirty minutes before flight time; can be picked up at destination thirty minutes after flight has arrived.

4. *Air Freight*
    Service: door to door.
    Weight limit: none, but governed by aircraft capability.
    Size limit: none, but governed by aircraft capability.
    Insurance: available.
    Remarks: delivery will be within forty-eight hours.

Freight Shipments

The use of motor-truck, rail, or air carriers for shipments creates some special situations. Such shipments are moved under a bill of lading, which is at once a receipt for the merchandise, evidence of title to the shipment, and a contract between the shipper and the carrier for the transportation of the shipment "with reasonable dispatch."

A bill of lading may be a "straight" bill of lading, which is nonnegotiable, or it may be an "order" bill of lading, which requires the consignee to pay a bank the invoice value shown on the bill of lading in order to obtain the shipment. Airwaybills are no less bills of lading than traditional bills of lading.

Bills of lading are drawn up subject to certain conditions. The so-called short form bill of lading may not show all the conditions. It is nevertheless subject to the same terms and conditions as are listed on the straight bill of lading.

Because a bill of lading is a contract and therefore a legal document, care should be taken in its preparation. For example, unless the word "Prepaid" is entered in the space provided, a shipment will be treated as a collect shipment, with the possibility that the consignee may refuse it.

To avoid the possibility of attempted delivery at the wrong place, the wise shipper includes not only the city or town and state in the address shown on the bill of lading but the county as well. As an example, take a destination named Mount Pleasant. There are nearly a hundred Mount Pleasants in the United States; in Pennsylvania alone, there are Mount Pleasants in at least sixteen of the state's sixty-seven counties. Other popular and widely distributed town names are Riverside, Five Points, and Fairview.

Because freight charges are based on the descriptions of the contents of the shipment shown in the bill of lading prepared by the shipper, the wise shipper can achieve substantial reductions in freight costs by studying freight classifications. If you make or receive frequent freight shipments, a freight consultant can verify that the cheapest freight classifications are being used by you and by those who ship to you regularly, if you are paying the freight charges.

The ownership of goods in transit with freight carriers is an important question. The governing factors are the terms quoted on the original purchase order and on the bill of lading. The magic letters are "F.O.B." (which stands for free on board). Table 28.1 shows who has title to freight shipments.

Table 28.1. Who Has Title to Freight Shipments?

Terms	Has Title	Picks Route	Determines Classification	Pays Charges	Files Claim
FOB shipping point	buyer	buyer	buyer	buyer	buyer
Freight prepaid and allowed	buyer	seller	seller	seller	buyer
Freight prepaid and added	buyer	buyer	buyer	seller	buyer
Freight equalized	buyer	seller	seller	both	buyer
FOB destination	seller	seller	seller	seller	seller

If you make shipments overseas or import goods from abroad, you may encounter the following terms and abbreviations:

Ex Works (also "Ex Factory," "Ex Mill," "Ex Plantation," or "Ex Warehouse") Seller makes goods available at the plant or other location, but is not responsible for loading or transporting them. Buyer assumes all risks and costs of transportation.

FOR/FOT (Free on Rail/Free on Truck at designated shipping point) These refer to railroad cars and motor trucks. Seller must place the goods on a specified carrier. Buyer assumes responsibility once goods are loaded.

FAS (Free Alongside Ship at designated shipping point) Seller must deliver the goods alongside the ship. Buyer assumes responsibility for loading goods on ship and all liability once goods are delivered alongside ship.

Free Carrier (at designated shipping point) Seller delivers goods to the initial carrier, at which time responsibility passes to the buyer and not necessarily at the ship's rail.

FOB (Free on Board vessel at designated port) Seller places goods on board ship; liability for loss or damage becomes the buyer's once goods pass the ship's rail.

FOB (Free on Board at designated airport) Not quite the same as FOB vessel; seller's responsibility ends when goods are delivered to an air carrier or its agent.

Freight/Carriage Paid (to designated destination) Seller pays freight, but responsibility for loss or damage becomes the buyer's when goods are delivered to the initial carrier.

C&F (Cost and Freight to designated destination) Seller pays costs of placing goods on board ship and freight to the destination. Responsibility passes to buyer once the goods pass the ship's rail.

Freight/Carriage & Insurance Paid (to designated destination) Same terms as Freight/Carriage Paid, but also includes insurance paid by seller.

CIF (Cost, Insurance, Freight to designated destination) Same terms as C & F, but also includes marine insurance, which is paid by the seller but must be transferable to the buyer.

Ex Ship (at named destination port) Seller makes goods available to buyer at destination, where liability passes to buyer.

Ex Quay (at designated destination port) Seller makes goods available on the dock at designated port of importation. Duty may be paid by the seller or the buyer, but the responsibility for this should be clearly stated.

Delivered Duty Free (at designated point) Seller delivers goods with all duties and inland transportation paid to buyer's premises at which point title passes to buyer.

Shipping Containers

Containers for shipping freight and express are of many types and have their own nomenclature. Here are some hints on what to use (and what those who make shipments to you should do).

Fiberboard boxes Light in weight and low in cost, these are the most widely used shipping container. You know them as "cartons." In selecting them, the first consideration should be the bursting-strength test. Turn a carton upside down and you'll find a circular printed "certificate" showing the name of the manufacturer and the carton's performance in a test of its resistance to bursting. The higher the number, the better. For books and similar heavy objects, this number should be 275 or more. This certificate also contains information on size limits and allowable gross weight.

To pack a carton properly, the contents should fill the container so as to support sides and top. Without sufficient resistance to compression, the carton might collapse if placed at the bottom of a stack of cartons. The most common error in packaging is not properly cushioning the contents within the container; shocks received on the outside can be transmitted to the contents.

Ideally, carton flaps should be stapled or glued with a water-resistant adhesive applied over the area of contact between the flaps. If there's a chance the shipment will be exposed to moisture, seams should be sealed on the inside and outside with water-resistant tape. If you reuse a carton, be sure that it's rigid and in good condition, with no punctures, tears, rips, or corner damage, and that all flaps are intact.

In the absence of commercial cushioning materials, heavy brown-paper grocery bags can be crumpled and stuffed around the item being shipped. Less desirable are crumpled sheets of newspaper. (It's a good idea to get in the habit of saving and reusing packing materials from shipments delivered to you.) Remember that the shipment should be protected on *all* sides, so several inches of cushioning material should also be placed on the bottom of the carton. Use enough cushioning material so that the contents are several inches from all sides and edges of the carton and cannot move if you shake the carton.

Proper closure of the carton is as important as adequate cushioning. Use strong tape, at least two inches wide. The tape can be pressure-sensitive plastic tape, gummed paper tape, or filament-reinforced tape. Avoid the use of string or rope on packages; not only isn't it an effective closure, but it may snag on conveyors and other automatic equipment.

For further reinforcement, use metal or plastic tension straps crossing at right angles at the top and bottom of the carton. Alternatively, apply two encircling girth straps of filament or similar tape.

Before labeling your shipment, be sure to cross out or remove all visible previous markings and address labels that might tend to mislead or confuse the shipping carrier's employees.

Your label should show the complete address of the consignee, including the ZIP code, which is now universally used in sorting operations. Include the apartment number with all multiunit dwelling addresses. As an extra precaution, show the recipient's telephone number on the label, especially if the shipment is addressed to a post-office box or rural route destination. Place the label on the top of the package. (The "top" is considered to be the most stable orientation of the package, as it might ride on a conveyor.) You'll only cause confusion if you place more than one label on the package. As an added precaution in case the label should become unreadable, include a duplicate label or address information inside the carton. Always show your return address, preferably a street address, and ZIP code.

If you bundle or strap cartons together, they should be of identical size and shape. Be sure a shipping label and return-address information are on and in each individual carton.

TWENTY-NINE

Please Take a Letter: Employees and Independent Contractors

You've been operating your home office by yourself, and everything has gone swimmingly. Now you've decided to have a staff— to add someone to help you with the work. Suddenly, the picture changes. You are now an employer and subject to a whole new set of rules.

But you don't *feel* like an employer. The person who is helping you only comes in occasionally, at odd hours, as needed; it's not regular work or a forty-hour week.

For tax purposes, you may be an employer, nevertheless. One thing you should not do is to pay this person "off the books," even if the worker asks to be paid this way. Government computers are becoming more sophisticated, and enforcement procedures are tightening up.

Generally speaking, an employer is someone for whom a worker performs a *service* as an employee. The employer (you) provides the tools (typewriter, drafting table, or other office machinery or equipment) and the place to work (your home office) and has the right to fire the employee. A person paying wages to a worker at the conclusion of the work period is an employer. If you meet these tests, you are an employer.

Similar tests apply to the determination of who is an employee. Employees can be defined either under common law or under special statutes.

A common-law employee is anyone who performs services that can be controlled by an employer—what will be done and how it will be done. Persons in business for themselves, such as doctors, lawyers, veterinarians, and consultants, are not employees.

Once an employer-employee relationship has been established, it makes no difference what the employee is called—partner or agent, for example. Nor does it matter whether the employee is employed full or part time.

As an employer, wages you pay to an employee or employees will probably be subject to withholding—in short, you may be required to withhold federal income taxes from their wages and remit these to the government. You and the employee may also be subject to social security taxes under the Federal Insurance Contributions Act (FICA); you may also be subject to contributions under the Federal Unemployment Tax Act (FUTA).

As an employer, you should do the following:

1. Complete and mail to the Internal Revenue Service a copy of Form SS-4, *Application for Employee Identification Number.* This form can be obtained at any IRS or Social Security Administration office.

   In addition to receiving notification of your employer identification number assigned to you, you will receive coupon books, Form 8109, *Federal Tax Deposit Coupon Book,* to be used when depositing taxes through the Federal Tax Deposit System.

2. Obtain the name and social security number of each employee as it appears on the employee's Social Security card. An employee without a Social Security card can obtain one from any Social Security Administration office by completing Form SS-5, *Application for a Social Security Card.* These forms are available at IRS and Social Security Administration offices.

3. You should obtain from each employee a completed Form

W-4, *Employee's Withholding Allowance Certificate*. These
should be kept in your files.

4. You are also required to keep detailed records for income
tax, social security tax, and unemployment tax purposes. For
income tax withholding, these must include: each employee's
name, address, and social security number; the total amount
and date of each wage payment, and the period of time each
payment covers; for each wage payment, the amount subject
to withholding; the amount of withholding tax collected on
each payment and the date it was collected; and if the taxable
amount is less than the total payment, the reason why it is.

For social security (FICA) tax purposes, you must keep the
following information in your records: the amount of each wage
payment subject to FICA tax; the amount of FICA tax collected
for each payment and the date collected; and if the total wage
payment and the taxable amount differ, the reason why they do.

Additional information you are required to keep in your records
under the Federal Unemployment Tax Act (FUTA) includes the
total amount paid to your employees during the calendar year; the
amount of such compensation subject to the unemployment tax;
the amount you paid into your state unemployment tax fund; any
other information required to be shown on the unemployment tax
return; and the amount of the tax.

Social security taxes and withheld income taxes are reported
and paid together on the same form—usually Form 942, *Employer's Quarterly Federal Tax Return*. You generally will have to
make deposits of FICA and withheld income tax before the return
is due. Each return period is divided into a number of shorter
deposit periods. Whether or not you have to make a deposit for a
particular deposit period will depend on the amount of tax you
owe at the end of the period. When the amount you owe reaches a
threshold level, a deposit is required. Deposits are made by sending your check or a postal money order to an authorized financial
institution or a federal reserve bank.

Sounds complicated? It is. But wait a minute—that's not all.
You may be required to withhold state and local income taxes, too.
In addition, you may be required to pay a state unemployment tax.
If so, you will receive a credit equal to the percentage of the state
unemployment tax against your federal unemployment tax. In-
formation on your state's income tax can be obtained from the

state tax department, and information on your state's unemployment tax can be obtained from the state labor department.

You may also be required to purchase workers' compensation and disability policies to cover your employees. Information on these can be obtained from the Workers' Compensation Commission or Division of Workers' Compensation of your state.

On top of this burdensome paper work, by January 31 of the following year (or when an employee's employment ends), you must give copies of Form W-2, *Wage and Tax Statement,* to each employee.

If this seems like more work than you want to take on, you may want to reconsider your decision and not undertake anything that will make you an employer. There is one way around the tax and paper-work problems created by having an employee or employees. That way is only to do business with those who are (or who represent that they are) independent contractors or by using temporary employees obtained from an employment agency.

Those who follow an independent trade or profession in which they offer their services to the public are generally not considered to be employees. The rule of thumb is that an individual is an independent contractor if you, the employer, have the right to control or direct the result of the work but not the means and methods of accomplishing results.

If the person who performs work for you is totally independent of direction from you, performs the work off your premises, and renders invoices for the work done, you may not be considered an employer. Independent contractors are responsible for paying their own income tax, social security tax, and unemployment tax. Workers you obtain from temporary office service agencies are also not your employees but employees of the agency, which is responsible for withholding their income taxes, paying their unemployment taxes, and paying for their workers' compensation insurance.

Therefore, you do not have to withhold income tax or FICA tax from amounts you pay an independent contractor. However, if you pay an independent contractor $600 or more during the course of a year in connection with the operation of your trade or business, you must file a copy of Form 1099—MISC, *Statement for Recipients of Miscellaneous Income*, with the nearest Internal Revenue Center.

Part Four

~~~~~~

IT'S NOT
ALL GRAVY

THIRTY

Look Before You Leap

~~~~~~

For those setting up a home office as a place to work away from a regular business office, there will be few problems. But for those who have decided to give up a regular job and work at home, some words of caution are in order.

"How can you stay at home and work every day—doesn't it drive you crazy?" This is the question asked most frequently of those with an office at home. But those with offices at home have to face up to many problems other than "cabin fever." Before you hand in your resignation, be sure that an office at home is what you want. Here are some other things to consider:

Discipline Do you have the necessary discipline to work without a boss standing over you? In your home office, you will be an employee without a boss or—looking at it another way—a boss without any employees. Either way, you will need enormous self-discipline.

Distractions Will you be tempted by such distractions to concentration and motivation as "the comforts of home" and "the great outdoors"? Can you work diligently when the world outside is beckoning? There may be some advantages to having a windowless office in your home and therefore no distracting view. The windows to my home office are curtained—to shut out both sunlight (which affects my ability to view the computer monitor) and noise.

Interruptions I happen to welcome an occasional interruption; you may not. For example, the electric- and gas-meter reader comes on the seventh of every month, and the newspaper deliverer collects for the week's deliveries on Thursday afternoons, offering me a brief respite from work and welcome contact with the outside world. Special-delivery mail and UPS deliveries are infrequent; when they occur, the knocks at the front door can be heard over the home intercom monitoring system described in chapter 8.

Isolation If you need the give-and-take of traditional office situations, a home office may not be for you. You may find yourself growing sterile of ideas without co-workers to confer with every day. According to David P. Boyd and David E. Gumpert, who have studied stress and loneliness in entrepreneurs, there are ways to combat the solitude that accompanies the isolation of the home office and small business. First, recognize that loneliness "goes with the territory" and cannot be entirely removed. Seek confidants, say Messrs. Boyd and Gumpert. Be attentive to the needs of family and friends. Balance office isolation with public or social activities.

Lack of Room for Expansion Space can be a crucial problem, especially if you need more room and it simply isn't available in your house or apartment—or if you are at the legal limit of space permitted under the local zoning ordinance.

Long Hours Time spent in the home office will be a problem only if you find yourself becoming a workaholic. Long hours can be offset by days off—so long as this does not cause you to miss deadlines.

Motivation Without the presence of colleagues to banter with at coffee breaks or at lunch or the challenge of the interplay of business meetings and conferences, will you have enough self-motivation to continue plugging away each day? Will you feel out of place—someone who remains at home every day in a world of those who go to work? Comedian George Gobel once expressed this by asking, "Did you ever get the feeling that the whole world was a tuxedo and you were a pair of brown shoes?"

Dr. Walter S. Neff, professor emeritus of psychiatry at New York University, described the dichotomy of the significance of work in a 1965 article in *Psychiatry:* "Mountaineering may be a very arduous activity, but it is play for the tourist and work for the guide."

Privacy Will customers or clients invade your privacy during non-working hours? When you have a home office, some people think nothing of calling you at three in the morning.

Professionalism Will others question your professionalism because you do not have an address in a business or office area? There was a time when an address that seemed residential discouraged business callers. With the proliferation of home-based businesses, these attitudes are changing. If your residential address presents a problem for any reason (for example, bringing salesmen to your home), you can always rent a post-office box. Studies have shown that buyers by mail tend to be reluctant to send money to a post-office box; therefore, if you are operating a mail-order business, a post-office-box address may work against you.

Support Are your spouse and children understanding and supportive of your decision, or will they always be making references to "the good old days when you used to work like other people?"

Above all, if you have a tyrant for a boss, don't think of a home office as the answer to an unpleasant job situation. Get another job.

Does a home office still sound like what you want? If it does and you decide to go through with it, remember that it's a big step you will be taking, one that can mean changing your entire lifestyle. In many cases, it means cutting the hawser with associates (who may now become your competitors). Unless your home office is only a place where you work part time, it almost always means giving up your dependence on a regular paycheck.

A home office may mean that you'll have to survive on savings or with the assistance of a working spouse while you establish a regular cash flow. Invoicing clients and waiting to be paid can be nerve-racking when you are the creditor.

In addition to being an executive directing the activities of your office (or the principal creative person in your studio), with an office at home, you will have the privilege of being your own typist, bookkeeper, mail clerk, messenger, cleaning person, janitor, and security guard.

If, despite these drawbacks, it still sounds like a pleasant prospect, welcome to the most challenging, most exciting, and most satisfying place to work: *your own home office.* And say hello to one who can be the best person in the world for whom to work: *you.*

Sources and Resources

Chapter 1

Many books have been written on the subject of small business, but only a few have touched on the advantages and disadvantages of alternative home-based work styles. Among these are *Women Working Home: The Homebased Business Guide and Directory*, 2nd ed., by Marion Behr and Wendy Lazar (Norwood, N.J.: WWH Press, 1983); *The Number One Home Business Book*, by George and Sandra Delany (Cockeyesville, Md.: Liberty Publishing Company, 1981); *Home, Inc.*, by Stuart Feldstein (New York: Grosset & Dunlap, 1981); and *Working Free: Practical Alternatives to the 9 to 5 Job*, by John Applegarth (New York: AMACOM, 1982).

Chapter 2

Center on National Labor Policy, 5211 Port Royal Road, North Springfield, VA 22151

Readers interested in learning more about the local regulation of home offices and home occupations should consult *Planning for Home Occupations*, by William Toner. Available from the American Planning Association, 1313 East 60th Street, Chicago, IL 60637, at a cost of $6. The booklet also contains excerpts from zoning ordinances showing how four different communities handle the problem of home occupations.

Some Useful Addresses When Getting Started

Small Business Administration
1441 L Street, NW
Washington, DC 20416

To Order Small Business Administration Publications

Small Business Administration
P.O. Box 15434
Fort Worth, TX 76119

Small Business Administration Field Offices

ALABAMA
Birmingham: Room 202, 908 South 20th Street, 35205
ALASKA
Anchorage: Federal Building, 701 C Street, 99513
Fairbanks: 101 12th Avenue, 99701
ARIZONA
Phoenix: Room 1201, Arizona Bank Building, 3030 North Central
    Avenue, 85012
Tucson: Room 3V, Federal Building, 301 West Congress Street, 85701
ARKANSAS
Little Rock: Room 601, 320 West Capitol Avenue, 72201
CALIFORNIA
Fresno: 2202 Monterey Street, 93721
Los Angeles: 6th floor, 350 South Figueroa Street, 90071
Oakland: Room 947, 1515 Clay Street, 94612
Sacramento: Room 215, 660 J Street, 95814
San Diego: Room 4-S-29, Federal Building, 880 Front Street, 92188
San Francisco: 4th floor, 211 Main Street, 94105
San Jose, Room 424, 111 West St. John Street, 95113
Santa Ana, 2700 North Main Street, 92701
COLORADO
Denver: Room 407, U.S. Customhouse, 721 19th Street, 80202
CONNECTICUT
Hartford: One Hartford Square West, 06106
DELAWARE
Wilmington: Room 5207, Federal Building, 844 North King Street,
    19801
DISTRICT OF COLUMBIA
Washington: 6th floor, 1111 18th Street, NW, 20416
FLORIDA
Jacksonville: Room 261, Federal Building, 400 Bay Street West, 32202
Miami: 5th floor, 2222 Ponce de Leon Boulevard, 33134
Tampa: Room 607, 700 Twiggs Street East, 33602
West Palm Beach: 701 Clematis Street, 33402
GEORGIA
Atlanta: 1720 Peachtree Street, NW, 30309
Statesboro: 127 North Main Street, 30458

GUAM
Agana: Room 508, Pacific Daily News Building, 96910
HAWAII
Honolulu: Room 2213, Prince Kalanianaole Federal Building, 300 Ala Moana Boulevard, 96850
IDAHO
Boise: 2nd floor, 1005 Main Street, 83702
ILLINOIS
Chicago: Room 437, Everett McKinley Dirksen Building, 219 South Dearborn Street, 60604
Springfield: 4 North, Old State Capitol Plaza, 65806
INDIANA
Indianapolis: Room 578, New Federal Office Building, 575 North Pennsylvania Street, 46204
South Bend: Room 160, 501 East Monroe Street, 46601
IOWA
Cedar Rapids: 373 Collins Road, NE, 52402
Des Moines: Room 749, Federal Office Building, 210 Walnut Street, 50309
KANSAS
Wichita: 110 East Waterman Street, 67202
KENTUCKY
Louisville: Room 188, Federal Building, 600 Federal Place, 40202
LOUISIANA
New Orleans: 2nd floor, 1661 Canal Street, 70112
Shreveport: Room 141, Federal Office Building, 500 Fannin Street, 71101
MAINE
Augusta: Room 512, 40 Western Avenue, 04330
MARYLAND
Towson: Room 630, Maryland Executive Park, 8600 LaSalle Road, 21204
MASSACHUSETTS
Boston: 10th floor, 150 Causeway Street, 02114
Holyoke: 4th floor, 302 High Street, 01040
MICHIGAN
Detroit: Room 515, 477 Michigan Avenue, 48226
Marquette: Room 310, 220 West Washington Street, 49855
MINNESOTA
Minneapolis: Butler Square Building, 100 6th Street North, 55403
MISSISSIPPI
Biloxi: 2nd floor, 111 Fred Haise Boulevard, 39530
Jackson: Suite 322, 100 West Capitol Street, 39269

MISSOURI
Kansas City: 1150 Grand Avenue, 64106
St. Louis: Room 242, 815 Olive Street, 63101
Sikeston: 731-A North Main Street, 63801
Springfield: Room 150, 309 North Jefferson Street, 65806
MONTANA
Helena: Room 528, 301 South Park Avenue, 59601
NEBRASKA
Omaha: Empire State Building, 300 South 19th Street, 68102
NEVADA
Las Vegas: 301 Stewart Avenue, 89101
Reno: Room 107, U.S. Courthouse, 50 South Virginia Street, 89501
NEW HAMPSHIRE
Concord: Room 211, Federal Building, 5 Pleasant Street, 03301
NEW JERSEY
Camden: Ferry Station Office Building, 1800 East Davis Street, 08104
Newark: Room 1635, Federal Building, 970 Broad Street, 07102
NEW MEXICO
Albuquerque: Room 320, 500 Marble Avenue, NE, 87110
NEW YORK
Albany: Room 236-A, Federal Building, 445 Broadway, 12207
Buffalo: Room 1311, Federal Building, 111 West Huron Street, 14202
Elmira: Room 412, Nixon Building, 180 Clemens Center Parkway, 14901
Melville: Room 102-E, 35 Pinelawn Road, 11747
New York: Room 3100, Federal Office Building, 26 Federal Plaza, 10278
Rochester: Room 601, Federal Building, 100 State Street, 14614
Syracuse: Room 1071, James M. Hanley Federal Building & Courthouse, 100 South Clinton Street, 13260
NORTH CAROLINA
Charlotte: Room 700, 230 South Tryon Street, 28202
Greenville: Room 206, 215 South Evans Street, 27834
NORTH DAKOTA
Fargo: Room 218, 657 2nd Avenue, North, 58102
OHIO
Cincinnati: Room 5028, Federal Office Building, 550 Main Street, 45202
Cleveland: Room 317, Federal Office Building, 1240 East 9th Street, 44199
Columbus: Federal Office Building, 85 Marconi Boulevard, 43215
OKLAHOMA
Oklahoma City: Room 670, 200 Northwest 5th Street, 73102
Tulsa: Room 3104, 333 West 4th Street, 74103

OREGON
Portland: Room 676, Green Wyatt Federal Building, 1220 Southwest 3rd Avenue, 97204
PENNSYLVANIA
Bala-Cynwyd: Suite 400, 231 St. Asaphs Road, 19004
Harrisburg: Suite 309, 100 Chestnut Street, 17101
Pittsburgh: 5th floor, 960 Penn Avenue, 15222
Wilkes-Barre: Penn Place, 20 North Pennsylvania Avenue, 19801
PUERTO RICO
Hato Rey: Room 691, Carlos A. Chardon Avenue, 00919
RHODE ISLAND
Providence: 40 Fountain Street, 02903
SOUTH CAROLINA
Columbia: 3rd floor, New U.S. Courthouse, 1835 Assembly Street, 29101
SOUTH DAKOTA
Sioux Falls: Suite 101, Security Building, 101 South Maine Avenue, 57102
TENNESSEE
Knoxville: Room 307, Fidelity-Bankers Trust Building, 502 Gay Street SW, 37902
Memphis: Room 43, Federal Office Building, 167 North Main Street, 38103
Nashville: Room 1012, Parkway Towers Building, 404 James Robertson Parkway, 37219
TEXAS
Austin: Room 780, Federal Building, 300 East 8th Street, 78701
Corpus Christi: 3105 Leopard Street, 78408
Dallas: Room 3C36, 1100 Commerce Street, 75242
El Paso: Room 300, 4100 Rio Bravo, 79902
Fort Worth: Room 1007, 221 West Lancaster, 76102
Harlingen: Room 500, 222 East Van Buren Street, 78550
Houston: Room 112, 2525 Murworth Drive, 77054
Lubbock: Suite 200, 1611 Tenth Street, 79401
Marshall: Room G-12, 100 South Washington Street, 79401
San Antonio: Room A-513, Federal Office Building, 727 East Durango Boulevard, 78206
UTAH
Salt Lake City: Room 2237, Federal Building, 125 South State Street, 84138
VERMONT
Montpelier: Room 205, 87 State Street, 05602
VIRGINIA
Richmond: Room 3015, Federal Building, 400 North 8th Street, 23240

VIRGIN ISLANDS
St. Thomas: Room 283, Veterans Drive, 00801
WASHINGTON
Seattle: 5th floor, Federal Building, 915 2nd Avenue, 98104
Spokane: Room 651, U.S. Courthouse, 920 West Riverside Avenue, 99201
WEST VIRGINIA
Charleston: Charleston National Plaza, 25301
Clarksburg: Room 302, 109 North Third Street, 26301
WISCONSIN
Eau Claire: Room 17, 500 South Barstow Street, 54701
Madison: Room 213, 212 East Washington Avenue, 53703
Milwaukee: Room 246, Federal Building, 517 East Wisconsin Avenue, 53202
WYOMING
Casper: Room 4001, Federal Building, 100 East B Street, 82601

Internal Revenue Service
Department of the Treasury
1111 Constitution Avenue, NW,
Washington, DC 20224

Federal Trade Commission
Pennsylvania Avenue at Sixth Street, NW
Washington, DC 20580

Department of Health and Human Services
Food and Drug Administration
200 Independence Avenue, SW
Washington, DC 20224

If you decide to incorporate rather than to operate as an individual owner or as a partnership, information about forms to be filed, minimum number of shareholders, and fees required by each state or territory may be obtained from:
ALABAMA
Judge of Probate (of county in which application will be filed)
ALASKA
Department of Commerce and Economic Development, State Office Building, Juneau, 99811
ARIZONA
Corporation Commission, Secretary of State, 2222 West Encanto Boulevard, Phoenix, 85009
ARKANSAS
Corporation Department, Secretary of State, State Capitol Building, Little Rock, 72201

CALIFORNIA
Secretary of State, 1230 J Street, Sacramento, 95814
COLORADO
Secretary of State, 1575 Sherman Street, Denver, 80203
CONNECTICUT
Secretary of State, 30 Trinity Street, Hartford, 06115
DELAWARE
Secretary of State, Townsend Building, Dover, 19901
DISTRICT OF COLUMBIA
Recorder of Deeds, Washington, DC 20004
FLORIDA
Charter Section, Secretary of State, Capitol Building, Tallahassee, 32301
GEORGIA
Secretary of State, State Capitol Building, Atlanta, 30303
HAWAII
Department of Regulatory Agencies, 1010 Richards Street, Honolulu, 96813
IDAHO
Division of Corporations, Secretary of State, Statehouse, Boise, 83720
ILLINOIS
Corporate Division, Secretary of State, State House, Springfield, 62706
INDIANA
Corporations Division, Secretary of State, State House, Indianapolis, 46204
IOWA
Corporation Division, Secretary of State, Capitol Building, Des Moines, 50319
KANSAS
Corporation Division, Secretary of State, Capitol Building, Topeka, 66612
KENTUCKY
Secretary of State, Capitol Building, Frankfort, 40601
LOUISIANA
Corporations Division, Secretary of State, State Capitol Building, Baton Rouge, 70804
MAINE
Secretary of State, State Office Building, Augusta, 04333
MARYLAND
Department of Assessments & Taxation, 301 West Preston Street, Baltimore, 21201
MASSACHUSETTS
Corporation Division, Secretary of the Commonwealth, One Ashburton Place, Boston, 02108

MICHIGAN
Corporation Division, Department of Commerce, Law Building, Lansing, 48909
MINNESOTA
Corporation Division, Secretary of State, State Office Building, St. Paul, 55155
MISSISSIPPI
Secretary of State, Heber Ladner Building, Jackson, 39205
MISSOURI
Secretary of State, Capitol Building, Jefferson City, 65101
MONTANA
Secretary of State, State Capitol Building, Helena, 59601
NEBRASKA
Corporation Division, Secretary of State, State Capitol Building, Lincoln, 68509
NEVADA
Corporation Division, Secretary of State, Heroes' Memorial Building, Carson City, 89701
NEW HAMPSHIRE
Secretary of State, State House, Concord, 03301
NEW JERSEY
Corporate Filing Department, Department of State, P.O. Box 1330, Trenton, 08625
NEW MEXICO
State Corporation Commission, Santa Fe, 87501
NEW YORK
Division of Corporations, Secretary of State, 162 Washington Avenue, Albany, 12231
NORTH CAROLINA
Corporations Division, Secretary of State, 116 West Jones Street, Raleigh, 27603
NORTH DAKOTA
Division of Corporations, Secretary of State, Capitol Building, Bismarck, 58505
OHIO
Division of Corporations, Secretary of State, 30 East Broad Street, Columbus, 43215
OKLAHOMA
Secretary of State, State Capitol Building, Oklahoma City, 73105
OREGON
Corporation Commissioner, Commerce Building, Salem, 97310
PENNSYLVANIA
Corporation Bureau, Commonwealth of Pennsylvania, Harrisburg 17120

RHODE ISLAND
Secretary of State, State House, Providence, 02903
SOUTH CAROLINA
Secretary of State, West Hampton Office Building, Columbia, 29101
SOUTH DAKOTA
Secretary of State, State Capitol Building, Pierre, 57501
TENNESSEE
Corporate Division, Secretary of State, State Capitol Building, Nashville, 37219
TEXAS
Corporation Division, Secretary of State, Sam Houston State Office Building, Austin, 78701
UTAH
Secretary of State, State Capitol Building, Salt Lake City, 84114
VERMONT
Secretary of State, 109 State Street, Montpelier, 05602
VIRGINIA
State Corporation Commission, P.O. Box 1197, Richmond, 23209
WASHINGTON
Corporations Division, Secretary of State, Legislative Building, Olympia, 98504
WEST VIRGINIA
Corporation Division, Secretary of State, Charleston, 25305
WISCONSIN
Corporation Division, Secretary of State, State Capitol Building, Madison, 53702
WYOMING
Division of Corporations, Secretary of State, State Capitol Building, Cheyenne, 82002

Chapter 3

Readers who wish to explore the subject of office design in greater detail should consult:

Becker, Franklin. *The Successful Office: How to Create a Workspace That's Right for You.* Reading, Mass.: Addison-Wesley, 1982.

Cohen, Elaine, and Aaron Cohen. *Planning the Electronic Office.* New York: McGraw-Hill, 1983.

Fracchia, Charles. *So This Is Where You Work!* New York: Viking Press, 1979.

Hewes, Jeremy Joan. *Worksteads: Living and Working in the Same Place.* Garden City, N.Y.: Doubleday, 1981.

Klein, Judy Graf. *The Office Book: Ideas and Designs for Contemporary Workspaces.* New York: Facts on File, 1982.

290 SOURCES AND RESOURCES

Naar, John, and Molly Siple. *Living in One Room.* New York: Vintage Books, 1976.

Palmer, Alvin E., and Susan M. Lewis. *Planning the Office Landscape.* New York: McGraw-Hill, 1978.

Price, Judith. *The Office Style Book: Design for the Successful Executive.* New York: Harmony Books, 1980 (previously published as *Executive Style*).

Russell, Beverly. *Designers' Workplaces: 33 Offices by Designers for Designers.* New York: Whitney Library of Design, 1983.

Saphier, Michael. *Planning the New Office.* New York: McGraw-Hill, 1978.

Smith, Randy Baca. *Setting Up Shop.* New York: McGraw-Hill, 1982.

Weiss, Jeffrey. *Working Places.* New York: St. Martin's, 1980.

Although it is targeted at a professional audience, *How to Read Architectural Drawings*, published by the United States Gypsum Company, will be useful to anyone who must deal with architects and contractors. Copies are obtainable from United States Gypsum Company, Department 122-ZZ, 101 South Wacker Drive, Chicago, IL 60606.

Organizations that can provide answers to specific questions:

American Institute of Architects
1735 New York Avenue, NW
Washington, DC 20006

American Institute of Building Design
1412 19th Street
Sacramento, CA 95814

American Society of Heating, Refrigerating and Air-Conditioning Engineers
1791 Tullie Circle, NE
Atlanta, GA 30329

American Society of Landscape Architects
1733 Connecticut Avenue, NW
Washington, DC 20009

Association of Home Appliance Manufacturers
20 North Wacker Drive
Chicago, IL 60606

Illuminating Engineering Society of North America
345 East 47th Street
New York, NY 10017

Chapter 4

Publications on insulation materials and techniques are offered by the Mineral Insulation Manufacturers Association. For a list of such publications, write to: Mineral Wool Manufacturers Association, 382 Springfield Avenue, Summit, NJ 07901.

The Edison Electric Institute publishes several instructional and reference booklets of interest to office planners and consumers. Address: Edison Electric Institute, 1111 19th Street, NW, Washington, DC 20036.

For publications about carpets and carpet care, including the comprehensive *Carpet Specifier's Handbook*, write to: The Carpet and Rug Institute, P.O. Box 2048, Dalton, GA 30720. The Carpet Cushion Council, a division of the Carpet and Rug Institute, publishes booklets describing the advantages of rug cushion underlayment. Write to: Carpet Cushion Council, P.O. Box 465, Southfield, MI 48037.

For information on the care and cleaning of rugs and carpeting, write to the Association of Specialists in Cleaning & Restoration, Suite 1408, 5205 Leesburg Pike, Falls Church, VA 22041.

Chapter 6

Contract Magazine, Gralla Publications, Inc., 1515 Broadway, New
    York, NY 10036
Interiors Magazine, Billboard Publications, Inc., 1515 Broadway, New
    York, NY 10036

Office Furniture and Equipment

All-Steel, Inc., Route 31 & Ashland Court, Aurora, IL 60507
American Seating, 901 Broadway Avenue, NW, Grand Rapids, MI
    49504
Atelier International, 595 Madison Avenue, New York, NY 10022
Bevis Custom Tables, Inc., P.O. Box 2280, Florence, AL 35630
The Boling Chair Company, 108 West Third Street, Siler City, NC
    27344
Brayton International Inc., 255 Strathnore Avenue, High Point, NC
    27264
The Brewster Corporation, 50 River Street, Old Saybrook, CT 06475
Brueton Industries, 979 Third Avenue, New York, NY 10022
Charvoz-Carsen Corporation, 5 Daniel Road East, Fairfield, NJ 07001
Chromcraft Corporation, One Quality Lane, Senatobia, MS 38668
Comforto, Inc., P.O. Box 917, Lincolnton, NC 28092
Conwed Corporation, Interior Products Division, 444 Cedar Street, St.
    Paul, MN 55164

Corry Jamestown Corporation, 844 East Columbus Avenue, Corry, PA 16407

Cramer Industries, Inc., 625 Adams Street, Kansas City, KS 66119

Cumberland Furniture Corporation, 40 East 49th Street, New York, NY 10017

Domore Corporation, 2400 Sterling Avenue, Elkhart, IN 46515

Eck-Adams Corporation, 10121 Paget Drive, St. Louis, MO 63132

Eppinger Furniture, Inc., 15 Very Merry Road, Stamford, CT 06903

Esselte/Pendaflex, 71 Clinton Road, Garden City, NY 11530

Executive Office Concepts, 1705 Anderson Avenue, Compton, CA 90220

Facit, Inc., 66 Field Point Road, Greenwich, CT 06836

Fixtures Furniture, 1642 Crystal, Kansas City, MO 64126

GF Business Equipment, Inc., 229 East Dennick Avenue, Youngstown, OH 44501

Gregson Furniture Industries, 206 East Frazier Avenue, Liberty, NC 27298

The Gunlocke Company, 11385 South Lackawanna Street, Wayland, NY 14572

Harter Corporation, P.O. Box 400, Sturgis, MI 49091

Haworth, One Haworth Center, Holland, MI 49423

Hiebert, Inc., 19801 South Santa Fe Avenue, Carson, CA 90749

The Hon Company, 200 Oak Street, Muscatine, IA 52761

iiL International, 7005 Fulton Industrial Boulevard, Atlanta, GA 30336

Indiana Desk Company, 1224 Mill Street, Jasper, IN 47546

International Contract Furnishings, 305 East 63rd Street, New York, NY 10021

Jasper Desk Company, Jasper, IN 47546

Jofco, 13th & Vine Streets, Jasper, IN 47546

Kimball Office Furniture Company, 5 Daniel Road East, Fairfield, NJ 07001

Knoll International, 655 Madison Avenue, New York, NY 10021

Krueger, Inc., P.O. Box 8100, Green Bay, WI 54308

Krug Furniture, Inc., 111 Ahrens Street West, Kitchener, Ontario, Canada N2H 4C2

Lehigh-Leopold Furniture, 2528 Mt. Pleasant Street, Burlington, IA 52601

Madison Furniture Industries, P.O. Drawer 111, Canton, MS 39046

Modern Mode, 6425 San Leandro Street, Oakland, CA 94603

Office Suites, Inc., 359 North Wells Street, Chicago, IL 60610

Panel Concepts, Inc., 30001 South Yale, Santa Ana, CA 92074

R-Way Furniture Company, 740 South Commerce, Sheboygan, WI 53081

Samsonite Corporation, Furniture Division, 11200 East 45th Avenue, Denver, CO 80239

Smith System Manufacturing Company, 1405 Silver Lake, St. Paul, MN 55164

Steelcase, Inc., 1120 36th Street, SE, Grand Rapids, MI 49501

Thonet Industries, Inc., 491 East Princess Street, York, PA 17405

Tiffany Stand & Furniture Company, 9666 Olive Boulevard, St. Louis, MO 63132

United Chair Company, 114 Churchill Avenue, NW, Leeds, AL 35094

Chapter 7

Telephones

Telephones are widely available at specialty stores. See the yellow pages of your telephone directory under "Telephone Equipment & Systems— Dealers."

Chapter 8

Facsimile Services

Federal Express, Box 727, Memphis, TN 38194

Graphnet Systems, Inc., 329 Alfred Avenue, Teaneck, NJ 07666

ITT World Communications, Inc., 67 Broad Street, New York, NY 10004 (FAXPAK)

MCI International, Inc., International Drive, Rye Brook, NY 10573

Radio Corporation of America, 60 Broad Street, New York, NY 10004 (Q-FAX)

Syndifax, 116 Nassau Street, New York, NY 10004

3M/DMS, 1700 Old Meadow Road, McLean, VA 22101

Chapter 9

Telephone Answering Machines

Code-A-Phone Corporation, P.O. Box 5656, Portland, OR 97228

Dictaphone Corporation, 120 Old Post Road, Rye, NY 10580 (Ansafone)

GTE Corporation, One Stamford Forum, Stamford, CT 06904

ITT Personal Communications, 133 Terminal Avenue, Clark, NJ 07066

Olympia USA, P.O. Box 22, Somerville, NJ 08876

Panasonic, One Panasonic Way, Secaucus, NJ 07094

Phone-Mate, Inc., 325 Torrance Avenue, Torrance, CA 90503
Phonesitter, 10381 West Jefferson Boulevard, Culver City, CA 90230
Quasar Micro-Systems, Inc., 448 Suffolk Avenue, Brentwood, NY 11717
Radio Shack, Tandy Corporation, One Tandy Center, Fort Worth, TX 76102
Sanyo Electric, Inc., 51 Joseph Street, Moonachie, NJ 07074
Sony Corporation of America, 9 West 57th Street, New York, NY 10019
TT Systems Corporation, 9 East 37th Street, New York, NY 10016 (Message-Minder)

Paging Services

Because paging services are usually locally owned and operated, you should consult the yellow pages of your telephone directory under "Paging & Signalling Service—Common Carrier" for the names of paging companies.

Chapter 10

Electronic Typewriters

Adler-Royal Business Machines, Inc., 1600 Route 22, Union, NJ 07083
BSI Office Equipment, Inc., 3361 Boyington Drive, Dallas, TX 75006
Brother International Corporation, 8 Corporate Place, Piscataway, NJ 08854
Canon USA, Inc., One Canon Plaza, Lake Success, NY 11042
Contitronix, Inc., 3848 Marquis Drive, Garland, TX 75042
A.B. Dick Company, 5700 West Touhy Avenue, Chicago, IL 60648
Docutel-Olivetti Corporation, 155 White Plains Road, Tarrytown, NY 10591
Exxon Office Systems Company, 777 Long Ridge Road, Stamford, CT 06902
Facit, Inc., 235 Main Dunstable Road, Nashua, NH 03061
· Hermes Products, Inc., 1900 Lower Road, Linden, NJ 07036
International Business Machines Corporation, 3000 Westchester Avenue, White Plains, NY 10604
Olympia USA, Inc., Route 22, Somerville, NJ 08876
Remington Rand Office Systems, One Penn Plaza, New York, NY 10019
Royal Division, ARBM, 1600 Route 22, Union, NJ 07083
Sharp Electronics Corporation, 10 Sharp Plaza, Paramus, NJ 07652
Silver-Reed America, Inc., 19600 South Vermont Avenue, Torrance, CA 90230

Smith-Corona Division, SCM Corporation, 65 Locust Avenue, New Canaan, CT 06840

Swintec Corporation, 23 Poplar Street, East Rutherford, NJ 07073

Syntrex, Inc., 246 Industrial Way West, Eatontown, NJ 07724

TEC America, Inc., 19250 Van Ness Avenue, Torrance, CA 90501

Teal Industries, Inc., 1741 Lomita Boulevavrd, Lomita, CA 90717

3M Company, Inc., 3M Center, St. Paul, MN 55144

Xerox Corporation, High Ridge Park, Stamford, CT 06904

Dvorak International Federation, 11 Pearl Street, Brandon, VT 05733

American National Standards Institute, 1430 Broadway, New York, NY 10018

Chapter 11

Adding Machines and Calculators

Adler-Royal Business Machines, Inc., 1600 Route 22, Union, NJ 07083

CRS Office Products Division, Division of Cash Register Sales, Inc., 2909 Anthony Lane, Minneapolis, MN 55418

Canon USA, Inc., One Canon Plaza, Lake Success, NY 11042

Casio, Inc., 15 Gardner Road, Fairfield, NJ 07006

Citizen America Corporation, 1710 22nd Street, Santa Monica, CA 90404

Docutel-Olivetti Corporation of America, 155 White Plains Road, Tarrytown, NY 10591

Facit, Inc., 235 Main Dunstable Road, Nashua, NH 03061

Hermes Products, Inc., 1900 Lower Road, Linden, NJ

Hewlett-Packard Company, 1000 NE Circle Boulevard, Corvallis, OR 97330

IBICO, Inc., 760 Bonnie Lane, Elk Grove Village, IL 60007

Max Business Machines Corporation, 585 Commercial Avenue, Garden City, NY 11530

Merchants Corporation of America, 689 Fifth Avenue, New York, NY 10022

Monroe Systems for Business, The American Road, Morris Plains, NJ 07950

Office Environment Co-operative, Inc., 2848 Cullen Street, Forth Worth, TX 76107

Olympia USA, Inc., Route 22, Somerville, NJ 08876

Panasonic Calculator Department, One Panasonic Way, Secaucus, NJ 07094

Royal Business Machines, Inc., 500 Day Hill Road, Windsor, CT 06095

Sanyo Electric, Inc., 200 Riser Road, Little Ferry, NJ 07643

Sharp Electronics Corporation, 10 Sharp Plaza, Paramus, NJ 07652

Silver-Reed America, Inc., 8665 Hayden Place, Culver City, CA 90230
Swintec Corporation, 23 Poplar Street, East Rutherford, NJ 07073
TCA, Inc., 1313 South Pennsylvania Avenue, Morrisville, PA 19067
Teal Industries, Inc., 1741 Lomita Boulevard, Lomita, CA 90717
Texas Instruments, Inc., Box 225474, Dallas, TX 75265
Toshiba America, Inc., 258 Route 46E, Fairfield, NJ 07006
Towa Corporation of America, 1313 South Pennsylvania Avenue, Morrisville, PA 19067
Victor Business Products, 3900 North Rockwell Street, Chicago, IL 60616
Wang Laboratories, Inc., One Industrial Avenue, Lowell, MA 01851

Chapter 12

Copying Machines

AES Technology Systems, Inc., 140 Lively Boulevard, Elk Grove Village, IL 60007
Adler-Royal Business Machines, Inc., 1600 Route 22, Union, NJ 07083
Albin Industries, Inc., P.O. Box 346, Farmington, MI 48024
Bell & Howell, Business Equipment Group, 6800 McCormick Road, Chicago, IL 60645
Canon USA, Inc., One Canon Drive, Lake Success, NY 11042
Clark Copy International Corporation, 1949 Cornell Avenue, Melrose Park, IL 60160
Deltek Business Machines, P.O. Box 18178, Pittsburgh, PA 15236
A.B. Dick Company, 5700 West Touhy Avenue, Chicago, IL 60648
Dietzgen Corporation, 250 Wille Road, Des Plaines, IL 60018
Ditto Division, ATF-Davidson, One Main Street, Whitinsville, MA 02143
Eastman Kodak Company, 343 State Street, Rochester, NY 14650
Eskofot America, Inc., 1019 Industrial Boulevard, San Carlos, CA 94070
Facit, Inc., 235 Main Dunstable Road, Nashua, NH 03061
Gestetner Corporation, Gestetner Park, Yonkers, NY 10703
Graphic Enterprises, Inc., 439 North Market, Canton, OH 44702
Heyer, Inc., 1850 South Kostner Avenue, Chicago, IL 60623
International Business Machines Corporation, 3000 Westchester Avenue, White Plains, NY 20604
KIP USA, Inc., 411 Northside Parkway, NW, Atlanta, GA 30327
Lanier Business Products, Inc., Division of Oxford Industries, Inc., 1700 Chantilly Drive, NE, Atlanta, GA 30324
Minolta Corporation, Business Equipment Division, 101 Williams Drive, Ramsey, NJ 07446

Mita Copystar America, Inc., 777 Terrace Avenue, Hasbrouck Heights, NJ 07604

Monroe Systems for Business, The American Road, Morris Plains, NJ 07950

Multigraphics, Inc., 1800 West Central Road, Mount Prospect, IL 00645

Nashua Corporation, Office Products Division, 44 Franklin Street, Nashua, NH 03060

Olympia USA, Inc., Route 22, Somerville, NJ 08876

Olympus Corporation of America, 4 Nevada Drive, Lake Success, NY 11042

Panasonic Industrial Company, Office Systems Division, One Panasonic Way, Secaucus, NJ 07094

Pitney Bowes, Walter H. Wheeler, Jr. Drive, Stamford, CT 06926

Radio Shack Division, Tandy Corporation, One Tandy Plaza, Fort Worth, TX 76102

Ricoh of America, Inc., 20 Gloria Lane, Fairfield, NJ 07006

Roneo Alcatel, Inc., One Alsan Way, Little Ferry, NJ 07643

Royal Business Machines, Inc., 500 Day Hill Road, Windsor, CT 06095

Savin Corporation, 420 Columbus Avenue, Valhalla, NY 10595

Saxon Business Products, Inc., 13900 Northwest 57th Court, Miami Lakes, FL 33014

Sharp Electronics Corporation, 10 Sharp Plaza, Paramus, NJ 07652

Speed-O-Print Business Machines Corporation, 1801 West Larchmont Avenue, Chicago, IL 60613

Standard Duplicating Machines Corporation, 10 Connector Road, Andover, MA 01810

3M Company, Copying Products Division, 3M Center, St. Paul, MN 55144

Toshiba America, Inc., Copier Products Division, 2441 Michelle Drive, Tustin, CA 92680

Van Dyk Research Corporation, 45 South Jefferson Road, Whippany, NJ 07981

Xerox Corporation, High Ridge Park, Stamford, CT 06904

Yorktown Industries Corporation, 330 Factory Road, Addison, IL 60101

Duplicating Machines

ATF-Davidson Company, Main Street, Whitinsville, MA 01588

A.B. Dick Company, 5700 West Touhy Avenue, Chicago, IL 60648

Heyer, Inc., 1850 South Koster Avenue, Chicago, IL 60623

Marsh Stencil Company, 707 East B Street, Belleville, IL 62222

Roneo Alcatel, Inc., One Alsan Way, Little Ferry, NJ 07643
Speed-O-Print Business Machines Corporation, 1801 West Larchmont
    Avenue, Chicago, IL 60613
Standard Rex-Rotary, 475 Dean Street, Englewood, NJ 07631
Vari-Color Duplicator Company, 437 South Lincoln, Shawnee, OK
    74801

Chapter 13

Dictation Equipment

All Makes Office Machine Company, 150 West 24th Street, Los
    Angeles, CA 90007 (Grundig-Stenorette)
Assmann Communications, 333 Fifth Avenue, New York, NY 10016
Craig Corporation, 921 West Artesia Boulevard, Compton, CA 90220
Dictaphone Corporation, 120 Old Post Road, Rye, NY 10580
Doro International Corporation, 467 Forbes Boulevard, South San
    Francisco, CA 94080
IBM Information Systems Group, 3000 Westchester Avenue, White
    Plains, NY 10604
Lanier Business Products, Inc., 1700 Chantilly Drive, NE, Atlanta,
    GA 30324
Memocord Division, Niktek, Inc., 10 Dwight Place, Fairfield, NJ
    07006
Mineroff Electronics, Inc., 946 Downing Road, Valley Stream, NY
    11580
NTI Business Equiment, Ltd., 180 Amber Street, Markham, Ontario,
    Canada L3R 3J8 (Grundig-Stenorette)
Norcom Division, Micom Electronics Corporation, 675 Third Avenue,
    New York, NY 10017
Norelco Dictation Systems, North American Philips Corp., 100 East
    42nd Street, New York, NY 10017
Office Environment Co-operative, Inc., 2848 Cullen Street, Fort Worth,
    TX 76107
Olympia USA, Inc., Route 22, Somerville, NJ 08876
Olympus Corporation of America, 4 Nevada Drive, Lake Success, NY
    11042
Sanyo Business Systems Corporation, 51 Joseph Drive, Moonachie,
    NJ 07074
Sony Corporation of America, 9 West 57th Street, New York, NY
    10019
Stenocord Dictation Systems, 2050 Oakstone Way, Los Angeles, CA
    90046

Tandy Corporation, One Tandy Center, Fort Worth, TX 76102
Toshiba America, Inc., 2441 Michelle Drive, Tustin, CA 92680

Chapter 14

Computers and Word Processors

Alpha Microsystems, 17332 Von Karman, Irvine, CA 92713
Altos Computer Systems, 2360 Bering Drive, San Jose, CA 95134
Apple Computer, 20525 Mariani Avenue, Cupertino, CA 95014
Atari, Inc., 1265 Borregas Avenue, Sunnyvale, CA 94086
BMC Computer Corporation, 860 East Walnut Street, Carson, CA 90746
Basis, Inc., 5435 Scotts Valley Drive, Scotts Valley, CA 95066
Billings Computer Corporation, 18600 37th Terrace East, Independence, MO 64057
Burroughs Corporation, One Burroughs Place, Detroit, MI 48232
California Computer Systems, 250 Caribbean Drive, Sunnyvale, CA 94086
Canon USA, Inc., One Canon Plaza, Lake Success, NY 11042
Coleco Industries, Inc., 999 Quaker Lane South, West Hartford, CT 06110
Columbia Data Products, Inc., 9150 Rumsey Road, Columbia, MD 21045
Commodore Business Machines, Inc., 1200 Wilson Drive, West Chester, PA 19380
Compal, 8500 Wilshire Boulevard, Beverly Hills, CA 90211
Compaq Computer Corporation, 2033 FM 149, Houston, TX 77070
CompuPro Systems, 3506 Breakwater Court, Hayward, CA 94545
Corona Data Systems, Inc., 31324 Via Colinas, Westlake Village, CA 91361
Corvus Systems, Inc., 2029 O'Toole Avenue, San Jose, CA 95131
Cromemco, Inc., 280 Bernardo Avenue, Mountain View, CA 94043
Datapoint Corporation, 9725 Datapoint Drive, San Antonio, TX 78284
Digital Equipment Corporation, 146 Main Street, Maynard, MA 01754
Dynabyte, Inc., 521 Cottonwood Drive, Milpitas, CA 95035
Eagle Computer, 983 University Avenue, Los Gatos, CA 95030
Epson America, Inc., 3415 Kashiwa Street, Torrance, CA 90505
Fortune Systems Corporation, 300 Harbor Boulevard, Belmont, CA 94002
Franklin Computer Corporation, 2138 Route 38, Cherry Hill, NJ 08002
Fujitsu Microelectronics, Inc., 3320 Scott Boulevard, Santa Clara, CA 95051

Grid Systems Corporation, 2535 Garcia Avenue, Mountain View, CA
94043

Heath Company, Benton Harbor, MI 49022

Hewlett-Packard Company, 1010 Northeast Circle Boulevard, Corvallis, OR 97330

IBM Corporation, Entry Business Systems, P.O. Box 1328, Boca Raton,
FL 33444

IMS International, 2800 Lockheed Way, Carson City, NV 89701

Intertec Data Systems Corporation, 2300 Broad River Road, Columbia,
SC 29210

Kaypro, 533 Stevens Avenue, Solana Beach, CA 92075

Lanier Business Products, Inc., 1700 Chantilly Drive Northeast, Atlanta, GA 30324

Monroe Systems for Business, The American Road, Morris Plains, NJ
07950

Morrow Designs, 600 McCormick Street, San Leandro, CA 94577

NEC Information Systems, Inc., 5 Militia Drive, Lexington, MA
02173

North Star Computers, Inc., 14440 Catalina Street, San Leandro, CA
94577

Ohio Scientific, 7 Oak Park, Bedford, MA 01730

Olympia USA, Route 22, Somerville, NJ 08876

Osborne Computer Corporation, 26538 Danti Court, Hayward CA
94545

Otrona Advanced Systems Corporation, 4755 Walnut Street, Boulder,
CO 80301

Panasonic Corporation, One Panasonic Way, Secaucus, NJ 07094

Polo Microsystems, Inc., 2570 El Camino Real, Mountain View, CA
94040

PolyMorphic Systems, 5730 Thornwood Drive, Santa Barbara, CA
93117

Radio Shack, Tandy Corporation, One Tandy Center, Fort Worth,
TX 76102

Sage Computer Technology, 35 North Edison Way, Reno, NV 89502

Sanyo Business Systems Corporation, 51 Joseph Street, Moonachie, NJ
07074

Seattle Computer Products, Inc., 1114 Industry Drive, Seattle, WA
98188

Seequa Computer Corporation, 8305 Telegraph Road, Odenton, MD
21113

Sharp Electronics Corporation, 10 Sharp Plaza, Paramus, NJ 07652

Sony Corporation of America, 7 West 57th Street, New York, NY
10019

Sord Computer of America, 200 Park Avenue, New York, NY 10166

Systel Computers, 399 West Trimble Road, San Jose, CA 95131

TAVA Corporation, 1711 Corinthian Way, Newport Beach, CA 92660
TeleVideo Systems, Inc., 1170 Morse Avenue, Sunnyvale, CA 94086
Texas Instruments, Inc., P.O. Box 402430, Dallas, TX 75240
3M, 3M Center, St. Paul, MN 55144
Timex Computer Corporation, P.O. Box 2655, Waterbury, CT 06725
Toshiba America, Inc., Information Systems Division, 2441 Michelle Drive, Tustin, CA 92680
Vector Graphic, Inc., 500 North Ventu Park Road, Thousand Oaks, CA 91320
Victor Technologies, 380 El Pueblo Road, Scotts Valley, CA 95066
Wang Laboratories, Inc., One Industrial Avenue, Lowell, MA 01851
Wicat Systems, Inc., 1875 South State Street, Orem, UT 84057
Xerox Corporation, Xerox Square, Rochester, NY 14644
Zenith Data Systems, 1000 Milwaukee Avenue, Glenview, IL 60025

Monitors

Amdek Corporation, 2201 Lively Boulevard, Elk Grove Village, IL 60007
Apple Computer, Inc., 20525 Mariani Avenue, Cupertino, CA 95014
BMC Computer Corporation, 860 East Walnut Street, Carson, CA 90746
Electrohome, Ltd., 809 Willington Street, North, Kitchener, ON, Canada M2G 4J6
Leading Edge Products, 225 Turnpike Street, Canton, MA 02021
NEC Home Electronics, 1401 Estes Street, Elk Grove Village, IL 60007
Panasonic, One Panasonic Way, Secaucus, NJ 07094
Princeton Graphic Systems, 1101-1 State Road, Princeton, NJ 08540
Quadram Corporation, 4357 Park Drive, Norcross, GA 30093
Sanyo, Communications Division, 1200 West Artesia Boulevard, Compton, CA 90225
Taxan Corporation, 18005 Cortney Court, City of Industry, CA 91748
USI International, 71 Park Lane, Brisbane, CA 95005
Zenith Data Systems, 1000 Milwaukee Avenue, Glenview, IL 60025

Printers

Anadex, Inc., 9825 De Soto Avenue, Chatsworth, CA 91311
Apple Computer, Inc., 20525 Mariani Avenue, Cupertino, CA 95014
Brother International Corp., 8 Corporate Place, Piscataway, NJ 08854
Bytewriter, 125 Northview Road, Ithaca, NY 14850
Computer Printers International, 340 East Middlefield Road, Mountain View, CA 94043

Daisywriter, Division of Computer International, Inc., 3540 Wilshire Boulevard, Los Angeles, CA 90010
Diablo Systems, 24500 Industrial Boulevard, Hayward, CA 94545
Epson America, Inc., 3415 Kashiwa Street, Torrance, CA 90505
Integral Data Systems, Inc., Route 12, South Milford, NH 03055
C. Itoh Electronics, 5301 Beethoven Street, Los Angeles, CA 90066
Mannesmann Tally Corporation, 8301 South 180th Street, Kent, WA 98032
NEC Home Electronics, 1401 Estes Avenue, Oak Grove Village, IL 60007
Okidata Corporation, 111 Gaither Drive, Mount Laurel, NJ 08054
Olympia USA, Inc., Box 22, Somerville, NJ 08876
Qume Corporation, 2350 Qume Drive, San Jose, CA 95131
Radio Shack, One Tandy Center, Fort Worth, TX 76102
Smith-Corona, 65 Locust Avenue, New Canaan, CT 06840
Zenith Data Systems, 1000 Milwaukee Avenue, Glenview, IL 60025

Modems

Anchor Automation, 6624 Valjean Avenue, Van Nuys, CA 91406
Anderson Jacobson, 521 Charcot Avenue, Chatsworth, CA 95131
Apple Computer, Inc., 20525 Mariani Avenue, Cupertino, CA 95014
Bizcomp Corporation, 532 Weddell Drive, Sunnyvale, CA 94089
BytCom, 2169 Francisco Boulevard, San Rafael, CA 94901
Cermetek Microelectronics, 1308 Borregos Avenue, Sunnyvale, CA 94086
Computer Development, Inc., 1440 Broadway, Oakland, CA 94901
Datec, Inc., 300 East Main Street, Carrboro, NC 27510
Digital Equipment Corporation, 146 Main Street, Maynard, MA 07154
General Datacom Industries, One Kennedy Avenue, Danbury, CT 06810
Hayes Microcomputer Products, 5835 Peachtree Corners East, Norcross, GA 30092
Microcom, 1400A Providence Highway, Norwood, MA 02062
Multi-Tech Systems, Inc., 82 2nd Avenue SE, New Brighton, MN 55112
Mura Corporation, 177 Cantiague Rock Road, Westbury, NY 11590
Novation, Inc., 20409 Prairie Street, Chatsworth, CA 91311
Omnitec Data, 2405 South 20th Street, Phoenix, AZ 85034
Racal-Vadic, Inc., 222 Caspian Drive, Sunnyvale, CA 94086
Radio Shack, One Tandy Center, Fort Worth, TX 76102
Rixon, Inc., 2120 Industrial Parkway, Silver Spring, MD 20904
Tek-Com, Inc., 2142 Paragon Drive, San Jose, CA 95131
Universal Data Systems, 5000 Bradford Drive, Huntsville, AL 35805

U.S. Robotics, Inc., 1123 West Washington Boulevard, Chicago, IL 80607

Ven-Tel, Inc., 2342 Walsh Avenue, Santa Clara, CA 95051

Visionary Electronics, Inc., 141 Parker Street, San Francisco, CA 94118

Zoom Telephonics, Inc., 207 South Street, Boston, MA 02111

Electronic Mail Services

CompuServe, Inc., 5000 Arlington Centre Boulevard, Columbus, OH 43220 (Infoplex)

GEISCO (General Electric Information Services Company), 401 North Washington Street, Rockville, MD 20850 (Quik-Comm)

GTE (General Telephone & Electronics) ADP Network Services, Inc., 175 Jackson Plaza, Ann Arbor, MI 48106 (Telemail)

ITT (International Telephone & Telegraph), Suite 410, 1109 Spring Street, Silver Spring, MD 20910 (Dialcom)

MCI Mail, 2000 M Street, NW, Washington, DC 20036 (MCI Mail)

The Source Telecomputing Corporation, 1616 Anderson Road, Mc-Lean, VA 22102 (SourceMail)

Tymshare, Inc., 20705 Valley Green Drive, Cupertino, CA 95014 (OnTyme)

Western Union, EasyLink Response Center, 1651 Old Meadow Road, McLean, VA 22102 (EasyLink)

Word Processing Programs

AlphaBit Communications, 13349 Michigan Avenue, Dearborn, MI 48126 (LazyWriter)

Apple Computer, 20525 Mariani Avenue, Cupertino, CA 95014 (Apple Writer, MacWrite)

Applied Microcomputer Systems, Box 150, Silver Lake, NH 03875 (Documate)

Artsci, Inc., 5547 Satsuma Avenue, North Hollywood, CA 91601 (Magic Window)

Broderbund Software, Inc., 1938 Fourth Street, San Rafael, CA 94903 (Bank Street Writer)

Bruce & James Program Publishers, 4500 Tuller Road, Dublin, OH 43017 (WordVision)

Dynacomp, Inc., 1427 Monroe Avenue, Rochester, NY 14618 (Text-master)

HFK Software, Old Danbury Road, Danbury, NH 03230 (QWERTY)

Hayden Software, 600 Suffolk Street, Lowell, MA 01853 (PIE Writer)

Information Unlimited Software, 2401 Marinship Way, Sausalito, CA 94965 (EasyWriter)

Innovative Software, 9300 West 110th Street, Overland Park, KS 66210 (The Smart Word Processor)

Leading Edge, 225 Turnpike Street, Canton, MA 02021 (Leading Edge Word Processor)

Lexisoft, Inc., P.O. Box 267, Davis, CA 95616 (Spellbinder)

Lifetree Software, 411 Pacific Street, Monterey, CA 93940 (Volkswriter Deluxe)

LJK Enterprises, Inc., 7852 Big Bend Boulevard, St. Louis, MO 63119 (Letter Perfect)

Mark of the Unicorn, Inc., 222 Third Street, Cambridge, MA 02139 (Mince, The Final Word)

Metasoft Corporation, 6509 West Frye Road, Chandler, AZ 85224 (Benchmark)

Micromation, Ltd., One Yorkdale Road, Toronto, Ontario, Canada M6A 3A1 (Gutenberg Word Processor)

MicroPro International Corporation, 33 San Pablo Avenue, San Rafael, CA 94903 (WordStar)

Microsoft, 10700 Northrup Way, Bellevue, WA 98004 (Microsoft Word)

Miller Microcomputer Services, 61 Lake Shore Road, Natick, MA 01760 (ForthWrite)

Muse Software, 347 North Charles Street, Baltimore, MD 21201 (Super/Text)

NBI, Inc., 3450 Mitchell Lane, Boulder, CO 80301 (NBI Word Processor)

Nemco, 9 Walnut Street, Rutherford, NJ 07070 (WordFlex)

Newstar Software, Inc., 2150 John Glenn Drive, Corcord, CA 94520 (Neword)

Palantir Software, Inc., 3400 Montrose Boulevard, Houston, TX 77006 (Palantir)

Peachtree Software, Inc., 3445 Peachtree Road Northeast, Atlanta, GA 30326 (PeachText 5000)

Perfect Software, Inc., 702 Harrison Street, Berkeley, CA 94710 (Perfect Writer)

Quick Brown Fox, Inc., 548 Broadway, New York, NY 10012 (Quick Brown Fox)

Quark, Inc., 2525 West Evans Drive, Denver, CO 80219 (Word Juggler)

Radio Shack, One Tandy Center, Fort Worth, TX 76102 (SCRIPSIT, SuperSCRIPSIT)

Satellite Software International, 288 West Center Street, Orem, UT 84057 (WordPerfect, P-Edit)

Sierra On-Line, Inc., 36575 Mudge Ranch Road, Coarsegold, CA 93614 (Screen Writer)

Silicon Valley Systems, 1636 El Camino Real, Belmont, CA 94002 (Word Handler)

Sof/Sys, Inc., 4306 Upton Avenue South, Minneapolis, MN 55410 (Executive Secretary)

Software Publishing Corporation, 1901 Landings Drive, Mountain View, CA 94043 (PFS:Write)

Softword Systems, 52 Oakland Avenue North, East Hartford, CT 06108 (MultiMate)

Sorcim Corporation, 2310 Lundy Avenue, San Jose, CA 95131 (Super-Writer)

TexaSoft, 1028 North Madison Avenue, Dallas, TX 75208 (Versa-Text)

Thorn EMI Computer Software, 3187-C Airway, Costa Mesa, CA 92626 (Perfect Writer)

VisiCorp, 2895 Zanker Road, San Jose, CA 95134 (VisiWord)

XyQuest, Inc., P.O. Box 372, Bedford, MA 01730 (XyWrite)

Database/File Management Programs

ASAP Systems, Inc., 2425 Porter Street, Soquel, CA 95073 (ASAP Five)

Apple Computer, Inc., 20525 Mariani Avenue, Cupertino, CA 95014 (Quick File)

Applied Software Technology, 170 Knowles Drive, Los Gatos, CA 95030 (VersaForm)

Ashton-Tate, 10150 West Jefferson Boulevard, Culver City, CA 90230 (dBase II, Friday!)

Avant Garde Creations, P.O. Box 30160, Eugene, OR 97403 (Small Business Trilogy)

Blanton Software Service, 4522 Briar Forest, San Antonio, TX 78217 (Data Base Manager)

Chang Laboratories, Inc., 5300 Stevens Creek Boulevard, San Jose, CA 95129 (File Plan)

Compumax, Inc., P.O. Box 7239, Menlo Park, CA 94025 (Micro Base)

Computer Headware, P.O. Box 14694, San Francisco, CA 94114 (Whatsit?)

Computer Software Design, Inc., 1904 Wright Circle, Anaheim, CA 92806 (Data Ace)

Condor Computer Corporation, 2051 South State Street, Ann Arbor, MI 48104 (Condor Series III)

DJR Associates, 303 South Broadway, Tarrytown, NY 10591 (FMS-80)

Digital Marketing Corporation, 2363 Boulevard Circle, Walnut Creek, CA 94595 (Notebook)

FYI, Inc., 4202 Spicewood Springs Road, Austin, TX 78759 (Superfile)

GMS Systems, Inc., 12 West 37th Street, New York, NY 10018 (Power-base)

High Technology Software Products, Inc., P.O. Box 14665, Oklahoma City, OK 73113 (Information Master)

Hoyle & Hoyle Software, 716 South Elam Avenue, Greensboro, NC 27403 (Query!²)

Information Unlimited Software, Inc., 2401 Marinship Way, Sausalito, CA 94965 (Easyfiler)

Innovative Software, 9300 West 110th Street, Overland Park, KS 66210 (The Smart Data Manager)

International Software Enterprises, Inc., 85 West Algonquin Road, Arlington Heights, IL 60005 (MDBS III)

Libra Laboratories, Inc., 495 Main Street, Metuchen, NJ 08840 (Master File)

Micro AP, Inc., 7033 Village Parkway, Dublin, CA 94566 (Selector V)

Micro Architect, Inc., 96 Dothan Street, Arlington, MA 02174 (IDM-X)

Micro Data Base Systems, P.O. Box 248, Lafayette, IN 47902 (The Knowledge Man)

Micro Lab, 2310 Skokie Valley Road, Highland Park, IL 60035 (Data Manager III)

MicroPro International, 33 San Pablo Avenue, San Rafael, CA 94901 (InfoStar)

Microstuf, 1845 The Exchange, Atlanta, GA 30339 (Infoscope)

Pacific Software Manufacturing Company, 2608 Eighth Street, Berkeley, CA 94710 (Sequitur)

Pearlsoft, P.O. Box 13850, Salem, OR 97309 (Personal Pearl)

Radio Shack, One Tandy Center, Fort Worth, TX 76102 (Profile)

SMC Software, 1011 Route 22, Bridgewater, NJ 08807 (Idol)

Savvy Marketing International, 10 South Ellsworth, San Mateo, CA 94401 (Savvy)

Sierra On-Line Systems, Inc., 36575 Mudge Ranch Road, Corsegold, CA 93614 (General Manager)

Software Publishing Corporation, 1901 Landings Drive, Mountain View, CA 94043 (PFS:File)

Stoneware, Inc., 50 Belvedere Street, San Rafael, CA 94901 (DB Master)

Systems Plus, Inc., 1120 San Antonio Road, Palo Alto, CA 94303 (FMS-80)

Vector Graphic, Inc., 500 North Ventu Park Road, Thousand Oaks, CA 91320 (Data Manager)

VisiCorp Software, 2895 Zanker Road, San Jose, CA 95134 (VisiFile)

Graphics Programs

Apple Computer, Inc., 20525 Mariani Avenue, Cuppertino, CA 95014 (Apple II Business Graphics)

Avant Garde Creations, P.O. 30160, Eugene, OR 97403 (Ultra Plot)

Business & Professional Software, Inc., 143 Binney Street, Cambridge, MA 02142 (BPS Graphics)

Chang Laboratories, Inc., 5300 Stevens Creek Boulevard, San Jose, CA 95129 (GraphPlan)

Decision Resources, P.O. Box 309, Westport, CT 06880 (Chart-Master)

Dickens Data Systems, 3050 Holcomb Ridge Road, Norcross, GA 30071 (Wall Street Plotter)

Graphic Communications, Inc., 200 Fifth Avenue, Waltham, MA 02254 (GraphWriter)

Graphics Software, Inc., 1972 Massachusetts Avenue, Cambridge, MA 02140 (Chartman II)

Innovative Software, Inc., 9300 West 110th Street, Overland Park, KS 66210 (FastGraph)

International Microcompter Software, Inc., P.O. Box 2643, San Anselmo, CA 94960 (Four-Point Graphics)

International Software Marketing, 120 East Washington Street, Syracuse, NY 13202 (Graph Magic)

Microcode, 683 Oak Street, Columbus, OH 43215 (Grafpak)

Peachtree Software, 3445 Peachtree Road, NE, Atlanta, GA 30326 (Business Graphics System)

Muse Software, 330 Charles Street, Baltimore, MD 21201 (Data Plot)

Prentice-Hall, Inc., Route 9W, Englewood Cliffs, NJ 07632 (Execu-Vision)

Software Publishing, 1901 Landings Drive, Mountain View, CA 94043 (PFS:Graph)

Strobe, Inc., 897 Independence Avenue, Mountain View, CA 94043 (Strobe Graphics System)

Super-Soft, Inc., P.O. Box 1628, Champaign, IL 61820 (Stats-graph)

VisiCorp, 2895 Zanker Road, San Jose, CA 95134 (VisiTrend/Plot)

Wiley Professional Software, 605 Third Avenue, New York, NY 10158 (Multigraph)

Personal Finance Programs

Acorn Software Products, Inc., 7655 Leesburg Pike, Falls Church, VA 22043 (Money Manager)

Advanced Digital Microsystems, P.O. Box 203, Dayton, OH 04509 (Total Finance Manager)

Adventure International, 155 Sabal Palm Road, Longwood, FL 32708 (MAXI-CRAS)

Apparat, Inc., 4401 South Tamarac Parkway, Denver, CO 80231 (IBM Home Finance)

BPI Systems, Inc., 3423 Guadalupe, Austin, TX 78705 (Personal Accounting System)

Best Programs, 5134 Leesburg Pike, Alexandria, VA 22302 (Personal Finance Program)

Computer Tax Service, Box 7915, Incline Village, NV 89450 (Money Street)

Computronics, 50 North Pascack Road, Spring Valley, NY 10977 (Versaledger)

Continental Software, 11223 South Hindry Avenue, Los Angeles, CA 90045 (Home Accountant)

Cortland Data Systems, Box 14414, Chicago, IL 60614 (Electronic Checkbook)

DEG Software, 11999 Katy Freeway, Houston, TX 77079 (Perfin)

Decision Support Software, 1438 Ironwood Drive, McLean, VA 22101 (The Accountant)

Design Data Systems Corporation, 5270 North Park Place, NE, Cedar Rapids, IA 52402 (Home Finance)

Douthett Enterprises, Inc., 200 West Douglas, Wichita, KS 67202 (Silver Budget)

Dynacomp, Inc., 1427 Monroe Avenue, Rochester, NY 14618 (Family Budget, Personal Finance System)

Ensign Software, 7337 Northview, Boise, ID 83704 (Checkbook Accounting)

Financier, Inc., 200 West Park Drive, Westboro, MA 01581 (Financier II)

Futurehouse, Inc., Box 3470, Chapel Hill, NC 27514 (Complete Personal Accountant)

High Technology Software Products, Inc., 1611 NW 23rd Street, Oklahoma City, OK 73146 (Disk-o-Check)

Howe Software, 14 Lexington Road, New City, NY 10956 (Home Budget)

Innosys, Inc., 2150 Shattuck Avenue, Berkeley, CA 94704 (Money Maestro)

Master Works Software, Inc., 25834 Narbonne Avenue, Lomita, CA 90717 (Cheque Mate Plus)

Micro Masters Software, Box 513, Edmonton, Alberta, Canada T5J 2K1 (Budget Master)

Monogram, 8295 La Cienega Boulevard, Inglewood, CA 90301 (Dollars and $ence)

Omni Software Systems, 146 North Broad Street, Griffith, IN 46319 (CASH)

Pacific Coast Software Corporation, 3220 South Brea Canyon Road, Diamond Bar, CA 91765 (Account Pac)

Radio Shack, One Tandy Center, Fort Worth, TX 76102 (Cash Budget Management)

Reichert Digital Systems, 29 Blazier Road, Warren, NJ 07060 (Computerized Personal Accounting)

Scitor Corporation, 710 Lakeway, Sunnyvale, CA 94086 (Personal Finance/Recordkeeping)

Silent Butler Software, 1423 Alameda Avenue, Burbank, CA 91501 (Silent Butler)

SoftLink, 3255 Scott Boulevard, Santa Clara, CA 95051 (Practical Accountant)

Softquest, Box 3456, McLean, VA 22103 (Smart Checkbook)

The Software Guild, 2935 Whipple Road, Union City, CA 94807 (Home Budget, Home Budgeter)

Spectrum Software, 690 West Fremont Avenue, Sunnyvale, CA 94807 (Personal Finance Master II)

Sundex Software, 3000 Pearl Street, Boulder, CO 80301 (Certified Personal Accountant)

Thorn Computer Software, 3187-C Airway, Costa Mesa, CA 92626 (Home Financial Management)

Turning Point Software, 11A Main Street, Watertown, MA 02172 (Time Is Money)

Spreadsheets and Integrated Programs

ARTSCI, 5547 Satsuma Avenue, North Hollywood, CA 91601 (Magi-Calc)

Addison-Wesley Publishing Company, One Jacob Way, Reading, MA 01867 (MICRO DSS/Analysis; MICRO DSS/Finance)

Ashton-Tate, 10150 West Jefferson Boulevard, Culver City, CA 90230 (Framework)

Business Planning Systems, Two North State Street, Dover, DE 19901 (Plan 80)

Business Solutions, Inc., 60 Main Street, Kings Park, NY 11754 (The Incredible Jack, Jack 2)

Chang Laboratories, Inc., 5300 Stevens Creek Boulevard, San Jose, CA 95129 (GraphPlan; MicroPlan; ProfitPlan)

Comshare, 1935 Cliff Valley Way, Atlanta, GA 30329 (Target Financial Modeling; PlannerCalc)

Context Management Systems, 2386 Hawthorn Boulevard, Torrance, CA 90505 (MBA)

Cromemco, Inc., 280 Bernardo Avenue, Mountain View, CA 94039 (Plan Master)

Fox & Geller, 604 Market Street, Elmwood Park, NJ 07407 (OZ)

Hayden Book Company, 50 Essex Street, Rochelle Park, NJ 07662 (FINPLAN)

Innovative Software, 9300 West 110th Street, Overland Park, KS 66210 (The Smart Spreadsheet)

Inter-Care, 2044 Armacost Avenue, Los Angeles, CA 90025 (PBAR—Patient Billing Accounts Receivable)

Lifeboat Associates, 16561 Third Avenue, New York, NY 10028 (FLP; UNICALC)

Logic eXtension Resources, 9651 Business Center Drive, Cucamonga, CA 91730 (MultiCalc)

Lotus Development Corporation, 161 First Street, Cambridge, MA 02142 (Lotus 1-2-3, Symphony)

MicroPro International Corporation, 33 San Pablo Avenue, San Rafael, CA 94903 (CalcStar; PlanStar)

Microsoft Corporation, 10700 Northrup Way, Bellevue, WA 98004 (Multiplan)

Norell Data Systems, 3400 Wilshire Boulevard, Los Angeles, CA 90010 (Easycalc)

Noumenon Corporation, 512 Westline Drive, Alameda, CA 94501 (Intuit)

Osborne/McGraw-Hill, 630 Bancroft Way, Berkeley, CA 94710 (MICROFINESS)

Peachtree Software, Inc., 3445 Peachtree Road, NE, Atlanta, GA 30326 (PeachText 5000)

Perfect Software, 702 Harrison Street, Berkeley, CA 94710 (Perfect Calc)

Racet Computers, Ltd., 1855 West Katella, Orange, CA 92667 (Electric Spreadsheet)

Radio Shack, One Tandy Center, Fort Worth, TX 76102 (VisiCalc Enhanced)

Softrend, Inc., 2 Main Parkway, Salem, NH 03079 (Aura)

Software Libraries, Inc., P.O. Box 844, Pasadena, CA 91102 (Prophit Planner)

Software Products International, 4582 Complex Street, San Diego, CA 92123 (LogiCalc, Open Access)

Software Toolworks, 15233 Ventura Boulevard, Sherman Oaks, CA 91403 (ZenCalc)

Sorcim Corporation, 2310 Lundy Avenue, San Jose, CA 95131 (Super-Calc)

Structured Systems Group, 5204 Claremont, Oakland, CA 94618 (Magic Worksheet)

Supersoft, P.O. Box 1628, Champaign, IL (Scratchpad)

T/Maker Company, 2115 Landings Drive, Mountain View, CA 94043 (T/Maker)

TexaSoft, 3415 Westminister, Dallas, TX 75205 (The Thinker)

Timex Sinclair, P.O. Box 2655, Fort Worth, TX 76102 (Vu-Calc)

Vector Graphic, Inc., 500 North Ventu Park Road, Thousand Oaks, CA 91320 (ExecuPlan)

VisiCorp, 2895 Zanker Road, San Jose, CA 95134 (VisiCalc: Advanced Version, VisiOn)

Westico, 25 Van Zant Street, Norwalk, CT 06855 (Minimodel)

Telecommunications Programs

Alpha Software Corporation, 12 New England Executive Park, Burlington, MA 01803 (IBM Connection)

Digital Marketing Corporation, 2363 Boulevard Circle, Walnut Creek, CA 94595 (Microlink)

Communications Research Group, Inc., 8939 Jefferson Highway, Baton Rouge, LA 70809 (BLAST)

Dynamic Microprocessor Associates, 545 Fifth Avenue, New York, NY 10017 (ASCOM)

Generic Software, P.O. Box 790, Marquette, MI 49855 (F-TRANS)

Hayes Microcomputer Products, Inc., 5923 Peachtree Industrial Boulevard, Norcross, GA 30092 (Smartcom II)

Hilgraeve, Inc., P.O. Box 941, Monroe, MI 48161 (Access)

IE Systems, 112 Main Street, Newmarket, NH 03857 (Acculink)

Mark of the Unicorn, P.O. Box 423, Arlington, MA 02174 (PC/Inter-Comm)

MicroCall Services, P.O. Box 650, Laurel, MD 20707 (AMCALL/MCCALL-II)

Microcom, 1400A Providence Highway, Norwood, MA 02062 (Micro-Courier)

Microstuf, 1845 The Exchange, Atlanta, GA 30339 (Crosstalk 16)

Micro-Systems Software, Inc., 4301-18 Oak Circle, Boca Raton, FL 33431 (MTERM)

SSM Microcomputer Products, Inc., 2190 Paragon Drive, San Jose, CA 95131 (Trans-send)

Southwestern Data Systems, 10761 Woodside Avenue, Santee, CA 92071 (ASCII Express)

U.S. Robotics, Inc., 1123 West Washington Boulevard, Chicago, IL 60607 (Telpac)

Ven-Tel, Inc., 2342 Walsh Avenue, Santa Clara, CA 95051 (PC-Modem)
VisiCorp, 2895 Zanker Road, San Jose, CA 95134 (VisiTerm)
Zoom Telephonics, Inc., 207 South Street, Boston, MA 02111 (Netmaster)

On-Line Information Services

Automatic Data Processing, Network Services Division, 175 Jackson Plaza, Ann Arbor, MI 48106
Bibliographic Retrieval Services, Inc., 1200 Route 7, Latham, NY 12110
Billboard Information Network, 1515 Broadway, New York, NY 10036
Business Information Services, 500 West Putnam Avenue, Greenwich, CT 06836
Chase Econometrics/Interactive Data Corporation, 486 Totten Pond Road, Waltham, MA 02154
CompuServe Incorporated, 5000 Arlington Centre Boulevard, Columbus, OH 43220
The Computer Company, 1905 Westmoreland Street, Richmond VA 23230
Computer Sciences Corporation, 650 North Sepulveda Boulevard, El Segundo, CA 90245
Comshare, Inc., 3001 South State Street, Ann Arbor, MI 48106
Control Data Corporation, Cybernet Services, P.O. Box O, Minneapolis, MN 55440
Data Resources, Inc., 24 Hartwell Avenue, Lexington, MA 02173
Dialog Information Services, Inc., 3460 Hillview Avenue, Palo Alto, CA 94304
Dow Jones & Company, P.O. Box 300, Princeton, NJ 08540
Dun & Bradstreet, Inc., 99 Church Street, New York, NY 10007
General Electric Information Services, 401 North Washington Street, Rockville, MD 20850
General Videotext Corporation, 3 Blackstone Street, Cambridge, MA 02131
I. P. Sharp Associates, 2 First Canadian Place, Toronto, Ontario, Canada M5X 1E2
Knowledge Index, 3460 Hillview Avenue, Palo Alto, CA 94304
Mead Data Central, 9333 Springboro Pike, Miamisburg, OH 45342
National CSS, 187 Danbury Road, Wilton, CT 06897
National Data Corporation, 20 New Dutch Lane, Fairfield, NJ 07006
National Library of Medicine, 8600 Rockville Pike, Bethesda, MD 20209

New York Times Information Service: See Mead Data Central
Newsnet, 945 Haverford Road, Bryn Mawr, PA 19010
Rapidata, Inc., 20 New Dutch Lane, Fairfield, NJ 07006
SDC Search Service, 2500 Colorado Avenue, Santa Monica, CA 90406
The Source Telecomputing Corporation, 1616 Anderson Road, Mc-
    Lean, VA 22102
Time Sharing Resources, 777 Northern Boulevard, Great Neck, NY
    11021
Tymshare, 20705 Valley Green Drive, Cupertino, CA 95014
United Information Service, 5454 West 110th Street, Overland Park,
    KS 66211

Computer Furniture

Adirondack Direct, 210 East 42nd Street, New York, NY 10017
Bretford Manufacturing, Inc., 9715 Soreng Avenue, Schiller Park,
    IL 60176
Burroughs Division, Lear Siegler, Inc., 30002 North Burdick Street,
    Kalamazoo, MI 49007
Bush Industries, Inc., 312 Fair Oak Street, Little Valley, NY 14755
Charvoz-Carsen, 5 Daniel Road East, Fairfield, NJ 07006
Computer Roomers, Inc., 2737 Seelcco Street, Dallas, TX 75235
DMI Furniture, Inc., State Road 64 East, Huntingburg, IN 47542
Daisy-Net International, P.O. Box 1152, Northbrook, IL 60002
James David, Inc., 1950 Craig Road, St. Louis, MO 63141
Eagle Computer Furniture Systems, 6226 West Howard Street, Niles,
    IL 60648
Fournier Accessory Furniture, Inc., 5040 North Winnetka Avenue,
    Minneapolis, MN 55428
Future Solutions, Inc., 3198-H Airport Loop Drive, Costa Mesa, CA
    92626
Gusdorf Corporation, 6900 Manchester Avenue, St. Louis, MO 63143
Health Science Products, P.O. Box 5545, Birmingham, AL 35207
The Hon Company, 200 Oak Street, Muscatine, IA 52761
INMAC, 2465 Augustine Drive, Santa Clara, CA 95051
M & J Desk Manufacturing Company, 12154 Montague Street, Paco-
    ima, CA 91331
Monarch Computer Products, P.O. Box 4081, New Windsor, NY
    12550
Realist Micrographic Systems, Megal Drive, Menomonee Falls, WI
    53051
Recreational Products Manufacturing, Inc., 2142 West Fulton, Chi-
    cago, IL 60612
Ring King Visibles, Inc., 215 West Second Street, Muscatine, IA 52761

Riverside Furniture Corporation, 1400 South 6th Street, Fort Smith,
    AR 72901
Sirco Manufacturing, Inc., 1919 North Avenue West, Missoula, MT
    59801
Sligh Furniture Company, Inc., 174 East 11th Street, Holland, MI
    49423
Steelcase, Inc., 1120 36th Street, SE, Grand Rapids, MI 49501
Systems Furniture Company, 2727 Maricopa Street, Torrance, CA
    90503
Tiffany Stand & Furniture Company, 9666 Olive Boulevard, St. Louis,
    MO 63132
Viking Acoustical Corporation, Airlake Industrial Park, Lakeville,
    MN 55044
Virco Manufacturing Corporation, 15134 South Vermont Avenue, Los
    Angeles, CA 90044
Windsor Hardwoods, 964 Piner Road, Santa Rosa, CA 95401
Wright Line, Inc., 160 Gold Star Boulevard, Worcester, MA 01606

Chapter 15

Bookkeeping Systems

The Blackbourn Systems, Inc., 366 Wacouta Street, St. Paul, MN
    55101
Columbia Bookkeeping Systems, 21 George Street, Lowell, MA 01852
Data Management, Inc., 537 New Britain Avenue, Farmington, CT
    06032
Dome Publishing Company, 10 New England Way, Warwick, RI 02887
Ekonomik Systems, P.O. Box 11413, Tacoma, WA 98411
Esselte Pendaflex, Clinton Road, Garden City, NY 11530
Four Seasons Business Service, Inc., 404-A Main Street, Kerrville, TX
    78028
General Business Services, Inc., 51 Monroe Street, Rockville, MD
    20850
The Greenwood Company, 843 West Adams Street, Chicago, IL 60607
The Johnson Systems, 230 West Wells, Milwaukee, WI 53203
Master-Craft Corporation, 831 Cobb Avenue, Kalamazoo, MI 49007
MB Systems Unlimited, Inc., P.O. Box 252, Williams Bay, WI 53191
Pegboard Business Forms, P.O. Box 6722, Providence, RI 02940
Simplified Business Services, Inc., 225 Presidential Boulevard, Bala
    Cynwyd, PA 19004
    For information about the federal government's retention require-
ments for its agencies and departments, consult the *Guide to Record
Retention Requirements*, published by the Office of the Federal Register

and available from the Superintendent of Documents, Government Printing Office. See also "Document Retention and Destruction: Practical, Legal, and Ethical Considerations," by John M. Fedders and Lauryn H. Guttenplan, in the October 1980 issue of *The Notre Dame Lawyer*.

Chapter 18

High-Security Locks

Abloy, Inc., 6212 Oakton Street, Morton Grove, IL 60053
Fichet, Inc., P.O. Box 767, Pasadena, CA 91105
Medeco Security Locks, Inc., U.S. Highway 11 West at Allegheny Drive, Salem, VA 24153

Locks for Sliding Doors

Adams Rite Manufacturing Company, 4040 South Capitol Avenue, City of Industry, CA 91749

Window Locks

Blaine Window Hardware, Inc., 1919 Blaine Drive, Hagerstown, MD 21740
Deerfield Lock Company, 520 Saunders Road, Deerfield, IL 60015

Safes

John D. Brush & Company, 900 Linden Avenue, Rochester, NY 14625
Major Safe Company, 300 East Olympic Boulevard, Los Angeles, CA 90023
Meilink Steel Safe Company, P.O. Box 2847, Toledo, OH 43606
The Mosler Safe Company, 1561 Grand Boulevard, Hamilton, OH 45012
Schwab Safe Company, 3000 Main Street, Lafayette, IN 47902

Chapter 19

Orders for or inquiries about publications for sale by the Government Printing Office should be sent to the Assistant Public Printer (Superintendent of Documents), Government Printing Office, North Capitol & H Streets, NW, Washington, DC 20402.

The Government Printing Office operates 26 GPO bookstores carrying the more popular titles at the following locations:
ALABAMA
Birmingham: Roebuck Shopping City, 9220-B Parkway East, 35206

CALIFORNIA
Los Angeles: ARCO Plaza, 505 South Flower Street, 90071
San Francisco: Federal Office Building, 450 Golden Gate Avenue, 94102
COLORADO
Denver: Federal Building, 1961 Stout Street, 80202
Pueblo: Majestic Building, 720 North Main Street, 81003
DISTRICT OF COLUMBIA
Main Bookstore: 710 North Capitol Street, 20402
Commerce Department: 14th & E Streets, NW, 20004
Health & Human Services Department: 330 Independence Avenue, SW, 20003
International Communication Agency, 1776 Pennsylvania Avenue, NW, 20006
State Department: 21st & C Streets, NW, 20006
FLORIDA
Jacksonville: Federal Building, 400 West Bay Street, 32202
GEORGIA
Atlanta: Federal Building, 275 Peachtree Street, NE, 30303
ILLINOIS
Chicago: Everett McKinley Dirksen Building, 219 South Dearborn Street, 60604
MARYLAND
Laurel: 8660 Cherry Lane, Laurel, MD 20707
MASSACHUSETTS
Boston: John F. Kennedy Federal Building, Government Center, 02203
MICHIGAN
Detroit: Patrick V. McNamara Federal Building, 477 Michigan Avenue, 48226
MISSOURI
Kansas City: New Federal Office Building, 601 East 12th Street, 64106
NEW YORK
New York: 26 Federal Plaza, 10007
OHIO
Cleveland: Federal Office Building, 1240 East 9th Street, 44199
Columbus: Federal Office Building, 200 North High Street, 43215
PENNSYLVANIA
Philadelphia: Federal Office Building, 600 Arch Street, 19106
Pittsburgh: Federal Building, 1000 Liberty Avenue, 15222
TEXAS
Dallas: Federal Building & U.S. Courthouse, 1100 Commerce Street, 75242
Houston: 45 College Center, 9319 Gulf Freeway, 77017
WASHINGTON
Seattle: Federal Office Building, 915 Second Avenue, 98104

WISCONSIN
Milwaukee: Federal Building, 517 East Wisconsin Avenue, 53202

Library Sources of Business Information

ALABAMA
Auburn: Auburn University, Ralph Brown Draughon Library, College Street, 36849

Birmingham: Samford University, Harwell Goodwin Davis Library, 800 Lakeshore Drive, 35229

University of Alabama in Birmingham, Mervyn H. Sterne Library, 917 South 13th Street, 35294

Florence: University of North Alabama, Collier Library, Wesleyan Avenue, 35630

Huntsville: University of Alabama in Huntsville, 35899

Jacksonville: Jacksonville State University, Library, North Pelham Road, 36265

Mobile: University of South Alabama, Library, 307 University Boulevard, 36688

Montgomery: Auburn University at Montgomery, Library, 36193

Normal: Alabama Agriculture & Mechanical University, Joseph F. Drake Memorial Learning Resources Center, P.O. Box 489, 35762

Troy: Troy State University, Library, 231 Montgomery Street, 36081

University: University of Alabama, School of Business Library, P.O. Box S, 35486

ALASKA
Anchorage: University of Alaska, Anchorage, Library, 3211 Providence Drive, 99508

Fairbanks: University of Alaska, Fairbanks, Elmer E. Rasmuson Library, 99701

ARIZONA
Flagstaff: Northern Arizona University, Library, CU Box 6022, 86011

Glendale: American Graduate School of International Management, Barton Kyle Yount Memorial Library, Thunderbird Campus, 59th Avenue & Greenway Road, 85306

Phoenix: Salt River Project Library, P.O. Box 1980, 85001

Western Electric Company, Library, 505 North 51st Street, P.O. Box 13369, 85002

Tempe: Arizona State University, College of Business Administration, Lloyd Bimson Memorial Library, 85287

Tucson: University of Arizona, Division of Business & Economic Research, Library, 85721

ARKANSAS
Arkadelphia: Henderson State University, Huie Library, 1100 Henderson Street, 71923

Conway: University of Central Arkansas, Torreyson Library, Do-
naghey at Bruce, 72032
El Dorado: Murphy Oil Corporation, Library, 200 Jefferson Avenue,
71730
Fayetteville: University of Arkansas, Library, 72701
Little Rock: University of Arkansas at Little Rock, Library, Univer-
sity Avenue at 33rd Street, 72204
Magnolia: Southern Arkansas University, Magale Library, P.O. Box
1228, 71753
State University: Arkansas State University, Dean B. Ellis Library,
Aggie & Caraway Roads, P.O. Box 2040, 72467
CALIFORNIA
Arcata: Humboldt State University, Library, 95521
Azusa: Azusa Pacific University, Marshburn Memorial Library, Alosta
at Citrus Avenue, 91702
Bakersfield: California State College, Bakersfield, Library, 9001 Stock-
dale Highway, 93309
Belmont: College of Notre Dame, Library, 1500 Ralston Avenue,
94002
Berkeley: Armstrong College, Library, 2222 Harold Way, 94704
University of California, Berkeley, School of Business Admin-
istration Library, 94720
Burbank: Lockheed Corporation, International Marketing Library,
Building 61, 2255 North Hollywood Way, P.O. Box 551, 91520
Carson: California State University, Dominguez Hills, Educational Re-
sources Center, 1000 East Victoria Street, 90747
Nissan Motor Corporation, Corporate Library, 18501 South
Figueroa Street, 90247
Chico: California State University, Chico, Meriam Library, 1st and
Hazel Streets, 95929
City of Commerce: City of Commerce Public Library, 5655 Jillson
Street, 90040
Claremont: Claremont Colleges, Libraries, 800 Dartmouth Street,
91711
Davis: University of California at Davis, Shields Library, 95616
Downey: Los Angeles County, Department of Data Processing, Tech-
nical Library, 9150 Imperial Highway, 90242
El Segundo: Pepperdine University, LAX Business Center, 360 North
Sepulveda Boulevard, 90245
Fresno: California State University, Fresno, Henry Madden Library,
5241 North Maple Avenue, 93740
Fullerton: California State University, Fullerton, Library, 800 North
State College Boulevard, P.O. Box 4150, 92364
Pacific Christian College, Hurst Memorial Library, 2500 East
Nutwood Avenue, 92631

Hayward: California State University, Hayward, Library, 25800 Carlos
    Bee Boulevard, 94542
Inglewood: Northrop University, Alumni Library, 1155 West Arbor
    Vitae Street, 90306
Irvine: University of California, Irvine, Library, P.O. Box 19557,
    92713
LaVerne: University of LaVerne, Wilson Library, 1950 Third Street,
    91750
Loma Linda: Loma Linda University, Del E. Webb Memorial Library,
    92350
Long Beach: California State University, Long Beach, Library, 1250
    North Bellflower Boulevard, 90840
Los Angeles: Atlantic-Richfield Company, Library, 515 South Flower
    Street, 90051
        California Federal Savings & Loan Association, Management
            Library, 6570 Wilshire Boulevard, 90036
        California State University, Los Angeles, John F. Kennedy
            Memorial Library, 5151 State University Drive, 90032
        Getty Oil Company, Library, 3810 Wilshire Boulevard, 90005
        Los Angeles Public Library, Business & Economics Depart-
            ment, 320 West Temple Street, 90053
        Loyola Marymount University, Charles Von Der Ahe Library,
            7101 West 80th Street, 90045
        Peat, Marwick, Mitchell & Company, Library, 55 South Flower
            Street, 90071
        Price Waterhouse & Company, Library, 606 South Olive Street,
            90014
        Prudential Insurance Company of America, Business Library,
            5757 Wilshire Boulevard, 90036
        Security Pacific National Bank, Library, 333 South Hope Street,
            90071
        First Interstate Bank of California, Library, 707 Wilshire Boule-
            vard, 90017
        University of California, Los Angeles, Graduate School of Man-
            agement Library, 405 Hilgard Avenue, 90024
        University of Southern California, Roy P. Crocker Business Li-
            brary, Hoffman Hall, University Park, 90007
        West Coast University, 440 Shatto Place, Library, 90020
        Woodbury University, 1027 Wilshire Boulevard, Library, 90017
Malibu: Pepperdine University, Central Library, 24255 Pacific Coast
    Highway, 90265
Menlo Park: Stanford Research Institute, Library & Research Informa-
    tion Services, 333 Ravenswood Avenue, 94025
Monterey: Monterey Institute of International Studies, William Tell
    Coleman Library, 425 Van Buren Street, P.O. Box 1978, 93940

320 SOURCES AND RESOURCES

Moraga: St. Mary's College, St. Albert Hall Library, P.O. Box N, 94575
Mountain View: Pacific Studies Center, Library, 867 West Dana, 94041
Northridge: California State University, Northridge, Oviatt/South Libraries, 18111 Nordhoff Street, 91330
Oakland: Alameda County Library, 2201 Broadway, 94612
  Oakland Public Library, Science-Sociology Department, 125 Fourteenth Street, 94612
Orinda: John F. Kennedy University, Library, 12 Altarinda Road, 94563
Orange: Chapman College, Thurmond Clark Memorial Library, 333 North Glassell Street, 92666
Pasadena: Pasadena Public Library, Business-Industry Division, 285 East Walnut Street, 91101
Pleasant Hill: Contra Costa County Library, 1750 Oak Park Boulevard, 94523
Pomona: California Polytechnic State University, Pomona, Library, 3801 West Temple, 91768
Riverside: University of California, Riverside, Library, 990 University Avenue, P.O. Box 5900, 92517
Rohnert Park: Sonoma State University, Ruben Salazar Library, 1801 East Cotati Avenue, 94928
Sacramento: California State University, Sacramento, Library, 2000 Jed Smith Drive, 95819
  Sacramento Public Library, Business & Municipal Department, 828 I Street, 95814
San Bernardino: California State College, San Bernardino, Library, 5500 State College Parkway, 92407
San Diego: National University, Library, 4007 Camino del Rio South, 92108
  San Diego Public Library, Science & Industry Section, 820 E Street, 92101
  San Diego State University, Bureau of Business & Economic Research, Library, 5300 Campanile Drive, 92115
  United States International University, Walter Library, 10455 East Pomerado Road, 92131
  University of San Diego, James S. Copley Library, 5998 Alcala Park, 92110
San Francisco: Bank of America, Reference Library, 555 California Street, 94137
  Bechtel Corporation, Central Library, 50 Beale Street, 94105
  City College of San Francisco, Alice Statler Library, 50 Phelan Avenue, 94112

Crown Zellerbach Corporation, Corporate Information Center, One Bush Street, 94119

Federal Reserve Bank of San Francisco, Research Library, 400 Sansome Street, 94120

Golden Gate University, Library, 536 Mission Street, 94105

Industrial Indemnity Company, Library, 255 California Street, 94111

Lincoln University, 281 Masonic Avenue, Library, 94118

Pacific Gas & Electric Company, Library, 77 Beale Street, 94106

San Francisco Public Library, Business Library, 530 Kearny Street, 94108

San Francisco State University, J. Paul Leonard Library, 1630 Holloway Avenue, 94132

Standard Oil Company of California, Library, 225 Bush Street, 94104

University of San Francisco, Richard A. Gleeson Library, Golden Gate & Parker Avenues, 94117

Wells Fargo Bank, Library, 475 Sansome Street, 94144

San Jose: San Jose State University, Library, Washington Square, 95192

San Luis Obispo: California Polytechnic State University, San Luis Obispo, Robert E. Kennedy Library, 93407

Santa Clara: University of Santa Clara, Michel Orradre Library, 95053

Sherman Oaks: Sunkist Growers, Inc., Corporate Library, 14130 Riverside Drive, 91423

Stanford: Stanford University, Graduate School of Business, J. Hugh Jackson Library, 94305

Thousand Oaks: California Lutheran College, Library, 60 West Olsen Road, 91360

Turlock: California State College, Stanislaus, Library, 801 West Monte Vista Avenue, 95380

Whittier: Whittier College, Bonnie Bell Wardman Library, 7031 Founders Hill Road, 90608

COLORADO

Boulder: University of Colorado at Boulder, William M. White Business Library, 341 Business Building, 80309

Colorado Springs: University of Colorado at Colorado Springs, Library, Austin Bluffs Parkway, P.O. Box 7150, 80933

Denver: Manville Corporation, Corporate Information Center, P.O. Box 5108, 80217

Mountain States Employers Council, Information Center Library, 1790 Logan Street, P.O. Box 539, 80201

Public Service Company of Colorado, Library, 550 15th Street, 80201

United Bank of Denver, N.A., Information Center Library, 1740 Broadway, 80217

Regis College, Dayton Memorial Library, 5000 Lowell Boulevard, 80221

U.S. Air Force Accounting & Financial Center, Technical Library, FL 7040, 80279

University of Colorado at Denver, Library, 1110 14th Street, 80202

University of Denver, Penrose Library, 2150 East Evans Avenue, 80210

Fort Collins: Colorado State University, William E. Morgan Library, 80523

Greeley: University of Northern Colorado, James A. Michener Library, 80639

Gunnison: Western State College of Colorado, Leslie J. Savage Library, 81230

CONNECTICUT

Bloomfield: CIGNA Company, Library, 900 Cottage Grove Road, 06152

Bridgeport: Bridgeport Public Library, Business & Technology Department, 925 Broad Street, 06604

Sacred Heart University, Library, 5229 Park Avenue, 06606

University of Bridgeport, Magnus Wahlstrom Library, 126 Park Avenue, 06602

Warnaco, Inc., Market Research Library, 350 Lafayette Street, 06602

Western Connecticut State University, Ruth A. Haas Library, 181 White Street, 06810

Fairfield: Fairfield University, Gustav & Dagmar Nyselius Library, North Benson Road, 06430

Greenwich: AMAX, Inc., Library, AMAX Center, 06836

American Can Company, Business Information Center, 1B-8 American Lane, 06830

Hamden: Quinnipiac College, Library, Mount Carmel Avenue, 06518

Hartford: Aetna Life & Casualty Company, Corporate Information Center, 151 Farmington Avenue, 06156

Arthur Andersen & Company, Library, One Financial Plaza, 06103

The Hartford Graduate Center, Library, 275 Windsor Street, 06120

Hartford Public Library, Business, Science & Technology Department, 500 Main Street, 06103

Phoenix Mutual Life Insurance Company, One American Row, 06115

Travelers Insurance Company, Corporate Library, One Tower Square, 06115

University of Connecticut, School of Business Administration, Library, 39 Woodland Street, 06105

Wilson, Haight & Welch, Inc., Business Library, 100 Constitution Plaza, 06103

Middlebury: Uniroyal, Inc., Oxford Management & Research Center, Corporate Library, Benson Road, 06749

New Haven: Southern Connecticut State College, Hilton C. Buley Library, 501 Crescent Street, 06515

Yale University, Social Science & Economic Growth Center, 140 Prospect Street, 06520

Stamford, Stamford Public Library, Ferguson Library, 96 Broad Street, 06901

Storrs: University of Connecticut, Library, 06268

West Hartford: University of Hartford, Mortensen Library, 200 Bloomfield Avenue, 06117

West Haven: University of New Haven, Marvin K. Peterson Library, 300 Orange Avenue, 06516

DELAWARE

Newark: Produce Marketing Association, Information Center, 700 Barksdale Road, 19711

University of Delaware, Library, 19711

New Castle: Wilmington College, Library, 320 South DuPont Highway, 19720

Wilmington: Goldey Beacom College, J. Wilbur Hirons Library, 4701 Limestone Road, 19808

DISTRICT OF COLUMBIA

Washington: American Bankers Association, Library Information Services, 1120 Connecticut Avenue, NW, 20036

American Council of Life Insurance, Library, 1850 K Street, NW, 20006

American Society of Association Executives, Information Central, 1575 Eye Street, NW, 20036

American Telephone & Telegraph Company, Government Communications Library, 1120 20th Street, NW, 20036

The American University, Jack I. & Dorothy G. Bender Library, 4400 Massachusetts Avenue, NW, 20016

Catholic University of America, John K. Mullen of Denver Memorial Library, 620 Michigan Avenue, NE, 20017

Chamber of Commerce of the U.S.A., Library, 1615 H Street, NW, 20062

Communications Workers of America, Library, 1925 K Street, NW, 20006

District of Columbia Public Library, Martin Luther King Memorial Library, 901 G Street, NW, 20001

Export-Import Bank of the United States, Library, 811 Vermont Avenue, NW, 20571

Georgetown University, Joseph Mark Lauinger Library, 37th & O Streets, NW, 20057

George Washington University, Melvin Gelman Library, 2130 H Street, NW, 20052

Howard University, School of Business & Public Administration, Library, 2345 Sherman Avenue, NW, 20059

International Monetary Fund/International Bank for Reconstruction & Development, Joint Bank Fund Library, 700 19th Street, NW, 20431

Mortgage Bankers Association of America, Library, 1125 15th Street, NW, 20005

National Coal Association, Library, 1130 17th Street, NW, 20036

National Tax Equality Association Library, 1000 Connecticut Avenue, NW, 20036

Overseas Private Investment Corporation, Library, 1129 20th Street, NW, 20527

Potomac Electric Power Company, Library, 1900 Pennsylvania Avenue, NW, 20068

J. W. Redmond Company, Library, 1750 Pennsylvania Avenue, NW, 20006

Southeastern University, Library, 501 I Street, SW, 20024

Tax Foundation, Inc., Library, 1875 Connecticut Avenue, NW, 20009

U.S. Consumer Product Safety Commission, Library, 5401 Westbard Avenue, 20207

U.S. Department of Commerce, Bureau of the Census, Library, Federal Office Building 3, 20233

U.S. Department of Commerce, Industry & Trade Administration, Library, 14th Street & Constitution Avenue, NW, 20230

U.S. Department of the Treasury, Comptroller of the Currency, Library, 490 L'Enfant Plaza, SW, 20219

U.S. Department of the Treasury, Library, Main Treasury Building, 1500 Pennsylvania Avenue, NW, 20220

U.S. Federal Deposit Insurance Corporation, Library, 550 17th Street, NW 20429

U.S. Federal Home Loan Bank Board, Research Library, 1700 G Street, NW, 20552

U.S. Federal Reserve System, Board of Governors, Research Library, 20th Street & Constitution Avenue, NW, 20551

U.S. Federal Trade Commission, Library, 6th Street & Pennsylvania Avenue, NW, 20580

U.S. Postal Service, Library, 475 L'Enfant Plaza, SW, 20260

U.S. Securities & Exchange Commission, Library, 450 5th Street, NW, 20549

U.S. Small Business Administration, Library, 1411 L Street, NW, 20416

University of the District of Columbia, College of Business & Public Management, Library, 929 E Street, NW, 20004

Washington Gas & Light Company, Library, 1100 H Street, NW, 20080

FLORIDA

Altamonte Springs: Institute of Internal Auditors, Inc., Library, 249 Maitland Avenue, 32701

Boca Raton: Florida Atlantic University, S.E. Wimberly Library, 500 Northwest 20th Street, P.O. Box 3092, 33431

Coral Gables: University of Miami, Otto G. Richter Library, Memorial Drive, P.O. Box 248214, 33124

Daytona Beach: Embry-Riddle Aeronautical University, Learning Resource Center, Regional Airport, 32014

DeLand: Stetson University, duPont-Ball Library, 421 North Boulevard, 32720

Fort Lauderdale: Nova University, Library, 3301 College Avenue, 33314

Gainesville: University of Florida, Library, SW 13th & West University Avenue, 32611

Jacksonville: University of North Florida, Thomas G. Carpenter Library, 4567 St. John's Bluff Road South, 32216

Melbourne: Florida Institute of Technology, Library, 2901 South Country Club Road, P.O. Box 1150, 32901

Miami: Amerifirst Savings & Loan Association of Miami, Research & Management Division, Library, One Southeast Avenue, 33131

Florida International University, Athenaeum, Tamiami Trail & Southwest 107th Avenue, 33199

Florida Power & Light Company, Corporate Library, 9250 West Flagler Street, 33152

Miami-Dade Public Library, Business, Science & Technology Department, One Biscayne Boulevard, 33132

Miami Shores: Barry University, Monsignor William Barry Memorial Library, 11300 NE Second Avenue, 33161

Orlando: University of Central Florida, Library, 4000 Central University Boulevard, 32816

Pensacola: University of West Florida, John C. Pace Library, 32514

Tallahassee: Florida Department of Commerce, Research Library,
    Fletcher Building, 32301
        Florida State University, Robert Manning Strozier Library, 600
            West College Avenue, 32306
Tampa: University of South Florida, Library, 4202 East Fowler Ave-
    nue, 33620
        University of Tampa, Merl Kelce Library, 401 West Kennedy
            Boulevard, 33606
Winter Park: Rollins College, Mills Memorial Library, 32789
GEORGIA
Albany: Albany State College, Margaret Rood Hazard Library, 504
    College Drive, 31705
Athens: University of Georgia, Library, 120 Herty Drive, 30602
Atlanta: Atlanta Public Library, Department of Science, Industry &
    Government, One Margaret Mitchell Square, NW, 30303
        Atlanta University, Robert W. Woodruff Library, 111 Chestnut
            Street, SW, 30314
        Coca-Cola USA, Marketing Information Center, 310 North
            Avenue, 30301
        Emory University, Library, 1364 Clifton Road, NE, 30322
        Equifax, Inc., Library, 1600 Peachtree Street, NW, 30302
        Federal Reserve Bank of Atlanta, 104 Marietta Street, NW,
            30303
        Georgia Institute of Technology, Price Gilbert Memorial Li-
            brary, 225 North Avenue, 30332
        Georgia State University, William Russell Pullen Library, Uni-
            versity Plaza, 30303
        Life Office Management Association, Information Center,
            1175 Peachtree Street, NE, 30361
        Mercer University in Atlanta, Monroe F. Swilley, Jr. Library,
            3000 Flowers Road South, NE, 30341
Augusta: Augusta College, Reese Library, 2500 Walton Way, 30910
Carrollton: West Georgia College, Irvine Sullivan Ingram Library,
    Maple Street, 30118
Columbus: Columbus College, Simon Schwob Memorial Library, Al-
    gonquin Drive, 31907
Gainesville: Brenau College, Leslie Southgate Simmons Memorial Li-
    brary, Washington Street, 30501
LaGrange: LaGrange College, William & Evelyn Banks Library, 30240
Macon: Mercer University, Stetson Memorial Library, 1330 Edge-
    wood Avenue, 31207
Milledgeville: Georgia College, Ina Dillard Russell Library, 231 West
    Hancock Street, 31061
Mount Berry: Berry College, Memorial Library, 30149

Rome: Sara Hightower Regional Library, Business Library, 606 West First Street, 30161

Savannah: Savannah State College, Library, 31404

Statesboro: Georgia Southern College, Library, Landrum Box 8074, 30460

Valdosta: Valdosta State College, Library, 1500 North Patterson Street, 31698

HAWAII

Honolulu: Bank of Hawaii, Information Center, Financial Plaza, Tower Building, 96846

> Chamber of Commerce of Hawaii, Reference Library, Dillingham Building, 735 Bishop Street, 96813

> Chaminade University of Honolulu, Library, 3140 Waialae Avenue, 96816

> Hawaii Pacific College, Meader Library, 1060 Bishop Street, 96813

> Hawaii State Library, Business-Science-Technology Unit, 478 South King Street, 96813

> Hawaiian Telephone Company, Library, 1177 Bishop Street, 96841

> University of Hawaii, Thomas Hale Hamilton Library, 2550 The Mall, 96822

IDAHO

Boise: Boise University, Library, 1910 University Drive, 83725

Moscow: University of Idaho, Library, 83843

Pocatello: Idaho State University, Library, P.O. Box 8089, 83209

ILLINOIS

Aurora: Aurora College, Charles B. Phillips Library, 347 South Gladstone Avenue, 60507

Berwyn: Olympic Savings & Loan Association, Library, 6201 West Cermak Road, 60402

Carbondale: Southern Illinois University at Carbondale, Delyte W. Morris Library, 62901

Charleston: Eastern Illinois University, Booth Library, 61920

Chicago: Adams Advertising Agency, Inc., Library, 427 West Randolph, 60606

> American Hospital Association, Asa S. Bacon Memorial Library, 840 North Lake Shore Wrive, 60611

> American Marketing Association, Information Center, 250 South Wacker Drive, 60606

> Arthur Andersen & Company, Library, 32 West Monroe Street, 60603

> Bank Marketing Association, Information Center, 309 West Washington Street, 60606

Blue Cross/Blue Shield Association, Library, 840 North St. Clair, 60611

Booz, Allen & Hamilton, Inc., Library, 3 First National Plaza, 60601

CNA Insurance Library, 35 CNA Plaza, 60685

Campbell-Mithun, Inc., Research Information Center, 11 East Wacker Drive, 60601

Chicago Board of Trade, Library, 141 West Jackson Street, 60604

Chicago Public Library, Business-Science-Technology Division, 425 North Michigan Avenue, 60611

Continental Illinois National Bank & Trust Company, Information Services Division, 231 South LaSalle Street, 60693

DePaul University, 25 East Jackson Boulevard, Library, 60611

Federal Reserve Bank of Chicago, Library, 230 South LaSalle Street, 60690

First National Bank of Chicago, Library, One First National Plaza, 60670

Illinois Institute of Technology, James S. Kemper Information & Learning Resource Center, 3300 South Federal Street, 60616

Illinois Institute of Technology, Harold Leonard Stuart School of Management & Finance, Library, 10 West 31st Street, 60616

Insurance School of Chicago, Library, 330 South Wells, 60606

International Association of Assessing Officers, Library, 1313 East 60th Street, 60637

Keller Graduate School of Management, Library, 10 South Riverside Plaza, 60606

Loyola University, Julia Deal Lewis Library, 820 North Michigan Avenue, 60611

Midwest Stock Exchange, Inc., Library, 120 South LaSalle Street, 60603

Montgomery Ward & Company, Information Services, One Montgomery Ward Plaza, 60671

National Association of Realtors, Herbert U. Nelson Memorial Library, 430 North Michigan Avenue, 60611

Needham, Harper & Steers Advertising, Inc., Library, 303 East Wacker Drive, 60611

Northern Trust Company, Library, 50 South LaSalle Street, 60603

Northwestern University, Chicago, Graduate School of Management, Joseph Schaffner Library, 339 East Chicago Avenue, 60611

People's Gas, Light & Coke Company, Library, 122 South Michigan Avenue, 60603

Price Waterhouse & Company, Library, 200 East Randolph Drive, 60601

Roosevelt University, Murray-Green Library, 430 South Michigan Avenue, 60605

Society of Real Estate Appraisers, Library, 645 North Michigan Avenue, 60611

Standard Oil Company (Indiana), Library-Information Center, 200 East Randolph Drive, 60601

Stein Roe & Farnham, Library, 150 South Wacker Drive, 60606

J. Walter Thompson Company, Information Center, 875 North Michigan Avenue, 60611

United Air Lines, Inc., Library Box 66100, 60666

University of Chicago, Graduate School of Business, Library, 1101 East 58th Street, 60637

University of Illinois at Chicago Circle, Library, 801 South Morgan Street, P.O. Box 8198, 60680

U.S. Securities & Exchange Commission, Public Reference Library, 219 South Dearborn, 60604

DeKalb: Northern Illinois University, Founders Memorial Library, 60115

Downers Grove: George Williams College, Library, 555 31st Street, 60515

Edwardsville: Southern Illinois University at Edwardsville, Elijah P. Lovejoy Library, 62026

Evanston: American Hospital Supply Organization, Corporate Information Center, One American Plaza, 60201

National College of Education, Learning Resources Center, 2840 Sheridan Road, 60201

Northwestern University, Library, 1935 Sheridan Road, 60201

Washington National Insurance Company, Information Resources Center, 1630 Chicago Avenue, 60201

Lake Forest: Lake Forest School of Management, Lake Forest College, Donnelley Library, 60045

Lincolnshire: Hewitt Associates, Library, 100 Half Day Road, 60015

Lisle: Illinois Benedictine College, Theodore F. Lownik Library, 5700 College Road, 60532

Long Grove: Kemper Group Insurance Companies, Library, 60049

Macomb: Western Illinois University, Library, 900 West Adams Street, 61455

Normal: Illinois State University, Milner Library, 61761

Park Forest South: Governors' State University, Library, 60466

Peoria: Caterpillar Tractor Company, Business Library, 100 Adams
    Street, NE, 61629
River Forest: Rosary College, Rebecca Crown Library, 7900 West Di-
    vision Street, 60305
Rockford: Rockford College, Howard Colman Library, 5050 East
    State Street, 61108
    Rockford Public Library, Business, Science & Technology, 215
        North Wyman Street, 61101
Romeoville: Lewis University, Library, Route 53, 60441
Skokie: Brunswick Corporation, Information Center, One Brunswick
    Plaza, 60077
Springfield: Sangamon State University, Norris L. Brookens Library,
    Shepherd Road, 62708
Urbana: University of Illinois at Urbana-Champaign, College of Com-
    merce & Business Administration, Commerce Library, 61801
INDIANA
Bloomington: Indiana University at Bloomington, Business Library,
    Business Building, 47405
Columbus: Cummins Engine Company, Inc., Technical Library, 1000
    Fifth Street, 47201
Elkhart: Miles Laboratories, Inc., Library Resources & Services, 1127
    Myrtle Street, 46515
Evansville: University of Evansville, Clifford Memorial Library, 1800
    Lincoln Avenue, 47702
Fort Wayne: First Federal Savings & Loan Association, Library, 719
    Court Street, 46802
    Indiana University-Purdue University at Fort Wayne, Walter
        E. Helmke Library, 2101 East Coliseum Boulevard, 46805
    Public Library of Fort Wayne & Allen County, Business & Tech-
        nology Department, 900 Webster Street, P.O. Box 2270,
        46802
    St. Francis College, Library, 2701 Spring Street, 46808
Gary: Indiana University Northwest, Library, 3400 Broadway, 46408
Gas City: Indiana Northern Graduate School of Professional Manage-
    ment, Library, 410 South 10th Street, 46933
Hammond: Purdue University-Calumet, Library, 2233 171st Street,
    46323
Indianapolis: American States Insurance Company, Library, 500 North
    Meridian Street, 46207
    Butler University, Irwin Library, 4600 Sunset Avenue, 46208
    Indiana Central University, Krannert Memorial Library, 1400
        East Hanna Avenue, 46227
    Indianapolis-Marion County Public Library, Business, Science &
        Technology Division, 40 East St. Clair Street, 46204

Eli Lilly & Company, Business Library, 307 East McCarty Street, 46225

Muncie: Ball Corporation, Corporate Information Center, 345 South High Street, 43702

Ball State University, Alexander M. Bracken Library, 2000 University Avenue, 47306

Notre Dame: University of Notre Dame, Memorial Library, 46556

South Bend: Indiana University at South Bend, Library, 1700 Mishawaka Avenue, P.O. Box 7111, 46615

Terre Haute: Indiana State University, Cunningham Memorial Library, 217 North 6th Street, 47809

West Lafayette: Purdue University, Management & Economics Library, Krannert Building, 47907

IOWA

Ames: Iowa State University, Library, 50011

Cedar Falls: University of Northern Iowa, Library, 23rd & College, 50614

Cedar Rapids Public Library, Business, Science & Technology Division, 40 East St. Clair Street, 52401

Davenport: St. Ambrose College, McMullen Library, 518 Locust Street, 52803

Des Moines: Drake University, Cowles Library, 28th Street & University Avenue, 50311

Iowa City: University of Iowa, Business Administration Library, Phillips Hall, 52242

KANSAS

Emporia: Emporia State University, William Allen White Library, 1200 Commercial Street, 66801

Hays: Fort Hays State University, Forsyth Library, 600 Park Street, 67601

Lawrence: University of Kansas, Watson Library, 66045

Manhattan: Kansas State University, Farrell Library, Manhattan & Anderson Avenues, 66506

Pittsburg: Pittsburg State University, Leonard H. Axe Library, 66762

Topeka: Security Benefit Life Insurance Company, Library, 700 Southwest Harrison Street, 66636

Wichita: Wichita Public Library, Business & Technology Service, 223 South Main Street, 67202

Wichita State University, Library & Media Resources Center, Ablah Library, 1845 Fairmont Street, P.O. Box 68, 67208

KENTUCKY

Bowling Green: Western Kentucky University, Helm-Cravens Library, College Heights, 42101

Frankfort: Kentucky Department of Economic Development, Research Library, Capitol Plaza Office Tower, 40601
Highland Heights: Northern Kentucky University, W. Frank Steely Library, Louie B. Nunn Drive, 41076
Lexington: University of Kentucky, Business & Economics Library, Commerce Building, 40506
Louisville: Bellarmine College, Library, 2001 Newburg Road, 40205
    University of Louisville, Ekstrom Library, Belknap Campus, 40292
Morehead: Morehead State University, Camden-Carroll Library, University Boulevard, 40351
Murray: Murray State University, Harry Lee Waterfield Library, 42071
Richmond: Eastern Kentucky University, John Grant Crabbe Library, Lancaster Avenue, 40475

LOUISIANA

Baton Rouge: Louisiana State University & Agricultural & Mechanical College, Troy H. Middleton Library, Highland Road, 70803
Hammond: Southeastern Louisiana University, Linus A. Sims Memorial Library, Western Avenue, P.O. Drawer 896, 70402
Lafayette: University of Southwestern Louisiana, Dupre Library, 302 East St. Mary Boulevard, 70504
Lake Charles: McNeese State University, Lether E. Frazar Memorial Library, 4300 Ryan Street, 70609
Monroe: Northeast Louisiana University, Sandel Library, 700 University Avenue, 71209
Nachitoches: Northwestern State University of Louisiana, Eugene P. Watson Memorial Library, College Avenue, 71457
New Orleans: Loyola University, Library, 6363 St. Charles Avenue, 70118
    New Orleans Public Library, Business & Science Division, 219 Loyola Avenue, 70140
    Tulane University, School of Business Administration, Norman Mayer Library, 6823 St. Charles Avenue, 70118
    University of New Orleans, Earl K. Long Library, Lakeshore Drive, 70148
Ruston: Louisiana Tech University, Prescott Memorial Library, P. O. Box 10408, 71272
Shreveport: Centenary College, Magale Library, Woodlawn Avenue at Columbia Street, 71104
    Louisiana State University in Shreveport, Library, 8515 Youree Drive, 71115
Thibodaux: Nicholls State University, Allen J. Ellender Memorial Library, 70310

MAINE

Bangor: Beal College, Library, 629 Main Street, 04401
   Husson College, Library, College Circle, 04401
Orono: University of Maine at Orono, Raymond H. Folger Library, 04469
Portland: Andover College, Library, 335 Forrest Avenue, 04101
   Union Mutual Life Insurance Company, Business Library, 2211 Congress Street, 04112
   University of Southern Maine, Library, 96 Falmouth Street, 04103
Waterville: Thomas College, Marriner Library, West River Road, 04901

MARYLAND

Baltimore: Chessie System Railroads, Research Department, Library, 100 North Charles Street, 21201
   Enoch Pratt Free Library, Business, Science & Technology Department, 400 Cathedral Street, 21201
   Johns Hopkins University, Milton S. Eisenhower Library, 21218
   Loyola College, Loyola-Notre Dame Library, 200 Winston Avenue, 21212
   Morgan State University, Morris A. Soper Library, Cold Spring Lane & Hillen Road, 21239
   University of Baltimore, Langsdale Library, 1420 Maryland Avenue, 21201
Bowie: Bowie State College, Thurgood Marshall Library, Jericho Park Road, 20715
College Park: University of Maryland, Theodore R. McKeldin Library, 20742
Emmitsburg: Mount Saint Mary's College, Hugh J. Phillips Library, 21727
Frederick: Hood College, Joseph Henry Apple Library, Rosemont Avenue, 21701
Frostburg: Frostburg State College, Library, 21532
Silver Spring: National Foundation for Consumer Credit, Library, 8701 Georgia Avenue, NW, 20910

MASSACHUSETTS

Amherst: University of Massachusetts at Amherst, Goodell Library, 01003
Boston: American Institute of Management, Library, 607 Boylston Street, 02116
   Arthur Andersen & Company, Library, 100 Federal Street, 02110
   Bank of New England, Corporate Library, One Washington Mall, 02108

Boston Public Library, Kirstein Business Branch, 20 City Hall
   Avenue, 02108
Boston University, Mugar Memorial Library, 771 Common-
   wealth Avenue, 02215
Coopers & Lybrand, Library, One Post Office Square, 02110
Federal Reserve Bank of Boston, Research Library, 600 At-
   lantic Avenue, 02106
Harvard University, Graduate School of Business Administra-
   tion, Baker Library, Soldiers Field Road, 02163
Insurance Library Association, 156 State Street, 02108
John Hancock Mutual Life Insurance Company, Library, John
   Hancock Plaza, 02117
Liberty Mutual Insurance Company, Education Information
   Resources, 175 Berkeley Street, 02117
Massachusetts Department of Commerce & Development, Li-
   brary, 100 Cambridge Street, 02202
New England Mutual Life Insurance Company, Business Li-
   brary, 501 Boylston Street, 02116
Northeastern University, Dodge Library, 360 Huntington Ave-
   nue, 02114
Price Waterhouse & Company, Information Center, One Fed-
   eral Street, 02110
Scudder, Stevens & Clark, Library, 175 Federal Street, 02110
Shawmut Bank of Boston, NA, Library, One Federal Street,
   02110
Simmons College, Beatley Library, 300 The Fenway, 02115
Suffolk University, Mildred F. Sawyer Library, 8 Ashburton
   Place, Beacon Hill, 02108
Burlington: Raytheon Service Company, Information Center, 2 Way-
   side Road, 01803
Cambridge: Arthur D. Little, Inc., Management Library, 35 Acorn
   Park, 02140
   Lesley College, Library, 29 Everett Street, 02138
   Massachusetts Institute of Technology, Dewey Library of Busi-
      ness & Management, Hermann Building, 02139
Chestnut Hill: Boston College, School of Management Library, Fulton
   Hall, 02167
Dudley: Nichols College, Conant Library, 01570
Lexington: Raytheon Company, Business Information Center, 141
   Spring Street, 02173
Lowell: University of Lowell, Alumi-Lydon Library, One University
   Avenue, 01854
Marlborough: New England Telephone Company, Learning Resource
   Center, 280 Locke Drive, 01752

Maynard: Digital Equipment Corporation, Maynard Library, 146 Main Street, 01754

North Dartmouth: Southeastern Massachusetts University, Library, Old Westport Road, P.O. Box 6, 02747

Paxton: Anna Maria College, Mondor-Eagen Library, Sunset Lane, 01612

Springfield: American International College, James J. Shea Memorial Library, 1000 State Street, 01109

    Massachusetts Mutual Life Insurance Company Library, 1295 State Street, 01111

    Western New England College, D'Amour Library, 1215 Wilbraham Road, 01119

Waltham: Bentley College, Solomon R. Baker Library, Beaver & Forest Streets, 02254

Wellesley: Babson College, Horn Library, Babson Park, 02157

Wellesley Hills: Sun Life Assurance Company of Canada, Reference Library, One Sun Life Executive Park, 02181

Worcester: Assumption College, Library, 500 Salisbury Street, 01609

    Clark University, Robert Hutchings Goddard Library, 950 Main Street, 01610

    State Mutual Life Assurance Company, Library, 440 Lincoln Street, 01605

    Worcester Polytechnic Institute, George C. Gordon Library, 100 Institute Road, 01609

MICHIGAN

Allendale: Grand Valley Colleges, James H. Zumberge Library, College Landing, 49401

Ann Arbor: University of Michigan, School of Business Administration, Library, 48109

Berrien Springs: Andrews University, James White Library, 49103

Dearborn: University of Michigan-Dearborn, Library, 4901 Evergreen Road, 48128

Detroit: Burroughs Corporation, Corporate Information Research Center, Burroughs Place, 48232

    Comerica Corporation, Research Library, 211 West Fort, 49231

    Detroit Public Library, Business & Finance Department, 5201 Woodward Avenue, 48202

    National Bank of Detroit, Library, P.O. Box 116, 48232

    Ross Roy, Inc., Library, 2751 East Jefferson Avenue, 48207

    University of Detroit, Library, 4001 West McNichols Road, 48221

    Wayne State University, G. Flint Purdy Library, 5265 Cass Avenue, 48202

East Lansing: Michigan State University, Business Library, 21 Epley
Center, 48824
Flint: Flint Public Library, Business & Industry Department, 1026 East
Kearsley Street, 48502
University of Michigan-Flint, Library, 303 Kearsley Street,
48503
Grand Rapids: Aquinas College, Learning Resource Center, 1607 Rob-
inson Road, 49506
Foremost Insurance Company, Centennial Library, 5800 Fore-
most Drive, SE, 49501
Grand Rapids Public Library, Science, Business, Sociology &
Education Department, 60 Library Plaza, NE, 49503
Holland: Donnelly Mirrors, Inc., Library, 49 West Third Street, 49423
Houghton: Michigan Technological University, Library, 49931
Kalamazoo: Upjohn Company, Business Library, 7000 Portage Road,
49001
Western Michigan University, Business Library, North Hall,
49008
Marquette: Northern Michigan University, Lydia M. Olson Library,
Elizabeth L. Harden Drive, 49855
Midland: Dow Corning Corporation, Information Center, South Sagi-
naw Road, 48640
Northwood Institute, Strosacker Library, North Hall, 3225
Cook Road, 49008
Mt. Pleasant: Central Michigan University, Charles V. Park Library,
48859
Rochester: Oakland University, Kresge Library, 48063
Saginaw: Hoyt Public Library, Business & Technology Department,
505 Janes Street, 48605
Sault Ste. Marie: Lake Superior State College, Kenneth Shouldice Li-
brary, 1000 College Drive, 49783
Southfield: Sandy Corporation, Research & Retrieval Center, 16025
Northland Drive, 48075
Troy: Rockwell International, Reference Center, 2135 West Maple
Road, 48084
Walsh College of Accountancy & Business Administration, Li-
brary, 3838 Livernois Road, 48084
University Center: Saginaw Valley State College, Library, 2250 Pierce
Road, 48710
Warren: Campbell-Ewald Company, Reference Center, 30400 Van
Dyke Avenue, 48093
Ypsilanti: Eastern Michigan University, Library, 48197
MINNESOTA
Duluth: University of Minnesota, Duluth, Library, 2400 Oakland Ave-
nue, 55812

Mankato: Mankato State University, Memorial Library, Maywood & Ellis Streets, P.O. Box 19, 56001

Minneapolis: Cargill, Inc., Information Center, P.O. Box 5670, 55440

Carlson Companies, Library, 12755 State Highway 55, 55441

Deloitte, Haskins & Sells, Library, 625 Fourth Avenue South, 55402

Federal Reserve Bank of Minneapolis, 250 Marquette Avenue South, 55480

General Mills, Inc., General Office Library, 9200 Wayzata Boulevard, P.O. Box 1113, 55426

Minneapolis Public Library & Information Center, Business & Science Department, 300 Nicollet Mall, 55401

Northwest Bancorporation, Library, Northwestern National Bank Building, 620 Marquette Avenue, 55480

Northwestern National Life Insurance Company, Library, 20 Washington Avenue South, P.O. Box 20, 55440

Peat, Marwick, Mitchell & Company, Library, IDS Center, 55402

Pillsbury Company, Business Reference Library, Pillsbury Center, 55402

University of Minnesota, Twin Cities, Business Reference Service, O. Meredith Wilson Library, 309 19th Avenue South, 55455

Moorhead: Moorhead State University, Livingston Lord Library, 56560

St. Cloud: St. Cloud State University, Centennial Hall Learning Resources Center, First Avenue South, 56301

St. Paul: College of St. Thomas, O'Shaughnessy Library, 2115 Summit Avenue, 55105

James Jerome Hill Reference Library, 4th Street at Market, 55102

St. Paul Fire & Marine Insurance Company, Technical Information Services, 385 Washington Street, 55102

St. Paul Public Library, Science & Industry Room, 90 West 4th Street, 55102

3M Company, Business Information Service, Building 220-1C-02, 3M Center, 55144

Winona: Winona State University, Maxwell Library, Sanborn & Johnson Streets, 55987

MISSISSIPPI

Cleveland: Delta State University, W. B. Roberts Library, 38733

Clinton: Mississippi College, Leland Speed Library, P.O. Box 127, 39058

Columbus: Mississippi University for Women, John Clayton Fant Memorial Library, 39701

Hattiesburg: University of Southern Mississippi, Joseph A. Cook Memorial Library, P.O. Box 5053, Southern Station, 39401

Jackson: Jackson State University, Henry Thomas Sampson Library, 1400 Lynch Street, 39203

>Millsaps College, Millsaps-Wilson Library, 1701 North State Street, 39203

>Mississippi Research & Development Center, Information Services Division, 3825 Ridgewood Road, 39211

Lorman: Alcorn State University, Boyd Library, P.O. Box 539, 39096

Mississippi State: Mississippi State University, Mitchell Memorial Library, P.O. Drawer 5408, 39762

Natchez: University of Southern Mississippi-Natchez, Library, Duncan Park, 39120

University: University of Mississippi, School of Business Administration, Library, Conner Hall, 38677

MISSOURI

Cape Girardeau: Southeast Missouri State University, Kent Library, 900 Normal, 63701

Columbia: University of Missouri-Columbia, Elmer Ellis Library, 65211

Jefferson City: Lincoln University, Inman E. Page Library, P.O. Box 29, 65101

Kansas City: Avila College, Hooley-Bundschu Library, 11901 Wornall Road, 64145

>Business Men's Assurance Company, Library, BMA Tower, 700 Karnes Boulevard, 64108

>Employers Reinsurance Corporation, Library, 21 West 10th Street, 64105

>Federal Reserve Bank of Kansas City, Research Library, 925 Grand Avenue, 64198

>Kansas City Public Library, 311 East Twelfth Street, 64106

>Old American Insurance Company, Library, 4900 Oak Street, 64112

>Rockhurst College, Greenlease Library, 5225 Troost Avenue, 64110

>University of Missouri-Kansas City, Library, 5100 Rockhill Road, 64110

>Waddell & Reed, Inc., Investment Management Division, Research Library, One Crown Center, P.O. Box 1343, 64141

Kirksville: Northeast Missouri State University, Pickler Memorial Library, 63501

Maryville: Northwest Missouri State University, Owens Library, 64468

St. Charles: The Lindenwood Colleges, Margaret L. Butler Library, 63301

St. Louis: Federal Reserve Bank of St. Louis, 411 Locust Street, 63166
  Gardner Advertising Company, Inc., Information Center, 10
    Broadway, 63102
  May Department Stores, Corporate Information Center, 611
    Olive Street, 63103
  St. Louis Public Library, Humanities & Social Sciences Department, 1301 Olive Street, 63103
  St. Louis University, Pius XII Memorial Library, 3655 West
    Pine Boulevard, 63108
  University of Missouri–St. Louis, Thomas Jefferson Library,
    8001 Natural Bridge Road, 63121
  Washington University, School of Business Administration,
    Business Administration Library, Prince Hall, 63130
Springfield: Drury College, Walker Library, 900 North Benton Avenue,
    65802
  Southwest Missouri State University, Library, 901 South National, P.O. Box 175, 65802
Warrensburg: Central Missouri State University, Ward Edwards Library, 64093

MONTANA

Bozeman: Montana State University, Roland R. Renne Library, 59717
Missoula: University of Montana, Maureen & Mike Mansfield Library,
  59812

NEBRASKA

Chadron: Chadron State College, Library, 10th & Main Streets, 69337
Kearney: Kearney State College, Calvin T. Ryan Library, 68849
Lincoln: University of Nebraska, D. L. Love Memorial Library, 68588
  Woodmen Accident & Life Company, Library, 1526 K. Street,
    68501
Omaha: Creighton University, Alumni Memorial Library, 2500 California Street, 68178
  Mutual of Omaha–United of Omaha, Library, 3301 Dodge
    Street, 68131
  Omaha Public Library, Business, Science & Technology Department, 215 South 15th Street, 68102
  Union Pacific Railroad, Marketing Library, 1416 Dodge Street,
    68179
  University of Nebraska at Omaha, Library, 60th & Dodge
    Streets, 68132
Wayne: Wayne State College, U.S. Conn Library, 200 East 10th Street,
  68787

NEVADA

Las Vegas: University of Nevada, Las Vegas, James R. Dickinson Library, 4505 Maryland Parkway South, 89154

Reno: University of Nevada, Reno, Noble H. Getchell Library, 9th & Center Streets, 89557

NEW HAMPSHIRE

Durham: University of New Hampshire, Ezekiel W. Dimond Library, 03824

Hanover: Dartmouth College, Feldberg Library, 03755

Manchester: New Hampshire College, H. A. B. Shapiro Memorial Library, 2500 North River Road, 03104

Nashua: Daniel Webster College, Library, University Drive, 03063

Rivier College, Regina Library, Main Street, 03060

Plymouth: Plymouth State College, Herbert H. Lamson Library, 03264

NEW JERSEY

Bedminster: AT&T, Inc., Long Lines Information Research Center, 07921

Camden: Rutgers University, Arts & Science Library, 300 North 4th Street, 08102

Hoboken: Stevens Institute of Technology, Samuel C. Williams Library, Castle Point Station, 07030

Kenilworth: Schering-Plough Corporation, Business Information Center, Galloping Hill Road, 07033

Lawrenceville: Rider College, Franklin F. Moore Library, 2083 Lawrenceville Road, P.O. Box 6400, 08648

Madison: Fairleigh Dickinson University, Florham-Mendham Campus Library, 07940

Morristown: AT&T, Inc., Advanced Information Systems Library, 1776 On the Green, 07960

Newark: Newark Public Library, 34 Commerce Street, 07102

Prudential Insurance Company, Business Library, Prudential Plaza, 07101

Rutgers University, Newark College of Arts & Sciences, John Cotton Dana Library, 185 University Avenue, 07102

Nutley: Hoffman-La Roche, Inc., Business Information Center, 07110

Piscataway: American Bell, Inc., Business & Technical Resources Center, 444 Hoes Lane, 08854

Princeton: Pliny Fisk Library of Economics & Finance, Firestone Library, 08544

Rutherford: Fairleigh Dickinson University, Rutherford Campus, Messler Library, 207 Montross Avenue, 07070

South Orange: Seton Hall University, McLaughlin Library, 405 South Orange Avenue, 07079

Teaneck: Fairleigh Dickinson University, Teaneck-Hackensack Campus, Weiner Library, 1000 River Road, 07666

Trenton: Free Public Library, Business & Technology Department, 120 Academy Street, P.O. Box 2448, 08608

Trenton State College, Roscoe L. West Library, Pennington Road, 08625

Upper Montclair: Montclair State College, Harry A. Sprague Library, 07043

Wayne: American Cyanamid Company, Business Information Center, One Cyanamid Plaza, 07470

William Paterson College, Sarah Byrd Askew Library, 300 Pompton Road, 07470

West Long Branch: Monmouth College, Guggenheim Library, Cedar Avenue, 07764

NEW MEXICO

Albuquerque: American Classical College, Stock Market Library, 607 McKnight Avenue, NW, P.O. Box 4526, 87102

University of New Mexico, Robert O. Anderson School of Management, William J. Parrish Memorial Library, 87131

University of New Mexico, Institute of Applied Research Services, Bureau of Business & Economic Research, Data Bank, 87131

Las Cruces: New Mexico State University, Library, P.O. Box 3475, 88003

Las Vegas: New Mexico Highlands University, Donnelly Library, National Avenue, 87701

Portales: Eastern New Mexico University, Golden Library, 88130

Santa Fe: New Mexico State Commerce & Industry Department, Library, Bataan Memorial Building, 87503

Silver City: Western New Mexico University, Miller Library, College Avenue at C Street, P.O. Box 85, 88061

NEW YORK

Albany: College of St. Rose, Neil Hellman Library, 432 Western Avenue, 12203

Key Bank, N.A., Library, 60 State Street, 12207

New York State Department of Audit & Control, Library, Alfred E. Smith Office Building, 12236

New York State Department of Commerce, Library, 99 Washington Street, 12245

New York State Department of Taxation & Finance, Bureau of Research & Statistics, Tax Library, Taxation & Finance Building, 12227

State University of New York at Albany, Library, 1400 Washington Avenue, 12222

Binghamton: State University of New York at Binghampton, Glenn G. Bartle Library, East Vestal Parkway, 13905

Bronx: Manhattan College, Cardinal Hayes Library, 4513 Manhattan College Parkway, 10471

State University of New York Maritime College, Stephen B. Luce Library, Fort Schuyler, 10465
Brooklyn: Brooklyn Public Library, Business Library, 280 Cadman Plaza West, 11201
Long Island University, Library, University Plaza, 11201
Polytechnic Institute of New York, Spicer Library, 333 Jay Street, 11201
Buffalo: Buffalo & Erie County Public Library, Business & Labor Department, Lafayette Square, 14203
Canisius College, Andrew L. Bowhuis Library, 2001 Main Street, 14208
State University of New York at Buffalo, Library, Capen Hall, 14260
Corning: College Center of the Finger Lakes, Library, 22 West 3rd Street, P.O. Box 180, 14830
Dobbs Ferry: Long Island University, Mercy College, Library, 555 Broadway, 10522
Garden City: Adelphi University, Swirbul Library, South Avenue, 11530
Greenvale: Long Island University, C. W. Post Center, B. Davis Schwartz Memorial Library, Northern Boulevard, 11548
Hamilton: American Management Associations, Inc., Center for Planning & Implementation, Donald W. Mitchell Memorial Library, West Lakes Moraine Road, 13346
Hempstead: Hofstra University, Library, 1000 Fulton Avenue, 11550
Ithaca: Cornell University, Graduate School of Business & Public Administration, Library, Malott Hall, 14853
Jamaica: Queens Borough Public Library, Social Sciences Division, 89-11 Merrick Boulevard, 11432
St. John's University, Library, Grand Central & Utopia Parkways, 11439
Mount Vernon: Consumer's Union of the U.S., Inc., Library, 256 Washington Street, 10550
New Rochelle: Iona College, Ryan Library, 715 North Avenue, 10801
New York: Advertising Research Foundation, Library, 3 East 45th Street, 10022
American Association of Advertising Agencies, Member Information Service, 666 Third Avenue, 10017
American Banker & Bond Buyer, Inc., Editorial Library, One State Street, 10004
AT&T, Inc., Corporate Research Library, 195 Broadway, 10007

American Institute of Banking, Herbert W. Trecarin Finance & Bank Management Library, 233 Broadway, 10007

American Institute of Certified Public Accountants, Library, 1211 Avenue of the Americas, 10036

American Management Associations, Library, 135 West 50th Street, 10020

American Stock Exchange, Martin J. Keena Memorial Library, 86 Trinity Place, 10006

Arthur Andersen & Company, Library, 2 Park Avenue, 10016

Babcock & Wilcox Company, Library, 161 East 42nd Street, 10017

Bankers Trust Company, Library, 280 Park Avenue, 10017

Benton & Bowles, Inc., Library, 909 Third Avenue, 10022

Bernard M. Baruch College of the City University of New York, Library, 156 East 25th Street, 10010

Black Economic Research Center, Reference Library, 112 West 120th Street, 10027

Booz, Allen & Hamilton, Inc., 101 Park Avenue, 10178

Bradford National Corporation, Library, 67 Broad Street, 10004

Brakeley, John Price Jones, Inc., Library, 420 Lexington Avenue, 10017

Business International, Research Library, One Dag Hammarskjold Plaza, 10017

Business Week Magazine, Library, 1221 Avenue of the Americas, 10020

Chase Manhattan Bank, NA, Information Center, One Chase Manhattan Plaza, 10081

Chemical Bank, Research Library, 277 Park Avenue, 10017

C.I.T. Financial Corporation, Reference Library, 650 Madison Avenue, 10022

Citibank, N. A., CitiInfo, 153 East 53rd Street, 10043

The College of Insurance, Library, 123 William Street, 10038

Columbia University, Thomas J. Watson Library of Business & Economics, 130 Uris Hall, 10027

Conference Board, Inc., Information Service Library, 845 Third Avenue, 10022

Coopers & Lybrand, National Library, 1251 Avenue of the Americas, 10020

Donaldson, Lufkin & Jenrette, Inc., Corporate Information Center, 140 Broadway, 10005

Dun & Bradstreet, Business Library, 99 Church Street, 10007

Equitable Life Assurance Society of the U.S., Technical Information Center, 1285 Avenue of the Americas, 10019

Federal Reserve Bank of New York, Research Library, 33 Liberty Street, 10045

Fordham University, Library, Leon Lowenstein Building, 60th Street & Columbus Avenue, 10023

General Motors Corporation, Public Relations Library, 767 Fifth Avenue, 10022

Insurance Society of New York, Library, 123 William Street, 10038

International Advertising Association, Library, 475 Fifth Avenue, 10017

International Paper Company, Corporate Information Center, 77 West 45th Street, 10036

W. J. Levy Consultants Corporation, Library, 30 Rockefeller Plaza, 10020

Lincoln Educational Foundation, Business History Library, 299 Madison Avenue, 10017

Marine Midland Banks, Inc., Research Library, 140 Broadway, 10015

Marsh & McLennan, Inc., Information Center, 1221 Avenue of the Americas, 10020

McGraw-Hill, Inc., Corporate Library, 1221 Avenue of the Americas, 10020

Merrill Lynch, Pierce, Fenner & Smith, Inc., Financial Library, One Liberty Plaza, 10080

Metropolitan Life Insurance Company, Corporate Information Center & Library, One Madison Avenue, 10010

Minority Business Information Institute, Inc., 295 Madison Avenue, 10017

Mobil Oil Company, Secretariat Library, 150 East 42nd Street, 10017

Morgan Guarantee Trust Company, Library, 23 Wall Street, 10015

Morgan Stanley & Company, Library, 1251 Avenue of the Americas, 10020

Mutual of New York, Library Information Service, 1740 Broadway, 10019

National Association of Accountants, Library, 919 Third Avenue, 10022

National Broadcasting Company, Information Services, Research Department, 30 Rockefeller Plaza, 10020

New School for Social Research, Raymond Fogelman Library, 65 Fifth Avenue, 10011

New York Life Insurance Company, Reference Library, 51 Madison Avenue, 10010

New York Public Library, Mid-Manhattan Library, 8 East 40th Street, 10016
New York Public Library, Research Libraries, Fifth Avenue and 42nd Street, 10036
New York Stock Exchange, Research Library, 11 Wall Street, 10005
New York University, Graduate School of Business Administration, Library, 19 Rector Street, 10006
Newsom, Earl, & Company, Library, 10 East 53rd Street, 10022
Newspaper Advertising Bureau, Inc., Information Center, 485 Lexington Avenue, 10017
Ogilvy & Mather, Inc., Library, 2 East 48th Street, 10017
Pace University, Library, One Pace Plaza, 10038
Peat, Marwick, Mitchell & Company, Information & Resource Center, 345 Park Avenue, 10154
Pershing & Company, Research Library, 120 Broadway, 10005
Price Waterhouse & Company, Library, 153 East 53rd Street, 10022
Price Waterhouse & Company, National Information Center, 1251 Avenue of the Americas, 10020
Radio Advertising Bureau, Marketing Information Center, 485 Lexington Avenue, 10017
Research Institute of America, Information Services Center, 589 Fifth Avenue, 10017
St. Regis Paper Company, Library, 150 East 42nd Street, 10017
Salomon Brothers, Inc., Library, One New York Plaza, 10004
Scudder, Stevens & Clark, Library, 345 Park Avenue, 10154
Joseph E. Seagram & Sons, Inc., Corporate Library, 375 Park Avenue, 10022
Shearson/American Express, Inc., Library, 2 World Trade Center, 10048
Smith, Barney, Harris, Upham & Company, Inc., Library, 1345 Avenue of the Americas, 10105
R. M. Smythe & Company, Inactive & Obsolete Securities Library, 170 Broadway, 10038
Standard & Poor's Corporation, Library, 25 Broadway, 10004
Stone & Webster Management Consultants, Inc., Information Center, 90 Broad Street, 10004
J. Walter Thompson Company, Information Center, 466 Lexington Avenue, 10017
Towers, Perrin, Forster & Crosby, Inc., Library & Information Center, 600 Third Avenue, 10016
Teachers Insurance & Annuity Association of America, Business Library, 730 Third Avenue, 10017

Touche Ross & Company, Business Library, 1633 Broadway, 10019

U.S. Trademark Association, Library, 6 East 45th Street, 10017

U.S. Trust Company of New York, Investment Library, 45 Wall Street, 10005

Wall Street Journal, Library, 22 Cortlandt Street, 10007

Western Electric Company, Headquarters Library, 222 Broadway, 10038

Arthur Young & Company, Library, 277 Park Avenue, 10172

Young & Rubicam, Inc., Library, 285 Madison Avenue, 10017

Niagara University: Niagara University, Library, 14109

Oakdale: Dowling College, Library, Idle Hour Boulevard, 11769

Old Westbury: New York Institute of Technology, Library, 11568

Potsdam: Clarkson College of Technology, Andrew S. Schuler Educational Resources Center, 13676

Poughkeepsie: Marist College, Library, 82 North Road, 12601

Rochester: Eastman Kodak Company, Business Information Center, 343 State Street, 14650

Lincoln First Bank, Library Services, One Lincoln First Square, 14643

Rochester Institute of Technology, Wallace Memorial Library, One Lomb Memorial Drive, 14623

Rochester Public Library, Business & Social Science Division, 115 South Avenue, 14604

University of Rochester, Rush Rhees Library, River Campus, 14627

Xerox Corporation, Library, Xerox Square, 14644

St. Bonaventure: St. Bonaventure University, Friedsam Memorial Library, Route 417, 14778

Schenectady: General Electric Company, Main Library, Building 2, 12345

Union University, Schaffer Library, 12308

Staten Island: Wagner College, Horrmann Library, 631 Howard Avenue, 10301

Syracuse: Onondaga County Public Library, Business & Industrial Department, 335 Montgomery Street, 13202

Syracuse University, E. S. Bird Library, 222 Waverly Avenue, 13210

Troy: Rensselaer Polytechnic Institute, Folsom Library, 110 8th Street, 12181

Whiite Plains: National Economic Research Associates, Inc., Library, 123 Main Street, 10601

Yonkers: Yonkers Public Library, 70 South Broadway, 10701

NORTH CAROLINA

Boone: Appalachian State University, Carol Grotnes Belk Library, 28608

Buies Creek: Campbell University, Carrie Rich Memorial Library, P.O. Box 98, 27506

Chapel Hill: University of North Carolina at Chapel Hill, School of Business Administration Library, 27514

Charlotte: North Carolina National Bank, Library, One NCNB Plaza, P.O. Box 120, 28255

    Queens College, Everett Library, 1900 Selwyn Avenue, 28274

    University of North Carolina at Charlotte, J. Murray Atkins Library, Highway 49, 28233

Cullowhee: Western Carolina University, Hunter Memorial Library, 28723

Durham: Duke University, William R. Perkins Library, 27706

    North Carolina Central University, James E. Shepard Memorial Library, 1801 Fayetteville Street, 27707

Enka: American Enka Company, Business & Technical Library, 28728

Greensboro: Cone Mills Corporation, Library, 1106 Maple Street, 27405

    Greensboro Public Library, Business Library, 201 North Greene Street, P.O. Box X-4, 27402

    University of North Carolina at Greensboro, Walter Clinton Jackson Library, 1000 Spring Garden Street, 27412

Greenville: East Carolina University, J. Y. Joyner Library, East 5th Street, 27834

High Point: Southern Furniture Manufacturers Association, Library, 235 South Wrenn Street, 27260

Raleigh: North Carolina State University, D. H. Hill Library, 2205 Hillsborough Street, P.O. Box 5007, 27650

Winston-Salem: Wake Forest University, Charles H. Babcock Graduate School of Management, Library, P.O. Box 7689, 27109

NORTH DAKOTA

Fargo: North Dakota State University, Library, 58105

Grand Forks: University of North Dakota, Chester Fritz Library, 58202

OHIO

Akron: Akron-Summit County Public Library, Business, Labor & Government Division, 55 South Main Street, 44326

    B. F. Goodrich Company, Akron Information Center, 500 South Main Street, 44318

    Goodyear Tire & Rubber Company, Business Information Center, 1144 East Market Street, 44316

University of Akron, Bierce Library, 302 East Buchtel Avenue, 44325
Ashland: Ashland College Library, College Avenue, 44805
Athens: Ohio University, Vernon R. Alden Library, Park Place, 45701
Berea: Baldwin-Wallace College, Ritter Library, 57 East Bagley Road, 44017
Bowling Green: Bowling Green State University, Library, 43403
Cincinnati: Drackett Company, Research & Development Library, 5020 Spring Grove Avenue, 45232
> Public Library of Cincinnati & Hamilton County, Government & Business Department, 800 Vine Street, 45202
> University of Cincinnati, Library, University & Woodside, 45221
> Western-Southern Life Insurance Company, Library, 400 Broadway, 45202
> Xavier University, McDonald Memorial Library, 3800 Victory Parkway, 45207
Cleveland: Case Western Reserve University, Sears Library, 2040 Adelbert Road, 44106
> Cleveland Public Library, Business & Economics Department, 325 Superior Avenue, 44114
> Cleveland State University, Library, 1860 East 22nd Street, 44115
> Ernst & Whinney, National Office Library, 2000 National City Center, 44114
> Federal Reserve Bank of Cleveland, Research Library, 1455 East 6th Street, 44101
> John Carroll University, Grasselli Library, North Park & Miramar Boulevards, 44118
> Meldrum & Fewsmith, Inc., Business Information Library, 1220 Huron Road, 44115
Columbus: Capital University, Library, 2199 East Main Street, 43209
> Nationwide Insurance Company, One Nationwide Plaza, 43216
> Ohio State University, Commerce Library, Page Hall, 1810 College Road, 43210
Dayton: Dayton & Montgomery County Public Library, Industry & Science Division, 215 East Third Street, 45402
> NCR Corporation, Technical Library, Building 28, Main & K Streets, 45479
> University of Dayton, Roesch Library, 300 College Park Avenue, 45469
> Wright State University, Library, 7751 Colonel Glenn Highway, 45435
Kent: Kent State University, Library, 44242

Middletown: Armco, Inc., Technical Information Services, Research Building, 45043

Oxford: Miami University, Edgar W. King Library, 45056

Painesville: Lake Erie College, James F. Lincoln Learning Resource Center, 391 West Washington Street, 44077

Toledo: Owens-Illinois, Inc. Business Library, World Headquarters Building, One Seagate, 43666

    Toledo Edison Company, Library, 300 Madison Avenue, 43652

    Toledo-Lucas County Public Library, Business Department, 325 Michigan Street, 43624

    University of Toledo, William S. Carlson Library, 2801 West Bancroft Street, 43606

Wright-Patterson AFB: USAF Institute of Technology, Academic Library, Building 640, Area B, 45433

Youngstown: Public Library of Youngstown & Mahoning County, Science & Industry Division, 305 Wick Avenue, 44503

    Youngstown State University, William F. Maag Library, 410 Wick Avenue, 44555

OKLAHOMA

Bethany: Bethany Nazarene College, R. T. Williams Learning Resources Center, 4115 North College, 73008

Durant: Southeastern Oklahoma State University, Henry G. Bennett Memorial Library, 74701

Edmond: Central State University, Library, 100 North University Drive, 73034

Enid: Phillips University, Zollars Memorial Library, P.O. Box 248, University Station, 73701

Norman: University of Oklahoma, Business-Economics Library, 401 West Brooks, 73019

    University of Oklahoma, Harry W. Bass Collection in Business History, 401 West Brooks Street, 73069

    University of Oklahoma, Center for Economic & Management Research, 307 West Brooks Street, 73069

Oklahoma City: Anta Corporation, Library, 101 North Robison Avenue, 73102

    Oklahoma City Metropolitan Library System, Business-Technical Department, 131 Dean A. McGee Avenue, 73102

    Oklahoma City University, Dulaney-Browne Library, 2501 North Blackwelder Avenue, 73106

Stillwater: Oklahoma State University, Library, 74078

Tulsa: Oklahoma School of Business, 4470 South Harvard, 74135

    Oral Roberts University, John D. Messick Learning Resources Center, 7777 South Lewis Avenue, 74171

350   SOURCES AND RESOURCES

University of Tulsa, McFarlin Library, 600 South College Ave-
    nue, 74104
Weatherford: Southwestern Oklahoma State University, Al Harris Li-
    brary, 100 Campus Drive, 73096
OREGON
Ashland: Southern Oregon State College, Library, 1250 Siskiyou
    Boulevard, 97520
Corvallis: Oregon State University, William Jasper Kerr Library, 97331
Eugene: University of Oregon, Library, 97403
        University of Oregon, Bureau of Business Research, Gilbert
        Hall, 97403
Portland: First Interstate Bank of Oregon, Library, 1300 Southwest
    5th Avenue, 97208
        Portland General Electric Company, Library, 121 SW Salmon
        Street, 97204
        Portland State University, Branford Price Miller Library, 934
        Southwest Harrison, P.O. Box 1151, 97207
        Standard Insurance Company, Home Office Library, 1100 SW
        Sixth Avenue, P.O. Box 711, 97207
        University of Portland, Wilson W. Clark Memorial Library,
        5000 North Willamette Boulevard, P.O. Box 03107, 97203
Salem: Willamette University, Library, 900 State Street, 97301
PENNSYLVANIA
Bethlehem: Bethlehem Steel Corporation, Schwab Information Center,
    Martin Tower, 18016
        Lehigh University, Library, Linderman Library, 18015
Bloomsburg: Bloomsburg State University, Harvey A. Andruss Library,
    17815
Bryn Mawr: American College, Vane B. Lucas Memorial Library, 270
    Bryn Mawr Avenue, 19010
California: California State College of Pennsylvania, Louis L. Mander-
    ino Library, 15419
Chester: Widener University, Wolfgram Memorial Library, 700 East
    14th Street, 19013
Clarion: Clarion State University, Rena M. Carlson Library, Wood
    Street, 16214
Coraopolis: Robert Morris College, Library, Narrows Run Road, 15108
Erie: Gannon University, Nash Library, 619 Sassafras Street, 16541
Indiana: Indiana University of Pennsylvania, Library, 15705
Lewisburg: Bucknell University, Ellen Clarke Bertrand Library, 17837
Loretto: St. Francis College, Pius XII Memorial Library, 15940
Middletown: Pennsylvania State University, Capitol Campus, Richard
    H. Heindel Library, 17057
Philadelphia: Deloitte, Haskins & Sells, Library, 3 Girard Plaza, 19102

Drexel University, Library, 32nd & Chestnut Streets, 19104

Federal Reserve Bank of Philadelphia, Library, 100 North Sixth Street, 19105

Fidelity Mutual Life Insurance Company, Library Archives, Fidelity Mutual Life Building, 123 South Broad Street, 19101

First Pennsylvania Bank, Marketing Information Center, First Pennsylvania Tower, Center Square, 19101

Free Library of Philadelphia, Business, Science & Industry Department, Logan Square, 19103

Free Library of Philadelphia, Mercantile Library, 1021 Chestnut Street, 19107

Insurance Company of North America, Business Information Resources, 1600 Arch Street, 19101

LaSalle College, David Leo Lawrence Library, 20th Street & Olney Avenue, 19141

Philadelphia College of Textiles & Science, Senator John O. Pastore Library, School House Lane & Henry Avenue, 19144

Provident Mutual Life Insurance Company, Library, 46th & Market Streets, 19101

Rohm & Haas Company, Library, Independence Mall West, 19105

St. Joseph's University, Drexel Library, 5600 City Avenue, 19131

Smith, Kline & French Laboratories, Marketing Research Library, 1500 Spring Garden Street, 19101

Temple University, Samuel Paley Library, Berks & 13th Streets, 19122

University of Pennsylvania, Wharton School, Lippincott Library, 3420 Walnut Street, 19104

Pittsburgh: Aluminum Company of America, Corporate Planning Library, Alcoa Building, 15219

Carnegie Library of Pittsburgh, Business Division, 4400 Forbes Avenue, 15213

Carnegie-Mellon University, Hunt Library, Schenley Park, 15213

Duquesne University, Library, 900 Locust Street, 15282

Federal Reserve Bank of Cleveland, Pittsburgh Branch, Library, 717 Grant Street, 15230

Gulf Oil Corporation, Business Research Library, 435 Seventh Avenue, 15230

La Roche College, John J. Wright Library, 9000 Babcock Boulevard, 15237

Mellon National Corporation, Library, Mellon Square, 15230

Mine Safety Appliances Company, Library, 600 Penn Center Boulevard, 15235

PPG Industries, Library, 600 Penn Center Boulevard, 15235

Rockwell International, Business Research Center, 600 Grant Street, 15219

University of Pittsburgh, Graduate School of Business, Library, Cathedral of Learning, 15260

Radnor: Chilton Book Company, Marketing & Advertising Information Center, One Chilton Way, 19089

Reading: Metropolitan Edison Company, System Library, 2800 Pottsville Pike, 19605

St. Davids: Eastern College, Frank Warner Memorial Library, Fairview Drive, 19087

Scranton: Marywood College, Library, 2300 Adams Avenue, 18509

Scranton Public Library, Albright Memorial Library, Vine Street & Washington Avenue, 18503

University of Scranton, Alumni Memorial Library, 4 Ridge Row, 18510

Shippensburg: Shippensburg State College, Ezra Lehman Memorial Library, North Prince Street, 17257

University Park: Pennsylvania State University, Fred Lewis Pattee Library, 16802

Villanova: Villanova University, Falvey Memorial Library, 19085

Wilkes-Barre: Wilkes College, Eugene Shedden Farley Library, Franklin & South Streets, 18766

York: York College, Schmidt Library, 321 Country Club Road, 17405

PUERTO RICO

Ponce: Catholic University of Puerto Rico, Encarnacion Valdes Library, Avenue Las Americas, 00731

Rio Piedras: Inter American University of Puerto Rico, Metropolitan Campus, Library, Carr. PR1 Esq Calle Francisco Sein, 00919

University of Puerto Rico, Library, 00931

San German: Inter American University of Puerto Rico, San German Campus, Library, Luna Abajo y Avenida Harris, 00753

RHODE ISLAND

Kingston: University of Rhode Island, Library, 02881

Providence: Providence College, Phillips Memorial Library, River Avenue at Eaton Street, 02918

Providence Public Library, Business-Industry-Science Department, 150 Empire Street, 02903

Smithfield: Bryant College of Business Administration, Edith M. Hodgson Memorial Library, Route 7, Douglas Pike, 02917

SOUTH CAROLINA

Charleston: The Citadel, Daniel Library, Citadel Station, 29409
Clemson: Clemson University, Robert Muldrow Cooper Library, 29632
Columbia: University of South Carolina, Thomas Cooper Library, 29208
Greenville: Clemson University-Furman University, James Buchanan Duke Building, Furman University Campus, Poinsett Highway, 29613
Orangeburg: South Carolina State College, Miller F. Whittaker Library, College Avenue, P.O. Box 1991, 29117
Rock Hill: Winthrop College, Ida Jane Dacus Library, 810 Oakland Avenue, 29733

SOUTH DAKOTA

Rapid City: National College of Business, Learning Center, 321 Kansas City Street, P.O. Box 1780, 57709
Vermillion: University of South Dakota, I. D. Weeks Library, 57069

TENNESSEE

Chattanooga: University of Tennessee at Chattanooga, Library, Vine Street, 37403
Clarksville: Austin Peay State University, Felix G. Woodward Library, College Street, 37040
Cookeville: Tennessee Technological University, Jere Whitson Memorial Library, Dixie Avenue, P.O. Box 5066, 38501
Johnson City: East Tennessee State University, Sherrod Library, P.O. Box 22450A, 37614
Kingsport: Tennessee Eastman Company, Business Library, Building 280, P.O. Box 511, 37662
Knoxville: University of Tennessee, Knoxville, James D. Hoskins Library, 37916
Martin: University of Tennessee at Martin, Paul Meek Library, 38238
Memphis: Memphis-Shelby County Public Library & Information Center, Science, Business & Social Sciences Department, 1850 Peabody Avenue, 38104
  Memphis State University, John W. Brister Library, 38152
Murfreesboro: Middle Tennessee University, Andrew L. Todd Library, 37132
Nashville: Public Library of Nashville & Davidson County, Business Information Services, Eighth Avenue North & Union, 37203
  Tennessee State University, Brown-Daniel Library, 3500 Centennial Boulevard, 37203
  Tennessee Valley Bancorp, Library, One Commerce Place, 37239
  Vanderbilt University, Owen Graduate School of Management, Walker Library, 2505 West End Avenue, 37240

TEXAS
Abilene: Abilene Christian University, Margaret & Herman Brown Library, 1600 Campus Court, P.O. Box 8177, ACU Station, 79699
   Hardin-Simmons University, Rupert & Pauline Richardson Library, 2200 Hickory, 79698
Alpine: Sul Ross State University, Bryan Wildenthal Memorial Library, 79832
Amarillo: Southwestern Public Service Company, Library, P.O. Box 1261, 79170
Arlington: University of Texas at Arlington, Library, P.O. Box 19497, 76019
Austin: St. Edward's University, Scarborough-Phillips Library, 3001 South Congress Avenue, 78704
   University of Texas at Austin, School of Business, Perry-Castañeda Library, 78712
Beaumont: Gulf States Utilities, Corporate Library, 350 Pine Street, P.O. Box 2951, 77701
   Lamar University, Mary & John Gray Library, 77710
Canyon: West Texas State University, Cornette Library, 2nd Avenue & 26th Street, 79016
Cedar Hill: Northwood Institute, Library, Highway 1382, P.O. Box 58, 75104
Commerce: East Texas State University at Commerce, James Gilliam Gee Library, 75428
Corpus Christi: Corpus Christi University, Library, 6300 Ocean Drive, 78412
Dallas: Dallas Baptist College, Vance Memorial Library, 7777 West Kiest Boulevard, 75211
   Dallas Public Library, Business & Technology Division, 1515 Young Street, 75201
   Federal Reserve Bank of Dallas, Research Library, 400 South Akard Street, 75222
   Southern Methodist University, Fondren Library, P.O. 296, 75275
   Southern Union Company, Library, First International Building, 75270
   Tracy-Locke, BBDO, Inc., Information Services Department, Library, Plaza of the Americas, 600 North Pearl Street, 75250
Denton: North Texas State University, Library, P.O. Box 5188, NT Station, 76203
   Texas Woman's University, Bralley Memorial Library, P.O. Box 23715, 76204

Edinburg: Pan American University, Learning Resource Center, 1201 West University Drive, 78539

El Paso: University of Texas at El Paso, Library, West University Avenue, 79968

Fort Worth: Fort Worth Public Library, Business & Technology Department, 300 Taylor Street, 76102

> Texas Christian University, Mary Couts Burnett Library, 2800 South University Drive, P.O. Box 32904, TCU Station, 76129

Galveston: Rosenberg Library, 2310 Sealy Avenue, 77550

Houston: Arthur Andersen & Company, Library, 711 Louisiana Street, 77002

> Esso Eastern, Inc., Library, 240 South Gessner, 77001
>
> Exxon Company, U.S.A., Library, P.O. Box 1415, 77001
>
> Gulf Oil Corporation, Library & Information Center, Box 2100, 77252
>
> Houston Baptist University, Moody Memorial Library, 7502 Fondren Road, 77074
>
> Houston Public Library, Business, Science & Technology Department, 500 McKinney Avenue, 77002
>
> Peat, Marwick, Mitchell & Company, One Shell Plaza, 77210
>
> Prudential Insurance Company, Business Library, P.O. Box 2075, 77001
>
> Rice University, Fondren Library, 6100 Main Street, P.O. Box 1892, 77251
>
> Tenneco, Inc., Corporate Library, P.O. Box 2511, 77001
>
> Texas Southern University, Library, 3201 Wheeler Avenue, 77004
>
> Trunkline Gas Company, General Library, 3000 Bissonnet, 77001
>
> University of Houston, Central Campus, M. D. Anderson Memorial Library, 4800 Calhoun Boulevard, 77004
>
> University of Houston at Clear Lake City, Library, 2700 Bay Area Boulevard, 77058
>
> University of St. Thomas, Pace-Doherty Library, 3812 Montrose Boulevard, 77006

Huntsville: Sam Houston State University, Library, P.O. Box 2179, 77341

Irving: University of Dallas, William A. Blakely Library, UD Station, 75061

Killeen: American Technological University, Library, Highway 190W, P.O. 1416, 76540

Kingsville: Texas Arts & Industries University, James C. Jernigan Library, West Santa Gertrudis Avenue, 78363

Laredo: Laredo State University, Harold R. Yeary Library, West End
    Washington Street, 78040
Lubbock: Texas Tech University, Library, Broadway & University,
    79409
Nacogdoches: Stephen F. Austin State University, Ralph W. Steen Li-
    brary, 1936 North Street, P.O. Box 13055, SFA Station, 75962
Odessa: University of Texas of the Permian Basin, Learning Resources
    Center, East University Boulevard, 79762
Prairie View: Prairie View A & M University, W. R. Banks Library,
    Third Street, P.O. Box T, 77445
Richardson: University of Texas at Dallas, Library, 2601 North Floyd
    Road, P. O. Box 643, 75080
San Angelo: Angelo State University, Porter Henderson Library, 2601
    West Avenue North, 76909
        General Telephone Company, E. H. Danner Library of Tele-
        phony, 2701 South Johnson Street, 76904
San Antonio: St. Mary's University, Library, One Camino Santa Maria,
    78284
        San Antonio Public Library, Business, Science & Technology
        Department, 203 South St. Mary's Street, 78205
        Trinity University, Library, 715 Stadium Drive, 78284
        United Services Automobile Association, Corporate Library,
        USAA Building, 78288
        University of Texas at San Antonio, Library, 6900 North Loop
        1604 W, 78285
        H. B. Zachry Company, Central Records & Library, 527 Long-
        wood, P.O. Box 21130, 78275
San Marcos: Southwest Texas State University, Learning Resource
    Center, 78666
Stephenville: Tarleton State University, Dick Smith Library, Box T-
    2003, Tarleton Station, 76402
Texarkana: East Texas State University at Texarkana, Palmer Memo-
    rial Library, 2500 Robison Road, P.O. Box 6187, 75501
        U.S. Army, DARCOM Intern Training Center, Technical Li-
        brary, Red River Army Depot, 75501
Tyler: University of Texas at Tyler, Robert E. Muntz Library, 3900
    University Boulevard, 75701
Victoria: University of Houston, Victoria Campus, Library, 2602
    North Ben Jordan Street, 77901
Waco: Baylor University, Moody Memorial Library, P.O. Box 6307,
    BU Station, 76706
Wichita Falls: Midwestern State University, George Moffett Library,
    3400 Taft Avenue, 76308

UTAH

Logan: Utah State University, Merrill Library, University Hill, 84322

Provo: Brigham Young University, Harold B. Lee Library, University Hill, 84602

Salt Lake City: University of Utah, John L. Firmage Library, Business Classroom Building, 84112

Westminster College, William T. Nightingale Memorial Library, 1840 South 13th Street East, 84105

VERMONT

Burlington: University of Vermont & State Agricultural College, Bailey-Howe Memorial Library, 85 South Prospect Street, 05405

Montpelier: National Life Insurance Company, Law Library, National Life Drive, 05602

Rutland: Central Vermont Public Service Corporation, Technical Information Center, 77 Grove Street, 05701

Winooski: St. Michael's College, Durick Library, 56 College Parkway, Route 15, 05404

VIRGINIA

Arlington: American Gas Association, Library, 1515 Wilson Boulevard, 22209

Marymount College of Virginia, Ireton Library, 2807 North Glebe Road, 22207

Blacksburg: Virginia Polytechnic Institute & State University, Carol M. Newman Library, 24061

Charlottesville: University of Virginia, Colgate Darden Graduate School of Business Administration, Library, Darden School Hall, 22904

Fairfax: Fairfax County Public Library, Business & Technical Center, 3915 Chain Bridge Road, 22030

George Mason University, Library, 4400 University Drive, 22030

Fredericksburg: Mary Washington College, E. Lee Trinkle Library, 22401

Hampton: Hampton Institute, Collis P. Huntington Library, East Queen Street, 23668

Harrisonburg: James Madison University, Madison Memorial Library, 22807

Lynchburg: Lynchburg College, Knight-Capron Library, Westwood Avenue, 24501

McLean: National Automobile Dealers Association, Library, 8400 Westpark Drive, 22102

Norfolk: Norfolk State University, Lyman Beecher Brooks Library, 2401 Corprew Avenue, 23504

Old Dominion University, Library, 5201 Hampton Boulevard, 23508

Virginia National Bank, Library, One Commercial Plaza, P.O. Box 600, 23501

Radford: Radford University, John Preston McConnell Library, 24142

Richmond: Federal Reserve Bank of Richmond, Research Library, 701 East Byrd Street, 23261

    Reynolds Metals Company, Corporate Information Center, 6601 West Broad Street, 23261

    Richmond Public Library, Business, Science & Technology Department, 101 East Franklin Street, 23219

    United Virginia Bank, Information Center, 900 East Main Street, 23261

    University of Richmond, Boatwright Memorial Library, 23173

    Virginia Commonwealth University, James Branch Cabell Library, 901 Park Avenue, 23284

Williamsburg: College of William & Mary, Earl Gregg Swem Library, 23186

Winchester: Shenandoah College & Conservatory of Music, Howe Library, Milwood Pike, 22601

WASHINGTON

Bellevue: Puget Sound Power & Light Company, Library, Puget Power Building, 98009

Bellingham: Western Washington University, Mabel Zoe Wilson Library, 516 High Street, 98225

Cheney: Eastern Washington University, John F. Kennedy Memorial Library, 99004

Federal Way: Weyerhaeuser Company, Corporate Library, 2525 South 336th Street, 98003

Pullman: Washington State University, Library, 99164

Seattle: City College, Library, 607 Third Avenue, 98104

    Pacific Coast Banking School Library, 2001 Sixth Avenue, 98121

    Port of Seattle, Library, P.O. Box 1209, 98111

    Rainier National Bank, Information Center, 1301 Fifth Avenue, 98124

    Safeco Insurance Company, Safeco Plaza, 98105

    Seattle-First National Bank, Library, 1001 Fourth Avenue, 98154

    Seattle Public Library, Science & Business Department, 1000 Fourth Avenue, 98104

    Seattle University, A. A. Lemieux Library, 900 Broadway Street, 98122

    University of Washington, Business Administration Library, Balmer Hall, 98195

Washington Mutual Savings Bank, Information Center & Dietrich Schmitz Memorial Library, 1101 Second Avenue, 98111

Spokane: Gonzaga University, Crosby Library, 502 East Boone Avenue, 99258

Tacoma: Pacific Lutheran University, Robert A. L. Mortvedt Library, South 121st Street & Park Avenue South, 98447

Weyerhaeuser Company, Corporate Library, 98401

University of Puget Sound, Collins Memorial Library, 1500 North Warner Street, 98416

WEST VIRGINIA

Huntington: Marshall University, James E. Morrow Library, 1655 Third Avenue, 25701

Institute: West Virginia College of Graduate Studies, Library, 25112

Morgantown: West Virginia University, Library, 26506

Wheeling: Wheeling College, Bishop Hodges Learning Center, 316 Washington Avenue, 26003

WISCONSIN

Eau Claire: University of Wisconsin-Eau Claire, William D. McIntyre Library, 105 Garfield Avenue, 54701

Kenosha: University of Wisconsin-Parkside, Library, 700 Wood Road, P.O. Box 2000, 53141

La Crosse: University of Wisconsin-La Crosse, Murphy Library, 1631 Pine Street, 54601

Madison: Credit Union National Association, Inc., Information Resource Center, 5710 West Mineral Point Road, P.O. Box 431, 53701

Madison Public Library, Business & Science Division, 201 West Mifflin Street, 53703

University of Wisconsin-Madison, School of Business Library, B25A Bascom Hall, 500 Lincoln Drive, 53706

Wisconsin Alumni Research Foundation, Library, 814 North Walnut Street, P.O. Box 7365, 53707

Milwaukee: First Wisconsin National Bank Library, 777 East Wisconsin Avenue, 53202

National Association of Insurance Commissioners, Library, 633 West Wisconsin Avenue, 53203

Marquette University, Memorial Library, 1415 West Wisconsin Avenue, 53233

Milwaukee Public Library, Business Information Service, 814 West Wisconsin Avenue, 53233

Northwestern Mutual Life Insurance Company, Reference Library, 720 East Wisconsin Avenue, 53202

Joseph Schlitz Brewing Company, Consumer Research Library, P.O. Box 614, 53201

University of Wisconsin-Milwaukee, Golda Meir Library, 2311
   East Hartford Avenue, P.O. 604, 53201
Wisconsin Gas Company, Corporate Library, 626 East Wiscon-
   sin Avenue, 53202
Oshkosh: University of Wisconsin-Oshkosh, Forest R. Polk Library,
   800 Algoma Boulevard, 54901
Stevens Point: Sentry Library, 1800 North Point Drive, 54481
Wausau: Wausau Insurance Companies, Library, 2000 Westwood
   Drive, 54401
Whitewater: University of Wisconsin-Whitewater, Harold Anderson
   Library, 800 West Main Street, 53190
WYOMING
Laramie: University of Wyoming, William Robertson Coe Library,
   13th & Ivinson, P.O. Box 3334, University Station, 82701

Canadian Library Sources of Business Information

BRITISH COLUMBIA
Vancouver: Vancouver Public Library, 750 Burrard Street, V6Z
   1X5
MANITOBA
Winnipeg: University of Manitoba, Administrative Studies Library,
   Administrative Studies Building, R3T 2N2
NEWFOUNDLAND
St. John's: Memorial University of Newfoundland, Queen Elizabeth II
   Library, Elizabeth Avenue, A1B 3Y1
NEW BRUNSWICK
Frederickton: University of New Brunswick, Harriet Irving Library,
   P.O. Box 4400, E3B 5A3
NOVA SCOTIA
Halifax: Dalhousie University, Izaak Walton Killam Memorial Library,
   B3H 4H8
   St. Mary's University, Patrick Power Library, B3H 3C3
ONTARIO
Hamilton: McMaster University, Library, 1280 Main Street West,
   L8S 4L6
Kingston: Queen's University at Kingston, Douglas Library, Corner of
   Union & University, K7L 5C4
Toronto: MacLean-Hunter, Ltd., Library, 77 Bay Street, M5W 1A7
   Metropolitan Toronto Library, 789 Yonge Street, M4W 2G8
   Ontario Ministry of Treasury & Economics, Library, Frost
      Building North, Queen's Park, M7A 1Y7
   Ryerson Polytechnic Institute, Donald Mordell Learning Re-
      sources Center, 350 Victoria Street, M5B 1E8

Toronto Dominion Bank, Department of Economic Research, 55 King Street West, M5K 1A2

University of Toronto, Faculty of Management Studies, Library, 246 Bloor Street West, M5S 1V4

Waterloo: Wilfrid Laurier University, Library, 75 Waterloo Avenue West, N2L 3C5

QUEBEC

Montreal: Concordia University, Library, 1455 de Maisonneuve Boulevard West, H3G 1M8

McGill University, Howard Ross Library of Management, Bronfman Building, 1001 Sherbrooke Street West, H3A 2K6

Federal Information Centers

ALASKA
Anchorage: 701 C Street, 99513
ARIZONA
Phoenix: 230 North First Avenue
CALIFORNIA
Los Angeles: 300 North Los Angeles Street, 90012
Sacramento: 650 Capitol Mall, 95814
San Diego: 880 Front Street, 92188
San Francisco: 450 Golden Gate Avenue, 94102
COLORADO
Denver: Building 41, Federal Center, 80225
FLORIDA
St. Petersburg: 144 First Avenue South, 33701
GEORGIA
Atlanta: 75 Spring Street, NW, 30303
HAWAII
Honolulu: 300 Ala Moana Boulevard, 96850
ILLINOIS
Chicago: 219 South Dearborn Street, 60604
INDIANA
Indianapolis: 575 North Pennsylvania, 46204
IOWA
Des Moines: 210 Walnut Street, 50309
KANSAS
Topeka: 444 Southeast Quincy, 66683
LOUISIANA
New Orleans: 423 Canal Street, 70130
MARYLAND
Baltimore: 31 Hopkins Plaza, 21201

MASSACHUSETTS
Boston: J. W. McCormack Post Office & U.S. Courthouse, 02109
MICHIGAN
Detroit: 477 Michigan Avenue, 48226
MINNESOTA
Minneapolis: 110 South Fourth Street, 55401
MISSOURI
Kansas City: 601 East 12th Street, 64106
NEBRASKA
215 North 17th Street, 68102
NEW JERSEY
Newark: 970 Broad Street, 07102
NEW MEXICO
Albuquerque: 500 Gold Avenue SW, 87102
NEW YORK
Buffalo: 111 West Huron, 14202
New York: 26 Federal Plaza, 10278
OHIO
Cincinnati: 550 Main Street, 45202
Cleveland: 1240 East 9th Street, 44199
OKLAHOMA
Oklahoma City: 201 NW Third Street, 73102
OREGON
1220 SW Third Avenue, 97204
PENNSYLVANIA
Philadelphia: 600 Arch Street, 19106
Pittsburgh: 1000 Liberty Avenue, 15222
TEXAS
Fort Worth: 819 Taylor Street, 76102
Houston: 515 Rusk Avenue, 77002
UTAH
Salt Lake City: 125 South State Street, 84138
VIRGINIA
Norfolk: 200 Granby Mall, 23510
WASHINGTON
Seattle: 915 Second Avenue, 98714

Chapter 27

Postage Meters

Friden-Alcatel, 30995 Huntwood Avenue, Hayward, CA 94544
International Mailing Systems, Division of Better Packages, Inc., 8
    Brook Street, Shelton, CT 04684

Pitney Bowes, Walter H. Wheeler, Jr. Drive, Stamford, CT 06926
Postalia, 1423 Centre Circle Drive, Downers Grove, IL 60515

Chapter 28

Air Express Companies

Airborne International, 190 Queen Anne Avenue North, Seattle, WA
98111
Emery Worldwide, Old Danbury Road, Wilton, CT 06897
DHL Corporation, 1000 Cherry Avenue, San Bruno, CA 94066
Federal Express Corporation, Box 727, Memphis, TN 38194
Purolator Courier Corporation, 3333 New Hyde Park Road, New Hyde
Park, NY 11042
United Parcel Service, 51 Weaver Street, Greenwich Office Park 5,
Greenwich, CT 06830

Index

367